STUDIES IN MODERNITY AND NATIONAL IDENTITY

Sibel Bozdoğan and Reşat Kasaba, Series Editors

Studies in Modernity and National Identity examine the relationships among modernity, the nation-state, and nationalism as these have evolved in the nineteenth and twentieth centuries. Titles in this interdisciplinary and transregional series also illuminate how the nation-state is being undermined by the forces of globalization, international migration, electronic information flows, as well as resurgent ethnic and religious affiliations. These books highlight historical parallels and continuities while documenting the social, cultural, and spatial expressions through which modern national identities have been constructed, contested, and reinvented.

Modernism and Nation Building: Turkish Architectural Culture in the Early Republic by Sibel Bozdoğan

Chandigarh's Le Corbusier: The Struggle for Modernity in Postcolonial India by Vikramaditya Prakash

Islamist Mobilization in Turkey: A Study in Vernacular Politics by Jenny B. White

The Landscape of Stalinism: The Art and Ideology of Soviet Space edited by Evgeny Dobrenko and Eric Naiman

Architecture and Tourism in Italian Colonial Libya: An Ambivalent Modernism by Brian L. McLaren

ALME SOL POSSIS

NIHIL VRBE ROMA

VISERE MAIVS

ARCHITECTURE AND TOURISM
IN ITALIAN COLONIAL LIBYA
AN AMBIVALENT MODERNISM

BRIAN L. McLAREN

University of Washington Press
Seattle and London

This book is published with the assistance of grants from the Graham Foundation for Advanced Studies in Fine Arts, the University of Washington Architecture Publications Fund, and the Johnston Hastings Endowment.

© 2006 by the University of Washington Press
Printed in China
Design and composition by Christina Merkelbach
12 11 10 09 08 07 06   5 4 3 2 1

University of Washington Press
P.O. Box 50096, Seattle, WA 98145 U.S.A.
www.washington.edu/uwpress

Library of Congress Cataloging-in-Publication Data
McLaren, Brian L.
Architecture and tourism in Italian colonial Libya : an ambivalent modernism / by Brian L. McLaren.— 1st ed.
    p. cm. — (Studies in modernity and national identity)
Includes bibliographical references and index.
ISBN 0-295-98542-9 (hardback : alk. paper)
1. Architecture and tourism—Libya. 2. Architecture, Colonial—Libya. 3. Architecture, Italian—Libya. 4. Fascism and architecture—Libya. 5. Libya—History—1912-1951. I. Title. II. Series.
NA2543.T68M35 2005
916.204'3—dc22   2005021508

CONTENTS

Preface   vii

Introduction   3

1. The Incorporation of Libya into Metropolitan Italy   17

2. Colonial Tourism and the Experience of Modernity   43

3. The Indigenous Politics of Italian Colonialism   79

4. Tourism and the Framing of Indigenous Culture   105

5. Toward a Modern Colonial Architecture   145

6. In Search of a Regionalist Expression   183

Conclusion   219

Notes   229

Bibliography   261

Figure Credits   273

Index   279

A NOTE ON TRANSLITERATIONS

In the case of Arabic proper names of persons and places, I have followed the transliteration system of the *International Journal of Middle East Studies.* Exceptions to this system are major sites with strong historical associations, such as Leptis Magna, and sites with widely used contemporary names, such as the Fezzan.

ABBREVIATIONS

ACS	Central State Archive
ASMAE	Historic Archive of the Ministry of Foreign Affairs
CIT	Italian Tourism Company
ECL	Libyan Colonization Association
ENIT	National Association of Tourist Industries
ETAL	Libyan Tourism and Hotel Association
FFSS	Italian State Railway
ICF	Fascist Colonial Institute
ICI	Italian Colonial Institute
INFPS	National Fascist Institute for Social Security
ISIAO	Italian Institute for Africa and the East
MAI	Ministry of Italian Africa
MCP	Ministry of Popular Culture
PCM	Chair of the Council of Ministers
TCI	Italian Touring Club

PREFACE

This book project began with my own experience as a foreign traveler to Libya in the summer of 1994. I had just completed my first year of graduate study in the History, Theory, and Criticism section of the Department of Architecture at MIT, having taken a seminar on architecture and modernization in the postcolonial world. That class provided me with the impetus to apply for a summer travel grant from the Aga Khan Program for Islamic Architecture at MIT—a grant that allowed me to spend a month in Tripoli. While the full details of securing a visa at the Libyan consulate in Rome during the period of United Nations sanctions is a subject too lengthy to present here, it is at least worth noting that I traveled to Tripoli—like most tourists did during the 1930s—aboard an ocean liner. Despite the unpleasantness of spending the overnight sail from Malta in the belly of a 1960s cruise ship, I had the great fortune of arriving in the Bay of Tripoli in the earliest moments of dawn—the sun just beginning to burn off the mist that seemed to cling to its shore.

That quite moving introduction to the southern shore of the Mediterranean, and the many positive experiences of my stay, compelled me to pursue research on the Italian colonial presence in the region. As someone who had prepared for many years to work on Italian architecture during the Fascist period, this was a slight change in direction, but one that was generated out of a genuine sense of the contemporary importance of the issues raised by the Italian colonial legacy in North Africa. In this sense, the invitation to travel provided by this book is not merely an act of historical interpretation of a troubled though distant past, despite my efforts to keep it so.

The research itinerary that led from that initial journey to Tripoli in July and August of 1994 to the present volume on architecture, tourism, and Italian colonial politics in Libya is itself quite complicated. I will do my best to represent its outlines and give proper recognition to the many individuals and institutions that have assisted me along the way. I should first acknowledge the emergence of this book project from my dissertation work at the Massachusetts Institute of Technology. Although this earlier work was much broader—encompassing architectural discourse and colonial exhibitions as well as tourism—it provided much of the material for this book. During that time I received the generous assistance of MIT's Department of Architecture and, in particular, Stanford Anderson, who has wholeheartedly supported my scholarly efforts over the past several years. A fellowship from the Social Science and Humanities Research Council of Canada allowed me to pursue my research through the initial years of these studies. I am also indebted to the intellectual guidance of several mentors whose influence can be seen throughout the book. Particularly helpful were Mark Jarzombek, for his sound direction of my research, and Ákos Moravánszky, whose intellectual curiosity has continued to inspire my work. I am equally grateful to Diane Ghirardo, whose critical insights on the relationship between architecture and politics in Fascist Italy have been extremely influential on this project. Finally, this book would not have been possible without Sibel Bozdoğan, whose intellectual and moral support have moved my work forward at each stage. Not only did she start me off on this journey; she was instrumental in establishing a destination—including my present relationship with the University of Washington Press. For this and more I shall be forever grateful.

This book has benefited from numerous research trips that were supported by institutions and individuals whose help was vital to the success of the project. For my visit to Tripoli, I am indebted to the Aga Khan Program for Islamic Architecture at MIT, and especially to Attilio Petruciolli, who has also helped publish some of the results of my research on Italian colonial architecture in Libya in the journal *Environmental Design*. During my stay I was assisted by faculty members of the Architecture Department at the al-Fateh University—including Dr. Hadi Kelani, Professor Ali Gana, and Dr. Abdul-Jawad H. Ben Swessi—without whose help I would not have been able to see (and document) the Italian legacy in Tripoli and its environs. Also important was the guidance of the Old City of Tripoli Restoration Project —including its director Fawzia Shalaby and Miriam Ahmed Salama, who patiently showed me through the extant courtyard houses in the medina. Although my research in Libya was not conducted in libraries and archives, it provided me with an intimate knowledge of the Italian presence and the local architecture.

My second research trip was supported by the Wolfsonian Foundation in Miami Beach, which awarded me an associate fellowship in the spring of 1997. During this time, I was assisted by Cathy Leff, Joel Hoffman, Pedro Figueredo, and Neil Harvey, who also provided me with an introduction to the world of the archive. Immediately following my stay in Miami, I embarked on the first of two major research trips to Italy, where most of the archival material on the colonial period in Libya is to be found. The first lasted three months and was sponsored by a travel grant from the Samuel H. Kress Foundation. A second, much longer sojourn, from October 1998 to December 1999, was made possible by a Fulbright grant through the Institute for International Education, and by an International Dissertation Research Fellowship from the Social Science Research Council (SSRC),whose funds were provided by the Andrew W. Mellon Foundation. I would particularly like to thank Luigi Filadoro, Rosanna Di Ronco, and the staff at the *Commissione per gli Scambi Culturali tra l'Italia e gli Stati Uniti* in Rome, who assisted me throughout this stay. I am also grateful to Kenneth Prewitt, Kenton Worcester, and the staff at the SSRC in New York for their kind support of my research.

During my visits to Italy, I consulted the following archives and libraries: the Central State Archive (ACS), the Historic Archive of the Ministry of Foreign Affairs (ASMAE), the Italian Institute for Africa and the East (IsIAO), and the State Publications Archive (APS), all in Rome; the Archive of the School of Architecture of the University of Florence; the Study Center and Archive (CSAC) at the University of Parma; the Museum of Modern and Contemporary Art (MART) in Rovereto; and the Wolfsonian Foundation in Genoa. This project would not have been possible without the assistance of the directors and staff of these institutions, in particular, Francesca Albani of the ACS, Stefania Ruggieri of the ASMAE, Carla Ghezzi of the IsIAO, Signor Adinolfi of the APS, Gianna Frosali of the Archive of the University of Florence, Simona Riva of the CSAC, and Carlo Prossar of MART. Special thanks go to Gianni Franzone of the Wolfsonian Foundation in Genoa, who kindly housed me and allowed me access to all of their books and archival material. I am also grateful to Anna Rava for our long conversations about her father's and grandfather's activities in Africa and for access to her private collection of photographs.

I am indebted to the following scholars and individuals in Italy who were of great help to me during these research trips: Claudia Conforti and Giuliano Gresleri provided references that were crucial to the development of this project. Marida Talamona advised me of the lack of attention to the issue of tourism in the Italian colonies and gave me access to her personal library. I am extremely grateful to Maristella Casciato, whose friendship and whose knowledge of modern Italian architecture were important resources for this project. Of the newer scholars in this field, I would like to thank Patrizia Bonifazio and Sara Protasoni; the latter allowed me to examine the private archive of the Milanese architects Luigi Figini and Gino Pollini. I am also thankful for the friendship and scholarly assistance of Paolo Scrivano and the hospitality of Carla Keyvanian, who generously housed me during my first research trip and for part of my second. Lastly, I benefited from the facilities of the Rome Program of the University of Waterloo, whose past and present directors—Eric Haldenby and Lorenzo Pignatti, respectively—have supported my Roman adventures over the past twenty years.

The next stage in the development of the book was supported by a postdoctoral fellowship at the Aga Khan Program for Islamic Architecture at Harvard University, which I was awarded for the 2000–2001 academic year. Given that the majority of my research was conducted in Italy, this work grounded my prior efforts in a more detailed understanding of the different historical periods of Arab and Ottoman cultural traditions of Libya and North Africa. Of particular importance to the present book was the development of a critical understanding of how the Islamic heritage in Libya was reinterpreted by the Italians, what traditions were "selected," and how these were changed. I am extremely grateful to Gülru Necipoglu for her kind sponsorship of this project, which not only allowed me to expand my understanding of Libyan architecture but also to present and publish my work. I am also indebted to David Roxburgh for his encouragement and support, to Jeff Spurr for his assistance with my research, and to the late Margaret Sevçenko for publishing my essay in the Aga Khan Program journal, *Muqarnas*.

Since that time, my research and the completion of this book have been supported by the Department of Architecture in the College of Architecture and Urban Planning at the University of Washington. In particular I would like to thank former chair Jeffrey Ochsner and present chair Vikram Prakash for providing me with the time and the resources to complete the project. I am similarly grateful to the dean, Bob Mugerauer, for his interest in, and personal support of, my research. The department and college have also helped me with the book through their financial assistance, including the Johnston/Hastings Publication Support in 2003 and money from the joint fund established by the Department of Architecture and the University of Washington Press. I also thank my colleagues for their encouragement and support. In addition to those already noted, I want to thank Alex Anderson for our many conversations about scholarship and research.

During the course of my research itinerary through Italian colonialism in Libya, my work has benefited from the many public presentations I have made at academic conferences and from the numerous colleagues who have responded to my work. These events allowed me to focus and develop the ideas that appear in the present volume. Particular thanks go to Dennis Doordan for his support of my talk at the Society of Architectural Historians annual meeting in St. Louis in the spring of 1996, which was my first attempt to examine the discourse on Italian colonial architecture. My research on tourist architecture in Libya was first presented at a session organized by Sibel Bozdoğan at the annual meeting of the Middle Eastern Studies Association in Chicago in December 1998. This paper was the backbone of the final two chapters of this book. I next presented this research at the College Art Association in New York in February 2000, thanks to the support of Nina Athanassoglou-Kallmyer. Of the many other occasions when I have made presentations, I am particularly grateful to Sibel Bozdoğan and Ulker Çopur for organizing the plenary session "Cross-cultural and Regionalist Practices" at the 12th Annual International Conference of the Association of Collegiate Schools of Architecture in Istanbul in June 2001; D. Medina Lasansky for putting together "Italian Modernisms: Architecture-Politics-Urban Identity" at Cornell University in October 2002; and Sandy Isenstadt, Eeva-Liisa Pelkonen, and Kishwar Rizvi for organizing "Local Sites of Global Practice: Modernism in the Middle East" at the Yale School of Architecture, April 4–5, 2003.

The ideas contained in this volume have been enriched by their publication in other venues. In addition to the essays noted above in *Environmental Design* and *Muqarnas*, I am grateful for the opportunity to publish in the *Journal of Decorative and Propaganda Arts* on the Tripoli Trade Fair and Italian colonial exhibitions. For this, I would like to thank guest editor Joel Hoffman and the staff at the journal for their patience and support. A book on architecture and tourism that I co-edited with D. Medina Lasansky has been central to the development of my research. This project began with our co-chairing a session on this topic at the College Art Association in Philadelphia in February 2002, after which we solicited additional papers, including my own essay on tourist architecture in Libya, for a book proposal. The book, published in the summer of 2004 by Berg Press, was an important step in the development of the theoretical perspective that has emerged in the final editing of the present volume.

The refinement of the manuscript and its smooth production have been due to the ongoing support of the University of Washington Press. This relationship began in the fall of 1998 when I was asked to submit a preliminary abstract for a book on this subject that could be included in the Studies in Modernity and National Identity Series. The abstract was submitted to the Press for a grant application that was being made to the Graham Foundation for Advanced Studies in the Fine Arts—and I am grateful to this group for their financial support. Since that time, I have continued to work with executive editor Michael Duckworth, who has patiently guided me through each step, from the first manuscript to the present book project, and to whom I am extremely grateful. I also thank managing editor Marilyn Trueblood, Ed Page for his careful editing of my manuscript, John Stevenson and Christina Merkelbach for directing the design and layout of the book, and Gigi Lamm for her assistance with funding and marketing issues. The production of the book has benefited from the fact that, as you will note in the image credits, much of the material is my own. For this I would like to thank the numerous book, postcard, and ephemera sellers at the Porta Portese Market, which I visited virtually every Sunday during my stays in Rome. I appreciate the various online booksellers around the globe through whom I was able to collect a substantial library of rare books. My next book may have to be a catalogue of these materials.

Finally, I would like to recognize the contribution of my family, whose patience and moral support throughout this book project have been a source of great strength. Although the subject of this book seems a long way for me to travel, both intellectually and culturally, it is not so far that it has separated me from those that I care about the most. In particular, I would like to give thanks to my mother, Lois, and mother-in-law, Josephine Iarocci, who have always shown great interest in my research. I must also acknowledge the support of my late father, Lloyd, and late father-in-law, Mario—both of whose unexpected loss during the course of this project caused a good deal of sadness. To my wife, Louisa, who for so many years has been my friend and my intellectual collaborator, I cannot possibly explain in how many ways this project is also hers. She has more than just endured my many travels and my eccentric scholarly interests; she has also been an important sounding board for my ideas. Perhaps most importantly, she has all too often helped my prose become more eloquent. It is to her and to our daughter, Lucia—who came along in time to see this work published—that this book is dedicated.

September 2005, Seattle

ARCHITECTURE AND TOURISM IN ITALIAN COLONIAL LIBYA

INTRODUCTION

Just yesterday we completed a second automobile raid from Tripoli to Ghadames led by General Graziani who established a new route, except for the large mobile dunes on the Sinouen Ghadames section. The people of Ghadames welcomed the Duke of Spoleto who was a principal participant in the raid, as well as the first [Italian] women who have visited Ghadames—namely my wife and daughter, Mrs. Graziani and the Contessa Bianconcini. Despite the tropical temperature, there were no remarkable incidents. This raid has demonstrated that the Tripoli Ghadames route can be completed in five days and that the extreme western territory [of the colony] is perfectly safe.
—Giuseppe Volpi, telegram to the Minister of the Colonies, 1925.[1]

Fig. I.1. Military plane with the convoy at Sultan during the automobile raid between Benghazi and Tripoli, June 1931.

On May 30, 1925, just one month before he would resign his post as governor of the Tripolitanian region of Libya to join the Ministry of Finance under Fascist dictator Benito Mussolini, Giuseppe Volpi returned to Tripoli from an automobile *raid* that had taken him to Ghadames and back in a total of ten travel days—a journey that he undertook along with a small entourage of guests that included General Rodolfo Graziani.[2] Although he participated in this expedition as a tourist, this was the same Graziani that presided over Volpi's reconquest of Tripolitania, a process that culminated just over one year earlier with a series of military exercises that recaptured this oasis settlement on the edge of the Sahara Desert.[3] With only seven passengers on board, this tourist caravan was composed of twelve officers guiding four passenger vehicles and one equipment truck—which gave it the appearance of an organized military operation. Although the conjunction of tourism and military control is an indication of the fragile hold the Italian colonial authorities had over this region, it also reflects what became one of the most characteristic features of tourism in Libya. The experience of the most authentic aspects of the indigenous culture was almost always filtered through the means and mechanisms of the modern metropole, thereby producing a liminal state in which the identities of East and West, indigenous and metropolitan, were fused into a single, though highly contested, reality.

The excursion of Volpi and Graziani was neither the first nor the last of its kind in the pre-Saharan region of Libya. A similar trip had been undertaken on Volpi's behalf by Major Valentino Babini at the beginning of March of the same year.[4] This first trip, which was preparatory for the second, had only two civilian passengers traveling with two officers, nine soldiers, and one military photographer.[5] As with the second itinerary, a convoy of five trucks was equipped with food, water, and gasoline for a trip that was some 600 kilometers in length in each direction. Other materials included

Fig. I.2. Map of the automobile raid between Tripoli and Ghadames, March 1926.

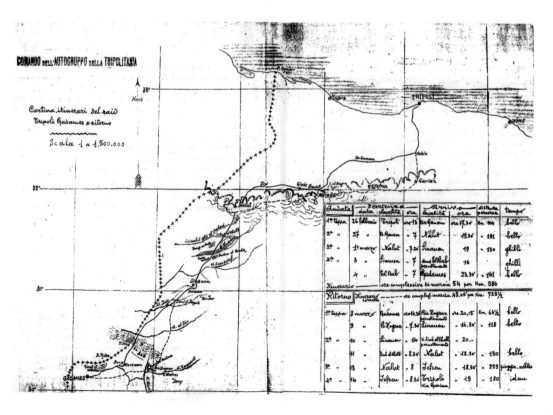

4

digging equipment and long metal channels for bridging difficult situations, both of which became indispensable to the success of the journey. The map drawn by Babini to document the trip resembles the planning of a military maneuver. This drawing also reveals the treacherous terrain of a region that was only traversable through the most advanced means of transportation available (fig. I.2). The organization and financial commitment made to such adventurous excursions reflects a desire to experience the exotic that would eventually lead to the tourist exploitation of the most remote regions of Libya—a development that quite naturally went hand in hand with its modernization.

The political dimension of colonial travel is evident in an even more elaborate excursion that General Graziani, then vice governor of the region of Cyrenaica, led in June of 1931. In this case Graziani traveled from Tripoli to Benghazi and back—a trip of 1,125 kilometers in each direction—in a total of six travel days. The journey was made with a prestigious group of government officials and business leaders, including Governor of Libya Marshall Pietro Badoglio, Undersecretary of the Colonies Alessandro Lessona, and officials from the Automobile Club of Benghazi.[6] This commemoration of the unification of Libya into a single colony free of rebellion was, in fact, a well-staged propaganda event. The complete suppression of rebel forces was not officially declared until January of 1932, some seven months after this voyage was completed.[7] A published account of the trip makes the intersection of commercial, tourist, and military discourses quite clear, stating: "The *raid* we are speaking of . . . establishes new currents of traffic, serving internal commerce as much as tourist propaganda, while even enhancing the security of military surveillance."[8] The photographs of the event provide visual testimony of this juxtaposition of tourism and colonial politics, with one particularly compelling image showing a small military plane encountering the long convoy of vehicles along the rugged coastal region of Sirt (fig. I.1).

The central argument of this book is that the tourist experience in Libya existed in a space of interaction where the modernization of this colony and the preservation of its indigenous culture were negotiated. In the first case, the creation of a tourist system was directly tied to, and dependent upon, the building and enhancement of ports, the regularization of a network of roads and related modes of transportation, and the creation of a system of modern public institutions. It is in this sense that, following military conquest and the creation of a viable infrastructure of transportation and public services, tourism can be considered the third wave of colonization. Organized travel in the Italian colonies was widely regarded as an important economic force that could facilitate the process of modernization. During the governorship of Volpi, it was argued that the presence of Italian and foreign travelers in Tripolitania would not only introduce money into the local economy, but had the potential to be the most important factor in the industrial development of the region.[9] The modernization of these overseas territories was an important backdrop to the creation of a positive image for colonial tourism. There was a considerable effort made by contemporary critics and commentators to represent the tourist system in these lands as modern—possessing the most perfect means of transportation, the most up-to-date facilities, and the most efficient organization. The emphasis on the modernity of this system was due, at least in part, to the fact that the tourist experience of Libya was a medium for the communication of Italy's status as a colonizing nation. The tourist system had the task of constructing an image of a modern and efficiently organized colony, thereby putting the accomplishments of Fascist colonization on display (fig. I.3).

This book also argues that tourism in Libya was an important vehicle for the direct experience of the indigenous culture. It brought Italian and foreign visitors to the most remote regions of this colony for the purpose of encountering its most characteristic aspects. This experience of difference was mediated through both colonial literature and research in scientific fields like anthropology.[10] These two means of dissemination reflect distinct, yet overlapping, conceptual models through which this culture was both communicated and understood. The indigenous culture of Libya was represented as an exotic and erotic projection of literary fantasy and as an important subject for serious academic inquiry. However, the idea of "native" culture is itself modern, the product of scientific disciplines that framed and contained these cultures in specific ways. Moreover, the Western experience of so-called primitive regions has often attempted to maintain and even supplement these cultures in a naturalized setting, in what has been described by art historian Griselda Pollock as a "spectacle of difference."[11] The self-conscious attempts by the Italian authorities in Libya to preserve the indigenous culture were reflected in the means by which the architecture of tourism attempted to appropriate its premodern opposite (fig. I.4).

The negotiation of the "modern" and the "indigenous" in the tourist system in Libya was closely tied to Fascist colonial politics—a politics that reached its most systematic developments under the governorship of Italo Balbo. His first priority was a

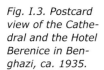

Fig. I.3. Postcard view of the Cathedral and the Hotel Berenice in Benghazi, ca. 1935.

series of administrative reforms that saw the unification of the single colony of Libya in April of 1935. This initial measure was merely the pretext for a more ambitious effort to integrate this colony and its bureaucratic structures into metropolitan Italy. This second aspiration came to fruition in January of 1939, when Libya became the nineteenth region of Italy.[12] Parallel to and supported by this modernization program was a *politica indigena*, or indigenous politics, that called for the preservation and protection of the environment and culture of the Libyans. Such colonial politics were clearly tactical in nature, aiming to disarm any dissent among the local populations through a series of carefully measured gestures of reconciliation. The approach taken to the indigenous populations by Balbo was understood as an alternative to what the Italian authorities argued were the failed attempts at assimilation on the part of the French colonies in North Africa.[13] In reality, their approach was not that different from the French in Morocco under Maréchal Hubert Lyautey. In respecting and preserving the cultural practices of the Libyan populations, the colonial administration was, at the same time, redefining those practices according to the demands of metropolitan society.

The discussion of the architecture of tourism in this book will be situated at the intersection of these touristic and political

Fig. I.4. Postcard view of the Berber Castle in Nalut, ca. 1935.

discourses. The same duality that was part of the Fascist colonial project in Africa was reified in the tourist facilities constructed in this region. The architecture of this tourist system balanced a need to project an image of a modern and efficient network of travel and accommodation, with the desire to preserve the experience of the indigenous culture. However, rather than view the tourist architecture in Libya as the product of a dialectical mediation of modernity and tradition, it will be seen that both of these terms—"modern" and "traditional"— were entirely constructed by the colonial authorities and, in that sense, are merely two different kinds of modernity. While the first of these deals with its structural and aesthetic principles, the second is tied to its objectivization and historicization of the "native."

The simultaneous experience of the modern and the indigenous placed the colonial tourist in an in-between realm. To be a tourist in Libya was to be contained within the mechanisms of modern metropolitan culture—the systems of transportation and accommodation as well as hierarchies of political and social control—at the same time as being removed from them. Even though one of the essential tourist experiences was escaping the moral and cultural boundaries of the West in favor of the experience of difference, that difference was framed and even defined by Western culture. This book investigates the condition of the modern and the indigenous as two overlapping experiences. Like the tourist system, this research cannot escape the ambivalence that is the very basis of Italian colonial rule in Libya. The marking of Libyan cultural identity as Western and non-Western is closely tied to a temporal dimension that alternately accepted and denied it a coevality with metropolitan culture. The temporal distancing of the "other" by the West has been examined by Johannes Fabian, who argues that there is a *persistent and systematic tendency to place the referent(s) of anthropology in a Time other than the present of the producer of anthropological discourse.*[14] In light of this view, I am careful to examine the status of the Libyans as alternating between that of colonial subjects—under the purview of the modern political structures of the Fascist authorities—and anthropological objects—both temporally and culturally distanced from the metropole as virtual specimens on display in an exhibition.[15]

In order to adequately deal with the liminal nature of colonial discourse in the Italian case, this book introduces the concept of an "ambivalent modernism." The idea that modernity is a complex and contradictory experience is certainly not new. In his book *All That Is Solid Melts into Air*, Marshall Berman argues that the "paradoxical unity" of modernity "pours us all into a maelstrom of perpetual disintegration and renewal, of struggle and contradiction, of ambiguity and anguish."[16] However, the use of the term "ambivalent modernism" *is* new. It is derived from the postcolonial theory of Homi Bhabha—an area of literary and cultural criticism that was largely initiated with the publication of Edward Said's *Orientalism* in 1978. Based upon the Foucauldian notion of discourse, Said argues that Orientalism is a dissemination of the politics of Western imperialism through all of its various cultural productions, which effectively creates and maintains hierarchies of domination of the West over the East.[17] By drawing in equal measure upon the psychoanalytic theory of Lacan, the writings of Frantz Fanon, the deconstructive theory of Jacques Derrida, and the cultural and political writings of Antonio Gramsci, Bhabha both advances and critiques the writings of Said. One of his primary assertions is that rather than being an expression of power and domination of the West over the East—an argument that had for many years been a source of criticism of Said's *Orientalism*—colonial discourse is, in fact, marked by an ambivalence. At the core of this argument is the assertion that the colonizer and colonized are not dialectically opposed, but rather linked in a relationship of repetition and difference—a relationship that, according to Bhabha, "does not merely 'rupture' the discourse, but becomes transformed into an uncertainty which fixes the colonial subject as a 'partial' presence."[18]

There are a number of reasons why Bhabha's discussion of the ambivalence of the colonial relationship is pertinent to the description of modern architecture in the Italian colonies, and particularly to the architecture of tourism. The first of these is its quite explicit rejection of a dialectical model for the examination of cultural difference. In "Of Mimicry and Man," Bhabha maintains that the colonial subject is a product of mimicry—its status in relation to the colonizer being *"almost the same, but not quite."*[19] According to this view, the colonial subject is produced metonymically, thus connecting it to a literary figure of speech where an object is substituted by a reference to its properties or qualities. Bhabha's description of a relationship of metonymy—where two unequal elements are closely linked—is similar to the imbrication of the modern and the indigenous in the tourist architecture of the Italian colonies. Second, the idea that colonial discourse is an ambivalent one communicates the complexity with which cultural identity is negotiated in the colonial context. In relating some of that complexity, Bhabha argues that mimicry is "at once a mode of appropriation and of resistance."[20] This argument is similar to that made by Lisa Lowe in her 1991 book *Critical Terrains: French and British Orientalisms*, where she reinterprets postcolonial theory through the filter of Antonio Gramsci's theories of cultural hegemony—a body of writings which recognize that mechanisms of power are not inevitable, as they are part of a complex process of consent and compromise.[21] The ambivalence of colonial discourse as theorized by Bhabha is a useful way to view the production of tourist space in Libya as a form of cultural hegemony that is neither uniform nor unchanging—existing in different forms in each domain and being subject to modification through time.

The idea of an "ambivalent modernism" is an extension of the writings on Fascist modernism in historical studies, whose earliest developments began in the 1970s. Arguing that this political regime was not guided by a monolithic ideological program, scholars like Roland Sarti posited Fascist politics as a form of reciprocal exchange between reactionary and revolutionary impulses.[22] More recently, Jeffrey Herf has offered the concept of "reactionary modernism" to describe the culture and politics of the Third Reich. Rejecting the dichotomy of tradition and modernity typical to these earlier historical models of Fascist politics and culture, Herf argues that reactionary modernists "incorporated modern technology into the cultural system of modern German nationalism, without diminishing the latter's romantic and anti-rational aspects."[23]

In the field of art and architectural history, one of the most significant contributions to the discussion of Fascist modernism has been made by Diane

Ghirardo, whose 1980 essay "Italian Architects and Fascist Politics: An Evaluation of the Rationalists' Role in Regime Building" attacks previous attempts to codify the Fascist content of architecture according to specific stylistic categories. She argues that architectural historians' attempts to identify the precepts of Italian Rationalism as revolutionary—and thus antithetical to the reactionary politics of Fascism—were seriously flawed. Ghirardo asserts that such dichotomies were not useful in examining cultural products during this period, as Italian Fascism was a political program that openly embraced diverse ideological and artistic tendencies. She illustrates this argument by examining how the projects and writings of Rationalist architects were, in fact, closely tied to Fascist concepts of mass society and social hierarchy.[24] Such studies are in support of this book's assertion that there is no incompatibility between the Italian colonial authorities' interest in the modernization of Libya and their attempts to preserve its indigenous culture. The tourist architecture of this colony was the product of a regime whose reactionary views of the local culture were carefully aligned with the integration of the region into metropolitan society. Rather than an oppositional model for reading the relation between these seemingly distinct and contradictory cultural and political forces, this book examines the experience of tourism and travel as a liminal state where such contested identities were negotiated in a continuous and seemingly naturalized setting.

The theoretical premises of this book are also related to recent research in tourist studies. One of the most crucial early writings in this area was Dean MacCannell's 1976 book *The Tourist: A New Theory of the Leisure Class*, which focuses upon the effects of tourist culture on questions of originality and authenticity.[25] In this argument, MacCannell asserts that the social conditions of modernity produce a separation between a given reality and its social representation—a separation that requires a kind of mystification that upholds a sense of authenticity in experience. According to this view, tourism is driven by a fruitless search for the authentic, a desire that is ultimately never satisfied, due to the contrived nature of such authenticity in the tourist environment. There are, however, some significant distinctions between the tourist experience in Libya during the period of Italian colonization and the model provided by MacCannell. In the Libyan case, this experience was more than the "staged authenticity" that he argues self-consciously presents the inner workings of a given tourist environment, thereby providing an experience of native culture that is purported to be free of all artifice.[26] Given that the Italian colonial authorities were presenting Libyan culture and not their own, this form of tourism represents a staging of cultural difference. The colonial authorities under Mussolini consistently argued that Libyan people and their culture were intricately linked with Mediterranean (and thus Western) culture—an assertion that went along with a recognition of their Arab (and thus non-Western) identity.[27]

The arguments of Tim Edensor in his 1998 book *Tourists at the Taj* offer a view of tourist space that is quite similar to that presented in this volume. While recognizing that colonial space was often clearly divided between colonizer and colonized, Edensor notes that a necessarily conflicted condition was produced out of the demands of modern tourism. In fact, he asserts that "the relationship between the regimented, domesticated European enclave and the 'other' space, that of the indigenous population, was complex, mirroring the ambivalence Europeans felt for colonized space and its inhabitants."[28] According to Edensor, the colonial tourist was torn between the fear of being outside the purview of the political and civic order of the colonial authority and the desire to experience a strange and even dangerous "other" culture. He goes on to remark that despite the colonial order that asserts the superiority of the West over the East, tourism in these regions is based upon the conception that the indigenous culture was more authentic—untouched by the progress that was destroying the cultural traditions of the West. In a recent essay written in conjunction with Uma Kothari, Edensor speaks about contemporary themed spaces on the tropical island of Mauritius—thereby extending his analysis to look at the constitution of tourist enclaves. In place of a model of tourism that opposes the authentic with the inauthentic, the authors offer a constellation of influences from historical to economic and cultural, as well as addressing many layers of significance, from those symbolized to those lived and performed. In a manner parallel to this book, Edensor and Kothari are interested in "the multiple consti-tution of place that facilitates varied and ambivalent readings."[29]

The idea of an ambivalent modernism is particularly important to a social and political analysis of the use of indigenous cultural references for a regional or national expression. This subject is discussed in great length by Antonio Gramsci in his *Prison Notebooks*, where he examines the concept of folklore as one of a series of what he calls "spontaneous philosophies," thereby connecting it with language, common sense, and popular religion. For Gramsci, folklore is spontaneous in that it has a direct correspondence with the members of a given social group at a specific moment in time. It is not a cultural activity that is imposed on the people, but rather an entire complex of historically conditioned practices and beliefs that emanate directly from an individual within a certain society. Folklore is a philosophy because, according to Gramsci, it is a practical activity that guides human conduct and, as such, implicitly contains within it a "conception of the world and of life."[30] Despite the almost exclusively local significance of such spontaneous philosophies, they play an important role in Gramsci's cultural writings. Although their weakness is an inability to have direct political implications, this characteristic allows for their resistance to the prevailing forces of society. Given that it is a form of cultural expression that is linked with a specific social group, Gramsci argues that the elevation of its implications to a broader scale would lead to "the birth of a new culture among the broad popular masses."[31] The term that he uses to describe such forms of cultural expression is "national-popular."

The Fascist regime clearly understood the important place of folklore in Italian culture and its potential political role. It was active in organizing a national conference on folklore studies in 1929 and even launched a journal on this subject in 1930 entitled *Lares*. A number of national and regional commit-tees were created to oversee this specific segment of the cultural sphere, and a National Museum of Popular Arts and Traditions was opened in Rome in 1941.[32] The Fascist intervention in folklore studies was characterized by a consider-able interest in its spiritual richness and diversity, and a grave suspicion of its potential to promote political disunity. Therefore, Mussolini employed a strategy of tapping into these long-standing popular traditions, while at the same time using them to constitute a national spirit. The Fascist promotion of folklore was certainly not a national-popular movement—that is, a popular movement formed *from below* that attains a national stature. It was intended to satisfy the desire for such regional manifestations while subverting their political potential. Moreover, in Gramsci's writings, the concept of "national," which implies the achievement of "a determinate world (or European) level of culture," is altogether different from that posed by Italian Fascism. In contrast with this Gramscian ideal—which is, in fact, an internationalism—the Fascist interest in regional culture was a form of what Gramsci referred to as "folkloristic provincialism."[33] It was the imposition *from above* of regional cultural norms on the people at a national level.

Gramsci's discussion of national-popular and folkloristic provincialism can be productively mapped onto the ambivalence of colonial discourse in Libya—and thus onto the architecture of the tourist system. In so doing, a series of questions can be raised about the political motivations of architects' appropriation of what were believed to be the most authentic forms of local culture—an appropriation that was closely tied with efforts to modernize the colony. Were architects attempting to elevate indigenous architecture to a national (or international) level (that is, as a national-popular expression) or merely imposing the appearance of regionalism as a national expression (that is, creating a folkloristic provincialism)? Can modern architects actually make use of indigenous references without violating the sense of authenticity and originality of these sources? This question is particularly pertinent when, as is the case of the tourist system in Libya, that indigenous reference is to an "other" culture.

What makes tourist architecture and the tourist experience in Libya distinct is the constant oscillation between modernizing and preservation tendencies. The movement between these seemingly conflicted forces has informed the structure of this book, which alternates between modernizing and preservation categories in moving from the broadest level of cultural and political inquiry into the Fascist colonial project in Libya to the tourist organization and finally to the architecture of the tourist environment. The book thereby presents a structure that derives quite directly from its theoretical premises: the first two chapters offering a coordinated argument about the connection between the modernization of Libya under Italian colonial rule and the creation of a modern tourist system, the second two chapters dealing with the connection between preservation initiatives and the experience of indigenous culture in the tourist system. Finally, the last two chapters examine the relationship between modernizing and preservation tendencies in the architecture of the tourist system.

More specifically, chapter 1 offers a historical examination of the political programs introduced by the colonial authorities in favor of the modernization of Libya, largely focusing on the period of Fascist rule. Beginning with the so-called rebirth of the region of Tripolitania during the governorship of Volpi, this discussion provides a chronological study of the efforts of the various colonial authorities to systematically organize the territory according to a Western standard—an effort that culminated during the governorship of Italo Balbo. In addition to discussing the creation of transportation systems and an infrastructure of public institutions, this chapter focuses on the political organization of Libya as Italy's so-called fourth shore, including the programs for demographic colonization. Another area of concern is the changing face of the city of Tripoli seen through the various master plans that dealt with its expansion. This general discussion is followed in chapter 2 by an examination of how a modern tourist system was created in Libya during this period. This effort built upon the modernization program through the construction of tourist accommodation and entertainment facilities and the foundation of a centralized authority for the supervision of tourist-related activities. The chapter concludes with a discussion of the experience of modernity in the tourist system of the Libyan Tourism and Hotel Association, or ETAL, an organization sponsored by the Fascist authorities that was responsible for all aspects of tourism during the second half of the 1930s.

The second pair of chapters opens with a historical examination of the Italian colonial government measures in favor of the indigenous populations of Libya. A crucial part of this discussion are the interventions into the native culture, whose guiding principle was the preservation of cultural traditions according to a modern Western conception. The chronology of chapter 3 begins with the earliest plans for the development of Tripoli and proceeds through the preservation initiatives of Volpi and the indigenous politics of Italo Balbo. In the case of this final stage of colonial rule, a series of parallel institutions were created for Libyan culture—a gesture that effectively incorporated "the natives" into the corporativist structures that were at the same time being applied to Fascist Italy. As a result, the distinction that has typically been made between modern (Western) and indigenous (non-Western) identities was in this case being blurred. Chapter 4 follows with a discussion of the two distinct modes through which the indigenous culture of Libya was presented in the tourist system. The first of these, colonial literature, suggests that the native culture would be experienced through a mysterious and even dangerous adventure. The second model through which the tourist experience of Libyan culture was structured was scientific research. In this case, the tourist was to encounter an unfamiliar culture through the objective lens of anthropology. This chapter ends with an examination of the presentation of indigenous culture in tourist publications and in the tourist system of the ETAL, including the creation of a number of experiences where this culture was staged for the purpose of its tourist consumption.

A similar structure is offered in the final two chapters, which examine architecture and tourism in Libya. In so doing, each of these chapters combines an examination of architectural discourse related to the Italian colonies with a discussion of the appropriation of local culture in the architecture of tourism. Chapter 5 offers a chronological investigation of the modernist discourse in tourist architecture, the first section beginning with the scholarly attitudes that shaped the understanding of indigenous culture in Libya in the 1920s. This period was remarkable for the relative lack of response to these scholarly views in colonial architecture and tourist facilities. This architectural and touristic discourse is then examined through the work of Alessandro Limongelli and the work and writings of Carlo Enrico Rava—a so-called Rationalist architect who was the most important figure in establishing the validity of the use of native forms by Italian architects working in the colonial context. Chapter 6 follows with a discussion of architectural discourse in the latter part of the 1930s, a period of time when the increasingly imperialist and racist rhetoric influenced contemporary scholars' interpretations of Libyan architecture. The central figure is the municipal architect Florestano Di Fausto, for whom the Mediterranean identity of Libyan architecture was tied to the specificity of its context and forms. The chapter concludes with the tourist buildings of Di Fausto, first examining the Mediterranean hotels constructed in the city of Tripoli and then ending with a tourist itinerary that linked the pre-Saharan hotels in Yifran, Nalut, and Ghadames. These last structures offer the most literal deployment of the indigenous culture of this region—a deployment that strongly questions the distinction between restoration and new construction.

Finally, a few points should be made about the material used to carry out this study of architecture and tourism in Libya and about the method of historical inquiry that informed the structure of this volume. In the first case, there has been quite deliberate use of a wide range of cultural productions as critical evidence to define the discourse on tourism in Libya. This material has included a variety of published sources, with a particular emphasis on tourist ephemera, from guide books to brochures and postcards. As Tim Edensor has argued, "such representations are part of a technology of enframing sights and cultures which forms the epistemological apparatus through which tourists see and interpret difference."[34] The exploration of the tourist experience has been supplemented by published material that intersected with this discourse, such as colonial novels and anthropological and ethnographic publications on the indigenous culture of Libya. The use of such a diverse array of tourist materials in historicizing architecture is related to a more general contention that these products are an important part of the cultural hegemony of Italian colonialism. This combination of material constitutes a larger context in which architectural objects can be understood. However, the diversity of research material examined in this book has been limited by the very nature of its object of study. This project explores the construction of tourist experience in Libya through representations produced *by* and *for* modern Italian society. Only in its critical perspective can this book deal with native voices.

In offering a succession of separate but overlapping arguments concerning the themes of modernization and preservation in the architecture and tourism in Libya, this book aims to avoid a monolithic theorization of this phenomenon. Rather, a larger historical field is produced in between these chapters, each of which traces its own separate chronology. The assertion is that architecture is a complex cultural formation that is part of a larger discursive field by which it is influenced and in which it actively participates. However, many of the specific architectural works that are examined here are seen to have certain aesthetic and theoretical qualities that transcend these discourses. Historicizing these architectural productions involves establishing a balance between their contextualization and the process of interweaving "disintegrated and fragmented constitutive units" in what the late architect and historian Manfredo Tafuri called "the labyrinthine path of historical study."[35] The historical method of this book is intended to respond to the interests of a diverse set of disciplinary fields—from historians of modern architecture to scholars of Fascism, colonialism, area studies, and tourism. This book proposes to engage those fields of inquiry through the breadth of its concerns, while maintaining its focus through an inquiry into a single, important phenomenon—the liminal state in which the experience of the modern West and of the indigenous culture of Libya interacted under the aegis of a modern tourist system.

**CHAPTER
ONE**

THE INCORPORATION OF LIBYA
INTO METROPOLITAN ITALY

Libya was, until a few decades or so ago, a stopping point, a blank space, or better still an interruption in the civilization, from the Atlantic to the Nile, that made much headway in the last century. The construction of the Litoranea, which completes an admirably disposed road network from the first period of the Fascist regime, has, more than any other work, contributed to the connection of North Africa to the rich and fervid life of the Mediterranean basin, that today in its size, with its ports and ancient and new trade centers, forms a large and unique system of transportation and commercial exchange.—Italo Balbo, "La Litoranea libica," 1938.[1]

Fig. 1.1. Aerial view of Tripoli, ca. 1925.

In October of 1938, the Alessandro Volta Foundation of the Italian Academy organized a conference in Tripoli on a series of topics related to the economic, religious, moral, and political status of Africa. The event was presided over by Air Marshall and Quadrumvir Italo Balbo, a charismatic military and political hero who was governor of Libya between 1934 and 1940. Some historians have argued that the popularity that Balbo enjoyed after leading an armada of twenty-four seaplanes on a mass flight across the Atlantic to New York and Chicago in 1933 eventually led to his being exiled by Fascist leader Benito Mussolini the following year.[2] Accepting his post in Libya, Balbo was able to apply his skill for organizing large scale spectacles of Fascist propaganda, like the transatlantic flight to America, to a more narrowly delimited political arena. The project for the *strada litoranea,* or "coastal highway," was just such a project—a massive work of engineering completed in 1937 that resulted in a continuous artery that connected Libya to Tunisia on the west and to Egypt on the east. At the Volta Conference, Balbo argued that this project was a modern infrastructure that facilitated communication along the Mediterranean coast within this colony and to its adjacent neighbors, thus enhancing the economic and civic progress of North Africa. He also noted that it reflected the "pride and glory of Imperial Italy" through recapturing the engineering prowess of ancient Rome.[3] What Balbo did not mention was that it was largely on the backs of Libyan laborers that this massive infrastructural project was completed.

The *strada litoranea* was one of the most prominent examples of the far-reaching modernization program that Balbo implemented in Libya—a program that prepared this region for its incorporation as a single and unified colony into the greater Italy. This integration was attempted through every possible means, from administrative and legislative restructuring, to public works and infrastructure improvements and a policy of demographic colonization. While one of the motivations behind this program was—as was the case for the French in Tunisia, Algeria, and Morocco—that of a mission intent on elevating the level of civilization of the various indigenous populations, the Italians had more profound ambitions. Libya was referred to as Italy's *quarta sponda,* or "fourth shore," an expression that reveals that this region was viewed as a piece of Italian soil on the other shore of the Mediterranean. Bringing Libya up to a European standard was necessary for the expansion of the borders of the metro-pole to encompass a region that for many was already Italian, much of it having been claimed as a Roman colony during the second and first centuries B.C. Quite obviously, this view would seem to take little account of the Libyans, who in this context were relegated to the status of passive caretakers of a region already dominated by Western culture.

Italian claims to the territory of Libya were the product of a long-standing belief that this region was part of Italy's "historic destiny"—a phrase auspiciously uttered by Liberal Prime Minister Giovanni Giolitti on the eve of the October 1911 invasion of this Ottoman territory.[4] The invasion of Libya was the last stage in a process that began in the initial days following the unification of Italy in 1860, during which time groups of colonial enthusiasts, such as the Italian Geographic Society, agitated for their country to join the "scramble for Africa." The two most influential arguments put forward by the early colonialist movements in Italy were that colonies in Africa would represent an affirmation of the country's status among the great powers of Europe, and that they would provide a solution to its emigration problems. These arguments were linked to and supported by an almost thirty-year effort of economic and cultural penetration prior to the initial invasion of Libya—an effort marked by accomplishments such as the opening of a branch of the Banco di Roma in Tripoli in 1907.[5] The general assertion of the economic and political importance of Libya was joined by the arguments of Nationalist commentators and intellectuals like Enrico Corradini, Giosuè Carducci, and Gabriele D'Annunzio, for whom the conquest of

this region could recapture the glories of Italy's Roman past.[6] Behind the imperialist rhetoric that viewed the remains of colonial towns like Leptis Magna
as symbols of a historic destiny, the Italians had a strategic aim in colonizing
North Africa. With the British protectorate in Egypt and the French in Tunisia,
the regions of Tripolitania and Cyrenaica could provide a beachhead that would
reinforce Italy's stake in the Mediterranean.

During the dictatorship of Benito Mussolini's Italian Fascist Party (1922–
43), when the Mediterranean was frequently referred to as an "Italian lake,"
Italy's Roman past was seen to give it a position of privilege in relation to other
European nations. This position was, at least in part, due to a distinction that
was made by the Fascists between a politics of action that was the logical heir
to the accomplishments of the Roman Empire, and the weak political programs
of either Liberal Democracy or Communism. In a speech given at the "Sciesa"
Regional Fascist Club in Milan on August 4, 1922, less than one month before
assuming the office of prime minister, Mussolini argued for a "tougher discipline" to be imposed on the bourgeoisie and the proletariat.[7] He further asserted
that the heroic actions of Italy in World War I revealed that while there was no
"state" in Italy, an Italian "nation" existed with a unity of customs, language,
and religion. According to this view, the "melancholic sunset" of Liberal politics
was giving way to a new Fascist era that offered a "politics of sternness and
reaction." In concluding this speech, Mussolini argued that one of the primary
goals of Italian Fascism was to direct the nation toward its "glorious destiny"
in the Mediterranean region—a goal stated with a rhetoric typical to such
bombastic pronouncements.[8]

The connection between the modernization program in Libya and the politics of Italian Fascism is evident in two prominent visits that Mussolini made
to the region. The first of these was in April of 1926, which, over the course of a
five-day trip, included a succession of highly staged ceremonies and rhetorical
speeches. This visit also included an itinerary that reached from the indigenous
settlement of Zuwarah near the Tunisian border to the Roman archeological
site of Leptis Magna on the east and the agricultural estates of the Gharyan
on the south.[9] One press report in the Fascist journal *Gerarchia* asserted the
importance of Italy's politics in Africa, stating: "Colonial politics should not be
considered, either in Italy or abroad, as a secondary politics but as an integral
part of its foreign policy."[10] The essay also speaks of the economic importance
of Libya, that is, that Fascist Italy had the ability to modernize this segment of
the African economy through its influence as a major European nation. Central
to this economic modernization was the agricultural development of Libya,
something that was the subject of Mussolini's final speech during this visit,
which was at the First National Conference of Colonial Agriculture, held at the
Miramare Theater in Tripoli. In recognizing the creation of a "new generation"
of individuals "shaped by Fascism," Mussolini argued that their fundamental
virtues of "tenacity, perseverance and method . . . must shine above all in the
Colonies."[11] In other words, the attributes that Fascism was espousing in its
political propaganda—such as unselfish sacrifice for one's nation—were exem-
plified in the pioneers of agricultural colonization in Tripolitania. As is made
clear in this speech, the modern Fascist individual was a colonist.

During Mussolini's second voyage to Libya—which took place from March 12 to March 21, 1937—his travel itinerary followed the length of the just completed *strada litoranea*, beginning near Tobruk at the eastern border with Egypt and traveling through Benghazi and Tripoli to Zuwarah and the western border with Tunisia. The strict adherence to this route and the political rhetoric of the visit reflect a shift from a Mediterranean politics to an imperial one. This political transformation took place following the Italian invasion of Ethiopia in October of 1935 and the declaration of an Italian empire in Africa in May of the following year. The tension between these two political views is evident in a speech Mussolini gave to his "Comrades of Tripoli," where he quite forcefully asserted that, despite a "campaign of alarmism" that was triggered by his visit to Libya, "we want to live in peace with everyone within the Mediterranean, and we offer our collaboration to all who demonstrate an identical will."[12] While a good amount of the speech was addressed to the issue of Italian foreign policy in Africa, it did not fail to recognize the substantial effort made to modernize the colony. Indeed, Mussolini noted that "the cities have been transformed and beautified" and that in the Libyan countryside "the virile Italians . . . awoke a land that had been sleeping for centuries."[13] Quite clearly, the Fascist policy in Libya continued to be one of incorporating this region into the metropole. By 1937 the governorship of Italo Balbo and the guidance of the Fascist authorities had brought Libya much closer to fulfilling its promise as Italy's fourth shore— that is, as both an outlet for demographic colonization and an extension of its borders within the Mediterranean.

It is important to note that the modernization program in Libya was parallel to the even more substantial commitment that the Fascist authorities made to the improvement and expansion of roads, railways, and transportation networks throughout Italy. These changes were accompanied by the reinforcement of existing public amenities, like post offices, rail stations, and universities, and the creation of new institutions, like the *Casa del Fascio*, the *Organizzazione Nazionale Dopolavoro*, and the *Gioventù Italiana del Littorio*.[14] However, even though the same effort to modernize that was taking place in Italy was being undertaken in Libya, and as such it was a testing ground for the metropole, there was a quite significant difference. Despite the view that Libya was an extension of Italy on the African shore of the Mediterranean—and in that sense it could be incorporated into the metropole—the modernization of the region was still an imperialist project of economic and cultural colonization. Moreover, it took little account of the Ottoman reforms in favor of economic development and European capitalist penetration in the latter half of the nineteenth century.[15] To make this situation more complicated, even if much of the work executed by the Italians in Libya was a projection of the modernity of the metropole, that modernity was said to be based upon, and harmonize with, the colonial context. In other words, the status of modernity in Libya was, from the beginning, an ambivalent one.

THE REBIRTH OF TRIPOLITANIA

The transformation of Libya from what the Italians regarded as a somewhat backward Ottoman possession began in January 1912, only a few months after

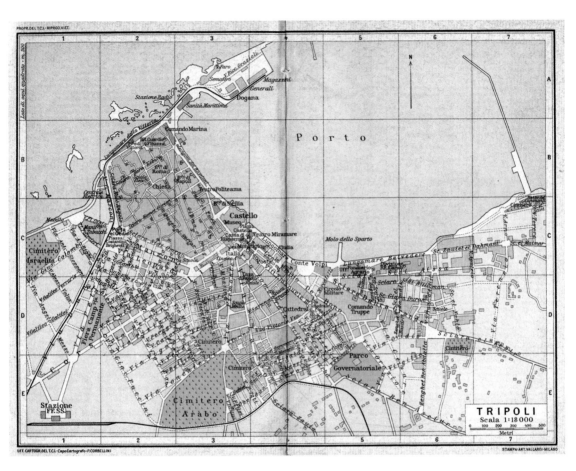

Plate 1. Map of Tripoli, from L.V. Bertarelli, *Guida d'Italia del Touring Club Italiano. Possedimenti e colonie* (Milan: Touring Club Italiano, 1929).

Plate 2. Cover of a brochure for Mediterranean cruises (1934), published by Italia Cosulich.

ALME SOL POSSIS
NIHIL VRBE ROMA
VISERE MAIVS

LA LIBIA
TVRISTICA

Plate 3. Cover design of the guidebook La Libia turistica (Milan: Prof. G. De Agostini, 1938),
published by the Libyan Tourism and Hotel Association.

Plate 4. Bruno Santi's cover design for Libia magazine (June 1937), published by the Libyan Tourism and Hotel Association.

Plate 5. Theater program for the Uaddan Hotel and Casino in Tripoli, January 31, 1937.

Plate 6. Drawing of Yifran from the valley with an automobile, from Itinerario Tripoli-Gadames (Milan: Tipo-Litografia Turati Lombardi, 1938).

Plate 7. Advertisement for the Hotel Derna (1937).

رحلة موسوليني الى ليبيا

Plate 8. Cover of an Arabic publication commemorating Mussolini's visit to Libya in March 1937.

Plate 9. Cover of the novel Piccolo amore Beduino (Milan: L'Eroica, 1926), by Mario dei Gaslini.

E/OTICA

Direttore: MARIO DEI GASLINI

| Anno I. - N. 1 | EDIZIONE PER L'ITALIA | C. C. con la Posta |

MENSILE DI LETTERATURA
COLONIALE

CRONACHE ARTISTICHE
E MONDANE

L. 5

MILANO
VIA LUCIANO MANARA, N. 2
Telefono 51-313

Plate 10. Cover of the journal Esotica (October 1926), published by Mario Dei Gaslini.

ENGLISH EDITION

Plate 11. Cover of the brochure Tripoli (Rome: Novissima, 1929), published by the National Association of Tourist Industries and the Italian State Railway.

Plate 12. Cover of the journal Difesa della Razza (20 August 1938).

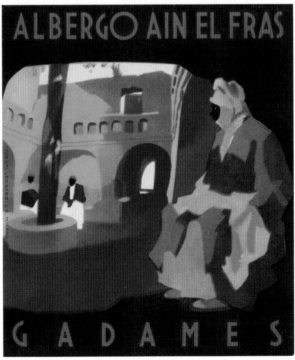

Plate 13. Baggage stickers for the Hotel Ain-el-Fras in Ghadames and the Hotel at the Excavations of Leptis Magna in Al-Khums, 1937.

Plate 14. Cover of the brochure Combinazioni di soggiorno in Libia (Tripoli: ETAL, 1937), published by the Libyan Tourism and Hotel Association.

Plate 15. Postcard view of the Uaddan Hotel and Casino in Tripoli.

Plate 16. Cover of the guidebook *Itinerario Tripoli-Gadames* (1938), published by the Libyan Tourism and Hotel Association.

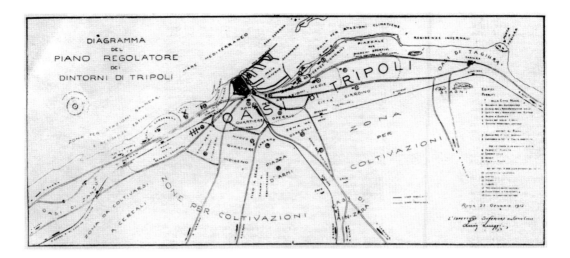

Fig. 1.2. Master plan
of Tripoli (1912), by
Luigi Luiggi.

the initial invasion. It was at this time that the Ministry of Public Works sent the engineer Luigi Luiggi to Tripoli.[16] His task was to both consider the administrative structure of the public works offices and identify the most important improvements to the infrastructure of the colony. The second part of this mission was published in the journal *Nuova Antologia* in March of 1912, where Luiggi recommended the restructuring of the port, the introduction of water and sewer systems, the regularization of streets, and the construction of public and private buildings in the city of Tripoli and its surrounding oasis.[17]

One of the key components of Luiggi's proposal was a master plan for the development of the city, whose organization was based upon the most modern principles of urban planning (fig. 1.2). The approach to structuring the colonial expansion of Tripoli was to create a new city for the metropolitan populations to the southeast of the medina—a program of separation that was common to both British and French colonies. The new Tripoli was to be a garden city whose urban center would be alongside the existing castle. In the surrounding oasis, the land to the southwest was reserved for industrial development while the remainder was given over to agriculture. The street network was based on the existing routes that radiated from the castle, with an additional connecting road that was likened by Luiggi to the "Ring" in Vienna, the boulevards of Paris, and the crescents in London. In addition to the new streets, a system of tramways was proposed that would make for easy movement between home and work in a manner that was "like all other modern cities."[18]

The proposal for the improvement of the public works of Tripoli in *Nuova Antologia* is the first document of what would become the official policy of the Italian colonial authorities in Libya. The goal was to modernize the region in order to make it suitable for a program of demographic colonization. Luigi's proposal is filled with references to metropolitan precedents, such as a comparison between his scheme for the Mediterranean seafront of Tripoli and the Promenade des Anglaises in Nice. It also makes note of the practices of other European nations: the separation of the new city from the old in French Tunisia and the British practice of building a Government House in its colonies. Notably, Luiggi does not fail to assert the value of Tripoli as a tourist destination. With its modern villas, hotels, and *pensioni*, it was seen to be less costly than the cities of Cairo or Algiers, while offering all of the benefits of a "mild climate and brilliant sun."[19]

In the years immediately following its adoption in January of 1914, the master plan of Tripoli was largely unrealized except for the partial completion of work on the water system and the repair of some of the major streets in the city and oasis. The failure of the plan was largely for reasons of political instability. Despite the successes of the year-long military campaign that began in October 1911—which resulted in the Italian forces capturing the most significant coastal enclaves of Tripoli, Benghazi, Derna, and Misurata Marina—the peace treaty with the Ottomans provided little security for the development of the region. The major reason behind the precarious situation in Tripolitania was that despite any problems the Libyans had with the Ottoman rule, they quite understandably never viewed their non-Muslim invaders as a liberating force. As one historian has argued, colonialism under the Italians quite profoundly disrupted the delicate balance that had developed between long-standing tribal allegiances and newly emerging economic and class formations.[20]

The initial military accomplishments by the Italian forces in the coastal region were followed by successive gains, which included the taking of the southern oases of Ghadames in the Jabal and Murzuq in the Fezzan. What followed, however, was a turbulent period of guerrilla warfare that included internal squabbling among the local leaders and active resistance by the Libyans. The advances of the Italian forces were swiftly countered by a number of humiliating defeats, leaving them in a poorer position in the fall of 1915 than they were at the time of the initial invasion.[21] In a desperate attempt to stabilize the situation, the Italian authorities reached a peace accord with the Sanusi tribes in the spring of 1917 and passed what was called the Fundamental Law in June 1919, which granted the right to a parliament, governing councils, and Italian citizenship to the Libyans. The system of indirect rule called for in this legislation, however, was never effectively implemented due to continuing instability.

The situation in Tripolitania changed following Giuseppe Volpi's appointment as governor in August of 1921, which ended what he called a politics of "humility, brotherhood and favors."[22] Volpi abolished the parliament and employed a more strict and hierarchical handling of the Libyans. The political changes were accompanied by a series of rather brutal military campaigns that were aimed at what the Italians termed the "reconquest" of Tripolitania. The operations began in January of 1922 with the invasion of Misurata Marina, a key port whose capture signaled a change in momentum in favor of the Italian forces. The military campaigns were primarily undertaken under the direction of a young colonel, Rodolfo Graziani, who was later dubbed "the butcher" by the Libyans for the cruelty of his military tactics in Cyrenaica.[23] It was under his direction that the Italian forces captured the coastal strip between Tripoli and the Tunisian border on the west and the oasis of Nalut on the south. With the rise to power of Mussolini in October of that year and the subsequent appointment of Luigi Federzoni as minister of the colonies, the military campaigns received greater political and financial support in Italy. As a result, by the end of Volpi's governorship, in July of 1925, all of the coastal regions and some of the most strategic posts within the interior of western Libya were under Italian control.[24]

These military campaigns were the necessary pretext for what was the first serious attempt to modernize the infrastructure and improve the colonial economy—an effort that was a central component of Volpi's attempt to revive Tripolitania. This modernization was largely based upon a firm political will and a careful consideration of the region's economic development. As a wealthy Venetian financier and industrialist who had considerable experience trading with the East, he was brought in for his business skills rather than for his political and military acumen.[25] The "rebirth" of the region under his direction was thus closely tied to the development of a viable economy, which, like military conquest, was an equally necessary precondition for the facilitation of tourism. The basis of the economic development of Tripolitania was largely agricultural, but this kind of economy did not develop spontaneously. Volpi was able to initiate a far-reaching program of land acquisition by taking advantage of the Islamic law that states that any agricultural land reverts to the public domain after lying fallow for three years.[26] In conjunction with this extremely dubious process of expropriating land, public offices were created to facilitate the development of agricultural estates by individual landowners and large-scale private companies, and the banking system was augmented through the formation of a credit institution for agriculture. However, the economic initiatives of Volpi went well beyond the agricultural development of Tripolitania. He was also responsible for setting up a more efficient and profitable system of taxation for Italians and the Libyans, which allowed the colony to develop in a more rapid and self-sufficient manner.[27]

Coincident with, and in support of, the economic development of Tripolitania, Volpi put a great emphasis on public works projects—an effort that was aimed at the improvement of the infrastructure and the construction of a network of public institutions. These projects had both practical and propagandistic value. They provided the necessary amenities to create the impression of a more modern and efficient colony, while giving an important visual corollary to the Italian military and administrative presence in the region. With the improvements to roads and modes of travel—what was called the "politics of transportation"—the intention was to assure military and civilian movement within the colony while also improving its connection with Italy and Europe.[28] These projects included the restructuring of the port and the creation of a wide tree-lined network of streets (fig. 1.1). The improvements in the infrastructure of Tripoli were, at least in part, conceived from the viewpoint of their political message—the intention being, among other things, to "communicate the sense of a stable reconquest."[29]

The image of a benevolent Italian presence in Libya was equally evidenced in the substantial remaking of the public face of Tripoli. Largely based upon the still unrealized master plan of 1912, a series of important public-works projects were completed.[30] A public open space, Piazza Italia, was created in front of the existing castle, and a major public artery, the Corso Vittorio Emanuele III, was built over the existing Sharah Azizia (fig. 1.3). This new street, which had a decidedly metropolitan character, was defined by a number of significant public institutions, including a town hall, courthouse, cathedral, and new governor's residence, thereby becoming the center of Italian civic life. A second infrastructural intervention was important to the definition of the public image of the city along the Mediterranean. A series of waterfront boulevards were created that stretched from the western portion of the old city along its northern edge and past the castle to form the seafront of the city. The last of these arteries, called the Lungomare Conte Volpi, was designed by the Roman architect Armando Brasini to create a distinct character to the Mediterranean face of Tripoli (fig. 1.4). It comprised a wide boulevard lined with palm trees and was defined on the water's edge by a stone balustrade. A number of new public institutions were constructed along this artery—including the Miramare Theater, the Bank of Italy, and the Grand Hotel—

Fig. 1.3. Corso Vittorio Emanuele III in Tripoli, ca. 1925.

Fig. 1.4. View of the Lungomare Conte Volpi in Tripoli (1922-24), by Armando Brasini.

thereby creating the impression that Italy was a modern colonial power in North Africa.

The full range of the modernization program of Volpi was captured in a beautifully illustrated commemorative volume entitled *La rinascità della Tripolitania*—a book that was fittingly presented to Mussolini during his 1926 visit.[31] This publication examines the renewal of the region within the context of a broader study of the landscape and people and a detailed discussion of its past, present, and future status. The central section is organized according to the major themes that informed the development of Tripolitania under Volpi—from the politics of colonization (agricultural development) to financial politics, the politics of transportation (the rail, road, and telephone systems), and the moral conquest (the school and justice systems, archeological research, and public-works projects). Volpi captured the main outlines of the four-year-long public-works campaign in the dedication to this volume, where he places a particular focus on its development for the purposes of agriculture. Echoing the political rhetoric on the colonies already developed by Mussolini, Volpi concludes his introduction by stating: "In the Mediterranean Italy has to complete the actions assigned by nature and by history, which, if it has paused for centuries, [today it] cannot be stopped."[32] Despite the rhetorical power of this statement and of this published volume—which suggests that Italy had already realized its historic destiny in

25

Libya—the military hold remained fragile and the substantial evidence of the modernization of the region had to wait for his successors.

BUILDING A MODERN COLONY

The modernization program of Governor Volpi was continued and expanded by Quadrumvir Emilio De Bono, who took office in July of 1925. These advances are largely attributable to the greater level of security provided by the ongoing military campaigns of Rodolfo Graziani—which were eventually able to claim the central coastal region of Sirt south to the oasis of Jufra and the 29th parallel.[33] The increasing importance of Libya to the Italian government was signaled by Mussolini's visit in April of 1926. The trip resulted in a number of new initiatives being undertaken in Italy, including the organization of the first Colonial Day by the Italian Colonial Institute on April 21, 1926—an annual event held in major Italian cities that celebrated the Italian colonies. This period also witnessed the creation of new publications on colonial matters, such as the journals *Rivista delle Colonie Italiane* and *L'Oltremare*—both of which were first issued in November of 1927.[34] In Tripolitania, the colonial government sponsored the continuing development of the agricultural industries, which De Bono asserted was crucial to the economic viability of the region.[35] In contrast with his predecessor, he favored government sponsorship of individual landowners over the large-scale agricultural concessions preferred by private speculators. De Bono was also a proponent of a more explicit specification of the demographic goals of this process. The result was the passing of the "De Bono Laws" for agricultural development in Tripolitania in 1928. While these laws fell short of a government-sponsored program for agriculture, it was the first step in a process that would lead to the systematic, government-organized influx of families onto individual farms that would happen in the mid-1930s.[36]

The economic development of Tripolitania was greatly assisted by a second major initiative undertaken by the De Bono administration—the foundation of the Tripoli Trade Fair. This presentation of metropolitan and colonial goods was held on an annual basis in this North African city between 1927 and 1939. The event was organized in a manner that was similar to exhibitions in Italy like the Milan Trade Fair, which presented the most recent advances in industrial and artisanal products. In Tripoli, the materials presented included Italian agricultural, mechanical, metallurgic, scientific, chemical, transportation, sports, and hygiene products. In this sense, the exhibition had a "strictly national character," with the purpose of increasing the level of trade between Libya and Italy.[37] The Tripoli Trade Fair was also an instrument of colonial propaganda that would demonstrate Italy's strength as a colonizing nation by encouraging development. The rhetorical dimension of the exhibition is evident in the various news reports, like that of Filippo Tajani in the *Corriere della Sera* that erroneously asserted that this was the only such event organized by a Western nation in the colonial context.[38] The architectural character of the first Tripoli Trade Fair also reflected its propagandistic function, combining rather indistinct industrial sheds with more monumental buildings like the Roman pavilion by the architect Felice Nori (fig. 1.5). The economic and political function of this exhibition was similarly manifest in its status as a major event on the tourist

calendar of Libya. By drawing metropolitan visitors to the region, it was supposed to bolster the economy and increase the knowledge of the colonial context.[39]

Fig. 1.5. Roman pavilion at the Tripoli Trade Fair (1927), by Felice Nori.

The economic development of Tripolitania under De Bono was accompanied by an extensive public-works program. Over the course of his governorship, almost 600 such projects were completed, including the improvement of ports; the extension of water and sewer systems; and the creation of a network of schools, post offices, hospitals, and government and military offices.[40] The result of this building campaign was the enhancement of the public services and infrastructure in the city of Tripoli and the extension of that network to smaller centers along the coast and into the interior of Tripolitania—including towns like Yifran, Nalut, and Ghadames that became important tourist destinations.[41] As the seat of the regional councils and military command for the southern area and an important center for agricultural colonization, the town of Gharyan, one hundred kilometers south of Tripoli, was provided with a police station, a postal and telegraph office, schools, a medical clinic, a mess hall, shops, and a hotel—all constructed between 1925 and 1928.[42] Equally important to the modernization program was the enhancement of the road network, an effort that was aimed at consolidating the areas that were gained during the ongoing military campaigns. These improvements included the road that followed the Mediterranean coast from Tunisia on the west to Sirt on the east—an artery whose presence signified the continuous control of these coastal territories by the Italian authorities. Also important was the construction of a system of roads within the interior of Libya south of Tripoli, a system that was conceived from the viewpoint of military surveillance.[43]

The policies carried out during the governorship of De Bono added considerably to the legacy of Volpi in the area of public works, introducing an infrastructure of modern amenities that was conceived according to metropolitan standards. In particular, a number of key appointments were made that had a substantial influence on the public face of Tripoli. The most important of these was the selection of Maurizio Rava as general secretary of Tripolitania in March of 1927.[44] As the father of Rationalist architect Carlo Enrico Rava, he had a direct knowledge of current trends in architecture and planning. It was under the elder Rava's guidance that the architect Alessandro Limongelli was appointed in 1928 to succeed Armando Brasini as art consultant to the City of Tripoli. In this capacity, Limongelli took the planning of the city in a new direction, as can be seen in his proposal for the restructuring of Piazza Italia in Tripoli from 1931 (fig. 1.6). As a young architect educated in the Roman school, the classicism of his work was tempered by an abstract modernist aesthetic. In the case of this proposal for Tripoli, the modern *romanità* of his work is adjusted to integrate with the environmental qualities and characteristic forms of the local architecture.

With the appointment of Marshall Pietro Badoglio as

Fig. 1.6. Proposal for the rearrangement of Piazza Italia in Tripoli (1931), by Alessandro Limongelli.

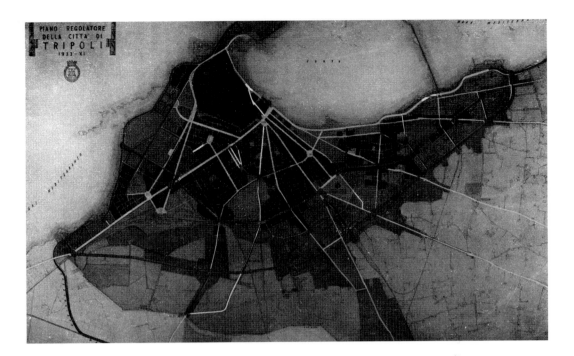

governor of the regions of Tripolitania and Cyrenaica in January of 1929, the colony of Libya and its related politics took a decisive step toward unification. It was under the guidance of Badoglio that the continuing military operations of General Graziani were concluded in January of 1932 after the complete "pacification" of these two colonies. However, this accomplishment came with a heavy price, particularly for the Libyans. In the region of Cyrenaica, the Sanusi tribes were bombed with mustard gas, 90,000 so-called rebels were put into concentration camps, and some of their leaders, like ʻUmar al-Mukhtar, were publicly executed. The Italians not only sacrificed lives and money in this struggle, their reputation in the Islamic world suffered greatly, and for good reason.[45]

The planning of the major cities in Libya received considerable attention as a result of the increasingly stable military control of the region. It was during Badoglio's governorship that the Milanese architects Alberto Alpago Novello, Ottavio Cabiati, and Guido Ferrazza were asked to prepare a new master plan for Tripoli and Benghazi. The concept of their proposal for Tripoli, which was completed in 1933, was to provide for the expansion of the city to approximately double its current size of 80,000 inhabitants, while maintaining the basic principles of the original plan of 1912, which called for a radial patterning for the main thoroughfares of the new city (fig. 1.7).[46] A series of transverse arteries were added to this radial system in order to provide better connections within the existing street network and divide the city into separate districts.

Fig. 1.7. Master plan of Tripoli (1933), by Alberto Alpago Novello, Ottavio Cabiati and Guido Ferrazza.

Fig. 1.8. Master plan of Casablanca (1914), by Henri Prost.

Fig. 1.9. Roman pavilion at the Tripoli Trade Fair (1929), by Alessandro Limongelli.

The approach taken in the proposal of Alpago Novello, Cabiati, and Ferrazza was not unique to the Italian context, as it bears a striking resemblance to that prepared in 1914 by Henri Prost for the city of Casablanca (fig. 1.8). This French colonial precedent has been referred to by Paul Rabinow as "techno-cosmopolitanism" for, among other things, its tendency to rationalize the order of the city into functional zones.[47] The major difference in the plan of Tripoli is that it offers an intricate scale of planning through the creation of a series of separate centers that were intended to decentralize the city while providing local amenities.[48] This structure was to act as a separation between areas of greater density, such as the waterfront district, and those on the periphery of the city that were to have a more equitable balance between built form and landscape. It was argued that the combination of this new structure and the related restrictions on building height and density would create a more orderly city and restrict the extent of new development so as to preserve the surrounding oasis.[49]

Badoglio was also active in the broader modernization program related to the development of the Libyan economy. On the issue of agriculture his policies followed directly from those of De Bono, who had begun a series of government sponsored programs to encourage Italians to settle in Libya as agricultural colonists. Despite some progress in the first year of his governorship, the demographic goals of private development and the initial efforts at state colonization were largely blunted by the financial drain of the ongoing resistance of the Libyans and the world economic depression.[50] The other major economic force in the Libyan economy, the Tripoli Trade Fair, was substantially expanded under Badoglio. These changes included its relocation to a new commercial and residential quarter along the Corso Sicilia in 1929 and the subsequent construction of a series of permanent buildings. One example of this change is Alessandro Limongelli's pavilion for the governorate of Rome, which was completed in 1929.[51] In contrast with the more theatrical use of classical forms in the temporary pavilion by Felice Nori, the simplified exterior volumes of Limongelli's project reveal a classical language organized according to a modern aesthetic sensibility (fig. 1.9). An equally significant change to the Fair was its opening in 1930 under the banner "First Inter-African Exhibit." This new title signified a shift in this exhibition from a national representation to a more international one—something that was achieved through the inclusion of a small group of African and European exhibitors.

In conjunction with the improvement of the Libyan economy, Badoglio pursued the continued development of the public-works infrastructure of Libya, for which he had considerable economic support from the Fascist government.[52] In Tripoli, these projects involved the enhancement of existing services, such as the expansion of hospital facilities and the introduction of new public amenities, such as an Italian-Arab School.[53] In remote locations in the colony, more basic services were improved or added, such as an electrical plant in Yifran, a Casa del Fascio in Nalut, and a health clinic and new barracks in Ghadames. This process of enhancement of the public infrastructure expanded considerably in 1932 after the military stabilization of the entire colony, particularly in remote areas like the Fezzan in southern Tripolitania.

The improvements to the public works and services under Badoglio were coincident with a substantial development of the road network.[54] These projects included extending the existing road system in the more populated regions along the coast and upgrading the coastal road between Zuwarah, Tripoli, and Misurata. On the interior, continued improvements were made to existing roads connecting Tripoli with Ghadames, and new roads were introduced in the recently claimed territories.[55] The new infrastructure served to improve the means of travel and the level of public amenities available—an enhancement that was closely tied to its tourist development. Among the buildings executed by the municipality was a series of eight hotels that were constructed throughout the colony.[56] While most of these were of a modest size, this was the beginning of what would become a substantial network of hotels that would make travel possible in the most remote locations.

At the end of the Badoglio era, the city of Tripoli was just beginning to resemble the modern colony that the Italians had envisioned at the time of the initial master plan of 1912. A commemorative volume published in 1933, entitled *La Nuova Italia d'Oltremare*, communicates the most important dimensions of that vision, in addition to presenting the political, economic, and cultural context of Italian colonization.[57] The scope of this book, which presents Libya in conjunction with Italy's other colonies of Eritrea and Somalia, underscores the fact that Mussolini increasingly saw Libya as part of a broader imperial politics. These ambitions are evident in the preface to the book, where Mussolini states: "Italy is a great colonizing nation, both in the field of economic development and in that of demographic population, and our modest claims [in the region] are fully justified."[58] The rhetorical bluster of the preface is followed by a 1,700-page two-volume book that presents a staggering accumulation of information on the past and current development of Italy's colonies. The material is divided up into eight different sections, beginning with the political and military history and including agricultural development; public works and transportation; education; economic, administrative and industrial development; and scientific research and propaganda. The bold ambitions of this book are a foreshadowing of attitudes that would take hold in the mid-1930s, that is, that "the fatherland has finally recovered its historical reality—the sense and the constructive capacity of Empire."[59]

THE POLITICS OF MODERNIZATION

The political modernization of Libya that eventually involved its incorporation into metropolitan Italy was the major accomplishment of the governorship of Italo Balbo, who was appointed to this position in January of 1934. The first step in this process was a series of administrative reforms that called for the unification of the regional governments of Tripolitania and Cyrenaica into a single authority.[60] These changes represent a consolidation of Balbo's powers in governing the colony and the creation of a system of government analogous to that found in Italy. While such adjustments had been proposed before, it was argued that the conditions were right for combining the economic development of the colony with its administrative redefinition along metropolitan lines. These proposals were initially met with a considerable amount of resistance on the part of Emilio De Bono—then Minister of the Colonies—who saw this as an effort to avoid being under his supervision. Mussolini was equally skeptical of the plan as he was reluctant to concede any substantial powers to Balbo.[61] The legislation that was passed into law in December of 1934 aimed to centralize the authority of Balbo and disseminate his power through a newly conceived regional structure. In order to accomplish this goal, the regional governments were eliminated in favor of a central authority in Tripoli. In becoming the governor general of Libya, Balbo assumed a position of absolute authority over all political, administrative, legislative, military, and financial matters.[62]

The dissemination of Balbo's power was related to the division of Libya into two distinct regions, the first of these comprising four provinces along the coast—Tripoli, Misurata, Benghazi, and Derna. Because these areas were believed to be more linked "with the Mediterranean world than to the African one," their governing was intended to "approach that of the regulation of the Mother country"—the goal being their eventual incorporation into Italy.[63] The area south of the 29th parallel, which included the remote oases of Jufra, al-Kufra, and Ghat in the desert regions of Libya, was considered African territory whose people and state of civilization were believed by the Italians to be inferior. As such, the Libyans in this region would always remain as colonial subjects, their government coming under the direct supervision of what was called the southern military command. The administrative structure of the four new provinces, which were called general provincial councils, created an intermediate level of government that more directly extended the powers of Balbo and his administration in Tripoli into these four regions of the colony.[64] This division of power was understood to be a parallel political and administrative subdivision to the provinces that existed within Italy.[65]

One important example of the increasingly close relationship between Libya and Italy was the 1935 passage of a law extending the structure of provincial corporativist councils from Italy to the colonial context.[66] This law formalized a gubernatorial directive given by Balbo to a meeting of the Federation of the Fascist Movement of Tripoli at the Miramare Theater in April 21, 1934, where he declared that in Libya, as in Italy, the party, the army, and the syndicate would be recognized as laws of citizenship. The logical conclusion of the modernization of Libya during the Balbo administration was reached in December of 1939, with the approval of the legislation that officially incorporated the four coastal provinces of Tripoli, Misurata, Benghazi, and Derna into the territory of the Kingdom of Italy.[67] This law originated from a deliberation of the Grand Council of Fascism, held on October 28, 1938—the sixteenth anniversary of the Fascist revolution. The incorporation of Libya into the larger Italian state and the completion of the idea of the colony as Italy's fourth shore was symbolically expressed in its appearance as one of the "Metropolitan Provinces" in the three-volume *Guida Breve* of Italy published by the *Consociazione Turistica Italiana* in 1940.[68]

In conjunction with the administrative and legislative changes that were aimed at bringing metropolitan standards to Libya, Balbo made a substantial effort to apply this same measure to the public-works infrastructure. The seriousness of this commitment is evidenced by the significant increase in expenditures on these projects, which almost doubled from that during the governorship of Badoglio.[69] These improvements involved the consolidation and expansion of public services and the construction of government institutions like post offices, schools, hospitals, government offices, prisons, and military barracks. These projects responded to the new administrative structure of the provincial councils and their subdivision into smaller districts—something that led to the creation of new regional centers in Misurata and Derna and the foundation of a network of district offices in towns like Nalut, Gharyan, al-Khums, Ghadames, and Sabratha.[70]

The reorganization of the bureaucracy in Libya also necessitated a substantial commitment to the construction of housing for officials, functionaries, and military personnel in these new regional and district centers. The National Institute for the Housing of State Employees (INCIS) worked in conjunction with the colonial administration to construct a substantial number of housing units in Libya between 1934 and 1940, including a sixty-three-unit project for city employees in Tripoli.[71] These efforts were reinforced by a similar commitment to improve the infrastructure of Libya. In larger centers like Tripoli and Benghazi, this included the extension and enhancement of the sewer and water systems, the paving of streets, the introduction of lighting, and the creation of parks as well as the more general development of the natural landscape.[72] Of particular importance in more remote locations, like Nalut and Ghadames, were enhancements in the water supply that resulted from geological expeditions to discover underground sources of water. Another area of considerable development was the road network, which continued the improvements begun in 1929 under Pietro Badoglio—an initiative that eventually created a road system in Libya that met the standards of metropolitan Italy.[73]

Fig. 1.10. Governor's Office in Tripoli (1937), by Florestano Di Fausto.

The architectural and planning implications of the public-works infrastructure of the colony of Libya—in fact, all building activity in this colony—was subject to a considerable level of scrutiny by the Balbo administration, which formed a building commission in February of 1934, just over one month after his arrival. This group had representatives from the colonial administration, the municipality, the technical office, and the Superintendency of Monuments and Excavations, and was asked to regulate the significant buildings constructed in the colonies.[74] In response to what was viewed by Balbo as a lack of a "civic aesthetic," this group was called upon to "participate in the task of aesthetic reorganization providing for the decoration of the most significant buildings with a sense of art."[75] As a result of this initiative, major public buildings, like the governor's own office building constructed in 1938 (fig. 1.10), were designed to create an image of the colony that combined the authoritarian aspirations of its leaders with attention to its Mediterranean and North African context.

In the first meeting of the building commission, which was presided over by Balbo himself, a series of eleven directives were formulated, most of which had to do with the regulation of the building process by his administration and the municipality. The most complex task given to this group was the review and implementation of the recently completed master plan for Tripoli. The proposal by Alpago Novello, Cabiati, and Ferrazza was eventually adopted by the Municipality of Tripoli in May of 1934 after an extensive period of review.[76] Several of the guidelines of the building commission referred to specific building projects, four of which were directly related to the construction or renovation of tourist facilities. Thus began an extensive program of restructuring the existing tourist infrastructure, including the renovation of the Grand Hotel and the construction of two new hotels in Tripoli and a network of buildings in the Libyan interior in Yifran, Nalut, and Ghadames.[77]

In addition to these general improvements that modernized the public-works and tourist infrastructure of Libya, the Balbo administration undertook two notable projects that were conceived and executed on a monumental scale: the construction of the *strada litoranea* and the *ventimila*—a mass emigration of 20,000 agricultural colonists from Italy to Libya in October of 1938. Exhibiting Balbo's organizational ability and his keen sense of the value of propaganda, these projects have come to symbolize the idea of Libya as Italy's fourth shore and to define the Fascist sense of monumentality and modern spectacle. The *strada litoranea* involved the completion of the remaining portion of just over 800 kilometers of the coastal highway that stretched from Tunisia to Egypt (fig. 1.11). Construction began in October 1935 and was completed in February 1937, just a few weeks before Mussolini's visit to Libya.[78] This project was the logical outcome of the political reforms that had unified Libya into a single administrative, military, and civic entity, providing an artery that gave physical and metaphoric form to this new reality. It was also intended to facilitate commercial and tourist development and respond to military demands. This road was not only built according to the most modern standards, it also contained modern amenities like roadside resthouses that would provide gas and lodging for travelers.[79] Viewed within the context of the ongoing military

Fig. 1.11. View from an automobile on the strada litoranea near Misurata, 1937.

campaign in Ethiopia, the *strada litoranea* was believed to be of great importance to the "security of the Mediterranean" by making possible the rapid movement of Italian troops for surveying the territory.[80] This project was also presented as a feat of engineering that underscored the ability of the Fascist regime to recapture the spirit and accomplishments of ancient Rome. The completion of this coastal artery was an effort of significant scope that required a considerable amount of organization in extremely difficult conditions.[81]

The *strada litoranea* was the product of colonial discourse, a fusion of modern exigencies with Fascist proclamations of the Roman origins of the region. This particular combination of influences is symbolically expressed in the design of the *Arae Philenorum*—a thirty-one-meter-high travertine-clad arch designed by the architect Florestano Di Fausto (fig. 1.12). Located in the Gulf of Sirt, this project marks the midpoint of the new coastal highway, thus affirming the Italian control and domination over this segment of the Mediterranean. It was intended to commemorate the legend from the fourth century B.C. of the Fileni brothers, who, as representatives of Carthage, agreed to be buried alive by the Cyrenians in order that a territorial dispute be settled. According to this legend, their tombs—the ruins of which were purported to be only a few meters from the location of this new arch—were to mark the new border between

Fig. 1.12. (Opposite) Postcard of the Arae Philenorum commemorative arch near Sirt (1937), by Florestano Di Fausto.

36

Carthage and Cyrene.[82] The project illustrates the synthesis of a number of regional sources, combining the monolithic and severe qualities of Egyptian monuments with more specific references to Roman triumphal arches and Libyan vernacular forms. Its iconography is also notable, as this arch includes two colossal bronze statues of the Fileni brothers and two travertine bas-reliefs that document the construction of this road and the founding of the Fascist Empire.[83]

The *Arae Philenorum* was an important backdrop to the inauguration of the *strada litoranea*, which coincided with Benito Mussolini's second visit to this region.[84] During the course of this visit, various events were staged for Italian and foreign journalists, one example being the stop made at this new Fascist monument. Given that Mussolini was arriving at dusk, Balbo arranged for the arch to be illuminated with searchlights that created columns of light in the darkness. A space was also created in front of the arch with a series of torches, a battalion of Libyan soldiers, and a group of indigenous military officers on camels.[85] In this context, the *Arae Philenorum* was a backdrop for a modern Fascist spectacle staged for an international audience.

The *ventimila*, or 20,000, was the culmination of a series of policies developed by the Balbo regime to create a state-sponsored program of agricultural colonization. While there had been some success during the previous governorships with govern-

Fig. 1.13. Aerial view of the agricultural village of Bianchi (1938), by Umberto Di Segni.

ment subsidies of private companies, by 1934 this system of land development had not fostered a substantial influx of colonist families. Balbo moved quickly to work with the organizations that facilitated the resettlement of families, such as the Libyan Colonization Organization (ECL) and the National Fascist Institute for Social Security (INFPS).[86] He also made a substantial investment in agricultural research and development, including programs to reclaim desert areas. After achieving only modest results in his first three years as governor, Balbo embarked on an ambitious project to populate the region. Conceived with the cooperation of Alessandro Lessona of the Ministry of the Colonies, this program was to settle 20,000 colonists annually for five years, beginning in 1938—the long-term goal being to create a population of 500,000 Italian colonists in Libya by 1950.[87]

At the time of the approval of the necessary legislation in May of 1938, the preparations for arrival of the first group of colonists in October of that same year were already under way. This was no small task, as it required an extensive process of review and selection of applicant families and a substantial effort to prepare suitable facilities for their settlement in Libya. A joint committee of ECL, INFPS, and government representatives was formed to undertake the difficult task of selecting 1,800 suitable families from a pool of approximately 6,000 applicants.[88] The preparations in Libya included the creation of roads, the subdivision and clearing of land, the digging of wells, the creation of drainage systems, and the construction of colonial villages, houses, and associated farm buildings. The design of these villages and farm houses is also notable. The product of well-known architects like Florestano Di Fausto, Giovanni Pellegrini, and Umberto Di Segni, their simple cubic massing and Libyan vernacular references place them squarely within the contemporary discourse on architecture in the Italian colonies (fig. 1.13).[89]

The *ventimila* was a powerful symbol of the incorporation of Libya as a modern colony into metropolitan Italy. It was a propaganda event that transformed the political policy of Balbo into a spectacle conceived on a monumental scale. This aspect was largely attributable to the conspicuous nature of this mass migration. Beginning in Genoa on October 27, 1938—the day before the annual celebration of the march on Rome—a flotilla of nine ships carried the colonist families to Naples, where they were joined by six other vessels. The crowning moment of the departure was Mussolini's inspection of these ships aboard a navy cruiser that traveled their full length. The arrival of the colonists in Tripoli and their transportation to their villages were no less orchestrated, as they were eventually loaded into convoys of army trucks that took them to their new homes (fig. 1.14).[90] There was also a well-organized publicity campaign that represented the *ventimila* to an Italian and European audience. The foreign press were given room aboard one of the vessels, allowing them to travel along with the colonists and report the entire event.[91] The propaganda in Italy was symbolically initiated by Balbo, who, in an article in *Nuova Antologia* from November 1938, described these colonists as "an army of rural infantry, who take stable possession of the land, already conquered by our armies and destined to be made fertile with our work"—a statement that clearly expresses the political policies of the Fascist government for the consolidation of Libya as Italy's fourth shore.[92]

Fig. 1.14. Colonists traveling to the agricultural village of Bianchi during the ventimila, October 1938.

The organization and execution of the *ventimila*, just like the construction of the *strada litoranea* and its related propaganda, are an indication of the fact that the introduction of the modernity of the metropole into the colonial context was fundamentally a political gesture. These projects were the culmination of a modernization process that had begun in the earliest days of the Italian occupation of Libya, but had only reached its final expression during the governorship of Italo Balbo—during which time four northern provinces of Libya became part of the Kingdom of Italy. However, this gesture of incorporation, just like the modernization that supported it, reflected an ambivalence that was at the core of Italian colonial politics. Despite the rhetorical statements that embraced this region as part of the larger Italy and the related efforts to bring Libya up to date with the standards of the metropole, the modernization program was conducted as an act of political and cultural colonization that considered this region and its people as an "other." This quality of treating Libya as "a subject of difference" is evident in the agricultural estates created for the Italian colonists; for example, the village of Bianchi, where a modern Mediterranean architecture of the Italian peninsula is combined with the indigenous buildings of the coastal regions of Libya.[93] Rather than a project of pure imitation, these villages derive from a process of substitution. The same ambivalent status was afforded the Libyans as colonial subjects.

While their land was embraced as part of the metropole—and in that sense it was continuous with the political and economic systems of modern Italy—their culture was always considered primitive and backward in relation to the West—that is, as "almost the same, but not quite."[94]

**CHAPTER
TWO**

COLONIAL TOURISM AND THE EXPERIENCE OF MODERNITY

The tourist organization of Libya is strictly tied to the rebirth and development of the Colony. With the indigenous populations subdued and large groups of Italian farmers introduced into the agricultural zones—that is to say, with the conclusive phase of the colonial arrangement being reached—the problem of tourist organization was born and namely, the necessity to bring the colonial environment in line with a tone and a level of civilization capable of establishing active currents of life with the outside, because these same propelling elements of civilization and wealth flow back.—Claudio Brunelli, "Ospitalità e turismo in Libia," 1937.[1]

Fig. 2.1. View of the rooftops of Tripoli, ca. 1925.

The modernization program that was in the process of remaking the network of roads and public services in Libya during the course of the 1920s and 1930s was, to a great extent, a necessary precondition for the creation of a tourist system in the region—a system that could offer a level of organization and comfort that was comparable to that found in the metropolitan context. The connection between the transformation of Libya under Italo Balbo and the tourist system was the subject of a press release written by Claudio Brunelli in preparation for Mussolini's 1937 visit.[2] As a longtime friend of Balbo, Brunelli had been appointed director of the Libyan Tourist and Hotel Association (ETAL) upon its founding in May of 1935. In his capacity as director of this group, Brunelli was responsible for the supervision of a system whose scope was unprecedented, even in the metropolitan context. In a press release he comments on the connection between tourism and the more general development of the colony, which he notes was aimed at the "civil, moral, political, and social elevation of the indigenous populations" who were thus "pervaded by Western civilization."[3] The creation of a tourist system that was equipped with modern facilities was, for Brunelli, a logical outcome of the fact that Libya was a political and geographical extension of Italy that needed to assert its position within the Mediterranean politics of European nations. In speaking about the modernization program of Balbo in Libya, he concludes this statement by arguing that the ETAL was a "mechanism [that was] indispensable to the realization of such an important and vast work of civilization."[4]

The connection between tourism in Libya and the modernization program under the Fascist colonial authorities can be traced back to the earliest guidebooks and publications related to this industry. One of the first of these, *Guida di Tripoli e dintorni*, was published in 1925 by the Milanese publisher Fratelli Treves under the sponsorship of the Volpi administration. This brochure seeks to represent the colonies in a favorable light to a potential tourist audience; in so doing, however, it does not provide guidance for the tourist experience of Tripoli so much as it documents the revival of this region under Italian colonial authority. After a brief eight-page itinerary of the major monuments and tourist facilities, including information on transportation to and within this colony, the book offers a comprehensive presentation of the accomplishments of Volpi in 140 pages of text and images. The information is structured according to different facets of the development of the colony, from the contemporary city and its municipal government, to public works, schools, archeological research, agricultural development and the economy.[5]

Guida di Tripoli e dintorni provides the reader with a detailed account of the state of development of this colony from a metropolitan point of view, its major concern being to illustrate what was described as "the civic function of the capital of Tripolitania."[6] The focus on the current accomplishments and the Western standards of civic organization, public services, and hygiene is evident in the illustrations to the guidebook, whose only references to local architecture, other than buildings of Roman origin, are a panorama of the rooftops of Tripoli and a view of the castle. The dominant image of the architecture of the buildings featured—like the newly constructed governor's house—is that of a neoclassical style typical to the Italian metropolitan context.[7] Not unlike *La rinascità della Tripolitania*, this tourist publication focuses on concrete accomplishments of Italian rule by providing a detailed presentation of its economic and political viability.[8] The political dimensions of this discourse are quite clear in the presentation of the "new city" in *Guida di Tripoli e dintorni*, which asserts that "Tripolitania . . . has validly resumed the path that will allow it to reach a development proportional to its function as a powerful colony—as an instrument for the demographic expansion of the Mother Country and the defense of its inescapably Mediterranean interests" (fig. 2.1).[9]

The belief that tourism was a projection of the accomplishments of Italian colonialism continued in the tourist literature throughout this period. One example of this attitude is a 1929 article in *Rivista delle Colonie Italiane* entitled "Turismo d'oltremare," which states that the tourist system had to "unveil the colony to the visitor, not only by means of Roman monuments and minarets, . . . but above all by our new works."[10] This article reflects the sense that tourism was believed to be a powerful instrument of colonial propaganda, and as such could overcome negative impressions of this colony. Critical of the perceptions of Libya as an "arid expanse of sand," the author Gennaro Pistolese asserts that the region "is not lacking for railways, streets, and is well advanced with the building of its urban centers, its ports, its churches, its aqueducts."[11] While lamenting that Italy had forgotten her colonies, he argues that due to the policies initiated by the Fascist government, the field of tourism had been revived and reinvigo- rated. According to this view, the consequence of this effort was that Tripoli was becoming one of the most important tourist centers in North Africa.

The sentiments expressed in this and other articles written during this period reflect the fact that the tourist discourse was closely tied to more general concerns about Italy's position as a colonizing nation. As a result, a great amount of attention was paid by the Italian colonial government to the need for a substantial propaganda effort. Not only was there a perceived lack of popular publications communicating the indigenous culture of Libya—such as illustrated journals, guidebooks, and brochures—the Italian efforts were seen to be deficient in relation to other colonial powers, like Britain and France (fig. 2.2).[12] The desire to see colonial tourism in this broader European context would seem natural, given Italy's late acquisition of Libya. The French had been in North Africa since the invasion of Algeria in 1835, later claiming Tunisia in 1881 and Morocco in 1911. Accordingly, there was a tendency to measure extent and organization of their tourist system against the accomplishments of these neighboring colonies.[13] The interest in a broader North African context mani- fested itself in a call by one commentator to coordinate and integrate these infrastructures into the more general system of travel within the region. In an essay published in 1931 in the journal *L'Italia Coloniale*, the author argued for the need to "graft the Libyan itineraries into the network of Mediterranean tourist crossings."[14]

The Italian ambitions for tourism in Libya were directly connected to the idea that its tourist infrastructure should be viewed in relation to a North African, and even a Mediterranean, context. While there was a recognition of the natural, historical, archeological, and folkloristic attractions that were the necessary preconditions for a viable tourist network, one of the constants in the early commentary on colonial tourism was the need for a modern and efficiently organized system. The focus was on the enhancement of tourist resources like hotels and transportation methods, which were intended to bring a metropolitan level of comfort to the colonial context.[15] There was also a perceived need to coordinate these facilities and services through a singular and more powerful organization. The necessity for more decisive control of colonial tourism was expressed in extremely bellicose terms in one article in which the author argues for "a person of authority and faith . . . to whom is given . . . the management of the battle for colonial tourism."[16]

Italiani,
Visitate la Tripolitania!

IL CASTELLO DI TRIPOLI

TRIPOLI, 1926

Fig. 2.2. Cover of the Italiani, Visitate la Tripolitania! brochure (1926), featuring the restored castle of Tripoli.

The first major guidebook on tourism in Libya was published by the Italian Touring Club (TCI) in 1929 in a volume that included all of the other Italian colonies. This publication of more than eight hundred pages profiles the tourist facilities in a format and presentation that was identical to the TCI guidebooks for

Italy. This structural parallel to tourist publications in Italy emphasizes the desire to view the tourist system in the colonies from a metropolitan standpoint.[17] This presentation includes a detailed accounting of the tourist facilities and itineraries, which at this time include locations as far west as the Tunisian border, as far south as Ghadames and the not-yet-conquered areas of the Fezzan, and as far east as Misurata and Sirt. As politically neutral as this presentation appears, one of the final sections of this general introduction is entitled "La rinascità delle Tripolitania." The literal intersection between Fascist colonization efforts and tourism is underscored in the insertion of an abbreviated form of this earlier publication into this guidebook.[18] The polemical nature of this gesture is evident in the concluding comments by the author Angelo Piccioli. Under the title "The Work of Tomorrow," he proclaims that "our colony is not, in fact, the 'gnawed bone' it was believed to be."[19]

The eventual integration of tourism with the politics of modernization during the Balbo era was foreshadowed by the book *Colonizzazione e turismo in Libia*, published in 1934.[20] In a manner derived quite directly from the political rhetoric of the time the author, Giuseppe Vedovato, asserts that tourism was one of the most important factors in the economic expansion of Libya as an agricultural colony and as an outlet for demographic colonization. In so doing, he argues that the conditions necessary for a viable tourist system in Libya—such as the creation of transportation systems and the construction of population centers along these itineraries—would open this system up for the movement of goods and the settlement of people for the purposes of agriculture. It is in this regard that tourism is referred to as the "catalyzing agent for the economic process."[21]

Tourism was also viewed by Vedovato as a civilizing and modernizing force. Not only did he argue that the exposure of the products of these agricultural activities to a tourist audience would potentially create new markets for these products back in Italy, he observed that "more frequent contact with interests and ideals carried by foreign and national tourist caravans" would create "a more elevated civil and economic level" in the colonies.[22] The key element in asserting the value of this modernity was an effective publicity campaign that would be gauged at demystifying the experience of the colonies. In listing the efforts that had to be made to clarify the great assets of Libya from a tourist point of view, the emphasis was on the most rational criteria, such as climate, transportation, and distribution of facilities. The desire for travel would thus be based on truth, not the distortion of reality—a view that runs parallel to the rise of objectivity in tourist representations like postcards, guidebooks, and brochures (fig. 2.3).

The assertive tone of Vedovato's book—which fuses the politics of Fascist modernization with a program for the development of tourism—largely anticipates the transformation of the tourist discourse after the conquest of Ethiopia in 1935. While there were always foreign travelers to Libya, their presence in the colonies after the victory in East Africa took on a heightened political significance. Colonial tourism was called on to do more than illustrate the legitimacy of Italy's colonial lands to its own people. It was asked to demonstrate the strength of the Fascist Empire in Africa to an international audience. Accordingly, there was an increasing recognition in tourist literature of the foreign audience for colonial tourism. This change can be seen in the revised guidebook

Fig. 2.3. Postcard of a characteristic mosque in Tripoli, ca. 1935.

to Libya, published in 1937 by the Italian Touring Club, this time put out as a separate volume.[23] The publication offers a strident endorsement of the achievements of the colonial authorities in the two-page introduction, which argues that Balbo had "transformed the face and the spirit" of Libya so that it was "the most tangible and indisputable documentation of [Italy's] colonizing capacity." Making reference to the cities in the interior of Libya, which "today offer to the tourist incredibly modern and comfortable hotels," a direct analogy is made between the broader colonial project in Libya and the changes to the tourist system under Balbo, described as "a construction site of will and of works."[24]

The transformation of the tourist discourse on the Italian colonies in this publication was characterized by a shift from a general presentation of the accomplishments of Italian colonization to the more specific focus on the agricultural development of the region. This change was evident in the renaming of the section "La rinascità della Tripolitania" as "Valorizzazione della Libia"—a change that implies a more confident and active process more closely allied with the intransigent Fascism of Balbo.[25] In the case of the first guidebook, the title was a direct reference to the renewal of Tripolitania that began under Volpi—a choice that was aimed at linking tourism with the project of legitimizing the Italian presence. In 1937, the connection was made to the modernization program of Balbo, which offered public-works improvements and a state-sponsored program of agricultural colonization. The guidebook pays particular attention to the latter, even providing detailed statistics on the number of colonist families and the amount of farmland involved.

In summarizing the accomplishments of agricultural colonization in this guidebook, the author states that it was "one of the most conclusive and concrete activities of Italian colonization." He goes on to remark that this program "has been able to create, *from absolutely nothing . . . a complex of agricultural real-estate works *of which not the slightest trace existed in the past and that today represents a conspicuous patrimony of indisputable economic and political value.*"[26] The extreme foregrounding of the Fascist colonization program under Balbo in the TCI guidebook to Libya reveals the extent of the transformation of the tourist discourse after the Italian conquest in Ethiopia. In this highly charged political context and amid bellicose assertions of Italy's imperial destiny, tourism increasingly became an instrument of the politics of colonial rule. The close connection between tourism in Libya and the Fascist politics of empire, though, should not be a surprising one. From the earliest days of the Italian occupation, there was a strong parallel between the military and political control of the territory and the tourist experience. As a system of accommodation and transportation that allowed the foreign traveler to experience characteristic attractions of the colony while maintaining a metropolitan level of comfort, the tourist system in Libya was marked by the same ambivalence with which the modernity of the West was projected onto the African shore of the Mediterranean.

CREATING A TOURIST SYSTEM

The initial stages in the development of a tourist system in Libya began during the governorship of Giuseppe Volpi, which was the first colonial administration to attend to this issue. Along with the reoccupation of land, the creation of an agricultural economy, and the construction of a suitable image to mark the Italian presence, the development of a tourist system was one of the four main components of the program of rebirth of Tripolitania under Volpi.[27] On the one hand, tourism was seen as being closely tied to travel to and within the colony. In the book *La rinascità della Tripolitania*, tourism was presented as an integral part of the "politics of transportation" and was referred to as a "new source of well-being and of activity for the colony."[28] On the other, tourism was viewed as a separate industry with its own issues and concerns. In this same publication, the tourist system was examined in an essay, entitled "Il problema industriale in Tripolitania," which discussed the industries in this colony that had the greatest potential for future development, including those related to the cultivation of agricultural products like tobacco, dates, and olives, and the harvesting of raw materials like salt, sulfur, phosphates, and petroleum.[29] The author of this essay took stock of the wide range of attractions that tourism in Tripolitania offered the foreign visitor, from hotels and modes of transportation to historic sites and special events, arguing that it could be an industry of considerable importance with the help of tourist publicity.

The foundation of a tourist system in Tripolitania during the Volpi era was largely the product of a series of government policies. These initiatives included the improvement of maritime connections between Italy and Tripolitania for both commercial and tourist purposes, which called for an extension of the itinerary of the weekly ships that sailed from Tripoli to Syracuse to include Naples.[30] The Volpi administration worked closely with the local Chamber of Commerce and the National Association of Tourist Industries (ENIT) to produce tourist publicity and guidebooks. A number of events were staged in this region to support the travel of foreigners, such as the archeological convention held in Tripoli in May of 1925.[31] In addition to a series of presentations by well-known Italian and foreign archeologists, this fifteen-day conference involved visits to the archeological sites at Leptis Magna and Sabratha. Volpi also made a substantial investment in the tourist infrastructure, with buildings like the luxurious Grand Hotel in Tripoli, for which construction began in 1925 (fig. 2.4). Despite these efforts, the tourist infrastructure during the Volpi era was still quite modest, with only three hotels in Tripoli—the Grand Hotel Savoia, the Hotel Moderno, and the Hotel del Commercio—and few forms of public entertainment, which at that time consisted of two theaters, some small movie houses, and three clubs.[32] A tourist itinerary in 1925 was similarly limited. It would have included only the city of Tripoli, whose major tourist sites were the old city, the museum, and the two archeological sites at Leptis Magna and Sabratha—the first being accessible only by passenger ship and the second only by train.[33]

Although the establishment of a tourist network was largely the product of the policies of the Volpi administration, the organization of travel during this period was primarily handled by private organizations. There were two major kinds of travel in this region corresponding to two distinct audiences, the first being dignitaries, government officials, and wealthy Italian and foreign travelers—all of whom had, or could afford, the logistical support to travel in a small group. The other mode of travel—although only available to a limited audience—were trips organized for larger groups. These excursions were arranged by various private groups, like the Italian Touring Club (TCI) or the Italian Colonial Institute (ICI), rather than by steamship companies and travel agencies, which would later become much more active in this sector of the tourist market.[34] One such example is a fourteen-day cruise to Libya in 1924 organized by the ICI for a group of 255 merchants, industrialists, and agriculturalists, an effort that was clearly aimed at encouraging investment in the region.[35] A product of economic demands and the need for safe travel, the predominance of large groups and the tendency for planned itineraries while within the colony became standard practice for tourism during the period.

The tourist system in this region enjoyed continuing growth during the governorships of De Bono and Badoglio. A review of the guidebook to the colonies published by the TCI in 1929 underscores the measure of that change (fig. 2.5). In the city of Tripoli, with the completion of the Grand Hotel and the construction of several others, there were five hotels that could provide lodging and meals to the most discriminating travelers, three for average tourists and three for more modest ones.[36] There was also a more substantial network of food and entertainment facilities for tourists, such as the 2,000-seat Miramare Theater, two cinemas, and many restaurants and cafés. In addition to the old city of Tripoli and the museum in the castle, beginning in 1927 the Tripoli Trade

Fig. 2.4. View of the Grand Hotel and the seafront of Tripoli, ca. 1925.

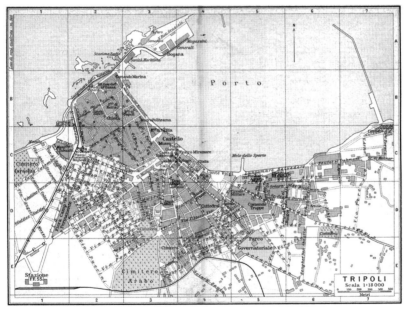

Fig. 2.5. Map of Tripoli, from L.V. Bertarelli, Guida d'Italia del Touring Club Italiano. Possedimenti e colonie (Milan: Touring Club Italiano, 1929). (See also Plate 1.)

Fair and its related activities became part of a tourist itinerary of the city. Another change in the tourist system was that travel outside of Tripoli to sites like Leptis Magna and Sabratha had become much more feasible (fig. 2.6). Daily car service was available to the first site, which now had the Hotel Le Venete. Tourist excursions to Sabratha were improved through changes to the

Fig. 2.6. Group of American tourists traveling to Leptis Magna, ca. 1932.

regularity of rail service and the addition of the Hotel Secchi, which provided extremely simple accommodation.[37] Tourism into the interior of Tripolitania also began during this period, with hotels being constructed in Gharyan and Nalut and bimonthly bus service from Tripoli to Ghadames beginning in January of 1929. This tourist itinerary, whose first trip was reported to have been completed on time and according to a preestablished program, took a total of four travel days in each direction with three days stationed in Ghadames.[38]

The tourist infrastructure achieved even more significant progress by the end of Badoglio's governorship in 1933. This progress is particularly noteworthy as it related to the development of tourism in less populated destinations in the southern desert regions of Tripolitania. To the existing Hotel Nefusa in Nalut were added hotels in Yifran (1930) and Ghadames (1931), though both were equally modest in scale. In the coastal region, new hotels were constructed in Ajdabiya (1932), Cyrene (1932), al-Khums (1931), Misurata (1930), Sirt (1933), and Zuwarah (1933). Many of these facilities were linked through a growing number of organized tourist itineraries, the longest of these involving a journey of over 1,500 kilometers in fifteen days. The mode of transportation for these excursions was so-called Saharan motor coaches, which could comfortably carry up to four people through the most demanding climate.[39] In the city of Tripoli, many of the existing tourist-related activities were improved and expanded, like the archeological museum in the castle, which was substantially renovated in 1930. The Tripoli Trade Fair moved to a new location southwest of the old city in 1929 and increasingly took on a more permanent appearance. Another significant addition to the tourist experience came with the construction of a municipal casino.[40] The result of this effort at improving the tourist system in Libya during the governorship of Badoglio was what Angelo Piccioli described as "a perfect system of accommodations in a climate that has no winter."[41]

There were also a number of significant developments in the tourist access to Libya between 1926 and 1933. The regularly scheduled marine transportation to Tripoli gradually improved from weekly service in 1924 to more-than-twice-weekly service in 1929. Another major change was the beginning of scheduled air service from Rome to Tripoli, which began in 1929 with seaplanes that carried up to nineteen passengers.[42] The early 1930s saw some of the initial efforts by Italian and foreign private steamship companies to make Tripoli a stop for some of their Mediterranean cruises. One of the primary examples is the Genovese company "Italia" of the Cosulich-Lloyd Sabaudo Line which, in 1931, began twice-yearly cruises that used Tripoli as a one-day stopping point.[43] There were also a number of organized excursions to Libya by groups like the Italian Touring Club, which organized excursions in Tripolitania in 1931 to commemorate the twentieth anniversary of the Italian invasion, and in Cyrenaica in 1933 to mark the subjugation of the region.[44] Even more active in the promotion of cruises was the Fascist Colonial Institute (ICF), which held cruises in 1929 and 1930 for farm workers and students—the intention being to link these excursions to the agricultural development of the colony.[45] A number of other organizations held excursions in this region, including the Dante Alighieri Society, which traveled to Tripolitania in 1927 to see the first Tripoli Trade Fair, and *Avanguardisti,* or fascist youth groups, which visited this region at least four times between 1928 and 1933.[46] Libya was thus becoming a more common destination for both Italian and foreign tourists, with the number of visitors to the city of Tripoli almost doubling between 1927 and 1933.[47]

The tourist system in Libya was moving toward a greater level of coordination and supervision and eventually adopted an organizational structure similar to that found in metropolitan Italy. This effort was largely the result of collaboration between Emilio De Bono, who was appointed to the Ministry of the Colonies in 1929, and Pietro Badoglio, then governor of Libya. Their relationship was responsible for a series of changes in government policy related to travel, including the simplification of passport and visa regulations for foreigners on cruise ships.[48] An even more significant contribution to the improvement of tourism was the creation of the Tripolitanian Tourism Association in November of 1929. Initiated by the Badoglio administration and the Chamber of Commerce of Tripoli, this group was modeled on the ENIT—a state-sponsored organization that was responsible for the coordination, control, and promotion of tourism in Italy.[49] The statute of the Tripolitanian Tourism Association called for a diverse array of activities, from coordinating the initiatives of various tourist-related companies, to developing propaganda for tourism in the colony, to reporting on tourist movement, and participating in congresses and exhibitions.[50] One specific initiative they launched was the creation of a special tourist season for Libya, which highlighted the best time for Italian and foreign tourists to travel to the region and provided them with reductions in the cost of travel.[51] The most important event they organized during this time was the Twelfth Congress of the International Federation of Travel Agencies in Tripoli from November 10 through November 14, 1931. Presided over by Fulvio Suvich, the Italian commissioner of tourism, this meeting was attended by representatives of travel agencies from thirty-four different countries and focused on the particular concerns of colonial tourism.[52]

A product of the initial attempts to systematically order tourism in the colonial context, the activities of the Tripolitanian Tourism Association reflect the need to provide a modern and efficient system of tourist amenities. This organization was, at least in part, based on a series of government measures that had already restructured the tourist system in Italy—a process that began with the creation of ENIT in 1919. The tourist network that was being established in Libya through the sponsorship of the Tripolitanian Tourism Association was also unquestionably based on the much earlier efforts of the French in their North African colonies. Under the direction of the private steamship company the *Compagnie Générale Transatlantique*, a coordinated system of transportation services that included rail travel was made available as early as 1913 in Algeria and Tunisia.[53] This modern tourist network grew quite rapidly, first by adding the colony of Morocco, and then through the creation of a system of accommodations that was linked through scheduled bus and auto transportation. By 1928 this system included forty-three hotels and nineteen automobile itineraries that covered a total of some 25,000 kilometers. The result was a continuous network of travel that connected Bordeaux and Marseilles with major centers like Marrakech, Casablanca, Tangier, Algiers, and Tunis, as well as more remote locations like the oases of Timimoun and Ghardaia in the Algerian Sahara. The publicity material that advertised this system speaks of a "unique chain of modern hotels" that made travel into the interior of Algeria, Tunisia, and Morocco possible (fig. 2.7).[54]

The organization of the tourist system in Libya reached its highest level of development under the auspices of the modernization program of Italo Balbo. The construction of an infrastructure of roads and public services undertaken during this period provided the necessary preconditions for the development of a well-organized and efficient tourist system. The intersection of the tourist discourse with the more general improvement of the colonial context was symbolically expressed in the "national excursion" organized by the TCI in Libya in April of 1937. As a reflection of the importance of the newly opened *strada litoranea*, one group of participants began in Tripoli heading east to Benghazi while a second took an equal and opposite itinerary, visiting virtually all of the significant historical sites from the Tunisian border to Egypt. A gesture of colonial propaganda not unlike the recent inauguration of this coastal artery by Mussolini, this excursion was meant to assert that with this new road, Libya was being organized for its future tourist demands. As was rhetorically stated in *Le Vie d'Italia* in June 1937, this tourist experience "offered a concrete demonstration of the great importance that the new imperial artery also assumes for tourist purposes."[55] The connection between the new infrastructure of roads constructed by Balbo and the tourist system was the subject of a second article, which in this case dealt with new arteries in the pre-Saharan region of Libya. This essay, entitled "L'autostrada del deserto libico," discusses a paved highway system that connected Tripoli with the towns of Gharyan, Yifran, Nalut, and the oasis of Ghadames. Though lamenting the loss of the "romantic aspect" of travel, the essayist referred to this road as "the most beautiful way of tourist penetration in our Mediterranean colony."[56]

The considerable financial investment that the Balbo administration made in the improvement of the road network was not an isolated gesture. The creation of a paved system of highways designed according to the most modern standards was undertaken

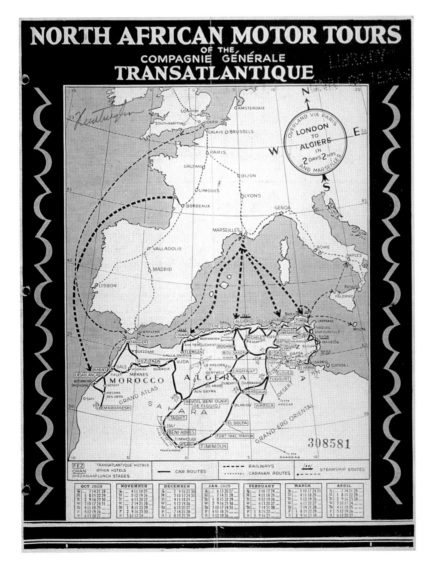

Fig. 2.7. Cover of a brochure for motor tours in the French colonies in North Africa (1928), published by the Compagnie Générale Transatlantique.

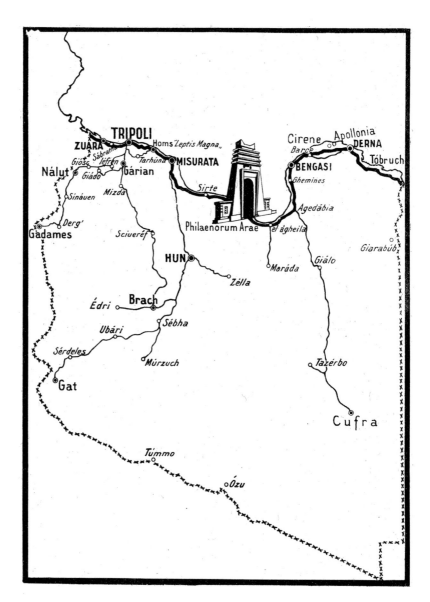

Fig. 2.8. Map of
the road system in
Libya, 1938.

in conjunction with a substantial program for the construction
of new tourist facilities that was initiated in the first days of
Balbo's governorship. In so doing, the tourist architecture during
the Balbo era participated quite directly in the broader political
discourse within architectural culture that called for the creation
of a more uniform appearance proper to both Libya's colonial
status and its Mediterranean setting. Four of the original directives given by Balbo to the Building Commission related to tourist
facilities. These were: the construction of hotels in the Libyan
interior, the renovation of the Grand Hotel, and the construction of a large tourist hotel and a luxury hotel in Tripoli.[57] As a
consequence, in 1934 four new hotels began construction and four
others were substantially renovated, all under the direction of
the colonial administration. These new projects were the luxu-

rious Uaddan and the more modest Mehari, both in Tripoli, the Hotel Rumia in Yifran, and the Hotel Nalut—all of which were designed by the architect Florestano Di Fausto. The renovation projects were the Hotel at the Excavations of Leptis Magna in al-Khums, the Hotel Sirt, the Hotel of the Gazelle in Zlitan, and the Hotel 'Ain el-Fras in Ghadames.[58]

It was during this same period that the project for the *strada litoranea* was being planned and a series of improvements in the road network in the Libyan interior were undertaken. These two initiatives resulted in the creation of a coordinated system of modern roads and hotels that described two basic itineraries that soon became the most desirable tourist experiences in this colony. The first of these reinforced Libya's Mediterranean status, following the *strada litoranea* from Zuwarah on the west to Tobruk on the east, linking Libya's largest cities of Tripoli and Benghazi and the major archeological sites of Sabratha, Leptis Magna, Cyrene, and Apollonia. The second route explored Libya's African and Saharan setting, traveling south from Tripoli into the Libyan interior, passing through Yifran and Nalut and ending in the oasis settlement of Ghadames (fig. 2.8).

The emphasis of the Balbo administration on the development of the tourist system also manifested a series of improvements related to transportation to and within this colony. These changes included increasing both the number and frequency of marine connections to Libya, which in 1929 included five steam-ship lines departing from Naples, Syracuse, and Tunis providing twice-weekly service. This system doubled by 1937 to four-times-weekly service and seven lines, including new departures from Genoa and Palermo.[59] Air travel to and within Libya, which began in 1929, was also improved, with the construction of seven new airports, the addition of three new lines, and a substantial increase in the frequency of travel and the number of passengers.[60] No less substantial were the attempts to improve automobile and bus transportation within Libya. In this case, three new motor-coach lines were created to link centers of major tourist interest like Yifran, Nalut, and Ghadames, and two new automobile lines were introduced to serve the archeological sites at Leptis Magna and Sabratha during the period of the Tripoli Trade Fair.[61]

The Balbo administration was equally active in encouraging cruise operators to visit Libya—an initiative that resulted in more than 30,000 tourists visiting this colony during the first six months of his governorship.[62] The Italian groups involved in these activities included the *Opera Nazionale Dopolavoro* (OND), which organized eleven different cruises for workers from different provinces of Italy, and the Fascist Colonial Institute, which had no fewer than four organized trips to Libya during the first year of Balbo's governorship.[63] Private cruise operators such as "Lloyd Triestino" and "Italia Cosulich" contributed to the growing interest in Libya as a tourist destination by providing passage to specific events, like the Tripoli Trade Fair, and offering Mediterranean cruises that included Libya on their itinerary (fig. 2.9).[64]

The creation of a coordinated tourist network in Libya was supported through the organization of a series of tourist-related attractions that catered to the demands of a metropolitan audience. The most important of these continued to be the Tripoli Trade Fair, which was expanded and substantially rebuilt between 1934 and 1936.[65] Some of the new features of this annual event included an exhibition of indigenous livestock and a newly constructed exhibition space for Libyan artisanry. The building program emphasized the construction of a series of permanent pavilions whose hybrid urban arrangement combined the regularity of a metropolitan street pattern with the variable qualities of the colonial landscape (fig. 2.10). A great effort was made to enhance other activities during the period of the Tripoli Fair, such as the annual Grand Prix automobile race and related lottery, an international fencing competition, held in 1934, and an annual air rally, begun in 1935.[66] Balbo was equally successful in attracting conventions and conferences to Libya which, although of scant tourist interest, were successful in bringing people to this region and thus reinforcing its status as a viable tourist destination for a metropolitan audience.[67]

The most crucial initiative that the Balbo administration pursued for the creation of an organized tourist system was the foundation of a centralized authority for the control of all tourist-related activities. Some of these responsibilities had been assumed by the Libyan Tourism Commission, which was created in November of 1933. The role of this government authority in Libya was two-fold: to direct and coordinate all tourist activities and to promote and control the development of all organizations or institutions involved in tourism.[68] Under the direction of Alessandro Melchiori, the Libyan Tourism Commission worked very closely with the Balbo administration to promote the tourist industry. These initiatives included the reduction in the price of hotels, restaurants, and transportation, the introduction of new transportation services within the colony, the facilitation of cruise ships, and the introduction of new events in the tourist calendar.[69] The structure was later modified with the creation of the Council of the Libyan Tourism Commission in 1934. This group was composed of members of all the major organizations involved in tourism, and their role was to advise and direct the activities of the commission—a role that was quite similar to that performed by the Provincial Councils of the Corporativist Economy in Italy.[70]

By the beginning of 1935, with the foundation of an organizational structure to regulate the tourist industry in Libya, the final element in the creation of a modern tourist system had been put into place. The Balbo administration had already begun an extensive program for the improvement of the system of transportation and the infrastructure of roads and public services—initiatives that were undertaken in conjunction with the construction and rehabilitation of a number of important tourist facilities and attractions. The result of these efforts, and of the newly founded administrative structure, is that it was possible for a Western traveler to experience the colonial context in a manner that was consistent with the expectations and standards of the metropole. The creation of this organizational structure was, however, only the first step in a development that would lead to the complete remaking of the tourist system in Libya in the latter half of the 1930s. It was during this period that the tension between modernity and indigenous culture was fused into a single, though highly contested, experience.

Fig. 2.9. Cover of a brochure for Mediterranean cruises (1934), published by Italia Cosulich. (See also Plate 2.)

Fig. 2.10. Aerial view of the Tripoli Trade Fair in 1939.

THE LIBYAN TOURISM AND HOTEL ASSOCIATION

After more than a year of working with the existing organization of the tourist system in Libya, Balbo decided to create a single group that could preside over and participate in all areas of the tourist economy. This ambition was realized with the creation of the Libyan Tourism and Hotel Association (ETAL) in 1935. As a state-sponsored corporation, the ETAL was offered as an alternative to the existing system where government agencies acted in promotional and supervisory roles over a series of private tourism companies. In so doing, industry and government were integrated into a single entity, thereby providing a more coordinated solution to the tourist industry in Libya.[71]

The formation of the ETAL needs to be understood in relation to the increasingly centralized efforts at coordinating and directing the Libyan economy according to Fascist corporativist principles. This group provided the services of a travel agency, organizing tourist itineraries involving all forms of travel. It acted as tour operator, providing car and motor-coach transportation throughout the region.[72] The ETAL was also responsible for the management of the eighteen hotels that belonged to the Libyan government and the municipality—including the most prominent hotels in Tripoli, Benghazi, and the Libyan interior—and for supervising a network of entertainment facilities that included a theater and casino. Finally, this group handled its own publicity campaigns, producing publications like brochures, guidebooks, and postcards, and organizing displays at exhibitions and fairs in Italy and abroad. This combination of activities and resources not only allowed this organization to provide an inclusive package of services for the tourist audience. It was able to conduct these activities with a unity of purpose that was not possible with the amalgam of private enterprise and public supervision that existed prior to its inception. The connection between the Fascist corporativist model and the ETAL was clearly evident in its publicity material, which argued that "the problem of tourism . . . is being resolved . . . with a solution that without exaggeration can be called totalitarian."[73]

The creation of the ETAL was closely tied to the corporativist politics in Libya under Balbo—a politics that was a projection of Fascist modernity in the colonial context. In organizing a group that was to both oversee and participate in all aspects of tourism, Balbo was clearly creating an equivalent to the organizations that, according to Mussolini, were "instruments that carry out the complete, organic and totalitarian regulation of production under the aegis of the State."[74] This connection is evident in the ETAL's participation in all sectors of the tourist industry, from those that were linked to its commercial and economic role, to those related to its political dimension in the colonial context and those associated with its promotion and propaganda in Italy and abroad. The degree of coordination of these goals with those of the Libyan government is confirmed by a list presented by Giuseppe Bruni, general secretary of the colonies, at the first meeting of this organization in October of 1935.[75] These objectives, which were generated by Balbo himself, illustrate a range of activities, from encouraging tourist travel to Libya to the creation of a system of hotels to deal with both mass and luxury tourism.

The Fascist and corporativist origins of the Libyan Tourism and Hotel Association are equally evident in the various pieces of legislation that were introduced for its creation and the specification of its administrative structure. The legislation that pertained to the institution of this group, which was passed into law on May 31, 1935, called for an organization that was able to operate in all of the different spheres of activity linked to tourism.[76] Assuming the role performed by both the Libyan government and the tourist commission, it was expected to "promote and increase the tourist movement in Libya" and "direct and coordinate the actions that institutes, organizations, corporations, committees and private companies pursue in this field."[77]

The ETAL was also intended to operate as a private corporation by being charged with the ability to manage hotels and develop other activities related to its perceived role in the tourist industry in Libya. One of the reasons offered for the conception of this organization was that there were flaws in the present combination of private industry and public supervision.[78] With the approval of its statute in June of 1935, this organization was given far-reaching powers to operate both tourism and travel offices that would be responsible for promotional and propaganda matters and travel and ticket agencies that would be involved in facilitating travel to and within this colony.[79] This group was also permitted to carry on these tourist-related activities outside of Libya, either by creating its own agencies or by working through representatives that would work within similar businesses abroad. In addition to this dual role in the tourist sector, this statute allowed it to both create and oversee "places of interest and sojourn" in Libya—which eventually included theaters, cafés, and bathing and sports facilities.[80]

The Libyan Tourism and Hotel Association was a fusion of the kinds of political, propagandistic, and commercial aspects of tourism that were handled by separate organizations in Italy. This phenomenon of extreme centralization of power in one organization is particularly interesting given the apparently opposite tendency in Italy at the time, where political and commercial aspects of tourism were separated from those related to propaganda.[81] The variable program of this group was reflected in its administrative structure, which was a composite of separate services held together by a central advisory group.[82] This coordinating role was performed by the General Administration, which regulated and oversaw the activities of the various departments. These smaller groups were the Publicity and Propaganda Service, the Tourism Service, the Hotel Service, the Transportation Service, and the Theater and Performance Service—each with their own administrative structure and their own independent responsibilities.[83] The General Administration assumed a political role, negotiating with different government departments and private companies involved in tourism on behalf of the individual groups within this organization.[84] These initiatives included an agreement with the Ministry of the Colonies to create an official tourist season in Libya from November to May, which granted up to 50 percent reductions in the cost of rail and ship travel.[85]

Two of the individual departments were concerned with issues that had a direct correspondence with existing tourist organizations in Italy. The Publicity and Propaganda Service performed a function similar to that of ENIT in Italy, communicating information about travel to Libya.[86] The means of this dissemination were multiple. The ETAL established relationships with Italian and foreign journals and publications and produced their own publicity material. In their promotional activities with other organizations, their role was largely one of facilitation—providing the most current information about tourism in Libya and the necessary supporting photographic material.[87] Other publicity activities included participation in fairs and exhibitions, commissioning billboards and lighted signs, creating radio propaganda, and working with the *Istituto Nazionale Luce* to make propaganda films on tourism in Libya.[88]

The second department modeled on a metropolitan precedent was the Tourism Service, whose activities were based on the Italian Tourism Company (CIT), which was the official state travel agency.[89] In addition to facilitating excursions within Libya, this group provided full travel assistance for Italy and abroad—including selling rail, maritime, and air tickets. The difference in this case, however, is that within Libya the Tourism Service was primarily able to use its own hotels, entertainment facilities, and means of travel. There were only two travel agencies in Libya, located in Tripoli and Benghazi, which provided transportation and travel services in an atmosphere that was more suggestive of the modernity of the metropole than the indigenous landscape of the colonial context (fig. 2.11). The ETAL also offered tourist information and reservations through a network of over a thousand affiliated travel agencies in Italy and abroad.[90]

Several of the departments of the Libyan Tourism and Hotel

Fig. 2.11. Libyan Tourism and Hotel Association travel agency in Tripoli (1935).

Fig. 2.12. Saharan
autobus used by the
Libyan Tourism and
Hotel Association,
ca. 1935.

Association offered tourism-related services that were more typical
to private companies in Italy. The Transportation Service provided
regular transportation throughout this colony.[91] In addition to
these scheduled routes, buses and smaller vehicles were available
for either special group outings or private rental (fig. 2.12). These
more modest vehicles were also used for an automobile service
that linked up Tripoli with Tunis with twice-weekly service. The
Hotel Service similarly fused modern enterprise with a government organization through the management of a coordinated
system of hotels that provided accommodation and related services
in the largest population centers and the most significant tourist
destinations.[92] While this kind of system was unprecedented in
Italy, a great majority of hotels in Libya were owned and operated by individual municipalities. Of the fourteen hotels that
were taken over by ETAL in November of 1935, all were either
municipal hotels or had recently been constructed by the colonial
administration.[93]

The Theater and Performance Service of the Libyan Tourism
and Hotel Association was equally involved in an area of the
tourist economy that was traditionally held by private enterprise.
The general mission of this group was to promote and, in many
cases, directly manage cultural and entertainment activities and
facilities that were aimed at a tourist audience.[94] One of the specific
events organized by this group was a production of Sophocles'
Oedipus Rex during Mussolini's visit in March of 1937, which was
the inaugural performance at the recently restored Roman amphitheater at the archeological site of Sabratha.[95] While the facilities
managed by this group were largely separate from the hotel
system, one exception was the theater in the Uaddan Hotel and

Casino in Tripoli.[96] Although all of the other venues of the Theater and Performance Service were independent, they were located in the principal centers of Tripoli and Benghazi and thus were part of a strategy of concentrating tourist activities in a manner that would make them mutually reinforcing. Some focused on cultural events and public entertainment, like the Arena of Sharah al-Shatt in Tripoli and the Berenice Theater and Nuova Italia Cinema in Benghazi. Others supported activities that were more recreational in nature, including the facilities at the Dirigible Beach in Tripoli and at the Giuliana Beach in Benghazi (fig. 2.13).[97]

By the end of the 1930s, the tourist system of the Libyan Tourism and Hotel Association comprised a network of eighteen hotels located throughout this colony, numerous affiliated entertainment and tourist facilities in Tripoli and Benghazi, and several offices dedicated to promoting the travel services of this organization. The administrative structure was conceived along metropolitan lines—based on a corporativist model for the dissemination of power from a centralized political authority. The relative success of these efforts can at least in part be measured by continued growth in the number of tourists traveling to this colony and, more particularly, by the financial stability of this organization and the relatively high occupancy rate of its hotels—which was almost 60 percent during the 1938–39 tourist season.[98]

Fig. 2.13. Libyan Tourism and Hotel Association bathing facility at Lido Giuliana in Benghazi (1935).

The tourist system that was presided over by the ETAL was closely tied to the modernization program initiated by Balbo to bring this region up to date with the standards of the metropole in order to incorporate it into the larger Italy. This system of tourist amenities stretched the full length of this colony and deep into the Libyan interior. Through the supervision of this network by a centralized authority whose point of reference was clearly metropolitan, a certain standard of services and amenities was almost universally available throughout the colony.[99]

MODERNITY AND THE TOURIST EXPERIENCE

The network of hotels, tourist facilities, transportation services, and tourist activities of the Libyan Tourism and Hotel Association fostered an experience of the colonial context that was fundamentally modern. Among the many facets of this tourist system, the activities of the Publicity and Propaganda Service—in particular, their participation in fairs and exhibitions—were instrumental in communicating the quality of that experience. This participation primarily consisted in regional trade fairs that took place on a yearly basis in Milan, Bari, and Tripoli.[100] In the case of this latter exhibition, the ETAL was first represented just months after their founding and continued until the final year of this event, in 1939. In 1936 this group was presented in a space that included a display of the Italian Touring Club and a diorama. The presentation of the ETAL system in this pavilion consisted of a modernist-inspired wall and counter display of photographs, travel itineraries, and tourist publications—a presentation that offered the image of a modern and efficiently ordered system of travel, transportation, and lodging at the expense of communicating the indigenous culture (fig. 2.14).[101]

The participation of this group at the Tripoli Trade Fair in 1937 included a substantial representation in the catalog of the exhibition. Their hotel and travel services were presented as part of a sixteen-page coverage of tourism that also provided general information on the climate and culture of Libya and the logistics of colonial travel. Among the services that the ETAL offered in this publication were comprehensive tourist packages that gave a choice of different programs that could be customized by the traveler based on the knowledge of the itinerary, the amount of travel time, and the cost of the trip.[102] This presentation was supported by information on the hotels and an extensive list of all of the available travel services. The description of the hotel system of the ETAL included information on prices and amenities for each facility. In a two-page spread that illustrated the hotels in Cyrene, Yifran, and Ghadames, this system was presented as "welcoming the traveler with every comfort" (fig. 2.15). In an analogy with the larger modernization program of Balbo, these facilities were seen to be "perfectly responsive to the necessity of tourism and to the modern demands of the traveler."[103]

The modernity of the tourist system in Libya is similarly communicated through the series of tourist-oriented materials and publications produced by the Publicity and Propaganda Service. These cultural productions shared a common purpose—to convince Italian and foreign tourists of the efficiency and comfort offered by the tourist system in Libya.[104] One example of this material is the tourist brochure La Libia, which was among ETAL's first publications, having

Fig. 2.14. Interior display in the Libyan Tourism and Hotel Association pavilion at the Tripoli Trade Fair in 1936.

been produced for the opening of the Tripoli Trade Fair in March of 1936. The textual presentation of this brochure offers a prosaic description of the physical and geographic reality of this colony in a manner that is intended to counteract preconceptions about its backwardness. This concern is apparent in the initial description of the colony, which states: "If at one time this immense territory may have merited being pejoratively called a 'large sand box,' today thanks to the provisions of the Fascist regime and the assiduous work of colonizers, it has been amply reclaimed and cultivated."[105] The accompanying visual representation contains a panorama of the old city of Tripoli and a view of the modern waterfront of Benghazi. Seen in conjunction with the text, this representation explicitly links the tourist identity of Libya and its traditional architecture with the modernization program in Libya under the Balbo administration (fig. 2.16).

The subsequent pages of the ETAL brochure *La Libia* provide a brief exposition of the history of the region. Naturally, this history is a history of colonization—from the Greek and Roman occupation, through the Ottoman domination, to the Italian conquest of 1911. The political overtones of this account are quite apparent when it is suggested that under Fascism this region had reached "that development and level of civilization that it had known during the Roman period."[106] The main body of this brochure contains a tourist itinerary that describes the major towns and historical sites

Fig. 2.15. (Opposite, top) Advertisement for the Libyan Tourism and Hotel Association in the catalog of the Tripoli Trade Fair in 1937.

in Libya, which is followed by a final section that deals with more practical matters relating to travel. The brochure concludes with a presentation of the hotels and travel services of the ETAL. Accompanied by photographs of most of the hotels and tourist facilities managed by this group, this brochure argues that this system was "sufficient to successfully confront every demand coming from the influx of tourists in the colony."[107]

The link between the new ETAL tourist network and the

Fig. 2.16. (Bottom) Presentation of Tripoli and Benghazi in the brochure La Libia (Milan: F. Milani, 1936), published by the Libyan Tourism and Hotel Association.

Fascist colonial project under Balbo is even more clearly manifest in a second brochure produced by the Publicity and Propaganda Service entitled *La Libia turistica*. This 1938 volume takes the format of an illustrated guidebook, giving considerable attention to the administrative, economic, and industrial organization of this colony.[108] Notably, the demographic colonization program under Balbo is presented as the "foundation of the Libyan economy." The heroic aspects of this reclamation project are depicted in the illustrations, which show new irrigation systems, methods of farming, and verdant fields of olives, grapes, and other crops. No less powerful is the representation of the public-works project of the *strada litoranea*, to which this volume dedicates a separate section of nine pages of text, numerous illustrations, and its cover (fig. 2.17).[109] The fusion of Fascist modernity and tourism is clearly expressed in the textual presentation of the *strada litoranea*, which refers to it as a "work of economic, political, touristic and military importance" that "connects the activity and initiative of Fascist Italy with the more pure Roman tradition, consecrated by the conquest of a mechanical and technical civilization like no other."[110] *La Libia turistica* is thus closely tied to the politics of modernization of this colony by associating itself with the symbolic and literal occupation of this region as an extension of metropolitan society.

The politics of colonialism is similarly evident in the general structure and content of *La Libia turistica*. The presentation of the regions of the colony directly corresponds with the administrative structure of the colonial government itself. The four coastal provinces of Tripoli, Misurata, Benghazi, and Derna—each with its own description—are treated separately from the southern regions of the "Territories of the Libyan Sahara." The larger structure of this publication is also significant, as it offers an objective presentation of this colony over a more literary or narrative model. This quality is particularly evident in the section of the guidebook that presents the major cities and towns in Libya. Rather than being ordered according to their regional location as part of a tourist itinerary, they are listed alphabetically—something that gives a dry and ascetic quality to this tourist representation. Adding to the sense of practicality of this guidebook is a section of tourist information and a brief Italian-Arabic dictionary. As a representation of the tourist system, *La Libia turistica* offers an image of Fascist modernity in the colonial context conceived according to a scientific model.

The Publicity and Propaganda Service of the ETAL also produced the journal *Libia* beginning in March of 1937. The representational mission of this monthly illustrated magazine was much broader than tourism, as it encompassed many current political and social developments related to the colonial project of Balbo. The link between this journal and Fascist colonial politics is quite apparent in the first issue, which was timed to coincide with Mussolini's 1937 visit. It opens with an impassioned dedication to Mussolini that asserts that his visit to the fourth shore of Italy was "a solemn consecration and affirmation of power and glory."[111] The political content of the journal continued through the span of its existence, and included the presentation of significant events and the communication of policy—such as the legislation that pertained to the incorporation of Libya into Italy.[112] The visual presentation of the magazine also conveys a

ALME SOL POSSIS
NIHIL VRBE ROMA
VISERE MAIVS

LA LIBIA
TVRISTICA

Fig. 2.17. Cover design of the guide-book La Libia turistica (Milan: Prof. G. De Agostini, 1938), published by the Libyan Tourism and Hotel Association. (See also Plate 3.)

powerful message very much in the manner of contemporary publications in Italy. The cover of the March 1937 issue, designed by the artist Bruno Santi, presents a characteristic street scene from an indigenous town viewed against the backdrop of an abstract graphic composition (fig. 2.18).

During the course of its several years of publication, the journal *Libia* paid considerable attention to the public-works accomplishments of the Balbo administration. The first issue of the magazine presents the *strada litoranea* through a combination of a highly rhetorical text written by Balbo and a series of images and titles that convey the reality of the realization of this artery. Through the use of images and text, the *strada litoranea* is offered as both an *opera romana* that conquered the desert that "terrorized Salust and the poets of the Imperial era" and a work of contemporary

Fig. 2.18. Bruno Santi's cover design for Libia magazine (June 1937), published by the Libyan Tourism and Hotel Association. (See also Plate 4.)

engineering prowess.[113] A second essay, entitled "Edificare in tempo fascista," presents significant public buildings like the governor's house and tourist-oriented projects of the Mehari and Uaddan hotels in Tripoli. The rhetoric of this article links this modernization effort to that of classical Rome, stating that "today Fascism presents to [Mussolini] a Libya ethically and profoundly Italian, ready to respond to the radiant destiny of the Nation."[114] At the same time, the author does not fail to recognize the modernity of these projects, stating that "in the fifteenth year of Fascism, Tripoli seems a beautiful Mediterranean, or better still, Italian city, where the green of its gardens and streets alternates or surrounds the clarity of the architecture, the purity of the arches, the loveliness of the porticoes."[115]

The connection between the modernization program of Balbo and the tourist system of the Libyan Tourism and Hotel Association was not limited to the promotional activities of the Publicity and Propaganda Service. This group was directly involved with the inauguration of the *strada litoranea*, through which it contributed to the sense of incorporation of this colony into Italy. One part of this relationship was quite direct. The ETAL actively participated in this event through the provision of accomodation and transportation for the entourage of journalists and guests that followed the inauguration by Mussolini. After the conclusion of the inauguration, it created regular transportation service between Tripoli and Benghazi, provided technical assistance for its service centers, and oversaw the roadside publicity for this artery, which it leased out to Italian companies.[116] In this sense, the tourist network of the ETAL was quite literally linked to, and dependent upon, the *strada litoranea* for both transportation and publicity regarding its activities. It can also be argued that in conjunction with the system of hotels, the *strada litoranea* was a potent symbol of the dedica-tion of the coastal region of this colony to tourist-related activities. This kind of rhetorical importance is evidenced by the fact that the ETAL issued a special series of postcards for the inauguration of the *strada litoranea* by Mussolini, such as one depicting the so-called "Charge of the *Savari*" at the military festival at 'Ain Zarah (fig. 2.19). These postcards transform a political event that symbolized the unification of the colony into a modern tourist spectacle.

The experience of modernity, however, was not limited to the *strada litoranea* and related publicity materials. It was quite literally suffused throughout the tourist system of the ETAL, which attempted to provide a network of modern travel services that met the expectations of the Italian and foreign traveler. While one of those expectations was, naturally, providing a well-organized system, of equal importance was creating an atmosphere that was familiar to the tourist. Despite the obvious cultural difference of its colo-nial setting, this system was intended to provide a tourist experience that was continuous with the metropolitan context. This quality can certainly be seen in the facilities of the Tourism Service, like the travel agency in Tripoli. Located in the very colony to which it provides services, the exoticism of its North African location is carefully tempered with the image of order and efficiency that would be expected in a travel office in Italy. To travel to Libya was thus not to leave the modern standards of Italian tourism behind.

The Libyan Tourism and Hotel Association provided a series of modern amenities and

Fig. 2.19. Post-card of the military festival of the "charge of the Savari," held in the presence of Benito Mussolini at 'Ain Zarah, March 1937.

Fig. 2.20. View of the Arena of Sharah al-Shatt in Tripoli (1936).

tourist related activities that effectively transported the metropolitan context to Libya. The primary source of this experience of the metro-pole was the Theater and Performance Service, which presided over the cultural, entertainment, and sports activities and venues in Libya. One such venue was the Arena of Sharah al-Shatt, an outdoor facility that could seat up to 2,000 people (fig. 2.20). This building was used for a summer film festival that ran between July and October each year and attracted some 60,000 visitors to see what were termed the "best Italian and foreign film productions."[117] In addition to such cultural events, it was used for sporting and recreation activities, including boxing matches and outdoor shooting competitions, both of which were held at an inter-national level. However, not only were a series of metropolitan events staged in the colonial context. The blank white surfaces and shaded patios of this facility provided an environment that was clearly based on the Mediterranean modernism that was prevalent in contemporary architectural discourse in Italy.

The Uaddan Theater of the Theater and Performance Service offered a similar confluence of event and setting. This group brought in actors and musicians from Italy to provide forms of entertainment that principally appealed to a highly cultured Western audience. During the 1938–39 tourist season, the program included nine different drama companies and four orchestral concerts.[118] The metropolitan aspect of this theater is evident in the architectural expression of the interior. Designed by the architect Di Fausto in conjunction with Stefano Gatti-Casazza, its highly polished wood surfaces provided an opulent but conventionally appropriate context for these performances—a space that would be just as much at home in Milan as it was in Tripoli (figs. 2.21, 2.22). In a similar manner, the strong horizontal lines and nautical themes of the restaurant of the Hotel Mehari, which was constructed in 1938, are suggestive of the kind of contemporary architecture that could be found along the Amalfian coast of Italy (fig. 2.23).[119] This facility is connected to the original hotel of 1936 through an underground passageway, allowing it to engage with the Mediterranean face of Tripoli—a face that had consciously been remade by the Italians as one of a modern colonial city. In this sense, this facility openly participates in the Italian identity of this North African colony.

In the experience of the colony provided by the ETAL system of hotels, entertainment facilities, and travel services, the key attraction was the provision of a Western standard of comfort. The idea that travel in the colonies was a virtual extension of a

Fig. 2.21. (Right) Theater program for the Uaddan Hotel and Casino in Tripoli, January 31, 1937. (See also Plate 5.)

Fig. 2.22. (Left) Interior of the Uaddan Theater in Tripoli (1935), by Florestano Di Fausto and Stefano Gatti-Casazza.

metropolitan system was particularly evident in the promotional material related to the Transportation Service, which was responsible for providing service throughout this colony. Prominent in this publicity material were the motor coaches that were used for travel into the pre-Saharan region of Libya—vehicles that were described as representing "the best automobile technology that has been realized."[120] Indeed, these vehicles were well insulated against the sun and were equipped with a small bar and bathroom facilities. Each passenger was provided with a separate seat that reclined and swiveled, and had individual tables and a private radio. The idea that travel in even the most remote regions of Libya could have all of the comforts of the West was conveyed in the ETAL publication *Itinerario Tripoli-Gadames*.[121] This guidebook offers a systematic description of the itinerary aboard the "spacious, comfortable, and luminous" ETAL motor coaches, which provided a five-day return trip to Ghadames with an overnight stay in Nalut. In contrast with the adventurous experience of the automobile *raid*, in this publication the difficult realities of travel in this colony had been rendered invisible. The series of watercolor images that accompany the text provide a narrative thread that reinforces the sense that travel in this region is almost effortless. One such example is the image of Yifran that counterposes a modern automobile in the foreground with the brilliantly white Hotel Rumia on the distant hillside (fig. 2.24).

Fig. 2.23. Exterior view of the restaurant of the Hotel Mehari in Tripoli (1938).

The idea of creating a metropolitan standard of comfort also extended to the network of hotel facilities that the Libyan Tourism and Hotel Association managed. This system of accommodation was seen to have a consistent level of amenity in centers of secondary tourist importance as well as in the major cities of Tripoli and Benghazi (fig. 2.25). All of the ETAL hotels provided first- or second-class lodging, the only exception being the luxury accommodation of the Uaddan Hotel and Casino. Moreover, all of the hotels had modern bathroom facilities, and all except the Hotel Tripolitania in Tripoli offered the option of three meals with a room. The importance of the modern amenities of their hotel system was certainly not lost on the ETAL, which in a news release stated: "To find a bathroom for each room and hot and cold running water 750 kilometers from the heart of Africa is undoubtedly a very pleasurable surprise."[122] In the publicity brochure *La Libia*, the universality was related to each of their hotels offering "comfortable rooms where the traveler can find that convenience and refinement that is quite welcome in distant countries and after uncomfortable journeys."[123] Their publicity photographs are equally imbued with the desire to convey an image of metropolitan comfort. One such example is an image of the dining room at the Hotel of the Gazelle in Zlitan, where the stark setting and contemporary furnishings and tableware communicate an image of hospitality and service, but without any substantial references

Fig. 2.24. Drawing of Yifran from the valley with an automobile, from Itinerario Tripoli-Gadames (Milan: Tipo-Litografia Turati Lombardi, 1938). (See also Plate 6.)

Fig. 2.25. Advertisement for the Hotel Derna (1937). (See also Plate 7.)

to the colonial context (fig. 2.26).

While an important part of tourism in Libya was the desire to experience an "other" culture, there is another equally significant and seemingly opposite aspect that determined the tourist experience in Libya. Colonial travel during the latter part of the 1930s was closely tied to the political program in Libya, which aimed to modernize this region in order to incorporate it into the larger Italy. The tourist system of the Libyan Tourism and Hotel Association was a projection of these modern standards of travel onto the colonial context. Thus, in a similar manner to the colonial politics of Balbo, it created a tourist experience that was continuous with the metropole. In a sense, tourism was a kind of propelling mechanism for the modernization process that was at this same time satisfying the expectation of metropolitan standards in the

Fig. 2.26. Dining room of the Hotel of the Gazelle in Zlitan (1936), by Umberto Di Segni.

civic life of Libya. Through its connection with this modernizing program, tourism in Libya was a means to reenact the colonial relationship; that is, it was instrumental in the suppression or erasure of cultural difference. Indeed, the experience of modernity in the tourist system in Libya seemed to specifically exclude any references to the indigenous culture. In this sense, the creation of an efficient system of travel and accommodation throughout Libya by the ETAL, through participating in this modernizing and colonizing program, was a means of escaping the colony for the "comfort" of the metropole, offering enclaves of modernity in a supposedly hostile colonial context.

**CHAPTER
THREE**

THE INDIGENOUS POLITICS
OF ITALIAN COLONIALISM

In Libya Italy faced its decisive test [against an] Islamic power. As a country of Muslim population whose fierceness has been amply demonstrated by centuries of indomitable warlike resistance, Libya represents a difficult and perilous field of action for a power that intends on harmonizing its Imperial laws with a politics of sympathy towards Islam. An Islamic politics based on the oppression of the Muslim populations would be . . . in contrast with the general direction of Italy in the East. Instead, those populations are considered not as an adversarial element but as a favorable instrument and necessary base to characterize our politics in the face of the Islamic world. That is the aim that Fascist Italy has pursued in Libya, overcoming all difficulties from internal ones . . . to those provoked by partisan foreign military operations.—Italo Balbo, "La politica sociale fascista verso gli arabi della Libia," 1938.[1]

Fig. 3.1. Photograph of Mussolini standing in his car responding to the cheers of the natives in Tobruk, March 1937.

Air Marshall and Quadrumvir Italo Balbo gave a second presentation at the Conference of the Alessandro Volta Foundation in Tripoli. In this speech, he spoke of the indigenous politics that the Italian authorities had established in Libya over the period of some twenty-five years of colonial rule. Arguing that Italy was free of the constraints of other European nations, whose actions in the East were tied to the determination of the colonial states by the League of Nations following World War I, Balbo suggested that "the populations of the Muslim East . . . not only did not have arguments to address to Italy, but they were bound to look at us with sympathy for our impartiality and unselfishness."[2] It was asserted that this impartiality was expressed in a foreign policy that offered "constant loyalty and honest friendship." According to Balbo, this general approach to the Islamic world found its natural corollary in a politics of "justice, religious respect, social elevation and economic well-being."[3] While these claims were quite obviously in open conflict with the military tactics employed by the colonial authorities against the Libyans, this discrepancy is an indication of the degree to which the indigenous politics of Balbo was a work of propaganda aimed at portraying a positive relationship between Fascist Italy and the Muslim world.

In its support of the culture of the Libyans, the indigenous politics in Libya under Balbo would seem to be the equal and opposite of the modernization program, which called for Libya to be Italy's fourth shore and thus an extension of Italian soil in North Africa. However, a policy of respect to the Libyans—including the preservation and reinforcement of their indigenous cultural institutions and practices—was, in fact, carefully coordinated with the incorporation of this region into metropolitan Italy. Just like the modernization program that was at this same time introducing a system of roads and public services, the indigenous politics were motivated by the desire to bring that culture into alignment with the standards of the metropole. In the context of his presentation at the Volta Congress, Balbo argued that the Italian authorities were pursuing an approach that called for the "transformation of the social structure of the people . . . to create the necessary conditions for a more direct participation of those people in our civic life."[4] The indigenous politics of Balbo was thus an ambivalent one. It allowed the Libyans to maintain their customs and religious practices while transforming their social structure to conform to a Western viewpoint. In this sense, the programs initiated for the preservation of indigenous culture in Libya were modern.

The Italian attitude to the indigenous populations in Libya was to a great extent shaped by the history of their colonial politics in Africa. Italy had been a relative latecomer to colonialism, not having participated in the 1884 conference in Berlin in which the major European powers agreed upon the division of Africa.[5] It was not until the election of Francesco Crispi as prime minister in 1887 that the Italian government actively pursued a coherent colonial policy. This initiative resulted in the consolidation of the existing settlements in East Africa to form the colony of Eritrea in 1890 and Somalia in 1905. Due to their status as a relatively new colonial nation, Italy's indigenous politics was largely shaped—and sometimes in a negative sense—by the prior experiences of Britain and France. In his 1933 book *La Politica indigena nelle colonie*, Aldobrandino Malvezzi makes a self-serving comparison of these nations: "The English have . . . the instinctive, physical repugnance for the man of color, while the French want them to conform too much to their own likeness. The Italians live and let live, without phobias, preconceptions, fanaticism, missionary spirit, or a proselytizing mania."[6]

In reality, the Italian policy toward the Libyans was quite close to that implemented by Maréchal Hubert Lyautey in Morocco, a colony whose "civilizing mission" was tempered by the hard lessons learned in Algeria and Tunisia. The colonial administration in Morocco sought to create a stable political situation through combining the modernization of the colony with the preservation of its indigenous cultural traditions.[7] It was at least in part due to the knowledge of these French precedents that the Italians pursued a policy of collaboration with the Libyans in the immediate aftermath of the initial occupation of 1911. It was during this period that the colonial government of the Italians existed as a parallel structure to an indigenous government stocked with many of the same officials that had worked within the Ottoman administration. Despite the violent resistance of the Libyans to the Italian presence, the argument that was advanced was that there was a close relationship between Italians and the Arab, Berber, and Jewish populations. In an essay published in *Rivista Coloniale* in July 1913, the author attributes this connection to an "anthropological substratum," noting that "in certain regions of Sardinia we still have authentic Berbers who were deported from Libya to this island during the Roman period."[8] Speaking of the political policy toward the indigenous populations, he argues that "each movement of the military advance in Libya should be preceded by a movement of spiritual penetration."[9] While educational initiatives were to avoid the sphere of religious instruction, it was suggested that the Libyans should be dissuaded from practicing religious beliefs that were contrary to Italian interests—a concept that would later inform official colonial policy.

The indigenous politics practiced in Libya were given more precise outlines during the course of Mussolini's two visits to Libya. Concerning the 1926 voyage, Undersecretary of the Colonies Roberto Cantalupo noted that one of the results for the region was to "provide a solemn manifestation of the ancient and insuppressible contact that the centuries have created between [Italy] and the Eastern Muslim Mediterranean."[10] For Cantalupo, as for Mussolini, the Italian policies towards the Muslim populations in Libya were tied to the more general relationship between Italy and the East. The political importance of this relationship is evident in the events connected with the visit, where in addition to recognizing the accomplishments of Italian colonization, the Fascist leader made a substantial effort to incorporate the local populations. One such gesture was a speech dedicated to Mussolini by Hasuna Qaramanli, the former Muslim mayor of Tripoli, who described the Italian colonization as a "day of light" in their history.[11] There were also a number of military exercises that involved the Arab and Berber populations, including a mock military battle with indigenous troops on horseback that was performed in the Fascist leader's honor in the town of Janzur. In complete contradiction with the ongoing military operations, Mussolini assured the Libyans of the benevolence of the Fascist administration, stating: "I know that if you are respectful of the laws of my august Italian King, you will be protected by his just laws."[12]

The message of support and mutual respect toward the Libyans was articulated more clearly during Mussolini's 1937 visit—a visit that was conceived and organized from the standpoint of its reception by an international (and particularly Muslim) audience (fig. 3.1). The attempt to appease the Libyans was evident in the speeches given by Mussolini, which spoke of "a new epoch in the history of Libya" that assured "peace, justice, well-being, and respect for the laws of the Prophet."[13] This relationship was conveyed in the publicity material related to this voyage, which asserted that "the international politics of Fascist Italy in relation to the Muslim East has always been, without any deviation, a politics of friendship."[14] As with the publications, this visit was a political gesture that was intended to convey the image of Mussolini as a protector of Islam—an objective that was communicated in the many events that incorporated the local populations, such as the ceremony of some two thousand Libyan soldiers on horseback entrusting the so-called sword of Islam to the Fascist leader. Not only was this visit the most prominent event to give symbolic expression to the incorporation of the Libyan populations into the Fascist colonial project; it was also the clearest expression of the dilemma posed by the Italian approach to indigenous politics. While the intention was to preserve the local culture, this effort was framed within the limits and according to the perspective of the Fascist authorities—an aspect that was evident in the details of this visit, such as in the fact that the sword of Islam was fabricated in Florence.[15]

In the years following these visits and leading up to the beginning of World War II, Italian policy toward the Libyans was influenced by the emergence of a racist discourse in Italian politics. Beginning in 1937, the Fascist leadership in Rome, through the Ministry of Popular Culture, began to study legislation that was largely aimed at the Jewish population of Italy. This effort came to fruition with the passing of the "Provisions for the defense of the Italian Race," in November of 1938.[16] This law called for the deportation of foreign Jews and for the prohibition of intermarriage between Jews and Italians—who in this law were described as an Aryan race. The repercussions of the law were just as significant in the colonial context, where the policy of separation of races that had sometimes been loosely practiced became more consistently observed—particularly in the East African colonies. Notably, it was at this same time that the Fascist journal *Difesa della Razza* began to publish articles on issues of race related to the Italian colonies by researchers like Edoardo Zavattari, who was director of the Institute of Zoology of the University of Rome. In his essay "Italia e islam di fronte al problema razzista," the author asserted that while Muslims are anti-racist, they are Islamists in that they only accept those that adhere to Islam in their community. According to this argument, the Italian desire to create a separation of the races was seen to coincide with the desire of the Muslim populations to segregate themselves based on religion.[17] Under the guise of anthropological research, this essay mobilized scientific arguments to justify a colonial politics of racism and exclusion.

In the latter part of the 1930s, the political policy of preserving the customs and practices of the Libyans was increasingly supported by a "science" whose aim was to assert the superiority of the Italian race. While these views had not always been explicitly stated in official colonial policy, they foregrounded the problematic relationship that existed between the Italians and the Libyans. While their land was deemed to be part of Italy's fourth shore, and as such subject to a modernizing program that was preparing the way for Libya's incorporation into the metropole, their society and culture was always viewed as an "other." However, as is quite clear during the governorship of Italo Balbo, even that status was defined by and subject to the standards of conduct of modern European culture. The indigenous politics of Italian colonialism was a modernizing and Westernizing politics that from the initial days of the occupation accorded the Libyans an ambivalent status.

A PROGRAM OF PRESERVATION

The first official public document that recognized the value of preserving the indigenous culture of Libya was the master plan of Tripoli prepared by the engineer Luigi Luiggi. Not only did this 1912 proposal call for the modernization of this colonial city—including restructuring the port, the introduction of public services, and the improvement of the street network—it also argued that it would be wise to respect the existing built fabric of the old city. Following the precedent of the French in Tunisia and the English in Egypt, this plan stated that the old city "should not be touched . . . in order to conserve the present character unaltered."[18] The sole exceptions to a preservationist approach to the old city were the recovery of Roman monuments like the second century A.D. Arch of Marcus Aurelius and the introduction of a modern network of water and sanitary services. While the first of these places the Roman cultural heritage of Libya on a higher plane than the Arab one, the second clearly values the modernization of the public infrastructure.

An interest in the hygienic condition of the old city found its planning equivalent in the strategy of creating a strong separation between the old city and the new. The walls of the medina and the existing castle were to be repaired, but isolated from the surrounding fabric through the construction of a "wide, beautiful and magnificent promenade, embellished with numerous trees" that would contrast with the "narrow, but picturesque lanes of the Arab city."[19] A similar preservation program was to be implemented in the surrounding oasis. Citing the precedent of the British in India, Luiggi argued that out of a broader policy of respecting the religious practices and primitive customs of the Muslim populations, their tombs, cemeteries, and the related landscape would be left alone. Notably, one of the motivations behind the conservation of what was described as a picturesque setting of gardens of palm trees, was the "local imprint that the aesthete and the tourist seek."[20]

Although the initial master plan of Tripoli was largely unrealized until the governorship of Giuseppe Volpi, it established a precedent for the preservation of the existing fabric of the old city that was part of a broader conservation effort taken up by this later colonial administration. This more general initiative of Volpi—and the most crucial component of his indigenous politics relative to tourism in the region—called for the preservation of the Roman and Muslim historical patrimony. This political policy had the aim of both appeasing the local populations and facilitating the tourist interest in the region.

Working with Rodolfo Micacchi of the Ministry of the Colonies, Volpi put a substantial effort into research, restoration, and propaganda related to Roman archeological sites.[21] In the case of the excavations at Leptis Magna—the Roman colony where Emperor Septimius Severus was born—although work had begun as early as 1920, it was not until around 1924 that a considerable financial investment was made by the colonial authorities.[22] Under the guidance of archeologist Pietro Romanelli—who was then director of the Superintendency of Monuments—the major landmarks of the fora, basilica, baths, and the surrounding fabric and port of the Roman colony of Leptis were recovered from the desert sands that had protected them for centuries, an effort that made possible their appreciation by a tourist audience (fig. 3.2). The Volpi administration's restoration of Roman archeological sites included Sabratha, where excavations began in 1923 under the direction of noted archeologist Roberto Paribeni.[23] In this instance, in addition to a collection of basilicas, temples, and baths, a spectacular theater and an elliptical amphitheater were discovered and eventually restored for public access and viewing.

In the city of Tripoli, the preservation program was supported by the creation of a commission to identify buildings and objects of historic, artistic, and archaeological interest. After an initial meeting in November of 1921, this group drew up a list that included two Roman monuments, the ancient castle and walls of the old city, thirteen Muslim religious buildings, and twenty-four private residences. The commitment of the Volpi administration to this restoration program was demonstrated through two legislative measures introduced in early 1922. The first allowed for government regulations that pertained to Roman antiquities to be applied to the conservation of the Islamic heritage of Libya, and the second established the list of buildings to be preserved.[24]

Fig. 3.2. View of the archeological site at Leptis Magna, ca. 1925.

Fig. 3.3. Restoration of the castle in Tripoli (1922-26), by Armando Brasini.

Among the first projects to be undertaken under this mandate was the restoration of the walls of the old city of Tripoli, the first stage of which was completed in 1923 under the supervision of Romanelli. Faced with the ruinous state of the walls—a situation that was a product of both the deterioration of the structure and its partial destruction by the Italian colonial authorities in 1914-1915—he chose to systematize them through a combination of restructuring existing elements and rebuilding selected portions.[25] One of the most substantial gestures made in the restoration of the western wall of Tripoli near the Bab al-Jedid was to reestab-lish its "true" height by excavating down to its lowest level, which was believed to have been from the Roman period. A similar approach was taken with the restoration of the castle of Tripoli by the architect Armando Brasini (fig. 3.3). It was during this time that, according to Italian scholars, the courtyard houses in Libya came closest to Italian Renaissance models. Working in conjunction with Renato Bartoccini of the Superintendency of Monuments, this project clearly favored a "classic" period of Libyan architecture over all others: that of the rule of Ahmad Pasha al-Qaramanli (1711–45).[26]

The Volpi administration undertook an equally significant preservation initiative related to the native artisanal industries of Tripolitania—a program that was aimed at improving the indigenous economy. The Government Office of Indigenous Applied Arts was founded in January of 1925, with the mission to study these industries, make proposals for their expansion, and promote their sales through exhibitions and displays.[27] In attempting to improve the artistic production of local craftsmen—who were seen to be practicing an "unclear and impure" interpretation of Arab art—

this office provided information, such as representative patterns taken from the indigenous craft industries of Algeria, Tunisia, and Morocco, and brought in master craftsmen from these French colonies. It was argued that the new methods were a return to the practices that "in past times they also performed in Tripoli, but of which almost all traces have been lost."[28] It should be noted, however, that these methods corresponded with the Italian authorities' view of the authentic culture of the region.

This government office was also active in improving the organizational and economic systems of these industries. The improvements involved, among other things, financial support for acquiring raw materials and the systematic upgrading of the quality and cost of these commodities. The enhancement of the distribution system for native artisanal products was largely connected with fairs and exhibitions. The displays included temporary installations at regional events in Italy and the creation of a permanent exhibition in Tripoli, which was organized in conjunction with the local chamber of commerce. This latter display was located in Corso Vittorio Emanuele III and had the appearance of a metropolitan shopfront reinterpreted through the use of arabizing motifs. This permanent exhibition is a perfect expression of the ambivalence of the preservation program that marked the Italian intervention into the indigenous culture of Libya, which was both historicized and modernized in conformance with a Western viewpoint (fig. 3.4).

The indigenous politics of the Volpi administration also provided for the restructuring of the educational system of the Libyans—what at that time was referred to as an important part of the "moral conquest" of Tripolitania.[29] The initial legislation that pertained to the creation of schools for the Muslim populations was passed into law in January of 1914. Although this law allowed both Koranic and private schools to continue to exist, it followed the approach taken by the French in Algeria in developing Italian schools that assimilated the Libyan children. A second piece of legislation, introduced in 1919, went in the opposite direction by severely restricting or eliminating the impact of the Italian educational system on the local populations. The situation changed rather dramatically under Volpi, who appointed Angelo Piccioli as superintendent of education. Rejecting the first approach on the basis that it did not recognize the difference between "the spirit of our race and that of the Arab race" and the second based on its assumption that "the indigenous populations [are] irreparably closed to the penetration of our civilization," Piccioli sought a middle ground.[30] Beginning with the 1922-23 academic year, a separate system of education was created for the Muslim populations, with the curriculum including mathematics, history, geography, and Italian-language training. Piccioli argued that while this system recognized the differences between Italian and Muslim races—and thus can be seen as a gesture of preservation of indigenous culture—"we should not forget that in the colonies a politics that aims at the moral and material elevation of the natives *cannot be made but in the interest of the colonizing power*."[31]

The governorship of Volpi was instrumental in establishing the direction of the indigenous politics of Italian colonial Libya—a direction that was followed by his successors De Bono and Badoglio. It set a precedent for intervention in

Fig. 3.4. Photograph of a window display in Corso Vittorio Emanuele III in Tripoli (ca. 1925), by the Government Office of Indigenous Applied Arts.

the indigenous culture of the Libyans with the preservation of historic buildings and sites. Notably, the choice of buildings and of how to preserve them was an operative one, often reflecting a desire to view Libyan culture as derived from Western (and Italian) precedents. A similar intervention took place in the artisanal industries, the motivation in this case being to keep the Libyans occupied with menial and labor-intensive jobs. A secondary benefit of this program was the improvement of the local economy and consequent elevation of the value of the colony to Italy. The changes in the education system were aimed at establishing precise limits for the level of education of the Libyans and indoctrinating them as colonial subjects. In all cases, these acts of preservation were carefully considered in relation to the demands of the colonial authorities and thereby were completely in line with the program of modernizing the colony for the purpose of its incorporation into the metropole.

Fig. 3.5. Interior of the Mosque of Ahmad Pasha al-Qaramanli in Tripoli (1736-37).

"WE MUST RESPECT THE CHARACTER OF TRIPOLI'S ARCHITECTURE"

During the governorship of Emilio De Bono, a substantial scholarly discourse on the indigenous architecture of Libya was created by a number of individuals who emerged as experts in this field of study. The most prominent of these scholars was Salvatore Aurigemma, who worked for the Superintendency of Monuments in Tripolitania between 1912 and 1919.[32] Although he returned to Italy several years before Volpi became governor, Aurigemma continued his research activities throughout the 1920s, eventually publishing essays on a number of prominent buildings in Tripoli, including the castle and the mosques of Ahmad Pasha al-Qaramanli (1736–37) and Mustafa Bey Gurgi (1833–34). In his essay on the Qaramanli mosque, published in the art journal *Dedalo* in January of 1927, Aurigemma provided a detailed account of the history of its founder and the Maghreb influences on its decorative traditions, while not failing to remark that there were "lines and decorative elements from eighteenth-century European art" (fig. 3.5).[33]

This research extended to the preservation of the Roman archeological patrimony of Libya, with a major publication on the baths at Leptis Magna in 1929.[34] The far greater commitment of the colonial authorities to the excavation and restoration of Roman sites is evidenced in the continuing excavations at Leptis Magna and Sabratha, the construction of museums at these two sites, and the renewed archeological missions at the sites of Apollonia and Cyrene in Cyrenaica.[35] The greater investment in these projects reflects the constant tension in Libya between the Italian interest in indigenous Muslim architecture and the compelling need for them to recover their Roman past. The tension between Roman monuments and local fabric was not isolated to the colonial context, however, as these values derived quite directly from the discourse on modernization and preservation in Italy. The question was, which history was to be preserved and at what cost? As early as December of 1925, in a speech given to the mayor of Rome, Mussolini made his opinions quite clear.[36] The city of Rome had two aspects, the Roman and early Christian monuments and the anonymous local fabric. The first was to be preserved and celebrated at the expense of the second—a dichotomy that transferred quite directly to Libya.

The discourse on the preservation of indigenous Muslim heritage of Libya emerged with renewed interest during the governorship of Pietro Badoglio. It was during this time that General Secretary of Tripolitania Maurizio Rava submitted a report on Tripoli's present and future development. It was published in the colonial journal *L'Oltremare* in November of 1929 under the title "Dobbiamo rispettare il carattere dell'edilizia tripolina," or "We Must Respect the Character of Tripoli's Architecture." This document provides a vigorous defense of the indigenous architecture and landscape of the city and oasis of Tripoli. It calls for the preservation of the local character through a careful program of conserving the most representative existing buildings and introducing new structures that would be in harmony with the existing environment. This contextualist method was to be implemented in the old Arab and Jewish quarters of Tripoli where, according to the author, "the impression of Africa and the East" could still be found. It was also applicable to the buildings of the surrounding oasis landscape, which "in their local *minor architecture . . .* represent the *true Arab style of Tripolitania.*"[37]

The timing of this report was extremely important, as it had a substantial influence on the master plan of Tripoli prepared by the architects Alpago Novello, Cabiati, and Ferrazza. While this 1933 plan was a document of the modernization of the city according to a set of technical considerations, not the least of which being its expansion to double its present size, it also reflected the long-standing interest in the status of the old city. One such regulation was the control of all new buildings within its walls, whose construction it stipulated as having to be of the "indigenous type." The surrounding oasis was given similar attention, the conservation of its scale and density being related to "both tourist

Fig. 3.6. Governor's
Palace in Rhodes
(1926), by Flores-
tano Di Fausto.

Fig. 3.7. Proposal
for restructuring
the Suq al-Mushir
in Tripoli (1932),
by Florestano Di
Fausto.

interests and hygienic demands of the city."[38] Another notable
aspect of this proposal was that the settlement of the indigenous
populations followed the decentralized model used to order the
new areas of the city. In so doing, the indigenous residential areas
outside the walls of the old city were distributed throughout the
plan rather than being located in a single district—an approach
that set this plan apart from the Prost plan for Casablanca of
1914. The preservation strategy that led to the dispersal of the

local populations was, however, no less destructive to the social fabric of Libya than that of tearing down large areas of the city. Preventing the Libyans from living in a dense urban enclave was simply a more subtle way of maintaining the public order.

Another key figure in this preservationist discourse was the architect Florestano Di Fausto, who was trained at the Academy of Fine Arts in Rome. His importance during the Badoglio era was due to his appointment as architectural consultant for the Municipality of Tripoli after the death of the Roman architect Alessandro Limongelli in 1932.[39] Prior to arriving in Libya, Di Fausto was well known for his efforts as director of the Technical Office of the Ministry of Foreign Affairs, where he was responsible for the construction or transformation of numerous embassies and cultural institutes in Europe and abroad, including Belgrade, Cairo, Algiers, Ankara, and Tunis.[40] His most notable work from this period is the substantial body of projects he realized in Rhodes beginning in the mid-1920s. In the Governor's Palace, Di Fausto illustrates his ability to synthesize a complex set of indigenous references—an effort that ran parallel to the Italian authorities' interests in fostering the peaceful coexistence of the different ethnic groups on this eastern Mediterranean island (fig. 3.6). Following his appointment in 1932, Di Fausto was involved in developing a number of proposals related to the ongoing master plan of Tripoli. While one set of projects were involved in creating public spaces within the new city, Di Fausto was also active in addressing the relationship between the new and the old city.[41] One such project is his 1932 proposal for the restructuring of the Suq al-Mushir, which obscures the distinction between the historic structure and the new construction based upon the demands of the tourist economy (fig. 3.7).

The indigenous artisanal industries in Tripolitania enjoyed a significant amount of attention in the years following the governorship of Volpi. The increasing interest in the native products was at least in part due to the participation of the Government Office of Indigenous Applied Arts in exhibitions and fairs, and particularly the Tripoli Trade Fair. Beginning in 1927, this event provided a popular venue for the representation of indigenous artisanry to a metropolitan audience. This annual representation often presented the native arts in a manner that was similar to contemporary museum practices.[42] There were also numerous public displays of the work of Libyan craft industries in Italy during this period, with a pavilion or stand appearing each year at the trade fairs in cities like Milan and Naples. One of the more notable examples of such displays was the Tripoli Village at the Turin International Exposition of 1928. This representation of an indigenous village included the so-called *Mercato di suk tripolino*—a fragment of the old city of Tripoli complete with vendors and their typical wares.[43] As a literal reenactment of the indigenous marketplace, this display is an example of the importance of a sense of authenticity to the value of native artisanal objects (fig. 3.8).

Equally significant to the advancement of the indigenous arts were a series of government initiatives introduced during the governorship of Badoglio. The first of these was a law passed in May of 1929 that changed the name of the Government Office of Indigenous Applied Arts to the School of Arts and Crafts. Although the mandate of this new group remained similar, it was to be an

Fig. 3.8. Reconstruction of Tripolitanian suq at the Colonial Exhibition in Turin (1928).

autonomous group that was more substantially involved in the instruction of indigenous arts in Tripolitania.[44] A second initiative saw the construction of a new building related to the School of Arts and Crafts in Tripoli in 1931. This new structure, which had the appearance of a building indigenous to the oasis of Tripoli, took the form of a *suq*, allowing space for thirty-four separate vendors to sell their goods (fig. 3.9). Badoglio was also active in promoting the study of the indigenous arts, commissioning Mario Scaparro to survey these industries. The report, which was published in 1932, painted a less than flattering picture, arguing that due to a number of factors, including "commercial disorganization" and "governmental agnosticism" there was an "abandonment and general decay of almost all of the arts."[45] This study was the impetus for the continuing efforts to improve the native industries—a preservation project that came to fruition under the direction of the Balbo administration.

Similar advances were made in the education of the Libyans during the De Bono and Badoglio administrations. While the general philosophy did not change dramatically—the Libyans continued to be educated in a separate system—the number of schools and students increased. What had been an extremely modest collection of twenty schools in Tripolitania in 1925—half of which were providing traditional religious education—had become a more substantial system of forty-two schools providing primary education, even in the most remote locations. The number of students reflects this change, with just over 1,700 Muslims in primary education in 1925 increasing to almost 5,000 by 1932.[46] Despite the modest growth in the educational system for the indigenous populations, three years of primary education were effectively eliminated by the De Bono administration in June 1927. This law suspended separate middle school education for the Libyans, instead offering them the option of metropolitan schools.[47] In conjunction with a greater emphasis on vocational education in the area of agriculture and artisanry, this legislation had the effect of limiting the options for the local populations at the same time as expanding the educational system.

The coexistence of modernization and preservation forces can be seen in the many publications that documented the accomplishments of this period, like Angelo Piccioli's *La nuova Italia d'oltremare*. In his concluding comments, he speaks of a Fascist government that imposes "the only conceivable politics for a people who want to dominate other people . . . an organic, direct and . . . linear politics: one that moves according to a preordained plan." At the same time, this rhetoric is tempered in the discussion of the indigenous populations, whom Fascism gave "the sense of a will to rule [that they were] not only called upon to affirm but also to construct."[48] In a manner that is entirely consistent with the indigenous politics that the Italian colonial authorities had been developing throughout this period in the area of planning, education, and the artisanal industries, gestures of reconciliation to the local populations went hand in hand with a greater level of manipulation and control. This

Fig. 3.9. School of Arts and Crafts in Tripoli (1931).

carefully measured policy of preserving indigenous culture unquestionably conferred an inferior status on that culture.

IMPERIAL POLITICS AND INDIGENOUS CULTURE

The political dimension of Italian colonial policy toward the Libyans was given a considerable emphasis during the governorship of Italo Balbo. His indigenous politics were a calculated attempt to counteract the negative impression, still lingering in the international community, of the reconquest of Libya during the governorship of Pietro Badoglio. Beginning as early as 1931, the Ministry of Foreign Affairs began to monitor the Islamic press through the Italian consulates in locations like Damascus, Jerusalem, and Cairo.[49] These practices continued throughout the Balbo era, and were conducted in conjunction with efforts by the Fascist authorities to create their own favorable press. The negative reports on the Italian colonial government began to change in early 1935 in response to a program of clemency by the Balbo administration, who freed 130 political prisoners in Cyrenaica in January of that year. This shift in opinion is also due to the systematic effort by the Italian consulates throughout the Middle East to disseminate the news of such gestures of leniency.[50]

The indigenous politics of Balbo evolved into a combination of firm rule and carefully conceived gestures of reconciliation. Indeed, Balbo maintained strict control of these populations, which he did not hesitate to punish for infractions that he regarded as either morally dangerous or contemptuous of colonial rule. In order to create a climate of mutual respect, he met with leaders of various indigenous groups on matters of education, public assistance, and religion. Balbo attempted to appease former dissidents through a 1936 program for the restitution of personal goods and property confiscated during the period of the concentration camps.[51] These political tactics were reinforced by a systematic propaganda effort—a campaign that reached new heights during the Balbo era. The most notable of these publicity materials are the publications that emerged at the time of Mussolini's visit to Libya in 1937. Among the most interesting of these are the pamphlets and flyers written in Arabic that quite obviously were aimed at the image of Italy in the larger Muslim world.[52] Through an extensive reporting of the policies in favor of the Islamic populations, these publications provided a false image of Italian benevolence (fig. 3.10).

The most comprehensive explanation of the indigenous politics of the Balbo administration in Libya can be found in the presentation he made at the Volta Conference in 1938. Entitled "La Politica sociale verso gli Arabi della Libia," it dealt with the problem of the negotiation between local traditions and the standards of modern Italian society. This problem had already been expressed by several commentators as a product of the inevitable conflict between European civilization and indigenous culture. Rejecting the idea that either of these had to be dominant, one particularly open-minded author offers the hybrid solution of "creating a condition for [the local populations] that permits the evolution of a new civilization, resulting from an adequate combination of living and dynamic elements of both their traditions and ours"—an approach that bears little resemblance to the actual policy of the Italians in Libya.[53]

In the case of the arguments of Balbo, the coexistence of Italian and Libyan

رحلة موسوليني الى ليبيا

Fig. 3.10. Cover of an Arabic publication commemorating Mussolini's visit to Libya in March 1937. (See also Plate 8.)

culture is given a more authoritarian solution. Although recognizing the need for a "vigilant defense of the manners" of the Libyans, he does not hesitate to speak of the eradication of "those old retrograde customs that oppose themselves to the social evolution of these same populations."[54] The qualified support of native customs was particularly true for religious practices, which were tolerated "as much as they are vital and derive from the laws of the Prophet," and prohibited if they were understood as "deviations of religious fanaticism."[55] Included in this second category was the Sanusi order, which was regarded as a religious sect that operated under a political motivation, and the practice of fakirism—both of which were outlawed by the Italian administration in Libya. This meant that while the Libyans were allowed, within certain limits and within the confines of religion and the family,

Fig. 3.11. Exterior view of the new Mosque of Sharah Bu-Harida in Tripoli (1937).

to practice according to their traditions, all larger forms of social and political organization were conceived according to the dictates of the colonial administration. Moreover, even explicitly private religious institutions like the Sharia tribunals that were allowed to continue were subject to considerable supervision.[56]

As Balbo argued in this speech, the incorporation of the Libyan populations into metropolitan Italy was to be undertaken in a selective manner. The governor asserted that there was a considerable difference between the Arab-Berber populations of the coastal regions—who he argued "possessed undeniable characteristics of nobility, of intelligence and of moral breadth"—and the "Negroid" races of the southern military zone—who were deemed to "need nothing other than material well-being and assistance."[57] It was on the basis of this distinction that the administration of this colony was divided into two regions—one metropolitan, the other colonial. This difference was extended to the legal status of these groups. While both would enjoy the benefit of the same laws in the areas of justice and social discipline, only the Muslim populations of the coastal region were deemed capable of exercising their spiritual and moral beliefs in the political and social arena. As such, only the Libyans of Arab and Berber descent would benefit from the creation of laws for their moral and civil elevation, and thus enjoy limited participation in the sphere of civic life and politics.[58] It is in this sense that the discourse on indigenous politics in Libya during the Balbo era represents a modern racial discourse. These policies apply scientific thought to politics by mobilizing ideas about the categorization of cultural advancement along racial lines. Balbo was not alone in this tendency, as the question of indigenous politics in the late 1930s was increasingly linked to the question of race. After the conquest of Ethiopia in 1936, there was heightened pressure, particularly in East Africa, to create a separation of the metropolitan and indigenous peoples based on racial difference.[59]

Although the indigenous politics of Balbo was largely a development of the policies of prior colonial administrations, its innovation was in offering a more rigorously Fascist corporativist structure to the colonial context. This approach to colonial politics resulted in the creation of a set of parallel organizations and practices for the local populations, thus giving form to the racial discourse that called for separation of metropolitan and colonial. This new approach to structuring indigenous political institutions had a profound influence on the initiatives related to the preservation of the architectural heritage of Libya, particularly religious buildings. The Balbo administration created the Provincial Council for the Administration of the Waqfs to oversee this traditional Muslim charitable endowment, which was responsible for funding the construction and administration of all religious facilities.[60] Due to the collaboration of this new council, the local religious leaders, and the Italian municipal authorities, twenty-nine different mosques and religious buildings were restored, reorganized, or newly constructed in the city of Tripoli alone.[61]

One such restoration project carried out under the direction of the Super-intendency of Monuments in Tripolitania is the Mosque of Ahmad Pasha al-Qaramanli in Tripoli—the largest and most well-known religious monument in the city. Completed in 1934, this restoration project was conducted according to the most advanced standards available at that time, the aim being to remove layers of recent additions so as to return this building to its original state.[62] This project in particular, and the restoration effort of the Italians in general, is coincident with an intense tourist interest in Muslim architecture—something that is underscored by the fact that most of these buildings were classified as national monuments. The historical interest in Muslim architecture was also manifest in new constructions, like the Mosque of Sharah Bu-Harida, which was completed by the municipality of Tripoli in 1937. As an abstract reinterpretation of traditional mosques, this project raises the problem of the relationship between historical preservation and modern innovations (fig. 3.11).

The exchange between archeological research and contemporary architecture was not only found in the colonial context of Libya. As William H. MacDonald has argued, there is a close connection between the undecorated Roman constructions that were being discovered in Ostia like the house of Diana (A.D. 160), where organized excavations began in 1909, and the anonymous urban buildings of the Fascist new towns of the Agro Pontino from the 1930s.[63] The question that he raises, which is an important one, is which architecture is influencing the other. That is, were the excavations at Ostia the basis for contemporary architecture or were archeologists interested in Ostia because of contemporary architectural discourse?

A similar level of ambiguity pervaded the activities of the building commission in its implementation of the master plan of Tripoli prepared by Alpago Novello, Cabiati, and Ferrazza. The principles of this plan were to create a new modern infrastructure of roads and public services that would preserve the existing character of the old city and surrounding oasis. Notably, the preservation program included a policy of *diradamento,* or thinning out, that was carried out in the indigenous housing zones in both of these areas.[64] These efforts involved giving order to the public infrastructure through the removal of some buildings and the introduction of modern amenities like new water and sewer lines. In some cases the demand for cleaning up these areas even superseded calls to preserve the local fabric. One such example was an amendment to the master plan that called for the destruction of an area of the indigenous settlement adjacent to the tourist district along the eastern seafront—the concern being for the squalid nature of this area and the danger of "the irreconcilable promiscuity of metropolitans and natives."[65]

An equally conflicted restoration initiative was the architect Di Fausto's design for the restructuring of the area around the Arch of Marcus Aurelius in Tripoli, an area that had been neglected since its initial excavation by archeologists between 1914 and 1918.[66] Completed in 1937, this project called for the creation of a linear space to frame the arch and link it to the seafront. This work of historic preservation actually created a considerable discontinuity in the adjacent fabric, requiring the demolition and restructuring of substantial portions of three of the city's most significant eighteenth-century *funduqs* (fig. 3.12).[67] The determination of what would be preserved was in the hands of the Building Commission, who in one case used modern principles of hygiene and urban order and in another chose to value one history (a Roman one) over another. The conflict between Libya's Roman legacy and its indigenous traditions was resolved in a manner that was entirely consistent with the values that informed Fascist planning in Rome, where monuments such as the Mausoleum of Augustus were "liberated" from centuries of anonymous built fabric.[68] In the colonial context of Libya, the native culture and its folkloric attraction, while desirable from the viewpoint of the tourist development, was carefully framed by the demands of Fascist colonial politics.

The indigenous politics of Balbo also embraced the problem of the education of the Libyans. To a great extent, these initiatives represent an extension of the efforts of previous governorships, which had gradually created a separate system of education. This system was delimited into four narrowly defined spheres of cultural activity—religion, family life, craft production, and agriculture—thus concretizing stereotypes about the religious devotion of Muslims, their patient dedication to menial forms of labor, and the domestic role of their women.

The tactics employed in these educational programs were multiple, as they included reinforcing existing institutions and creating new ones.[69] New schools were almost exclusively in the area of primary education, something which, as in previous administrations, unquestionably limited the educational opportunities for the Libyans. One of the few exceptions to the focus on primary education was the construction of a *madrasa* in Tripoli. Instituted by legislation passed by Balbo in 1935, this school provided education in judicial and religious doctrine of Islam so as to produce the next generation of Libyan functionaries for the Italian colonial administration.[70] A second exception to the predominance of primary education for the local populations was a Women's School for Instruction and Work, which dealt with the delicate issue of the education of Muslim women. The program comprised a series of separate institutions located in major towns, such as Tripoli, al-Khums, Misurata, Benghazi, and Derna—the intention being to prepare women for their role in family life. The courses of study included general instruction in subjects such as languages, religion, domestic economy, and hygiene, and specific training in domestic skills such as cooking, sewing, and weaving (fig. 3.13).[71]

The educational initiatives of the Balbo administration were equally focused on the indigenous arts, for which a new facility was constructed at the Suq al-Mushir in Tripoli in 1935. This institution, called the Muslim School of Indigenous Arts and Crafts, was the educational component of a much broader effort to restructure the indigenous artisanal industries according to a Fascist corporativist model. Although this effort began as early as

Fig. 3.12. Project for restructuring the area surrounding the Arch of Marcus Aurelius in Tripoli (1938), by Florestano Di Fausto.

Fig. 3.13. Muslim women at work in the women's section of the Muslim School of Arts and Crafts in Tripoli, ca. 1939.

1934, it was with the creation of the Fascist Institute of Libyan Artisans in 1935 that the indigenous sector of this industry came under this structure—providing technical, economic, commercial, and social assistance to its members.[72] As with other corporativist structures introduced into the colonial economy, this organization controlled the labor force by instituting a system of permits for each company and licenses for each member.

Although the Fascist Institute of Libyan Artisans was intended for both Italian and indigenous artisanry, a clear distinction was made in the potential contribution of these two groups. In the case of Italian artisanry in Libya, it was naturally seen as an extension of these industries in Italy, with a greater capacity for artistic innovation, technical developments, and economic output.[73] The exact opposite was the case for the indigenous part of this industry, as the call to improve techniques was in the interest of recuperating past traditions that had been lost or abandoned. This emphasis was related to two areas of concern in the indigenous arts: the impact of mass-produced goods and the potential loss of traditional techniques—something for which a considerable research effort was made in all regions of this colony.[74] The dilemma was that, while there was a desire to improve the indigenous industries according to modern and Fascist exigencies, this could not be conducted at the expense of the perceived function that they performed as a register for the authentic traditions of each region.

Although a much later development, the Balbo administration was active in the stimulation of the indigenous agricultural economy. Along with the indigenous arts, agriculture was one of the two major sectors of the economy in which the colonial administration encouraged the participation of the local populations.

Fig. 3.14. View of the Muslim coloniza-tion village of Alba or El-Fager (1939).

The educational part of this mission included the Hasuna Qara-manli Orphanage and Shelter, which provided instruction and training to the local populations in agricultural development.[75] The second was organizational and infrastructural, the Libyans being afforded a parallel system to that of the Italian agricultural colonists. While these initiatives were initially in the form of subsidies for Libyan entrepreneurs, by 1939 they were expanded to include the creation of a series of agricultural centers.[76] One such example is the town of Alba (al-Fager) in eastern Libya, which consisted of a modest series of buildings that included public services and a mosque, designed according to an abstract vernacular vocabulary. However, given their metonymic rela-tionship to the Italian demographic villages, these Muslim agricultural villages conformed to neither the patterns of settle-ment nor the farming practices of the indigenous peoples and, as such, failed to achieve any significant results (fig. 3.14).[77]

A similar program of replicating a metropolitan institution was the foundation of the Gioventù araba del Littorio (GAL) in August of 1935.[78] This group provided for the education of young Arabs in a structure that was analogous to that of the Fascist youth clubs in Italy—providing cultural instruction and premilitary training under the watchful eye of Fascist militia officers. According to a letter written by Balbo to Mussolini, its aims were "to accomplish *a work of penetration of the indigenous masses*, obtaining disci-plined subjects from its new generations, that are more interested in us, proud of belonging to a nation that returns to dominate with the sign of the Fascist party" (fig. 3.15).[79]

The most ambitious policy initiative undertaken by the Balbo administration in favor of the indigenous populations was the attempt to give them full Italian citizenship. The process began during the administrative restructuring of the colony in December of 1935 with an appeal by Balbo to Mussolini for the approval of a temporary measure for granting citizenship to the Libyans and some foreign nationals.[80] This proposition almost immediately met with considerable opposition from the Ministry of the Colonies, which noted "the irreconcilability on the part of Muslim religious law and the profession of Islamism with a European citizenship."[81] Although the objections blocked the passage of this proposal, it was revived immediately following the visit of Mussolini to Libya—a process that eventually led to the creation of a special Italian citizenship for the Libyans in 1939.[82] This new citizenship status meant that the local populations could participate in Fascist organizations, the military, and, in a limited way, in politics. Although these new rights represented a greater recognition by the Italian government, they were only valid within the territorial limits of Libya. Moreover, in order to apply for this special status, all rights to full citizenship were lost. While the four provinces of Libya had been incorporated into the "greater Italy," the Italians had a metropolitan identity while the Libyans were given a colonial one.

The policy related to the granting of Italian citizenship to the Libyans is a poignant illustration of the difficulty of resolving the conflict between the incorporation of this colony into a modern Western nation and the maintenance of its native customs and practices. Even though Balbo achieved his goal of creating a fourth shore for his own people, he incorporated the Libyans into larger Italy in such a manner that they remained entirely within the

Fig. 3.15. Arab Gioventù araba del Littorio in Libya, ca. 1939.

colonial frame of the Fascist authorities. Indeed, the policy toward the Libyans, in allowing them citizenship but denying them equivalent rights, is a perfect demonstration of the ambivalence of the indigenous politics in Libya. Through a double gesture of incorporation and discrimination, the Libyans were marked by modern metropolitan culture as Western, while remaining primitive, backward, and non-Western.

**CHAPTER
FOUR**

TOURISM AND THE FRAMING
OF INDIGENOUS CULTURE

For its Oriental, indigenous and primitive fascination, Trip-
olitania has preeminence over all of the regions of the African
Mediterranean, being less profoundly penetrated by the cosmo-
politanism that radiates from the cities of Egypt, Tunisia,
Algeria and Morocco. The Arab, devoted to traditions, lives in
his psychological and social climate, without mystifications and
contaminations. Moreover, the faith that the Italians inspire in
the natives permits us to experience their way of living.—L.V.
Bertarelli, Guida d'Italia del Touring Club Italiano, 1929.[1]

Fig. 4.1. View of an excursion in the Libyan Sahara near El Bab, from Raffaele Calzini, Da Leptis Magna a Gadames (Milan: Fratelli Treves Editori, 1926).

Just as the modernization program in Libya was necessary for
the establishment of a tourist network, the efforts of the colonial
authorities to preserve Libyan culture made a significant contribution to the tourist experience. The most important distinguishing
feature of colonial tourism—as opposed to tourism within the
metropole—is the conjunction of a modern tourist system with a
strange, exotic, and even dangerous setting. The tension between
this "other" culture and the necessary level of organization and
comfort produced an experience in which the modern metropolitan
observer was able to escape their cultural norms while safely
remaining within the colonial system. Another important consideration related to the tourist experience of Libyan culture was
the authenticity of that experience—something that is directly

alluded to in the Italian Touring Club (TCI) guidebook to the Italian colonies. In this context it is asserted that this colony offers a genuine experience of the native culture that is free of Westernization. According to this argument, the creation of a modern tourist system in Libya had the obligation to maintain, and even enhance, the most authentic experiences of the indigenous culture. It is important to note, however, that the authenticity of native culture was itself a Western construction—linked as it was to the view that so-called primitive societies existed in a manner that was untouched by modernity.

The experience of local culture in the tourist system in Libya was captured in the book *Da Leptis Magna a Gadames* of 1926.[2] This publication was written by Raffaele Calzini, who visited the colony just prior to the end of Volpi's governorship. Written as a compilation of his experience in Tripolitania, the book recounts Calzini's excursion to the archeological site at Leptis Magna and a journey from Tripoli to the oasis settlement of Ghadames (fig. 4.1). The precise nature of the book as a piece of writing is ambiguous, even by the account of its own author who notes: "My book . . . is not about archeological discoveries or wonderful adventures—it puts together daily notations where men, landscape and things appear projected in a motion of cars and accelerated thought."[3]

The intersection of tourist experience, literary description, and scientific documentation is strikingly conveyed in the second part of the book, which provides a detailed recounting of Calzini's participation in the automobile *raid* of Major Babini in rich and descriptive prose. A good amount of his description dealt with the difficulty of travel in what was an often hostile desert context— what was referred to by Calzini as "kilometers and kilometers of desolate whiteness of a barren polar landscape."[4] However, this book was more than just a travelogue of an excursion to Ghadames or a detailed study of the colonial landscape. *Da Leptis Magna a Gadames* offers a number of carefully written examinations of the indigenous populations and their native culture. A particularly extensive passage was dedicated to the Tuareghs of the southern regions of Tripolitania, who are described as "the most fierce and most bellicose population of this African world."[5]

As an early text presenting the native culture of the colonial context, *Da Leptis Magna a Gadames* is a combination of a literary recounting of the experience of the indigenous landscape and an ethnographic description of the indigenous body. This publication reflects the state of colonial tourism during the late 1920s, whose demand for authenticity was carefully interwoven with the mechanisms of modern travel—a tourist experience that was increasingly organized to stage the native culture for the purposes of tourist consumption. The value of Libyan culture to the tourist experience was noted by Enrico Niccoli in *La rinascità della Tripolitania*, where he stated that "all of the indigenous aspects of the country" were available to the tourist.[6] These experiences of local culture included the characteristic elements of the Tripolitanian landscape, from the palm trees of the oasis to the vast plains of the Gharyan. Notably, in describing the attractions of the region, Niccoli referred to "the possibility of seeing and studying the simple life of the nomads."[7] This statement is compelling testimony to the fact that the tourist experience of indigenous culture of Tripolitania was seen as being coincident with the objective practices of scientific study. It also accords the indigenous body the status of an ethnographic object removed from the passage of time—a silent marker of the primeval origins of the Libyan people.

The importance of local culture to the tourist interest in the colonies is consistently conveyed in the large body of tourist-oriented material that was produced during this period. One prominent example of this material is the guidebook *Tripoli*, which was published in 1929. The emphasis on indigenous culture is evident in the text of this brochure, which argues that the city of Tripoli—through the combination of its "picturesque and suggestive local color" and the archeological excavations in Leptis Magna and Sabratha—offers something unique to the "thirst for novelty of the modern tourist." In addition to the focus on the indigenous attractions of Tripoli, the contemporary accomplishments of colonization are recognized—an effort that is attributed to "the will and faith resolutely impressed by the new Regime on all forms of activity."[8] The duality of metropolitan and indigenous culture is evident in the format and presentation of the guidebook, whose text includes a detailed history of the medina in addition to information on the contemporary city and its tourist attractions.[9] This twofold aspect is conveyed in the section on the tourist highlights, which features both the newly restored castle and archeological museum and the annual Tripoli Trade Fair.

Like the tourist brochure *Tripoli*, much of the early publicity material relative to travel in the colonial context affirms the intersection of modern tourist organization with the experience of native culture. This is no less the case with the Italian Touring Club guidebook to the colonies, which carefully balances its presentation of the politics of the Fascist colonial project in Africa with references to the indigenous landscape. In the section on Tripolitania, a series of practical notes recommend that those traveling outside of normal tourist itineraries consult with the colonial authorities to determine a safe route —something that underscores the fact that travel in this region was still dangerous. This section is accompanied by a comprehensive overview of topics from the climate, flora, fauna, and geology of this region, to the historical, artistic, linguistic, and cultural practices of its people, and the recent Italian administrative and economic developments.[10] The information resembles a series of entries in the *Enciclopedia Italiana*—an observation that is supported by the fact that this guidebook boasts the participation of well-known academics and scholars like Renato Bartoccini and Angelo Piccioli. The evidence of the desire to view the Libyan physical and cultural landscape as an unmediated experience is apparent in the discussion of the inhabitants of Ghadames in this guidebook, who are described as having "maintained their original characteristics intact, so that even today they constitute an interesting topic of study."[11]

The objectivity with which the indigenous culture of Libya was represented in guidebooks to the Italian colonies reveals the importance of this culture to the tourist experience—an experience in which modern Western culture was rendered invisible. According to this view, the tourist would enjoy a seamless experience of the primitive origins of Libyan culture—a culture that was at the same time being preserved by the Italian colonial authorities. This approach permeated many of the brochures from this period, including the Libyan Tourism

Commission leaflet *Libia itinerari* of 1935 (fig. 4.2).[12] While the cover would seem to offer an exotic and mysterious experience of an unfamiliar culture, the colony was presented in a quite opposite manner. Published in Italian, French, English, and German, this 126-page brochure offers a detailed presentation of travel itineraries with practical information on tourist events and various travel and transportation options. The introductory text notes that "we will not use words of allurement for the purpose of enticing tourists." Instead, it is suggested that "what must be taken into account are photographs and facts as well as the facilitation of travel, the itineraries of excursions, the certainty of having every comfort and the attraction of important folkloristic, sports and cultural events."[13] Of particular note is the middle section of the brochure in which a general map of travel itineraries is followed by a series of photographic images that create a narrative sequence of constantly unfolding visual panoramas that emphasize the experience of these locations and their distinctive culture (fig. 4.3).

The brochure *Libia Itinerari* signals the rise of objectivity as a value in the tourist experience of indigenous culture in the latter half of the 1930s—a development that ran parallel to the preservation efforts of the colonial authorities. The tourist experience was the result of a mediation of the "comfort" provided by the modern tourist system of the Libyan Tourism and Hotel Association (ETAL) by a carefully staged encounter with the

Fig. 4.2. Cover of the brochure Libia itinerari (Milano: S. A. Arti Grafiche Bertarelli, 1935), published by the Libyan Tourism Commission.

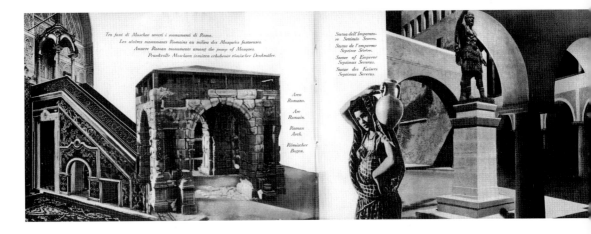

Fig. 4.3. "Austere Roman monuments among the pomp of the Mosques," from Libia itinerari (1935).

indigenous culture. This encounter, however, was just as modern as the system of hotels and tourist amenities that were designed to accommodate the needs of the metropolitan traveler. It was at this same time that the Libyans and their culture were subject to systematic study by anthropologists and other modern scientific fields—study that largely reinforced the Fascist politics of empire. As a result, the Libyans were simultaneously providers of comfort for the metropolitan traveler and bearers of indigenous cultural significance—as virtual objects in an ethnographic museum. The tourist experience in Libya existed in a space where two different kinds of modernity interacted—one determined by the demands of the modern tourist, the other by the need for an authentic experience of an "other" culture.

LITERARY AND SCIENTIFIC PARADIGMS

Although colonial tourism was a relatively direct projection of Fascist modernity in the colonial context, it could be argued that the framing of the indigenous culture is what gives colonial tourism some of its most distinguishing features. While this presentation was no less important for the creation of a successful tourist system in Italy, there was a simple but significant difference in the colonies—that is, the culture being presented was not Italian. One trajectory of this discourse, based on the influence of contemporary colonial literature, suggests that the tourist would encounter Libyan culture through a mysterious, exotic, and even dangerous adventure. A second and seemingly opposite vehicle for the appropriation of local culture was through the filter of scientific research and representation. In this case, the knowledge of the indigenous culture by the tourist was an analogue to its objective study, which leads to viewing the Libyans and their culture as temporally removed from contemporary society. Although both of these representations are clearly Orientalist ones—establishing the local populations and their culture as primitive and backward in relation to the West—there are some important distinctions. They place the Western subject in a specific relationship to the object of study—the first being romantic and literary; the second, objective and scientific. It is along the lines of difference between these two modes of transmission that attitudes toward North African culture, and ultimately the means of reenacting it for a tourist audience, were determined.

The first of these interpretive mechanisms, colonial literature, was a form of writing that emerged in the mid-1920s in conjunction with the increased attention given to the colonies after Mussolini's first visit. Although many of the experiences recounted in the earliest of these novels were from the period following the initial Italian invasion of this region, it was not until the colonies enjoyed broad popular appeal—and the support of the Fascist government—that such writings were both conceived and published. This was, however, only one of the factors that contributed to the emergence of colonial literature. There were a number of already existing journalistic and literary tendencies that laid the groundwork for the development of this genre of writing. One such group of references are the travel accounts of Italian and foreign explorers that traveled to Africa in the late nineteenth and early twentieth centuries.[14] This vast body of literature was frequently published in popular journals in the 1880s, like Manfredo Camperio's *L'Esploratore*, the *Bollettino della Società Geografica Italiana*, and *Nuova Antologia*.[15] These early writings contributed to a preoccupation in Italian colonial literature with themes of heroism and discovery. The work of colonial authors also exhibited an interest in the descriptive realism of this journalistic writing—a "realism" that was in constant tension with its more romantic literary tendencies.

Equally formative to Italian colonial literature of the mid-1920s was the work of two important authors, Gabriele D'Annunzio and Filippo Tommaso Marinetti. The first of these figures was a poet, novelist, dramatist, and journalist who was the leading Italian writer of the late nineteenth and early twentieth centuries. D'Annunzio was also a mythical figure in Italian Nationalist political circles, leading a military coup for the occupation of the Dalmatian port of Fiume in 1919—a protest against the incorporation of the town into the new Yugoslav state by the Treaty of Versailles after World War I.[16] The influence of the writings of D'Annunzio on colonial literature can be found in his distinctive writing style, which was filled with exuberant, passionate, and sensuous descriptive prose that captures the turmoil and restlessness of Italian intellectual culture around the turn of the twentieth century. There are also a number of specific themes from his literary work that found their place in colonial literature, such as the figure of the "superman" from Nietzsche and a focus on aestheticism, decadentism, and sensual gratification.[17] The most important individual work for literary discourse on the colonies was D'Annunzio's play *Più che l'amore* of 1906, which was written as a classical tragedy set in the context of contemporary Rome.[18] The play explores the end of the protagonist, Corrado Brando—the typical superman cast by D'Annunzio as an explorer of Africa. Corrado forsakes his love to accept his tragic fate, thereby articulating themes of heroism and social transgression that became standard in colonial novels. Another influential aspect of this work was its portrayal of Africa as both *terra incognita*—an atavistic terrain where Corrado could exist outside of the restrictive morals of contemporary society—and *terra promessa*, a land already latent with the call for Italian colonial expansion.

The second figure, Filippo Tommaso Marinetti, had a similar range of literary and journalistic experience, although he was from a younger generation of Italian intellectuals and artists. He was best known as the leader of the Futurist movement, for which he wrote the original "Manifeste de Futurisme" that was published in the Paris newspaper *Le Figaro* on February 20, 1909. Futurism was a wide-ranging artistic and literary movement that rejected academicism in the arts in favor of the chaos, dynamism, and destructive power of twentieth-century urban life. Despite the fact that the group espoused a politics of anarchy and violence and participated in irredentist demonstrations that called for Italy to enter World War I, Marinetti joined the Fascist party in 1919

Fig. 4.4. Cover of the novel Piccolo amore Beduino (Milano: L'Eroica, 1926), by Mario Dei Gaslini. (See also Plate 9.)

111

and eventually became a member of the Italian Academy in 1929.[19] Although the literary tendencies of Marinetti were an explicit attack on figures like D'Annunzio, his themes of heroism and social transgression were the basis for much of this Futurist writer's work. The connection to D'Annunzio can be seen in Marinetti's first African novel, *Mafarka le futuriste* of 1909, which recounts the tragic end of its protagonist, African warrior king Mafarka el Bar.[20] This novel develops the figure of the superman to embrace the Futurist fascination with the machine through Mafarka's creation of a mechanical and immortal son, Gazurmah, in which he transfused the soul of his brother Magamal, who was slain in battle. The representation of Africa in this work is also significant, as it elides the imperialist and colonialist connotations of *Più che l'amore*. Instead, only one-half of the D'Annunzian dialectic is portrayed. In *Mafarka le futuriste*, Africa is a primitive or virgin territory separate from the decadence of the West in which the birth of the Futurist man was possible.[21]

The publication of one of the first colonial novels, *Piccolo amore Beduino*, and the notoriety of its author, Mario Dei Gaslini, were a direct result of a national competition organized by the Ministry of the Colonies in 1926. This novel brings together the literary themes and tendencies of D'Annunzio and Marinetti, with a descriptive and documentary viewpoint of the colonial context. Despite its fascination with the exotic, this novel of Dei Gaslini offers itself as a semiautobiographical story of the experiences of a rather ordinary military officer in Tripolitania just prior to World War I. It thus relates quite directly to the documentary mode of writing found in travel accounts and diaries—representing the banal reality of the everyday experience of the colonial context during this period. At the same time, *Piccolo amore Beduino* borrows its basic plot and structure from D'Annunzio and Marinetti, chronicling an ill-fated love relationship between the protagonist (and author) and a young Bedouin woman Nica (fig. 4.4). This novel recounts the misdeeds of the hero, who violates the moral boundaries of his society by having this relationship, and who obtains his eventual redemption by forsaking his love to follow his orders to return to fight for his country in World War I.[22] The story also conveys the tragic circumstances of the young Nica, who was disgraced to her own people and thus destined to suffer in relative solitude.

The most influential qualities of *Piccolo amore Beduino* are not only in its combination of the "modern tragedy" of D'Annunzio with the autobiographical mode of travel accounts. The style of prose used in the novel is also extremely important, and is heavily indebted to the "decadent exoticism" of D'Annunzio.[23] Dei Gaslini's book relies on intense description and a disruptive syntax to convey the protagonist's fascination and unease with his context. One such example is his description of a meeting with the local tribal leader, Sheik Abd el-Kefi, which is described as having "a dizzying atmosphere in which everything that is seen is adulterated by hallucination and assumes a clandestine aspect of love, of intrigue, of tenderness."[24] The evocative qualities of this literary style are intensified by the illustrations to the text, whose dark and primitivist imagery draws on the work of Edoardo del Neri (fig. 4.5). The prints of this well-known colonial artist show a primitivism preoccupied with surface and texture rather than depth.[25]

Fig. 4.5. Image of Sheik Abd el Kefi, from Piccolo amore Beduino (1926).

The exoticism of this imagery is part of what is perhaps the most innovative and influential part of this work—its Orientalist depiction of a strong cultural contrast between East and West and its almost fetishistic representation of this other culture. This quality of *Piccolo amore Beduino* is largely established through the relationship between the protagonist and Nica, which sets a Western man and his culture against that of Islam and the East. His rationality and sense of duty are constantly at odds with his emotions, although it remains clear throughout that he regards this as an impossible love.[26] The experiences of the protagonist provide the reader with a vicarious exploration of the mysteries of the East—from the confusion of a crowded *suq*, to the sensuous eroticism of the young Nica. However, the terms of this relationship are always unequal, as the young Bedouin woman is consistently depicted as an "imprisoned queen" of her Italian officer whose love represents a civilizing and modernizing force.[27] The fact that the hero of the novel is not merely a fictional char-

Fig. 4.6. Cover of
the journal Esotica
(October 1926),
published by Mario
Dei Gaslini. (See
also Plate 10.)

acter but also the author of the work enhances the significance.
The novel is both a representation and a product of a process
of colonization and domination over what is depicted as a more
passive and culturally backward society.

Following the publication of *Piccolo amore Beduino,* the
literature of exoticism in general and the work of Dei Gaslini in
particular were extremely influential on Italian cultural discourse
related to the representation of its colonies. Not only did he
publish other novels that explored similar themes; he started his
own publishing house and edited a new journal, *Esotica,* beginning in 1926.[28] The first issue of this monthly journal came out just

Fig. 4.7. Cover of the brochure Tripoli (Roma: Novissima, 1929), published by the National Association of Tourist Industries and the Italian State Railway. (See also Plate 11.)

following Mussolini's visit to Libya, with many pages dedicated to communicating the present activities in each of the Italian colonies. Well over half of the magazine was dedicated to literary and cultural matters related to the colonies, such as poetry, literature, and art. This journal also contained a section on current women's and men's fashion, which it was noted was chosen according to "good Latin taste."[29] In the section on colonial literature, in addition to incorporating other authors, Dei Gaslini was not averse to promoting his own work. Each issue included an installment of his serial novel "Le Ombre dell'Harem" (The Shades of the Harem), which narrates the life of two young Arab women who live with

Fig. 4.8. Postcard of a street in the Arab quarter, Tripoli, ca. 1930.

their widowed father in a modest courtyard house in the old section of Beng-hazi. Their life is described in rich and florid prose: "Even their steps appear restrained by the inertia of a dream, struck by that sense of silence and myste-rious twilight that fills the house where light does not enter, where love has yet to call."[30] The graphic appearance of the magazine is similarly suffused with the image of exoticism, such as the cover of the first issue, which depicts a solitary traveler with camel viewed from the palm canopy of a desert oasis (fig. 4.6).

The prose style and literary devices of colonial novels enjoyed a wide dissemi-nation in published material related to colonial travel during the late 1920s. Even the Italian Touring Club guidebook to the Italian colonies, a publication whose reputation was based on the accuracy of its information, participated in this discourse. In a general section under tourism in Tripolitania entitled "Le principali attrative," the landscape of the region is recounted in prose that is suggestive of colonial literature. One such passage describes "the oasis with its colonnades of palm trees, which raises its star-shaped fan in the fiery sunset or in the peaceful nights or in the enchantment of the pearly dawn."[31] A similar style of writing is employed in the main section of the guidebook, which provides information on the different tourist destinations. One particu-larly striking example is a description of the town of Ghadames, which states: "The appearance of the town is extremely unique, with a very irregular plan, with mysterious covered streets, the arches crowned with notches, the violent contrast between the dazzling reflections from the white walls in the sun and the dense shade of the covered passages."[32]

The literature of exoticism had an equally substantial effect on the iconog-raphy of the publicity material related to tourism in Libya. This printed matter shared a common fascination with the exotic aspects of the culture of this region—providing a visual corollary to the prose of authors like Dei Gaslini. One such example is the brochure published by the National Association of Tourist Industries (ENIT) and the Italian State Railway (FFSS) that presented the city of Tripoli. The cover of this publication depicts an aerial view of the old city as a vernacular scene. The realism of this image and its use of strongly contrasting tones and colors borrows directly from the artistic techniques found in colonial art and in popular representations of Italy's Mediterranean tourist destinations like Amalfi and Capri (fig. 4.7).[33] This same preoccupation with the exotic and the dangerous certainly applies to the large volume of postcards that were produced during this period. These images are often set in "characteristic" areas, along narrow streets or in crowded markets or *suqs*. By employing complex staging and strong contrasts of light and dark, these postcards present the indigenous landscape and culture of Libya through a vision of the chaos and confusion of the East (fig. 4.8). In giving visual form to these well established literary devices, this publicity material participates in an Orientalist discourse that was aimed at fueling the desire to travel in a strange and even dangerous land.

The second mechanism through which the indigenous culture of Libya was appropriated and disseminated was scientific research and study, an activity that both motivated and benefited from the colonization process. The most significant research expeditions took place during the Fascist era, and, in particular, after the military reconquest of Libya. It was not until after 1932 that areas of interest to researchers, other than those in the coastal regions, were under firm military control. This work eventually encompassed a number of separate disciplinary fields, including anthropology, archeology, ethnography, folklore studies, geography, and geology.[34] Prior to this time, these efforts had been limited to the travels of Italian explorers during the nineteenth century, which produced little in the way of serious research. Despite their lack of scientific import, these early expeditions laid the groundwork for later research. They also increased the popular knowledge of Africa and in so doing contributed to the Italian interest in the region. The early period of exploration thus fueled the initial desire to travel to the colonies under the auspices of tourism and influenced the nature of this experience. In the same manner, the exploration conducted during the Fascist period provided the conceptual model for travel in the colonies that eventually made a profound impact on the development of the tourist panorama during the 1930s.

Not surprisingly, the scientific research in Libya during the Fascist period was a form of validation of the politics of Italian colonial rule. The politicization of this research is due to the fact that many of the organizations involved had long been supporters of Italy's colonies, like the Italian Geographic Society of Florence, which sponsored missions by Ardito Desio in Al-Jaghbub (1926-27) and the Fezzan (1932). Moreover, most of the other missions were directly sponsored by the Ministry of the Colonies, like the ethnographic research of Raffaele Corso in Ghat in 1935.[35] Much of this scientific work can thus be seen as a literal extension of the Italian control over these regions.

One particularly striking example of the use of scientific research as a validation of colonial policy is the representation of the colonies in the *Enciclopedia italiana*, which was published by Giovanni Treccani in 1934. The fact that this encyclopedia was an extension of Fascist politics was, at least in part, due to the presence of Fascist philosopher Giovanni Gentile on the editorial board.[36] In recounting the ancient ethnography of Libya, Francesco Beguinot, director of the Oriental Institute of Naples, clearly seems to be attempting to find a scholarly justification for Italy's colonization of this region. In this encyclopedia entry, Beguinot dismissed the Berber culture, which he criticized for its "inability to progress beyond the initial levels of civil life."[37] Beguinot also questioned the originality of much of what was taken to be indigenous to North Africa, arguing that the most important civilizing influences were from outside the region, which he called "a leavening of a superior form of life."

The most important venue for the presentation of this research was a series of Colonial Studies Conferences, which were held in Florence (1931 and 1937), Naples (1934 and 1940), and Asmara (1940). Organized by the Center of Colonial Studies and the Cesare Alfieri Institute of Social and Political Science in Florence with substantial representation and support by the Fascist government, these five-day conferences brought together the most current research of Italian and foreign scholars on a full range of topics related to the Italian colonies.[38] The rhetorical nature of this effort is evidenced in the representation of its political intentions, which were clearly aimed at creating a scientific pretext for Italian colonization. In reporting on the first congress in the journal *L'Oltremare*, Guido Valensin stated that "the great colonizing nations find in research a spiritual preparation for their colonial expansion, and they feel the need then to support it on a robust scientific basis."[39] The scheduling of these events was also carefully considered, the first of which was timed to precede a similar gathering related to the Paris Colonial Exhibition in 1931. Though not aimed at a broad audience, the publication of the proceedings constitutes an important record of the varied research interests of this period and the ongoing relationship between scientific research and Fascist colonial politics.[40]

In the first Colonial Studies Conference, the indigenous culture of Libya was represented through a variety of topics presented under the general category of ethnography. This session was moderated by Francesco Beguinot and offered investigations of the indigenous populations through their ethnic and racial identities, their cultural practices, and their forms of inhabitation. One such presentation, entitled "Etnografia delle popolazione libiche," was made by Colonel Enrico De Agostini, who led a scientific mission to Cyrenaica in 1922-23.[41] This study looked at the Arab, Berber, and other populations in terms of their origins, distribution, and social and political characteristics. Despite the allegedly scientific basis of this research, a clear sense of the colonial interest is maintained throughout—their ethnic and cultural identities being largely defined with regard to concerns for the colonial order. The intersection of scientific research and colonial politics is particularly evident in Professor Costanzo Di Marzo's presentation, entitled "L'atteggiamento psicologico degli indigeni nord-africani di fronte alla colonizzazione."[42] This paper argues that the psychology of the indigenous populations should be studied through their writings. This body of research, according to Di Marzo, would foster an understanding of their resistance to colonization that would allow the colonial authorities to devise a successful political program. In a similar manner, Emilio Scarin notes in the introduction to his essay on human settlement in western Tripolitania that "such a study is the best means to know the indigenous mentality more profoundly . . . and should also be taken into account by colonial legislators."[43]

The discourse on the study and representation of indigenous culture under the aegis of scientific research had a great influence on the evolution of the tourist experience in Libya. The research conducted during the 1930s was one of the most important sources of information on the indigenous culture, and thus it disseminated this information directly or infiltrated tourist-related publications like guidebooks and brochures. Moreover, the object of attention of this research—the human and material culture of Libya—was the same culture that the tourist audience was seeking to experience. Accordingly, the activities that these fields of research undertook were often directly inserted into tourist-related representations, such as the identification, classification, and localization of different racial groups within the local populations.[44] The assumptions underlying these disciplines—the presumed organic relationship between so-called primitive societies and their cultural artifacts, and even their scientific method—that these cultures should be viewed in a manner that is undisturbed by modern influences, became operative metaphors for the determination of the tourist experience.

One of the most interesting results of the intersection of tourism and scientific study is that the research expedition became a model for structuring the

679

PANORAMA DI GHAT.

UNA MISSIONE SCIENTIFICA ITALIANA

NEL FEZZÀN

DEL Fezzàn, la bella regione dell'estremo meridionale della Tripolitania, dopo un lungo periodo di silenzio, si è finalmente ripreso a parlare parecchio in questi ultimi tempi. Può dirsi che dal 1877 al momento della nostra occupazione quasi si sia taciuto intorno a quella terra; in particolare, poi, per quanto concerne la sua conoscenza scientifica, poco fu fatto oltre la pura e semplice esplorazione geografica, che cominciò dalla fine del XVIII secolo col Hornemann, seguito poi da altri, di cui parecchi lasciarono la vita per avversità di clima, o di genti.

Ora, con quanto ha intrapreso a fare la Reale Società Geografica Italiana su ideazione dovuta a S. A. R. il Duca d'Aosta, cotesta conoscenza verrà aumentata di parecchio. Infatti già tre diverse missioni scientifiche si sono recate nel Fezzàn, e molte altre ne seguiranno, ciascuna con programmi e itinerari prefissati, sì da non lasciare senza almeno un principio di indagine nessuna parte di quell'esteso territorio.

Come partecipante alla prima di coteste missioni, svoltasi con intendimenti antropologici ed etnografici, ebbi occasione di ampiamente percorrere il Fezzàn. Non starò qui a riferire, nemmeno per quanto mi concerne, le risultanze dei miei studi e soltanto accennerò ai percorsi della missione, nonchè ad alcune delle caratteristiche principali di quella nostra terra lontana e delle sue genti.

La missione, composta dal N. H. Antonio Mordini e da me, con aggiunto il sergente maggiore Francesco Tagliapietra, più due autisti (uno italiano ed uno indigeno) ed un attendente eritreo, prese le mosse da Tripoli al principio del settembre scorso per rientrar-

Fig. 4.9. Publication of the scientific mission to the Fezzan in Le Vie d'Italia (September 1933), led by Lidio Cipriani and Antonio Mordini.

tourist expedition. In some cases, tourism so thoroughly assumed the procedures of anthropology that it became a form of analogous research. An example of this phenomenon can be found in the "National Excursion" to the Fezzan in the southwestern desert region of Libya held by the TCI in April of 1935, which visited the oases of Suknah, Brak, Sabha, and Murzuq—one of several such trips this group organized for its members in Libya. One of the significant aspects of this excursion is that it followed an itinerary that was almost identical to that of an anthropological and ethnographic mission led by Lidio Cipriani and Antonio Mordini in 1933. In fact, the research from this mission, which was sponsored by the Italian Geographic Society, was even published in the official TCI magazine in September of 1933, under the title "una missione scientifica italiana nel Fezzan" (fig. 4.9).[45] In looking at the subsequent report of the National Excursion in the same journal, it is quite apparent that not only was this tourist itinerary inspired by and following the route of a scientific expedition, it was also clearly organized according to the same logic—showing the same kind of "systematic and patient inquiry."[46] This connection is particularly clear in the illustrations of the article, which prominently feature scenes of the cultural practices of the local populations being put on display for a tourist audience.

Not unlike the relationship between tourism and colonial literature, scientific research was thoroughly suffused into the tourist practices in the Italian colony of Libya in the 1930s. The nature of this "science" and its influence on colonial tourism took a decisive shift in the latter part of this decade. It was during this period that the specifically racial connotations of these scientific projects—connotations that were always latent in this work—were foregrounded in a significant way. This shift can be detected in the TCI guidebook to Libya from 1937, where the interpretation of indigenous culture had become increasingly imbedded in a racially encoded discourse borrowed from contemporary academic research. One example of this connection is a new section entitled "Preistoria," which was written by Professor Paolo Graziosi of the National Museum of Anthropology and Ethnography in Florence. While this information represents his most current research, it is important to recognize that in inquiring into the primordial origins of the region and its people, Graziosi was defining the identity of the region prior to the influence of Islam.[47] A second example of the imbrication of tourism and scientific research is a section entitled "Etnografia e demografia," which provides a historical account of the Berbers, Arabs, Jews, and Africans. As with the section on the prehistory of Libya, this discussion places considerable emphasis on the Berber origins of the "original" populations of Libya, a group that was converted to Islam following the Arab invasions of the seventh and eighth centuries.[48] Not only is this focus on the Berbers a self-serving way of dealing with the colonial politics in Libya, it also pretends to create clear racial categories among a population where such categories were a complete fiction.[49]

The representation of indigenous culture in the 1937 TCI guidebook to Libya reflects the fact that by this time "the native" had become both an object of racial classification and a fixture within the tourist experience. Although it has been argued that the field of anthropology was politicized in Fascist Italy, in this case the opposite also appears to be true. Under the aegis of the "Provisions for the defense of the Italian Race," political discourse was becoming more scientific.[50] The Italian colonial authorities deployed a number of firmly entrenched arguments about the primitive state of cultural advancement of the local populations in Africa in order to justify a racist politics. Such research was advanced in books like Raffaele Corso's *Africa Italiana. Genti e costumi* of 1940, which suggests that in relation to the problem of the contact between white and black cultures in the colonies, "racist ethnography" was part of the "fundamental task that interests the life, the administration and the politics of colonial domains."[51]

Similar arguments were advanced by Lidio Cipriani, professor at the University of Florence and director of the National Museum of Anthropology and Ethnography in Florence. One such article published in the journal *Difesa della Razza* entitled "Razzismo Coloniale" presents the dangers of mixing between "racial elements that are too disparate and distant"—effectively

Fig. 4.10. Cover of the journal Difesa della Razza (20 August 1938). (See also Plate 12.)

providing a scientific justification for the Fascist policy that discouraged racial mixing in the Italian colonies.[52] The connection between racist views of the local populations and even the most conventional forms of tourist representation can be seen throughout the 1930s. One such example, a postcard entitled "Mendicanti di Tagiura" that depicts a group of beggars and street urchins, appears like a documentary image intended to support a scientific research project or to illustrate a case of racial and cultural degeneration. Through this and other similar tourist representations, the eye of the tourist was increasingly becoming the eye of the anthropologist (figs. 4.10, 4.11).

The turn toward a more scientific reading of the indigenous culture during this period even made its impact on colonial literature. It was during this time that Mario dei Gaslini published *Paradiso nell'inferno: Uso e costumi abissini* (1937), which offers itself as an objective representation of the indigenous populations and their cultural practices.[53] The change in literary discourse toward more scientific prose was also reflected in Filippo Tommaso Marinetti's presentation at the Volta Conference, which was entitled "L'Africa generatrice e ispiratrice di poesia e arti." This contribution was written in the form of a manifesto, with Futurist prose interspersed with statements of colonial domination. One example of the latter is a call to "reveal the new psychic mysteries provoked by European civilization in the static and customary souls of the African people."[54] The contribution of Marinetti to the Volta Conference reveals the fact that during the latter part

Fig. 4.11. Postcard showing a group of beggars in Tajurah, ca. 1930.

of the 1930s, the difference between literary and scientific representations of indigenous culture had been blurred. All forms of representation, including these two forms of Orientalism, had been subjected to the same racial discourse that was in the process of redefining the politics of Italian colonialism and, ultimately, the tourist experience of Libya.

CONSTRUCTING THE TOURIST PANORAMA

From the earliest developments of a tourist system in Libya during the governorship of Volpi—a development that focused on the creation of a modern network of roads and public services—an equally serious effort was made to put its indigenous culture on display. One of the first attempts to construct the tourist panorama was the creation of the Museum as part of Armando Brasini's restoration of the ancient castle in Tripoli.[55] This new attraction, which opened in 1924, was seen as a supplement to the excavations at Leptis Magna and Sabratha, being dedicated to statuary, mosaics, and small objects taken from these two archeological sites (fig. 4.12). The focus of the Museum on the sites of Leptis Magna and Sabratha reflects the fact that the preservation program of Volpi was largely directed toward the Roman antiquities. The location of this museum in an existing structure at the base of the castle placed this Roman museum in close proximity with the old city, which interestingly enough was itself described in tourist literature as a museum of indigenous culture.

Fig. 4.12. Archeological museum in Tripoli (1926).

In the guidebook *Guida di Tripoli e dintorni* of 1925, the area

of the Suq al-Turk was presented as "the most characteristic of indigenous life." This covered market space contained two rows of shops where "Arab and Jewish merchants in their picturesque costumes sell the most varying goods."[56] Another area of the old city that was seen to be of significant tourist interest was the fabric and carpet market of the Suq al-Kebir adjacent to the Qara-manli mosque, where a series of small workshops of indigenous craftsmen both produced and sold their wares (fig. 4.13). Of considerable importance is the fact that these were the same artisanal industries that were in the process of being restructured by the Government Office of Indigenous Applied Arts—the ancient industry of carpet making in Misurata being singled out as the most artistically and economically promising. The workshops and markets of the Suq al-Kebir in Tripoli can thus be regarded as having a relatively equivalent status to the displays of Roman statuary in the Museum. It was tied to the preservation program of Volpi and, in that sense, represents a self-conscious staging of the indigenous culture.

The significance of the intervention of the Volpi administration in the native arts reached far beyond its primary intention, which was to improve the local economy. The Government Office of Indigenous Applied Arts was responsible for the historicization of the indigenous arts and its artisans, both of which became objects on display for the benefit of a tourist audience. The close relationship between the presentation of indigenous culture and tourist experience is most clearly expressed in its annual representation at the Tripoli Trade Fair. In 1927, Libyan culture was presented in the Colonial Village, which was an eclectic collection of different pavilions that presented the characteristic products from the different regions. This walled precinct was located on the far eastern end of the exhibition site and was intended to "offer a summarizing but extremely faithful vision of the Tripolitanian landscape" through a collection of buildings that included display spaces, artisanal workshops, a *suq*, and an Arab house.[57] While the scientific reenactment of a colonial environment is consistent with those of previous exhibitions like the Eritrean Village at the 1911 International Exhibition in Turin, in this case there is a very important difference. This indigenous village at the Tripoli Trade Fair was located within the very context that it purported to represent. Not unlike the workshops in the Suq al-Kebir, it offered more than a mere image of the indigenous landscape and culture. It was a heterotopic domain of native culture that screened out all contradictory aspects.

The artisanal workshops in the Suq al-Kebir are a crystallization of the means through which the tourist experience of local culture was increasingly structured during the course of the 1930s. At the same time that a modern and efficient system of transportation services and tourist facilities was being created in Libya, a seemingly opposite effort was taking place—an effort that was aimed at conserving and even enhancing the indigenous culture of the region. Largely a product of the objective practices through which this culture was being studied by Italian academics, the tourist panorama was constructed as an enclave of authentic experience. Although the inspiration for such an approach can be traced back to the preservation program that began during the governorship of Volpi, the most concrete measures for the preservation of the indigenous culture for tourist purposes began in the late 1930s under the

Fig. 4.13. Fabric and carpet market at the Suq al-Kebir in Tripoli, ca. 1925.

auspices of the greater level of coordination and supervision of tourism in Libya.

The foundation of the Tripolitanian Tourism Association was a key catalyst to this development, as one of the primary tasks of this group was to "further the development, conservation, improvement and embellishment of the localities in the colony that offer particular tourist interest."[58] With the collaboration and support of the colonial government of Badoglio and the Chamber of Commerce of Tripoli, the activities of this state-sponsored organization went beyond the coordination and promotion of tourist activities provided by private companies. Faced with a lack of evening entertainment in the city of Tripoli, the Tripolitanian Tourism Association established a nightclub with Arab women performing native dance.[59] Similar kinds of performances were provided for large groups of tourists visiting the region aboard cruise ships. One such example is an excursion to Cyrenaica organized by the Fascist Colonial Institute in May of 1933, for which a "characteristic" indigenous ceremony was performed.[60]

The appointment of Italo Balbo to the post of governor of Libya in 1934 resulted in an even more substantial commitment to a program of preserving and enhancing the native culture for the purposes of tourism. From the first months of his governorship, Balbo worked with Alessandro Melchiori of the newly formed Libyan Tourism Commission to enhance the tourist system in this colony. In a meeting between Melchiori and the Minister of the Colonies Emilio De Bono, one of the major initiatives identified was to "include some characteristic and attractive manifestations of a strictly local and colorful order."[61] A list of possible demonstrations of indigenous culture was subsequently sent from the colonial administration in Tripoli to the Ministry of the Colonies. These events included a Jewish engagement festival—for which the best couple would receive a monetary prize—a ceremony of Arab horsemen staged for the arrival of cruises in Tripoli, a performance of Sudanese singers and musicians, an indigenous supernatural ceremony with an exhibition of rhythmic dancing, an Arab restaurant offering the most characteristic local food, and a competition for decorating areas of the old city on the occasion of the arrival of important cruise ships.[62] A more definitive listing was made in the tourist brochure *Libia Itinerari*, where in addition to the ceremonies noted above, an "Oriental" theater, a folkloristic horseracing exhibit, and a camel race were mentioned.[63] This program is presented in this tourist publication as part of a calendar that was divided into three categories: cultural events, folkloristic events, and sporting events. What this calendar makes clear is that the cultural activities of the indigenous populations are viewed as folkloristic and thus outside of the ambit of modern Western culture.

Although the Balbo administration in Libya was extremely active in the organization of indigenous ceremonies and special events that would satisfy the demands of a tourist audience in search of an authentic experience of native culture, they were quite careful to promote only those manifestations that were coincident with the political policies of the colonial administration. One example of this policy is the indigenous supernatural ceremony that was originally planned to be one of the native cultural manifestations organized by the Libyan Tourism Commission. This ceremony involved the participation of marabouts—Arab dervishes who performed rhythmic dancing and who were purported to stab their flesh and eat nails. Due to the objections of the Ministry of the Colonies, this ceremony never became one of the folkloristic events on the tourist calendar of Libya.[64]

In fact, just over a year after the initial proposal of Melchiori, Balbo moved to ban the religious practice of fakirism and its related ceremonies with a gubernatorial decree. This piece of legislation was critical of Muslim confraternities that were considered barbaric and that held pseudomystical ceremonies that included "crushing glass with their teeth, eating the thorny branches of Indian figs, and bending nails on their heads." Although this decree noted that local authorities had from time to time allowed these confraternities to perform in public for tourist groups, it asserts: "We believe it is opportune to abolish any pseudo-religious manifestations [as] a residue of customs that offends morals and that for their form of exaltation . . . can constitute a danger to the public order."[65] This legislation reveals the fact that the indigenous ceremonies organized in Libya during the governorship of Balbo, like the annual celebration of Ramadan, were carried out within the strictest interpretation of public morality (fig. 4.14). This approach reveals an inherent conflict between the tourist demand for the most authentic forms of native culture and the need for the colonial administration to control all cultural manifestations.

Fig. 4.14. Postcard of an indigenous celebration of Ramadan, ca. 1935.

The absolute control of the experience of indigenous culture during the Balbo administration extended to the design and preservation of the physical context. The coordinated tourist network in Libya that was part of Balbo's modernization program was reinforced by a systematic campaign to restore historical sites and implement tourism-related civic improvements. In addition to the program undertaken with the Provincial Council for the Administration of the Waqfs that involved Muslim religious buildings in Libya, historical sites like the Berber castle in Nalut were restored for the benefit of a tourist audience—the restoration of this castle being completed just two months after the completion of the hotel in 1935. Equally important to the preservation of the existing character of tourist destinations were improvements to the local streets and, in some cases, the enhancement of the existing landscape, all of which were intended to reinforce the character of these locations.[66]

This program certainly applied to the city of Ghadames, which, in part due to the complete unfamiliarity of its culture and the remoteness of its location, became one of the most desirable destinations for travel within the interior of Libya. During the Balbo era, this city was the beneficiary of a considerable preservation effort that was aimed at intensifying its characteristic qualities. These enhancements include the planting of some 150 palm trees in the town at the same time as the 1935 renovation of the Hotel 'Ain el-Fras, which itself appears to be a conscious effort to reinforce and even enhance the exoticism of its oasis setting (fig. 4.15).[67] The preservation program under Balbo was thus closely tied to the tourist experience of indigenous culture. Not unlike the various manifestations of local culture organized by the Libyan Tourism Commission, the physical context of the native settlements in Libya was becoming increasingly staged in order to

Fig. 4.15. View of a veranda at the Hotel 'Ain el-Fras in Ghadames (1931).

create an authentic experience for the foreign traveler.

With the formation of the Libyan Tourism and Hotel Association (ETAL), the measures taken by the Balbo administration and the Libyan Tourism Commission in favor of the preservation of the native culture of this colony reached new levels of development. While this group was created to offer a modern and efficient system of travel, accommodation, and entertainment, one of its most important missions was to strengthen the value of the indigenous culture of the region. The ability to improve this aspect of the tourist panorama was facilitated by the initial legislation that formed this group, which authorized it to carry out a wide range of activities related to the promotion and enhancement of tourist movement in Libya.[68] These activities were not restricted to the provision of modern tourist services, as they included the kinds of folkloristic tourist events that the tourism commission and the Balbo administration had been staging.

The Hotel Service of the ETAL was particularly engaged in the presentation of indigenous culture through a system of modern hotels that responded to the landscape and culture of the various regions of Libya. Immediately following its formation, this group assumed control of all of the municipal and governmental hotels that had been constructed up until that time.[69] By 1937, with the construction of new hotels in Derna and Tobruk in Cyrenaica, the ETAL was responsible for a network of hotels that provided a metropolitan level of accommodation throughout the colony.[70] In incorporating the most recently constructed tourist facilities, these hotels offered a coherent system through which the foreign traveler could experience the indigenous culture of Libya. This quality is particularly evident in publicity material like the baggage stickers, which prominently feature the characteristic landscape of each region (fig. 4.16). Through a careful attention to design in relation to the native architectural styles, the system of hotels in Libya provided a continuous experience of "the native" that was intended to act as an analogue to the actual experience of the indigenous landscape.

The tourist program of the Libyan Tourism and Hotel Association was clearly framed within the political discourse of the governorship of Balbo—that of mediating between the modernization of this colony on the one hand and the preservation of its indigenous culture on the other. Not only was the administrative structure of this organization conceived along metropolitan lines, the facilities and services of the ETAL were themselves, conceptually and materially, linked to and part of the process of modernization. It was, however, through the means of that modernity—through its ability to negotiate between the realms of government and private industry—that the tourist system in Libya was able to provide a more comprehensive experience of native culture. This group oversaw a unique combination of transportation services, accommodation, and entertainment facilities. Through these suggestive settings and a number of carefully staged events—all determined according to a desire to maintain a continuous relationship between the tourist system and the native culture—this system was able to heighten the experience of the colonial context for the metropolitan traveler. In some notable cases, the tourist system was itself so authentic that it became a kind of substitution for the "real" experience. However, just like the indigenous politics of the Balbo administration in Libya, the preservation of

the native culture in the tourist system was politically motivated. In creating an authentic experience of the Libyan culture for the foreign traveler, and placing it within an organized system of facilities and attractions, this culture was being subjected to the direct supervision and control of the colonial authorities.

Fig. 4.16. Baggage stickers for the Hotel at the Excavations of Leptis Magna in al-Khums and the Hotel 'Ain el-Fras in Ghadames, 1937. (See also Plate 13.)

RE-PRESENTATIONS OF "THE NATIVE"

The modern network of tourist activities and facilities that reached the most remote locations in this colony was not necessarily an end in itself so much as it provided a mechanism for the experience of the Libyan environment and culture, an experience that was, after all, the motivation for travel in this region. The importance of the native landscape to the tourist experience of Libya was duly noted in a press release from the ETAL, which states: "The tourist that remains enchanted by the vision of white Tripoli then has the magnificent attraction of the superb palm groves of the oasis." This document is no less cognizant of the appeal of what was described as "the always varying manifestations of the indigenous life that present such great diversity of usages, customs and habits from one place to another."[71] What remains to be examined is the various means through which this culture was re-presented to a tourist audience and the experience that this presentation supported.

One of the most prevalent venues for the communication of Libyan culture was the publicity and propaganda program of the Libyan Tourism and Hotel Association, which used the most varied and advanced techniques of communication available. Among the most influential mechanisms for this dissemination

Fig. 4.17. Exterior view of the Libyan Tourism and Hotel Association pavilion at the Tripoli Trade Fair in 1936.

was the participation at regional fairs and exhibitions like the annual Tripoli Trade Fair. In the catalog to the 1937 exhibition, considerable attention was paid to communicating "the charm of its desert zones" and "the variety of its customs" through a combination of images and text.[72] The same can be said for the design of its pavilions and interior displays. In 1936 the exterior of the ETAL pavilion was a collage of references to the indigenous architecture of North Africa—an appearance that most closely resembles the so-called Saharan style that was used to represent French West Africa at the colonial exhibition in Paris in 1931 (fig. 4.17).[73] In the interior of the building, the exhibits included a diorama that depicted the tourist system in Libya within the physical landscape of this colony (fig. 4.18). The form of this exhibit is notable, as it employed a representational technique often used in colonial exhibitions for the display of indigenous culture, but here it is put in service of a tourist presentation of "the native."[74] This diorama is more than a representation of the tourist experience in Libya. It is its direct analogue—a modern tourist system in a seamless relationship with the local culture.

This diorama is an indication of the scientific and museological nature of the representation of indigenous culture at fairs and exhibitions in the latter part of the 1930s. This same quality can be traced in the continuing presence of the ETAL at the Tripoli Trade Fair, which after 1937 was within the pavilion of the Libyan

government. This context is extremely significant to the experience of these displays, as this building contained a presentation of photography of the transformation of Tripoli since 1911 and exhibits of Libyan artisanry and Roman antiquities.[75] Not unlike this photographic exhibition, the wall displays of the ETAL room focus on the building program of hotels and entertainment facilities and general tourist infrastructure like the *strada litoranea*. This presentation is completed with a model of the Uaddan Hotel and Casino, which was placed on a podium in the manner of a historical artifact in a museum. However, these modern displays are set within an architectural frame that is an abstract reinterpretation of the indigenous architecture (fig. 4.19). To complete the image of Libyan culture, the ceiling and wall openings are screened with traditional *mashrabiya* (wooden screens), and the space is furnished with two palm trees and two groupings of tables and stools produced by local artisans. By including these artisanal objects, the representation of a modern tourist system was fused with an ethnographic reading of the indigenous culture.

A second and equally effective venue for the dissemination of indigenous culture was the tourist-oriented material of the Publicity and Propaganda Service of the Libyan Tourism and Hotel Association. These visual and cultural productions, though covering a wide range of formats, shared the common purpose of communicating the value of the indigenous culture of this colony.

Fig. 4.18. View of the diorama in the Libyan Tourism and Hotel Association pavilion at the Tripoli Trade Fair in 1936.

Fig. 4.19. View of the Libyan Tourism and Hotel Association display at the Tripoli Trade Fair in 1937.

A more specifically literary interpretation is provided by the brochure *Combinazioni di soggiorno in Libia* from 1937.[76] This publication was intended to provide individual travelers with detailed information on a series of predetermined travel itineraries for which this group was offering a complete package of travel and accommodation services. Despite the greater similarity of these itineraries to the mass tourism of the cruise ship than to the spirit of adventure of the automobile *raid*, this brochure makes a considerable effort to balance the organizational and practical concerns of tourists with the need to convey a compelling image of Libyan culture. This aspect is evident in the text of this brochure, which, although primarily aimed at communicating information to the traveler, does not fail to underscore the importance of the customs and folklore of Libya, placing particular importance on the voyage to Ghadames, which is described as being "an extremely original city."[77]

The combination of practical information with an image of exoticism is powerfully conveyed on the colored front and rear panel, which superimposes a palm tree, an Arab woman in native dress, and a vision of the characteristic architecture of the medina against a backdrop of a map of the colony (fig. 4.20). An even more synthetic presentation is offered in a central section of this brochure, entitled "Visioni della Libia." This large foldout collage combines images of the indigenous landscape and culture with those of the travel, accommodation, and entertainment facilities of the ETAL—which are fused through a graphic frame that suggests the native architecture (fig. 4.21). This collage provides a compelling image of the continuous relationship between the tourist system in Libya and the characteristic aspects of the native culture.

The publicity material of this group is equally suggestive of

Fig. 4.20. Cover of the brochure Combinazioni di soggiorno in Libia (Tripoli: ETAL, 1937), published by the Libyan Tourism and Hotel Association. (See also Plate 14.)

Fig. 4.21. "Visioni della Libia," from Combinazioni di soggiorno in Libia (1937).

a more scientific view of the indigenous culture of Libya. This quality can be found in the guidebook *La Libia turistica* by Giovanni De Agostini, who was a professor and scholar in the field of geography. His discussion of the local populations in this publication is done according to the most rigorous logic, with each ethnic group being discussed according to their origins, settlements, artisanry, language, and social practices. The reading of all Libyans according to a racially encoded scientific interpretation is evident in the text which argues that "characteristic practices, secular traditions, complicated customs and superstitions govern the principal manifestations of the social life of the Libyan populations."[78] The visual presentation of this guidebook follows this tendency quite directly, with populations like the Bedouins being typified along racial lines and depicted in characteristic dress. The insistently uniform presentation of all subjects in this guidebook—from the physical description of this colony to the discussion of its racial and ethnic composition—reflects a shift in the indigenous politics in the late 1930s.

These increasingly racially encoded politics were the subject of considerable attention in the journal *Libia*, which offered a combination of historical and contemporary representations.[79] One such example is a 1937 essay entitled "Femminismo arabo," where the author rejects the depiction of women by authors of colonial literature who "narrated fantastical stories of voluptuous women, living in a life of dreams." Instead, he argues that a Muslim woman "lives the greatest part of her life closed between the walls of her modest house."[80] It was then asserted that the Italian policy of reinforcing their role through instruction in domestic skills was understood to be a form of feminism. In this discussion, particular attention is paid to the lack of hygiene of the Libyans which, among other things, was seen to be the source of problems such as infant mortality and various contagious diseases. The modernization and preservation of the local populations were thus connected in this essay with "the elements of hygiene penetrating the Arab household."[81] While this essay was attempting to demystify Islamic culture, it was in fact doing the opposite. Muslim women were depicted as being regulated by a monolithic and unchanging belief system that ruled all aspects of the life of its adherents.

The journal *Libia*, like the larger publicity and propaganda efforts of the ETAL, reveals the imbrication of the tourist discourse on indigenous culture with the larger political discourse of the Fascist colonial project in Libya. In the space of the pages of this magazine, the native culture of this region was subject to the essentializing gaze of the colonial tourist, just as the preservation of Libyan culture under the auspices of the indigenous politics of the Balbo administration resulted in the legislation of the most "authentic" artifacts and cultural practices.

A similar connection between the representation of indigenous culture in the tourist system and contemporary political and scientific discourse can be detected in another publication of the Publicity and Propaganda Service, *Itinerario Tripoli-Gadames* of 1938. This guidebook was published to advertise the itinerary that would take tourists from Tripoli to Ghadames and back as part of a five-day excursion. The organization and content of this publication are decidedly complex. The text is divided into a series of sections that describe the basic itinerary of the trip. This narrative structure is overlaid with a series of watercolor images of the actual experience of the excursion—images that prominently feature the system of hotels and amenities provided by the ETAL. While this approach would suggest the literary model prominent in the representation of indigenous culture, this tendency is counteracted with the dry and often "scientific" prose of the text, and a series of black-and-white images that provide objective documentation of the narrative experience of this tourist itinerary.

The connection between *Itinerario Tripoli-Gadames* and contemporary politics is evident in its depiction of the accomplishments of Fascist colonization. While placing a considerable emphasis on the characteristic architecture and culture of the region, this publication does not fail to refer to more contemporary accomplishments. In discussing the plain of the Jabal Nafusah, this book argues that "no longer the domain of slow camels, nor abandoned to the lazy unrefined shepherds, the Jifarah has been put into cultivation by Italian farmers, who have crossed the Mediterranean to make Libya the fourth shore of the fatherland" (fig. 4.22).[82] This itinerary is thus more than a tourist excursion into the Libyan interior that was intended to provide an experience of indigenous culture; it is also a way of reifying the Fascist colonial project in Libya.

The parallel between this text and contemporary scientific

Fig. 4.22. View of the outskirts of Gharyan, from Itinerario Tripoli-Gadames (1938).

Fig. 4.23. Interior of the Berber castle in Nalut, from Itiner-ario Tripoli-Gadames (1938).

discourse can be found in the approach taken to the prose. Despite the detailed nature of the descriptions contained in this guidebook, it is not treated as a romantic portrayal of travel—a form of writing found both in colonial literature and travel diaries. *Itinerario Tripoli-Gadames* contains the kind of dispassionate description that is employed in more obviously objective tourist aids, like the guidebooks of the Italian Touring Club. Moreover, its description of indigenous culture provides a historical, cultural, and racial understanding in the manner of an anthropologist or ethnographer.

This publication is an indication of the intersection of the tourist discourse on the representation of the indigenous and contemporary activities in various fields of scientific research. One such example in the text is a presentation of the Berber populations, who were described both for their appearance—being "predominantly blond, light colored eyes, tall and thin stature" —and their customs—being "more severe, more rigid, more bound to the observance of law."[83] The movement toward a more scientific model of depiction of the indigenous populations is also found in the postcard itineraries produced by the ETAL, one of which represented the same route from Tripoli to Ghadames.[84] Acting as both an inducement to travel and the documentation of a potential experience, this series of postcards represented various indigenous settlements, the people, and their culture in a manner that was in a continuous relationship with the general tourist infrastructure (figs. 4.23, 4.24). *Itinerario Tripoli-Gadames*, like the larger system of accommodation, entertainment, and transportation services, adopts the objective means through which contemporary scientific discourse re-presented the indigenous populations to a metropolitan audience. Under the guise of this "science," this publication theorizes the tourist experience as a form of objective research that allows the traveler to view the native environment and culture without any interference by modern Western culture.

The scientific means of presenting native culture was not limited to the publicity activities of the Libyan Tourism and Hotel Association, as it also informed the creation of a number of tourist environments that were owned and operated by this group. The interest in the authenticity of experience of indigenous culture extended to the conception of the larger tourist system, which was intended to re-present, rather than merely frame, the experience of the native culture. The meeting places and recreation facilities of the Theater and Performance Service were particularly instrumental to this experience—facilities that, according to a press release from 1938, were "one of the most appreciated attractions for the foreigner."[85] The most well-noted of these tourist settings was the so-called Arab Café designed by the architect Di Fausto. This facility was located in the Artisanal Quarter that this architect executed in 1935 under the mandate of the Building Commission of Tripoli. This larger project was one of the most important restoration works carried out during the Balbo administration due to its location within the nineteenth-century Suq al-Mushir just inside the walls of the medina and adjacent to the castle and the Qaramanli mosque.[86] This educational and entertainment facility was important because of its close connection with the Balbo administration's reorganization of the indigenous craft industries of Libya. In addition to the Arab Café, the program of the larger project accommodated the new facilities for the School of Arts and Crafts, which required a combination of classrooms and workshops and some small shops for selling goods.[87]

The Artisanal Quarter at the Suq al-Mushir provided a tourist experience in which the indigenous architecture and culture of Libya was presented in an authentic environment. The facility was so carefully interwoven into the existing context as to create a continuous relationship with the historic architecture of the castle and the surrounding fabric of the old city. This connection was also more figurative. The aesthetic expression of this project, described as exhibiting a "modern sense of architecture associated with eastern Mediterranean motifs," shows a careful assimilation of traditional spaces like the Qaramanli courtyard in the nearby castle.[88] This courtyard, which was surrounded by the workshops and classrooms, contained a large reflecting pool and was decorated by ceramic tile produced by the students (fig. 4.25). The decoration of the courtyard with the products of Balbo's

Fig. 4.24. Postcard of a vase maker in Ghadames, ca. 1935.

restoration program connects the historical reference to the castle with the present program of redefining the native culture of Libya. The conflation of the historical past with attempts to reenact it in the present applies more broadly to the tourist experience of this facility. Such a seamless relationship is created between the existing context and associated restoration work and the new intervention, they are impossible to separate. Just like the artisanal wares that were being offered in the shops of this new tourist facility, the forms of the building so closely follow precedent that it can be argued that they are themselves part of a program of historical restoration.

In a similar manner, the Arab Café offered the metropolitan traveler an experience of native culture in an authentic environment. Operated by the Theater and Performance Service of the ETAL, this facility presented "characteristic" Arab musical and dance performances in a setting that one commentator argued "fully reproduces the suggestive local environment."[89] Just like the larger project for the Artisanal Quarter, the project is a carefully studied reinterpretation of the local forms, expressed through a restrained and simplified architectural vocabulary (fig. 4.26). The sense of authenticity of the space was reinforced through the use of decorative tiles produced in the adjacent Muslim School of Indigenous Arts and Crafts, which reenacted traditional forms and patterns. The interest in creating an authentic experience for the tourists extended to the music and dance performances, which

Fig. 4.25. View of the courtyard of the artisanal quarter at the Suq al-Mushir in Tripoli (1935), designed by Florestano Di Fausto.

included the eroticism of traditional Oriental dance—where Arab women were clad in thin layers of revealing clothing (fig. 4.27).

Not unlike the broader restoration project of Balbo in Libya, this "authentic" experience was assembled according to the same eminent logic that pervaded the Italian intervention in the Libyan artisanal industries. Indeed, in response to a lack of qualified local musicians and dancers—the initial performers largely being from Tunisia—the ETAL created an Arab music school to train the Libyans.[90] It would seem that in the tourist system in Libya, "the native" was not presented so much as it was re-presented according to the demands of the modern tourist and the politics of colonial rule. At the same time that certain indigenous practices were being outlawed by the Libyan government, a whole new set were being created for the benefit of the metropolitan traveler.

The incorporation of the indigenous as part of the tourist

Fig. 4.26. Arab Café at the Suq al-Mushir in Tripoli (1935), designed by Florestano Di Fausto.

experience was not limited to manifestations of local culture or the system of tourist facilities in the colonial context. The Libyan Tourism and Hotel Association had a store in Rome that sold cigarettes, tobacco, and products of Libyan artisanry—a business that was overseen by the Tourism Service (fig. 4.28).[91] In a setting that was suggestive of a dark and mysterious "Oriental" interior, the products of the indigenous artisans of Libya were seemingly reduced to mere commodities for sale to a metropolitan audience. However, given the location of this shop in Rome, this business was intended to be an inducement to travel—the artisanal products having the status of ethnographic objects through which the Libyan culture could be experienced and understood. In this sense, the display of these products is more closely tied to contemporary museum practices than modern merchandising.

While the appeal of the indigenous culture of Libya in the tourist system was in its exotic qualities—in its difference—it is also clear that this presentation had to conform to a contemporary Western understanding. The ethnographic discourse related to these artisanal objects and the rational logic with which the indigenous events in the tourist network in Libya were planned and staged, underscore the fact that in the tourist system in Libya the apparent opposition between the modern and the indigenous has every appearance of being false. Rather than a mediation of opposites—that of modernization and preservation—this system was, in fact, a dual embrace of modernity. The first of these was the exten-

Fig. 4.27. Postcard of a dance performance in the Arab Café at the Suq al-Mushir in Tripoli, ca. 1935.

sion of an efficient system of travel and accommodation throughout this colony related to the demands of modern tourism. The second was closely tied to the indigenous politics of Balbo and the rise of scientific discourse in the realm of colonial culture and called for the systematic preservation and control of the indigenous landscape. The preservation and presentation of local culture is itself modern, conceived according to the modern demands of tourism, and presented through means that, despite their appearance, were modern. In this sense it can be argued that in the context of the tourist system in Libya, the indigenous was also modern.

Fig. 4.28. Libyan Tourism and Hotel Association tobacco shop in Rome (1937).

**CHAPTER
FIVE**

TOWARD A MODERN COLONIAL ARCHITECTURE

The native architecture of our Mediterranean colonies presents, for those who may know how to recognize it, all the necessary requirements from which to deduce a perfect modern colonial architecture: rationality in planning, contemporary simplicity of form in exterior appearance, perfect adherence to the necessity of the African climate, perfect harmony with the Libyan nature. When the frequent examples that they propose to us of vivid polychromy applied to affect and brighten up the nudity of the cubic masses and smooth walls are added to these qualities, it will be shown that the native architecture of Libya offers us all of the desirable elements for creating our present-day colonial architecture.—Carlo Enrico Rava, "Di un'architettura coloniale moderna – Parte seconda," 1931.[1]

Fig. 5.1. Pavilion of the Colonies at the Milan Trade Fair (1928), designed by Sebastiano Larco and Carlo Enrico Rava.

In an eight-part "Panorama of Rationalism" published in *Domus* magazine between January and November of 1931, Italian architect Carlo Enrico Rava included a two-part essay, in which he argued that the problem of a modern colonial architecture was closely tied to the more general question of architectural modernity.[2] Rava was one of the founding members of the *Gruppo Sette*, which was an affiliation of recent graduates from the Milan Polytechnic University who published a series of manifestos in the political and cultural journal *Rassegna Italiana* beginning in

December of 1926.[3] In these essays, Rava, as the *mente pensante* of this group of Rationalist architects, argued that "the new architecture" was to be based on logic and rationality, deriving its aesthetic value "exclusively from the character of necessity." Rejecting the idea of creating a style, these architects asserted that a style would be born through a process of "selection"—an approach which called for "the constant use of rationality" in the creation of a few fundamental types.[4]

In his essays on a modern colonial architecture, Rava noted that there was an almost total ignorance of the problem of building in the colonial context. In reaction to much of what had already been built, he stated that Italian architects should avoid the direct copying of Roman models. He was also critical of the use of Moorish motifs, arguing their presence in Libya could only be found in the "false and monstrous" constructions built in the years following the Italian conquest.[5] Instead of following these historicist approaches, Rava asserted that Italian architects should adapt the forms and materials of the "native architecture" of Libya, which had all of the desirable qualities for the creation of a modern colonial architecture proper to Fascist Italy. One of the crucial reasons behind the appropriation of these sources, he notes, was that they were modern. This modernity was to be found

Fig. 5.2. Photograph of Carlo Enrico Rava in front of a tent with Hag Muchtar (March 1930), by an unidentified photographer.

in their suitability to climatic conditions, their lack of superfluous elements, and their ability to harmonize with the colonial context.[6] These indigenous constructions were also seen as an appropriate reference for a modern colonial architecture due to their connection with the Roman colonization of North Africa. In this discussion, Rava makes a distinction between the monumental ruins of sites like Leptis Magna—which he refers to as being "already dead," and having only "a purely archaeological-touristic value"—and the native architecture of the region.[7] According to this view, the so-called Arab house was a reinterpretation of the Roman domus, inheriting both its classical plan and its central courtyard. To borrow from these indigenous forms was borrowing from the surviving traces of Italy's own building traditions.

The interpretation of indigenous architecture in Libya offered by Rava in "Di un'architettura coloniale moderna" was derived from, and participated in, a specifically colonial discourse—that of the representation of this architecture by Italian scholars in the 1920s who asserted its Western and Roman origins. This architect's interest in the question of a modern colonial architecture based on indigenous sources was greatly facilitated by the activities of his father, Maurizio, whose administrative position in Libya created work opportunities. It also allowed him to undertake six extended visits to this colony during his father's tenure (fig. 5.2).[8] The intersection of this experience of the colonies with the younger Rava's theoretical arguments on Italian Rationalism is evident in the use of his travel photographs as the visual illustrations for his polemical writings on colonial architecture.

Carlo Enrico Rava's theoretical interest in the indigenous architecture of Libya was also closely tied to his early professional activities. One of the most important of these works was his design, with his partner Sebastiano Larco, for a Pavilion of the Colonies at the Milan Trade Fair. This project was the result of a national competition sponsored by the Italian Colonial Institute in 1927, whose jury characterized the facade as being "inspired by elements of Arab minor architecture" that were in turn "developed with a completely modern clarity and refinement."[9] These comments were echoed in the pages of *Architettura e Arti Decorative*, where Marcello Piacentini described the project as "compact, pure, schematic" with "beautiful light cut out in the white, smooth and bare material."[10] The appropriation of indigenous Libyan architecture is evident in the unadorned stucco surfaces and simple cubic volumes on the exterior of the building and its allusion to buttressed wall construction (fig. 5.1). The arrangement of the interior of this pavilion into two linear display rooms that flank a small domed exhibition space links these visual references to planning principles derived from these same vernacular constructions.

The arguments of "Di un'architettura coloniale moderna" were also closely tied to architectural discourse in Italy due to their publication in a "Panorama of Rationalism" that theorized a new direction for contemporary architecture. In the first article in this series, published in January of 1931 under the title "Svolta pericolosa: Situazione dell'Italia di fronte al razionalismo Europeo," Rava argued that Italian Rationalist architects were at a crucial turning point, wherein two distinct views were emerging within current European tendencies. The first of these approaches had been elaborated by "intransigent" architects like Walter

Gropius, Erich Mendelsohn, Ludwig Mies van der Rohe, and Le Corbusier, whom Rava referred to as "pure," "dogmatic," and "absolute abolishers of individualism."[11] The second of these positions was evident in the work of "independent" architects like Emil Fahrenkamp, Heinrich Tessenow, and Alfred Soulek, whom he argued had "reclaimed the right to preserve their own personality through Rationalism," while being vigilant in their affirmation of "the distinctive national characteristics of culture and race."[12]

Linking the founding manifestos of Italian Rationalism with this first line of thought—with the renunciation of individualism, the inevitability of production standards, and the spirit of the series—Rava asserted that this movement had made such great progress, that it was both possible and necessary for it to pursue a more independent approach. According to this argument, the source of this more independent direction was to be found in the "smooth white cubes" and "large terraces" of the indigenous architecture of Italy's coastal regions, that is, in the "Mediterranean spirit" of Italy's ancient and modern civilization.[13] This *mediterraneità*, as it was referred to by contemporary architects and critics, was one of several terms, like *latinità* and *romanità*, that entered the contemporary debate concerning the appropriate identity for a modern architecture proper to Fascist Italy.[14]

The idea of a modern architecture based on the indigenous constructions of the Italian Mediterranean was tied to the tradition of modern European architects, who viewed these vernacular sources as a suitable inspiration for their contemporary works. However, in so doing, Rava was both reevaluating his own position within Italian Rationalism and providing an explicit critique of the dogmatism of his colleagues. Rava's participation in the debate concerning a modern Fascist architecture is evidenced in the final essay of the "Panorama of Rationalism," where he defends himself against the accusation of "having washed the dirty linen of Rationalism in public." Instead, he asserts that "our precise purpose was to discern, in the rationalist tendency, the good and the useful from the bad and the harmful . . . to distinguish them from the vain, empty formulas." Rava concludes his response by stating: "Today it is no longer a question of being 'rationalists,' it is only a question of being modern Italian architects . . . each searching within themselves for the most profound, sincere and independent expression."[15]

For Rava, a modern Italian architecture was to be a product of a fusion of technical developments, environmental demands, and the influence of Latin civilization. The appropriation of indigenous Mediterranean sources addressed certain ambiguities in the relationship between the modern and the traditional for which his early Rationalist manifestos were severely criticized. In so doing, he attempted to forge a specifically national identity for modern Italian architecture.[16] The nationalist dimension of this recourse to indigenous forms was itself the subject of criticism in the press. In an article reflecting on the theoretical discourse within modern Italian architecture in *Domus* magazine in 1934, critic Edoardo Persico bluntly asked: "What had happened in two years to lead Rava from the Europeanism of 1928 to the *mediterraneità* of 1930?"[17]

The arguments of Carlo Enrico Rava concerning the derivation of a modern colonial architecture from the indigenous heritage of Libya marked the beginning of a discourse on this subject that continued to evolve through the course of the

1930s. This discourse, however, was not without its contradictions. By making reference to indigenous Libyan architecture under the guise of a Mediterranean architecture, Rava was constituting a modernist and imperialist project. In the first case, he was following an already well-established tendency to interpret indigenous sources according to a modern aesthetic sensibility—that is, through the simplification and abstraction of the local architecture. In the second, he was mirroring Italian colonial politics by incorporating the Libyan architectural heritage into a broader political and aesthetic category—which is that of a Mediterranean architecture. According to Rava, Italian colonial architecture was to be modern and indigenous, timeless and rooted in a specific time and place. The ambivalence of this modernist architectural discourse is a perfect match for the political project of the colonial authorities in Libya in the early 1930s.

THE DISCOURSE ON LOCAL CULTURE

The theory for a contemporary colonial architecture in Libya was not conceived in isolation. It was a relatively direct product of a scholarly discourse connected with the preservation program that the Volpi administration began in 1921. It was under the auspices of this political initiative that a number of monuments and historical sites were restored and that these projects were eventually published in prominent Italian journals like *Bolletino d'Arte* and *Dedalo*.[18] As a consequence of this program, the local architecture of Libya become a valid topic of scholarly interest. The early research into the indigenous architecture of Tripolitania culminated with the publication of Salvatore Aurigemma's *Tripoli e le sue opere d'arte* of 1927.[19] As in his other essays, the book recognizes the complex interaction of numerous decorative traditions in the native architecture and artisanry of Tripoli. It includes a historical account of the region and the development of its arts followed by a detailed description of a number of individual buildings and artworks. These works include the Roman monument of the Arch of Marcus Aurelius, the fifth-century Christian tombs at 'Ain Zarah, the mosque of Murad Agha from the first Ottoman period (1511-1711), the Qaramanli and Gurgi mosques from the Qaramanli period (1711-1834), and examples of contemporary Jewish, Arab, and Berber artisanry (see fig. 5.3).

Despite the breadth and sophistication of this presentation of local traditions, *Tripoli e le sue opere d'arte* reflects the operative nature of Italian scholarly work on Libya during this period. The first section of the book, which describes the Roman colonization effort, closely resembles the Italian colonial authorities' vision of their own political policies. In discussing the success of the Roman empire in Africa, Aurigemma argued that "the campaigns prospered by virtue of the Roman element being established in the territory, or the indigenous element renewing itself within the Romans and then becoming part of the great Roman state."[20] In this sense, Aurigemma was using a historical and scholarly study of the artistic traditions of Tripoli to link the greatness of its Roman past with the potential of its colonial present. This approach was very much in line with academic discourse in Italy, which was largely determined by the political policies of the Fascist regime. It was during this period that the scholarly research into Roman architecture within the Mediterranean published in well-respected official journals on art and architectural history

*Fig. 5.3. View of the
majolica tile at the
Gurgi mosque in
Tripoli, ca. 1925.*

like *Le Arti* and *Palladio* was used to justify Fascism's imperialist
politics in the region.[21]

The scholarly interest in the indigenous culture of the Italian
colonies was itself profoundly influenced by a parallel discourse
that had emerged much earlier in the French colonies in North
Africa. In addition to the cultural nationalism of the "civilizing
mission" that historians have argued was carried out by the French
in Algeria, Tunisia, and Morocco—that is, in their indoctrination of
the local populations as French subjects—the colonial authorities
in this region initiated educational and research programs related
to its indigenous language and culture. One of the most prominent
figures in this work was Prosper Ricard, who began his academic
and scholarly career in North Africa in 1900 teaching the local
populations of Algeria.[22] After becoming inspector of artistic and
industrial teaching for all indigenous schools in this colony in 1909,

Fig. 5.4. Courtyard of Dar Adîyel in Fez (restored 1920), published in Prosper Ricard, "Il rinnovamento artistico del Marocco," Dedalo (May 1929).

Ricard embarked on a series of research missions that led him to Morocco, where he eventually became inspector of indigenous arts of the regions of Fez and Meknès in 1915. Throughout this period and well into the 1920s, Ricard established himself as a leading expert on the Muslim arts of the French colonies in North Africa by publishing numerous essays and books on the subject.[23] Notably, Ricard also published an essay entitled "Il rinnovamento artistico del Marocco" in *Dedalo* in 1929, whose appearance in this Italian art journal underscores his international reputation as an expert on Muslim artistic traditions.[24] This well-illustrated essay provides an extensive presentation of the renewal of artistic and artisanal production of Morocco under the guidance of Ricard and the Indigenous Arts Service of the Department of Public Instruction of Arts and Antiquities, including the recently renovated courtyard of Dar Adîyel in Fez (fig. 5.4).

One of Ricard's most productive relationships was with Hachette, the Paris-based company that produced the *Guides Bleus* and other tourist-oriented publications. The collaboration of Ricard with Hachette included guidebooks to Algeria, Tunisia, and Morocco and a large illustrated volume on these French colonies that provides an extensive documentation of the French colonial project in North Africa.[25] The most influential of his publications on the interpretation of Islamic art and architecture, and also the most widely disseminated, was *Pour comprendre l'art musulman dans l'Afrique du Nord et en Espagne* (1924). This book presents Muslim art in North Africa and Spain according to a modern Western viewpoint, systematically cataloging its constituent elements within a taxonomic system. The importance of this publication to the Italian discourse on indigenous culture in Libya lay not only in its popularizing of Muslim arts and architecture, but also in the particular views it advanced about those traditions. In *Pour comprendre l'art musulman,* Ricard furnishes arguments about the Roman origins of the Muslim culture of North Africa that would later be taken up by Italian scholars. The connection between these origins and the contemporary presence of the West in North Africa is made in the preface to this publication, where Ricard boldly states: "Roman Africa continues to live, in effect, through its hundreds of thousands of settlers returning from Sicilian, Mahonian, Maltese, Italian, Spanish and French shores to populate its towns and make its Numidian countryside fertile."[26]

The research of Prosper Ricard on the Muslim arts of North Africa also had a more direct impact on the interpretation of Italian scholars of the indigenous culture of Tripolitania in the 1920s. As director of indigenous arts in Morocco, Ricard was hired by Giuseppe Volpi to research the native artisanal industries. The results of this project appeared in two issues of the journal *Rivista della Tripolitania* in early 1926 and were later published in book form.[27] In these publications, Ricard surveys a range of artistic and artisanal production, from architecture and decoration to its regional craft traditions, contextualizing these arts in relation to those of the French North African colonies. In so doing, he laid the interpretive groundwork for future scholarship on the architectural and decorative traditions of Tripolitania, by alluding to their relationship with Roman and Western precedents.[28]

In discussing the indigenous craft traditions of this region, Ricard places great emphasis on the influence of the Berbers, a group which held a great interest for the Italians as a "primitive" society whose culture preceded the Arab invasion of North Africa. The discussion of the Berber origins of indigenous craft traditions can be understood as a not-so-subtle validation of the Italian interest in viewing the Libyan culture as built upon Roman foundations. Ricard's essay was clearly the basis of the policies instituted by the Italian colonial authorities under Giuseppe Volpi relative to the native artisanal industries. It argued for a program of preservation that returned to more ancient authentic practices, and a program of modernization that called for the systematic study of these practices for the purposes of improving the quality and production of these industries.[29] The arguments of Ricard reflect the ambivalence of the indigenous politics of Volpi, for whom the preservation of local culture was closely tied to a policy of economic modernization.

Although the early scholarly research on the native arts of Libya formed a general backdrop to the views of Carlo Enrico Rava, a more direct influence was the construction of regional identity in contemporary Italian architectural periodicals. The interest in local architecture was cultivated in the pages of *Architettura e Arti Decorative*, a journal which began publication in September of 1921 under the direction of Gustavo Giovannoni and Marcello Piacentini. This magazine was the official organ of the *Associazione artistica fra i cultori di architettura*, a group which was founded in Rome in 1890 to preserve the historical patrimony of Italian cities.[30] Under the guidance of its two editors, this publication provided both critical commentary on contemporary activities in Italy and abroad, and scholarly reviews of the history of Italian architecture. It argued for an appreciation of the indigenous traditions of the various regions of Italy through the presentation of current building projects, competitions, and exhibitions. These local and national representations were carefully measured against European and international tendencies, which were given ample space in the magazine. More importantly, *Architettura e Arti Decorative* was a valuable resource for a more profound appreciation of the historical value of Italy's architectural heritage. It provided important documentation of the architecture of each province and chronicled recent activities in the area of historic preservation.[31]

The heterogeneous nature of the presentation of local architecture in *Architettura e Arti Decorative* was largely due to the divergent backgrounds and interests of its two editors. Giovannoni's contribution was directly tied to the preservation activities of the *Associazione artistica*. In his writings, he espoused a scholarly defense of the importance of *architettura minore*, or "minor architecture," a term that became synonymous with this journal and was defined as the anonymous architectural organisms that expressed the distinctive character of particular cities. While this concept was primarily related to housing, it was also applied to public or religious buildings that were indigenous to a specific place or region. The culmination of his collaboration with the *Associazione artistica* was the publication of a series of books beginning in 1926 entitled *Architettura minore in Italia*. By documenting these anonymous buildings, these publications were intended to fill a lacuna in the history of Italian architecture.[32] They were also used as an intellectual justification for a policy of contextualism in the modernization of historic centers of Italian cities, an approach that Giovannoni himself had developed in his proposals for the reorganization of the Renaissance quarter of Rome of 1913 (fig. 5.5). Largely inspired by Camillo Sitte's *Der Städtebau nach seinen kunstlerischen Grundsätzen* of 1889, this proposal called for the thinning out of the area surrounding the Via dei Coronari, an approach that responded both to modern demands and to the desire for the preservation of the picturesque qualities of this quarter of Rome.[33] Through the writings and proposals of Giovannoni, an historical interest in minor architecture was closely tied to the contemporary debate on the importance of considering historical context in the modernization of Italian cities.

The concept of *architettura minore* in the writings of Marcello Piacentini was more clearly related to the theoretical discourse concerning the development of a modern architectural aesthetic. In the first issue of *Architettura e Arti Decorative*, Piacentini argued that, along with classicism and abstraction, minor

Fig. 5.5. Proposal
for the restoration of
via dei Coronari and
piazza San Salvatore
in Lauro in Rome
(1913), by Gustavo
Giovannoni.

architecture, or what he called "rusticism," was one of the key
developments in contemporary architecture in Italy and abroad.[34]
For Piacentini, a modern Italian architecture would derive from
a mediation of the fundamental characteristics common to all
countries, which he asserted were "sobriety, synthesis, and
renunciation," and the permanent principles that resided in the
architecture of Italy's past.[35] In a subsequent article, entitled
"Influssi d'arte italiana nel Nord-America," he examines the influence of the local architecture of Italy on the domestic architecture
of North America. Piacentini argues that this minor architecture
reflected a "response to the modest needs of life common to all
men" and, as such, was an art that was "simple and spontaneous,

free of any presumptions." In considering the contemporary value of these indigenous sources, he states: "This architectonic prose, of little personal content, but collective, anonymous, must be revived against the sterile attempts of the architectonic fashions of recent decades."[36] The connection between indigenous sources and contemporary artistic production was expressed in a very direct way in a villa in the Parioli quarter designed by Piacentini, dating from 1916 to 1918, whose dynamic composition is expressed through an architectural language derived from anonymous rural buildings in the Roman countryside (fig. 5.6).[37]

Giovannoni and Piacentini not only theorized a concept of minor architecture that was influential in modern architectural discourse and thus indirectly fueled the interest of Italians in the native architecture of Libya, but their journal *Architettura e Arti Decorative* had a more direct influence on this discourse. Several important essays on Libyan architecture were published during the early 1920s, where it was presented as a particular regional manifestation of the concept of minor architecture. In one of these essays, published in April of 1924, Renato Bartoccini examined the mosque of Murad Agha in Tajura (1553) according to the same historical practices that Giovannoni used to study indigenous architecture in Italy. The essay combined a detailed history of this mosque from the first Ottoman period with drawings and photographs that documented its form and structure. Notwithstanding the apparent objectivity of this presentation, it is quite clear that the reasoning behind the selection of this Muslim religious building was that, as Bartoccini argued, "the architectonic type of the mosque is clearly Western."[38] The designation of the general configuration of this mosque as Western by Bartoccini was tied to its conformance with what he argued were Maghreb precedents, and thus to the Italian sector of the Mediterranean region. The clear implication was that, for Bartoccini and numerous other Italian scholars, the true indigenous style of Tripolitania was determined by North African (and thus Roman) rather than Ottoman influences. The fact that the columns of the mosque were scavenged from the town of Leptis Magna was merely a confirmation of its Western designation.

An equally operative view of the minor architecture of Libya is provided by Pietro Romanelli in his article "Vecchie case arabe di Tripoli," which was published in the January 1924 issue of *Architettura e Arti Decorative*. The essay was a direct result of the preservation program of the Volpi administration, presenting eleven of the twenty-four private residences that had been singled out for conservation in November of 1921.[39] In so doing, it followed the approach taken by other scholars of architecture, categorizing these courtyard houses into three distinct groups based upon their age and their architectural influences. Romanelli also overlaid a political agenda on this scholarly one, arguing that "the plan of the Tripolitanian house, in its simplicity, is closer than any other Eastern house to the Roman one."[40] In discussing the Roman origins of the Arab house, Romanelli asserts that this was the underlying type of all houses in the East, while at the same time noting that this type developed, amplified, and modified itself to better correspond to the customs and habits of the local populations. The attempt to connect the native architecture of this region to specifically Italian influences persisted throughout the essay, which asserted that the decorative schemes of buildings like the Qaramanli house in Tripoli (ca.

1790) were related to seventeenth-century Italian sources and that the craftsmen that built many of these projects were "without a doubt Italian" (fig. 5.7).[41] The arguments advanced by Romanelli in this essay—that the indigenous house in Tripolitania was based upon Roman precedents and related to the practices of the Italian building trades—provided intellectual and scholarly justification for the arguments of Rava about the use of these local forms for a contemporary colonial architecture.

Despite the theorization of minor architecture in the pages of *Architettura e Arti Decorative* and a preservation program that fostered a scholarly discourse on the Libyan vernacular, Italian

Fig. 5.6. Villa in the Parioli quarter of Rome (1916-18), by Marcello Piacentini.

Fig. 5.7. Courtyard of the Qaramanli house in Tripoli (ca. 1790), published in Pietro Romanelli, "Vecchie case arabe di Tripoli," Architettura e Arti Decorative (January 1924).

architects practicing in Libya in the early 1920s showed little
interest in indigenous constructions. Instead, the colonial architecture was characterized by an eclecticism that alternated between
various received forms of Eastern culture—the most prominent
of these being Moorish, Byzantine, Pisan, and Venetian—and
overt references to Roman classical architecture. These tendencies were a product of two factors, the first being the need to
legitimize the Italian presence—thus the adoption of an already
established architectural style. Second, as some historians have
argued, the Venetian origins of Volpi had a profound influence.[42]
One example of contemporary colonial architecture is the mosque

Fig. 5.8. Exterior
view of the mosque
of Sidi Hamuda in
Tripoli, ca. 1925.

of Sidi Hamuda in Tripoli. This building, constructed during the late Ottoman period, was substantially remade during the 1920s, with considerable attention paid to the enhancement of its exterior and interior. The relatively simple cubic massing of the building is elaborated through the employment of a rich decorative surface development of colorful ceramic tiles (fig. 5.8). The Italian approach to colonial architecture during the Volpi era is largely derivative of the *arabisances* practiced by the French in North Africa—a term that François Béguin uses to refer to the "numerous traces of arabisation of architectural forms imported by Europe."[43] Just like the mosque of Sidi Hamuda, the majority of these French precedents maintained a clear separation between local decorative patterns and modern forms.

The most prominent architect active in Tripolitania during the governorship of Volpi was Armando Brasini, who practiced a form of eclecticism inspired by antique sources. Brasini was one of a group of influential academic architects working in Rome, one of his most significant accomplishments being his participation, along with architects Giovannoni, Piacentini, Alberto Calza-Bini, and archeologist Roberto Paribeni, in the commission that produced the 1931 master plan of Rome.[44] Although he had executed few projects at the time, Brasini was given a number of significant commissions in Libya during the Volpi era, his position being that of the municipal architect for Tripoli. His projects in the colonial context, according to one commentator, express an interest in Roman architecture through a "scenographic union of great monumental architecture."[45]

The first work constructed by Brasini in Tripoli is the Monument to the Fallen and to Victory of 1923-25—a memorial to the soldiers lost in the initial conquest of Tripoli that was located on the west seafront of the old city (fig. 5.9). Architecturally, this design has been connected with the fifth-century Mausoleum of Theodoric in Ravenna, which is widely regarded as a point of connection between West and East. Notably, Brasini's relationship to this monument is more than incidental, as he designed the costumes and stage sets for the film, *Teodoro*, in 1919.[46] The work of Brasini was the product of an approach to colonial architecture that asserted a specifically Roman identity in the colonial context. However, the *romanità* of Brasini, a term used by artists and critics to refer to the self-conscious use of classicism as a political statement, was more than a commemoration of the metropole in the colony. This project can be understood as a gesture of aesthetic and cultural colonization. It was a reification of Fascist colonial politics, which viewed the present activities of Italy in North Africa as being a continuation of ancient practices.

One example of a tourist facility in Libya from the mid-1920s that followed an eclectic approach to design is the Hotel Italia in Benghazi. This building was one of the largest and most luxurious of such tourist facilities, providing more than fifty rooms with hot and cold running water and the additional facilities of a restaurant, a small theater, some shops, and a café.[47] The hotel was designed to offer such luxuries despite the fact that the region of Cyrenaica was a much less common tourist destination. Under the governorships of General Ernesto Mombelli (1924-26) and General Attilio Teruzzi (1926-28), Benghazi followed a very similar tendency to that found in Tripoli in the design of its major public institutions—pursuing an eclectic architectural language that offers a Western conception of Eastern architecture.

The Hotel Italia, or the *Palazzo Nobile* as it was called, is a prime example of such an approach. This building presented a monumental public facade that formed the southeastern edge of the Piazza del Ré—a public space and garden that was the symbolic center of the new Benghazi (fig. 5.10). The simple and symmetrical disposition of this facade was punctuated by a delicately scaled arcaded entryway and a series of decorative spandrel

Fig. 5.9. Monument to the Fallen and to Victory in Tripoli (1923-25), by Armando Brasini.

Fig. 5.10. Postcard of the Hotel Italia in Benghazi, ca. 1925.

Fig. 5.11. Postcard of the Municipal Palace in Benghazi (1923-24).

panels. The symmetrical design of the Hotel Italia and its decorative program is quite similar to the Municipal Palace (1923-24), which was described in the tourist literature as having a "Moorish style with a sumptuous stair and rich rooms on the interior" (fig. 5.11). In the case of the Hotel Italia, the central rhythm of the building is enhanced by two large octagonal towers that are more reminiscent of the monumental architecture of the Mughal period in South Asia than anything found in North Africa. In an effort to create an image of the East that is familiar to the foreign tourist, the Hotel Italia offers an assimilation of various non-Western traditions.

The most prominent example of the eclectic approach to the design of a tourist facility is the Grand Hotel in Tripoli (1925-27), which was planned and executed by the municipality (fig. 5.12). Located along the Lungomare Conte Volpi just four blocks from the Piazza Italia, this hotel provided luxury accommodation for up to 120 guests through facilities that included a restaurant, bar, tennis courts, and a private garden.[48] The exterior of the building is typical of the tourist architecture of this period—offering a thin veneer of Moorish horseshoe arches and delicate columns placed over a massing scheme whose well-ordered composition reflects Beaux-Arts planning principles. The thinness of the stylistic application of the exterior is particularly evident in the decorative cornice, a detail that emphasizes the surface of the building rather than its depth. The exoticism of the exterior of the building is greatly enhanced by its seafront location, which allowed for the development of a garden space that is punctuated by a small grove of palm trees. Although it was not the only hotel in Tripoli during this period, it was the most luxurious and, as such, the Grand Hotel was the most crucial in defining the character of the tourist architecture.

The Hotel Gebel in Gharyan, which was managed by the same group as the Grand Hotel in Tripoli, was conceived according to a similar eclectic architectural program. Designed to accommodate the rather modest tourist needs of this newly developed area of agricultural colonization of the Jifarah Plain, this facility provided second-class accommodation for up to thirty visitors.[49] The exterior of the hotel provides allusions to the indigenous architecture through its cubic massing and the decorative treatments of the cornice, which vaguely resemble building details from the pre-Saharan settlement of Ghadames. In a similar manner, the Hotel Nefusa in Nalut of 1928, perhaps due to the extreme modesty of its means, has the appearance of an anonymous local construction (figs. 5.13, 5.14). These last projects illustrate the fact that during this early period of Italian colonialism in Libya, architects were still struggling to find the appropriate language for the architecture of the tourist system. Virtually all of the hotel facilities constructed during this period pursued an architectural eclecticism that would eventually be displaced when architectural

Fig. 5.12. Seafront view of the Grand Hotel in Tripoli (1925-27).

Fig. 5.13. Exterior view of the Hotel Gebel in Gharyan (1927).

Fig. 5.14. Postcard view of the Hotel Nefusa in Nalut (1928).

developments in Libya were more directly influenced by contemporary architectural discourse in Italy.

EARLY SIGNS OF MODERNITY

The approach to a contemporary colonial architecture underwent a gradual transformation during the latter part of the 1920s. This process began with the appointment of Pietro Badoglio as the governor of the colony in 1928 and the subsequent hiring of Alessandro Limongelli as art consultant to the municipality of Tripoli. In replacing Brasini as the most influential architect in this colony, Limongelli's early work, like the triumphal arch designed for the visit of the King of Italy to Tripoli (1928), pursued a *romanità* that was clearly penetrated by the use of formal abstraction (fig. 5.15). Moreover, in contrast with Brasini's work, which remained in a detached eclectic mode throughout his career in Tripolitania, the later projects of Limongelli, like his unexecuted

Fig. 5.15. Triumphal arch for the visit of the King of Italy to Tripoli (1928), by Alessandro Limongelli.

Fig. 5.16. Proposal for a housing project in Tripoli (1931), by Alessandro Limongelli.

1931 proposal for a residential project in Tripoli, illustrate a complex knowledge of the formal characteristics of the indigenous architecture (fig. 5.16).[50]
The tension between the modern *romanità* of Limongelli and his interest in
the Islamic architecture of Tripolitania is expressed in his statement to Angelo
Piccioli: "I can even admire and exalt . . . some types of Eastern architecture, but
I cannot forget that, here in Libya, much earlier than an Islamic architecture
based on thin columns and decorative majolica tile was introduced, there was
the majestic architecture of the legionnaires of Rome."[51] The trajectory of the
work of Limongelli in Tripolitania is the perfect paradigm for the transformation of colonial architecture during this period, which was moving away from the
imposition of an eclectic vocabulary derived from the metropolitan context and
toward a closer attention to the characteristic qualities of both the indigenous
architecture and the larger context of North Africa.

One of the factors contributing to this shift was a theoretical discourse on
colonial architecture that was just emerging. In writing a report to the Mayor of
Tripoli in 1929 concerning the future development of this Italian colonial city,
Maurizio Rava argued that not only was the indigenous architecture of Tripoli
an asset to be preserved for economic and political reasons; it was an appropriate model for the creation of a contemporary architecture.[52] The intersection
of a preservationist discourse with questions of modern colonial architecture
is evident throughout this essay, which argues that "the simple house of local
architecture . . . born in the same locus, offers an exemplary and characteristic example of how one can construct in North Africa."[53] The bases for this
suitability were multiple, the first being the visual effect of these indigenous
constructions. There was also a typological basis for the appropriation of the
Arab house, which was organized around an outdoor courtyard. Moreover, the
courtyard was understood as an important means by which these local constructions accommodated the climatic demands of the North African environment, a
concern that was evident in the contrast between the utilization of verandahs or
covered spaces and ample greenery within this interior space, and the restricted
use of openings in relatively mute exterior walls. In concluding this essay,
Rava makes the connection between modernity of the "simple linear and cubic
combinations" and "smooth and bare walls" of these vernacular sources and
the problem of a contemporary architecture, quite clearly stating that "it will
be simple to fuse all of the technical specialization and practical comfort of the
most modern European constructions with the local characteristics."[54]

Another important factor in establishing the direction for a modern colonial
architecture was Limongelli's attempt to open architectural discourse in Libya to
the influences of contemporary architecture in Italy. His contribution included the
appointment of Marcello Piacentini to design the *Riunione Adriatica di Sicurtà* in
Tripoli and, along with the much younger Luigi Piccinato, the Berenice Theater
in Benghazi—a project that began at virtually the same time as his appointment
to the municipality. Like the work of Limongelli, this last project exemplifies the
adaptation of a modern neoclassical language to the environmental context of
North Africa (fig. 5.17). Limongelli was also active in creating a context in which
young Italian architects, and in particular Rationalist ones, could participate.
The work of these architects was initially brought to Libya through Limongelli's

Fig. 5.17. Berenice Theater in Benghazi (begun 1928), by Marcello Piacentini and Luigi Piccinato.

organization of a number of national competitions for the design of public projects. The most significant of these was a proposal for the Piazza della Cattedrale in Tripoli. This national competition was organized by the municipality of Tripoli and the Ministry of the Colonies and called for the design of three buildings that would form the remaining sides of the existing public space in front of the neo-Romanesque cathedral of San Cuore di Gesù (1923-28) designed by Saffo Panteri.[55]

Originally due in January of 1930, the jury ruled the results of the competition inconclusive despite giving four awards of merit, and reopened it with a submission date in December of the same year. The second competition, though similar in scope, was more explicit in its desires. Its announcement in *Architettura e Arti Decorative* called for a "fusion of the local architectonic character with that of our artistic tradition."[56] The first prize was awarded to the *Pentagono Group*—a group of Milanese architects headed by Mario Lombardi whose project was described by the jury as "an architectural ensemble expressively and monumentally inspired by the Roman tradition" (fig. 5.18).[57] One of three second-prize winners was the scheme of *Gruppo Sette* member Adalberto Libera. In this case, the jury stated that of the awarded submissions, only this project was modern in its approach through its preoccupation with "harmonizing the new architecture with that of the old city, but without repeating its folkloric motifs" (fig. 5.19).[58]

Despite the fact that the winning scheme for the Piazza della Cattedrale competition was strongly influenced by Italy's Roman tradition, the acknowledgment of Libera's project by a jury composed of powerful and well-established officials like Undersecretary of the Colonies Alessandro Lessona, Roman Director of Antiquities and Fine Arts Roberto Paribeni, and architect Vincenzo Fasolo, delegate of the National Syndicate of Fascist Architects, is an indication of the transformation that was taking place within architectural culture in Italy's colonies. It was during this same time that the master plans of Tripoli and Benghazi were taken up by the Milanese architects Alpago Novello, Cabiati, and Ferrazza—proposals that clearly advanced the cause of modern architecture at an urban scale. Equally significant to the development of architectural discourse in Libya was the arrival of two young Italian architects, Umberto Di Segni and Giovanni Pellegrini, who began an extended period of work for the municipality of Tripoli. During the course of the 1930s, these two architects were able to execute numerous public buildings through the Public Works office—including many of the agricultural villages constructed to support the official policy of demographic colonization.[59]

The emergence of a discourse for a modern colonial architecture had a quite direct influence on tourist architecture in Libya through Limongelli's own design for the Grand Hotel at the Excavations in Cyrene, which was proposed in 1930 and completed after his premature death in 1932.[60] This project provided accom-

Fig. 5.18. Proposal for the competition for Piazza della Cattedrale in Tripoli (1930), by the Pentagono Group (Natale Morandi, Mario Lombardi, Giambattista Cosmacini, Alberto del Corno, Oddone Cavallini and Dante Alziati).

modation and tourist facilities for travelers to the adjacent fourth-century B.C. Roman archeological site of Cyrene—which was among the most desirable tourist destinations in Libya. This building responded to the demands of tourist visits to this archeological site by providing for a combination of day travelers and overnight guests.[61] In the first case, the ground floor of the project was largely given over to a large restaurant, offering meals to these casual tourists in a classically inspired modern interior. The upper floor of the building was given over to more permanent travelers, who were provided with first-class accommodation in thirty rooms with shared baths that provided hot and cold running water. These modern amenities were quite directly related to the function of the building as an introduction to the adjacent archeological site. The water in the building was taken from the font of Apollo, a feature that was duly noted in the tourist literature as being "the best in all of Cyrenaica."[62] Another striking feature of the project in relation to the tourist demands of the archeological site was its location on a large plateau that overlooked the necropolis, the sanctuary of Apollo, and the Mediterranean sea. The front facade of the building responded to this spectacular location

Fig. 5.19. Proposal for the competition for Piazza della Cattedrale in Tripoli (1930), by Adalberto Libera.

Fig. 5.20. Main facade of the Grand Hotel at the Excavations in Cyrene (1932), by Alessandro Limongelli.

Fig. 5.21. Rear facade view of the Grand Hotel at the Excavations in Cyrene.

through creating a large covered terrace that overlooked this view of the ancient site of Cyrene (fig. 5.20).

The design of the Grand Hotel at the Excavations in Cyrene harmonized with the indigenous constructions of the local environment, although it did so through a vocabulary that is closely linked with Roman precedents. While the simplicity of its massing shows an affinity for the unadorned cubic volumes of the indigenous architecture found in Libya, the scale of the project and its formal arrangements are more closely allied with the *romanità*

that is characteristic of the work of Limongelli in Libya.[63] The
fusion of a modern interpretation of the local architecture with
a classical language is most evident in the difference between
the two main faces of the building. The simple cubic massing of
the rear facade shows a great affinity with indigenous architecture, while the facade that faces the archeological site presents a
more clearly monumental scale (fig. 5.21). In the case of the main
facade, the two-story columns that frame the covered terrace and
the more prominent central bay give the project a classical rhythm
that responds to the need of the building to provide an introduction to the archeological site for the foreign traveler. At the same
time, a subtle reference to the indigenous architecture is evident
in the small tower that recalls the minarets that are found on
the more modest examples of religious architecture and in the
scale and relief brought to the main facade by the covered terrace
spaces that face the Mediterranean. These vernacular themes are
more fully explored in the central atrium space in the interior,
whose simple geometries, though based on Roman precedent, can
also be related to indigenous forms (fig. 5.22).

The *romanità* of the Grand Hotel at the Excavations by Limongelli, unlike that employed by the architect Brasini, was more
than a rhetorical statement of the Italian legacy in the region and
the need to recapture that legacy. It prepared the foreign traveler
for the experience of the classical ruins that they were about to
explore. At the same time, the use of classicism by Limongelli was
not absolute. Like the majority of the late projects of this architect,
the modern classicism of the hotel is tempered by an understanding of the indigenous architecture of the region. Within the
realm of the tourist infrastructure, the project was the first signifi-

*Fig. 5.22. Atrium of
the Grand Hotel at
the Excavations in
Cyrene.*

cant example of an architect using the hotel to engage foreign visitors with the surrounding environment and culture. It is also one of the first signs of modernity in the tourist architecture—a modernity that would become the norm for almost all of the tourist projects constructed during the early 1930s.

THE *MEDITERRANEITÀ* OF LIBYAN ARCHITECTURE

The most significant contribution to the discourse on a modern colonial architecture in Libya was provided by the writings and projects of Carlo Enrico Rava. The essays he published in *Domus* magazine in 1931 provide a relatively heterogeneous reading of the local architecture, arguing that it was the product of a complex exchange of influences. He notes that during what he called the Maghreb Middle Ages, this exchange took the form of "a continual movement of ebb and tide between the always vital Roman-Byzantine traditions" and "the new primitive but vigorous constructions of the black populations of the Sudan."[64] He illustrates the first of these sources with a discussion of the Berber castle at Qasr

Fig. 5.23. Photograph of the castle of Qasr al-Hajj (February 1930), by Carlo Enrico Rava, published in "Di un'architettura coloniale moderna – parte prima," Domus (May 1931).

al-Hajj, whose circular arrangement, he argued, derived from the Roman amphi-
theaters whose monumental ruins still existed along the Mediterranean coast
(fig. 5.23). For Rava, the impression of the Sahara and the Sudan was evident
in constructions like the ancient citadel at Mizdah, which he connected to the
villages discovered by the Seabrook expedition southeast of Timbuktu. The most
compelling repository for the interaction between Roman and African influences
were, according to Rava, the settlements constructed by the Berber populations
of the pre-Saharan regions of Libya. In fact, he argued that it was "through the
long narrow alliance of the Byzantine principles of the coast with the Berber
principles of the Jabal (mountain) against the Arab invader, that the primitive Berber architecture was transfused with numerous elements of Roman
derivation, elements which the Berbers, in their turn, then passed on to the
Arab-Libyan architecture, in which they are still today evident and viable."[65]

The most concrete example offered in this essay was the city of Ghadames,
whose status as one of the most important stopping points along the caravan
routes from the heart of Africa to the Mediterranean was a metaphor for the
interaction between Roman and African sources.[66] Rava stated that, like the
city itself, the architecture of Ghadames "has also been a place of transition and
exchange between the forms of *latinità* and those of Saharan-Sudanese Africa."[67]
Although he notes that the Sudanese stylistic characteristics were most evident
in the crenellated towers of its houses, he also describes the central mosque of
Ghadames as a "bewildering example of Byzantine penetration."[68] In summarizing this general discussion, Rava notes there was a more recent, but no less
important, influence on the indigenous architecture in Libya. He argued that
during the period of its domination by Ottoman governors, the introduction of
wooden loggias and roof terraces into the patio of the Arab house led to a reinterpretation of this essentially Roman source that adapted it to the necessities
of the African and Mediterranean climate, a contribution that was presented as
an architectural corollary to the colonial status of this region.[69]

In concluding this first essay, Rava provided a synthetic summary of what
he regarded to be the principal qualities that made Libyan architecture a suitable model for a modern colonial architecture. The first of these was its Roman
influence; however, rather than an archaeological or stylistic connection to this
classical tradition, he was interested in the "practical and organizing spirit of
Rome" that was "still very vital in the scheme of the Arab-Turkish house."[70] For
Rava, the rationality of this indigenous source had to do with both its derivation
from a Roman precedent and its correspondence with the functional and climatic
demands of the colonial context. A second quality that he identified in Libyan
architecture was what he described as "the impulse of a vigorous primitivism
that . . . derives from its relations with the populations of the South."[71] This
tendency could be traced in the use of simple geometric forms in buildings like
the mosque in Qasr al-Hajj, a building whose cubic massing and spherical and
pyramidal roof features were linked to the abstract works of Russian construc-
tivism (fig. 5.24). The final characteristic Rava identifies in the indigenous
architecture of this region was what he described as the "composition of blank
rhythms of cubes and parallelepipeds—opposing the cool shade of the patio with
the sun and the blue of the large superimposed and alternating verandahs and

Fig. 5.24 . Photograph of the mosque of Qasr al-Hajj (February 1930), by Carlo Enrico Rava, published in "Di un'architettura coloniale moderna – parte prima," Domus (May 1931).

roof terraces."[72] These qualities, which he argued could be found in the simplest Arab house in the oasis of Tripoli, linked these sources to the indigenous architecture of the Italian Mediterranean (fig. 5.25).

After defining the primary characteristics of Libyan monumental and domestic architecture in "Di un'architettura coloniale moderna– Parte prima," Rava dedicates the second part to establishing a direction for the architecture of Libya. After noting that almost everything that was constructed by Italy in these territories was not colonial architecture, Rava proceeds to offer some suggestions through a discussion of the architecture of North America and that of British colonialism. In the first case, he argues that the domestic buildings of California, "with their cubic masses and their white walls, and their wooden loggias and balconies," would be perfectly at home in Libya.[73] According to Rava, a similar formal solution was provided by the bungalow, which the British used as an almost universal type to house the metropolitan populations in the colonies. He then connects this contemporary colonial architecture with the indigenous architecture of Libya, comparing the wooden pergola of the Cutting house in Los Angeles by Garvin Hodson with the garden pavilion from the villa of Hassan Pasha near Tripoli. For Rava, all of these structures were "incredibly rational" in relation to their solution to the problem of the colonial environment.[74]

Fig. 5.25. Photo-
graph of an Arab
house in the
oasis of Tripoli
(December 1929),
by Carlo Enrico
Rava, published in
"Di un'architettura
coloniale moderna
– parte seconda,"
Domus (June 1931).

This inquiry into the contemporary value of Libyan architecture
was not just closely tied to modern architectural discourse, its very
means of analysis was also modern. It was through the detached
mode of encounter of the metropolitan traveler in the colonies and
the lens of the camera that this "indigenous architecture" was
appropriated and eventually deployed. The primitivism of the pure
geometries of the cubic, spherical, and pyramidal forms of the
mosque of Qasr al-Hajj was not so much present in the original
structure as it was crystallized in its image, which was already
determined by a modern photographic aesthetic.[75] Moreover, terms
like primitivism that informed Rava's analysis of the Libyan
architecture were similarly a product of modern modes of cultural
inquiry. Through an emerging body of research, the Libyan people
were constructed as a "primitive" society that could be understood
through a direct reading of their customs and cultural artifacts. The
empiricism of this scientific project was the almost universal basis
by which the indigenous culture of Libya was examined by Italian
scholars. It also formed an important backdrop against which
writers like Rava formulated their own subjective views of this
culture.

The interpretation of Libyan architecture offered by Rava in
"Di un'architettura coloniale moderna" was also derived from and
participated in a specifically political discourse. It was the theoretical manifestation within architectural discourse of a Fascist
politics which asserted that Libya "was Roman and returns to
Rome."[76] In a similar manner, in asserting the fundamentally
Roman basis for the indigenous architecture, Rava was defining
the identity of this architecture as the inevitable product of this
past colonialism. His *mediterraneità* was not only deploying the
kind of imperialist rhetoric typical to Fascist Italy, it was constituting an imperialist project by claiming the indigenous identity
of this architecture as Italian. Despite the genuine interest in the

Libyan architecture that these arguments illustrate, the writings of Rava represent a fundamental erasure of the Arab identity of this architecture in favor of emphasizing its *latinità* and *mediterraneità*—qualities that explicitly link these indigenous sources with Italian Mediterranean culture. In deference to the political demands of the colonial context, Rava asserted that this gesture of incorporation was not aimed at adopting the "characteristic architecture of the conquered populations." Rava alludes to this ambivalence in concluding this essay, stating that "we are not at all inspired . . . by an Arab architecture, but we recover, through it, the undying traces of the *latinità* of an architecture that is, first of all, profoundly Mediterranean."[77]

The discourse on a modern colonial architecture based on indigenous Mediterranean sources had a quite direct influence on the professional work of Larco and Rava, like their submission to the first competition for the restructuring of the area around Piazza della Cattedrale. Despite the fact that this project was not awarded

Fig. 5.26. Proposal for the competition for Piazza della Cattedrale in Tripoli (1930), by Sebastiano Larco and Carlo Enrico Rava.

first prize, it was the only submission from the first competition published in *Architettura e Arti Decorative.*[78] In this essay of August 1930, the project was praised for its utilization of the modern planning criterion found in the grouping of apartments around common staircases. This proposal was also commended for its attention to the necessities of the North African climate, which was evidenced in the creation of ample covered terraces that allowed for proper ventilation of the apartments. In summarizing its evaluation of this project, the author states, "The rationality of the forms is not cool or absolute, and appears tempered by their combination . . . with Tripolitanian and Mediterranean stylistic elements."[79] The assimilation of indigenous forms is particularly evident in the towers that mark the corner of the new piazza, which are derivative of the native architecture of the town of Ghadames (fig. 5.26). Notably, these observations are entirely coincident with Rava's own evaluation of this project. In a letter sent to the critic Roberto Papini in March of 1930, he describes this project as "a *fusion* of the most modern and rational exigencies, with the local character and *colonial* demands." He goes on to state, "This work (which is one of my favorites) perhaps indicates the moment of an important evolution in my architecture."[80]

Rava's interest in combining a modern rational architecture with references to the indigenous architecture of Libya was also explored through one of his tourist projects, the Hotel at the Excavations of Leptis Magna in al-Khums—a project whose drawings were exhibited at the first exhibition of Rationalist architecture in 1928 (fig. 5.27). That the architecture of tourism in Libya participated in such an important way in the discourse for a modern Italian architecture was a product of the fact that there was a close fit between the demands of tourist architecture and the ideological program of Rava's early Rationalist arguments. The need for tourist architecture to respond to modern exigencies while also relating to the local culture was mirrored in the polemics of the *Gruppo Sette*. In the first manifesto, which was written primarily by Rava, these architects were concerned with both creating an architecture of logic and rationality and recognizing the inevitably national dimension of Italian architecture. This last aspect was clearly asserted by Rava in this manifesto in the statement "There is no incompatibility between our past and our present. We do not want to break with tradition, it is tradition that transforms itself and assumes new aspects."[81] The attempt to negotiate the relationship between the aesthetics of simplicity and renunciation of the "new spirit" and the classical foundation of "the spirit of tradition" characterizes both the Rationalist writings of Rava and the tourist architecture of the hotel project in al-Khums.

The connection between the Hotel at the Excavations of Leptis Magna and the principles of Italian Rationalism was recognized upon its publication in *Architettura e Arti Decorative* in 1931. This article argues that this project was a direct derivation of "the most sane and acceptable" rationalist principles— that is: "pure architectonic constructivity and functionality" and "the total and exclusive response of the external expression to the internal organism."[82] Other attributes of this project that this essay associated with Italian Rationalist architecture include a "unity, compactness and continuity of masses"; a "cubicness of volumes, perpendicularity of planes, and longitudinality and rectilinearity of profiles"; and "the abandonment of pleonastic and pseudo-

Fig. 5.27. Preliminary drawings for the Hotel at the Excavations of Leptis Magna in al-Khums (1928), by Sebastiano Larco and Carlo Enrico Rava.

constructive structuring elements."[83] Several of the photographs that accompanied this article emphasize these qualities through closely cropped images that bring out the abstract geometric qualities of the project (fig. 5.28).

The independence of the hotel at Leptis Magna from these same Rationalist principles was understood as a deliberate attempt on the part of Larco and Rava to not follow what was considered the new rhetoric in architecture. The authors of the project were deemed to have "soundly avoided the application of some characteristic manners of modern international architecture

Fig. 5.28. Side view of the Hotel at the Excavations of Leptis Magna in al-Khums (completed 1931).

in their hotel."[84] Rather, so this article argues, the project was "completely contextualized to a Mediterranean country"—having "conserved in the voids the sense of proportion typical to the houses of Libya."[85] An article on the project in *Domus* magazine recognizes this same acclimatization to the Libyan environment— a quality which it associates with, among other elements, the large verandah that faced the Mediterranean.[86] The visual presentation of both of these articles emphasizes the environmental quality of the hotel at Leptis Magna through images that present it within its larger context and focus on particular spaces that were understood as being conceived according to the particularities of the Libyan climate and this building's seafront location.

The project of Larco and Rava was credited with the same selectivity that Rava himself had argued was necessary to create a more independent direction for Italian Rationalism. The Hotel at the Excavations of Leptis Magna, designed in 1928, would thus seem to have had a direct influence on the theoretical position that Rava later published in *Domus*. That is, this project was "rational but Italian, modern but colonial"—a fusion of the theoretical, formal, and technical concerns typical to Italian Rationalism with abstract typological, climatic, and aesthetic references to the vernacular architecture of the coastal regions of Libya.[87] A closer examination of the plan of this project would seem to support this double reading, as it illustrates a clear and logical organization of the program, and is indicative of a broader typological reference to Libyan vernacular architecture (fig. 5.29).

Constructed to cater to the tourist interest in the archeological site at Leptis Magna, this project had to accommodate both larger groups of tourists who would be visiting the site on day trips and a smaller number of people who would remain overnight. The ground floor is organized around a central covered courtyard that links a series of large public rooms, with their own entrance facing the oasis of al-Khums and the archeological site. Diagonally opposite the entrance is the area on the ground floor dedicated to the residents—its orientation being toward the Mediterranean—a space which then connects to a second level that contains all of the hotel rooms.[88] As well as providing the point of intersection between these two distinct audiences, the courtyard was intended to refer to the vernacular tradition of the so-called Arab house of this region. This indigenous source was, for Rava, both derived from Roman origins and reflected the modern exigencies where, as he argued in "Di un'architettura coloniale moderna": "The conditions of nature and climate are . . . the generators of architectonic form."[89]

The three-dimensional development of this project follows directly from the logic of its plan—the diagonal relationship of the plan manifesting itself in the asymmetrical massing of the higher block related to the seafront. The frontality of the building to the Mediterranean is reinforced by the large covered verandah, which also acts as a terrace for the hotel rooms on the upper floor (fig. 5.30). The facades of the project largely reflect the influence

Fig. 5.29. Floor plans of the Hotel at the Excavations of Leptis Magna in al-Khums.

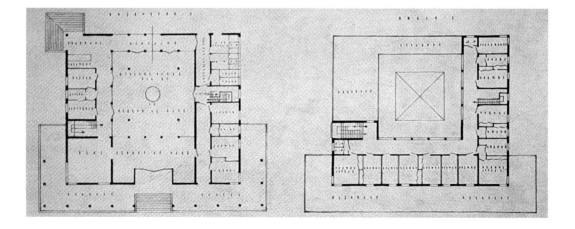

Fig. 5.30. Seafront view of the Hotel at the Excavations of Leptis Magna in al-Khums.

of Rationalist architecture through their direct mapping of the function of the interior spaces onto the exterior surface, as is particularly evident in the spacing of the windows on the main facade. The relatively blank nature of the surfaces and the variable nature of its massing—which terraces down away from the seafront—seem intended to suggest vernacular constructions (fig. 5.31). Other gestures, which included the large verandah and a system of brightly colored canvas panels that allowed for various exterior spaces to be protected from the sun and the wind, integrate this project with its immediate context and the demands of the Libyan environment.[90]

Despite all of its attempts to relate to its North African context, the Hotel at the Excavations of Leptis Magna was inextricably linked to architectural discourse in Italy. It was designed and constructed during a period when that discourse was operative in the field of tourism, but the temporary nature of this relationship can be measured, at least in part, by the fact that it was among the first buildings to be renovated by Balbo in 1934 due to the irrationality of what was called its "Nordic character."[91] Ultimately, this project participated in the tourist discourse as much through the experience of Rava himself as a traveler— through the process of abstraction through which he viewed and appropriated the indigenous architecture of Libya—as through its detailed consideration of tourist demands. While clearly attempting to contextualize his projects with the local environment and culture, the *mediterraneità* of Rava effectively erased the Arab content of the Libyan vernacular. Like his "Panorama of Rationalism," the Hotel at the Excavations of Leptis Magna was the product of an attempt to incorporate the local architecture

Fig. 5.31. View from the oasis of the Hotel at the Excavations of Leptis Magna in al-Khums.

into a broader, supra-regional expression—an expression that was, in its essence, already Italian.

The tourist projects of Larco and Rava and Limongelli reveal the fact that the contemporary architectural discourse in Italy—which was a discourse of a modernism seeking a specifically Italian identity—was beginning to influence tourist architecture in Libya. However, the support for modernism as the official language of the tourist system was neither unanimous nor long-lasting. A memorandum on the subject of colonial tourism sent to Mussolini in November 1931 by Tourism Commissioner Fulvio Suvich was preoccupied with the problem of local culture, and the perceived loss of it due to "the ugly constructions of European character"—something that underscores the indifference with which modern architecture was viewed in the colonial context.[92]

Notwithstanding the criticism of the use of a modern architectural language by such an important government official, the Hotel at the Excavations of Leptis Magna responded to the emerging demands of the tourist system. On the one hand, it is a product of the need for this architecture to project an image of civilization and modern comfort that would be familiar to a metropolitan audience. On the other, references to the indigenous constructions of this region satisfied a desire to link the tourist infrastructure to its context. This project is also a powerful demonstration of the political ambivalence of colonial politics being mapped onto the architecture of tourism. Rather than an eclectic reinterpretation or literal reconstruction, the Hotel at the Excavations by Larco and Rava produces a sort of fusion of indigenous Libyan architecture with a quintessentially modern language. The project is, at once, indigenous and modern, local and supra-regional. But is this, in fact, possible? It would seem that the incorporation of indigenous references into an architecture designed to host European tourists in Libya would destroy both the authenticity of the indigenous sources and the integrity of the language of modern Italian architecture.

**CHAPTER
SIX**

IN SEARCH OF A
REGIONALIST EXPRESSION

*Architectonic forms vary in their relation to the peculiar condi-
tions of the historical moment and the spiritual conditions of
each population, but nothing takes away from the influence of
the climate and the action that the sacred and fatal basin of
the Mediterranean exercises, everywhere—cradle and crucible
of the highest human civilization. Working on the coast or on
the Mediterranean islands, I felt these traditions revive in me
and passed on the necessity of respecting them to my buildings.—Florestano Di Fausto, "Visione mediterranea della mia
architettura," 1937.*[1]

*Fig. 6.1. Photograph
of an isolated house
in Tripoli (1936), by
Giovanni Pellegrini.*

In an article published in *Libia* magazine, architect Florestano
Di Fausto speaks of his approach to an architecture for Italy's
Mediterranean colonies—an architecture that he asserts had
always been, and should continue to be, based on a careful
reading of the local architecture. In an impassioned discussion
of the sizable body of works that he constructed throughout this
region—in Italy, Rhodes, Kos, as well as in Libya—he emphasizes
the deliberate and studied process of design by which he developed a reciprocal relationship between these projects and their
historical and environmental context. The "Visione mediterranea"
of Di Fausto—which calls for a relatively direct appropriation of
indigenous forms—is in strong contrast with the approach prof-

fered by Carlo Enrico Rava and other Rationalist architects working in Libya in the early 1930s. While similarly inspired by the native architecture, these architects proposed an abstract process of assimilation of indigenous references. They suggested that the typological approach to the environment found in these local constructions provided the basis for a rational solution to the problem of a modern Fascist architecture in the colonial context.

The transformation of the discourse on modern colonial architecture found in the writings of architects like Di Fausto was largely the result of new political exigencies. Following the Italian invasion of Ethiopia, the emphasis of the Fascist government shifted to its territories in East Africa. These colonies were the most recent trophies of Italian imperialism, and as such they enjoyed a more substantial financial commitment from the Fascist government.[2] A major part of this investment was made in the rapid development of the urban infrastructure. In order to facilitate this effort, the Ministry of the Colonies created the Central Council for Architecture and Urbanism in November of 1936, a group whose primary task was the approval of master plans for the new Fascist cities in East Africa.[3] The attention of Italian architects and engineers was thus directed to the issue of colonial planning, an emphasis that is registered in the prominence of this theme at the first National Congress of Urbanism, held in Rome in April of 1937. The importance of this subject was noted in final declarations at the conclusion of this conference, which affirmed "the necessity and urgency of the integral and unitary urban planning of Italian East Africa."[4]

In part owing to the imperial rhetoric generated by the conquest of the East African colonies, the indigenous politics of Libya under Italo Balbo took on a more authoritarian tone.[5] Under the weight of these increasingly racially encoded colonial politics, the theories of Rava on the contemporary value of Libyan architecture—in which various indigenous, Mediterranean and Latin influences interacted—gave way to a number of considerably more narrow readings. One of these, theorized by Giovanni Pellegrini, was a continuation of the arguments of Rava, although in a more limited form. His theoretical writings instrumentalized the indigenous architecture of Libya in relation to an already existing vocabulary of modern forms, creating an architecture determined almost exclusively by technical and climatic demands.[6] A second and far more influential direction was established by the work and writings of Di Fausto, who called for a direct incorporation of indigenous sources and led to an architecture that reenacted these historical forms. In his position as municipal architect and member of the Building Commission founded by Balbo, this architect established the direction for much of the public architecture in Libya during the latter part of the 1930s.

In comparison to the Rationalist views of Rava, Di Fausto offers a geographical and climatic argument about the characteristic qualities of architecture within the Mediterranean basin. In so doing, he was making a cultural and historical assertion of the primacy of this region which "seems in its beat to almost be confused with the heartbeat of the world."[7] This argument is not without its imperialist overtones. In discussing the indigenous architecture of Libya, Di Fausto claims that "architecture was born in the Mediterranean and triumphed in Rome in the eternal monuments created from the genius of our birth: it must, therefore, remain Mediterranean and Italian."[8] In examining his various projects in the region, Di Fausto speaks about a careful process of design, where the "spirit of the place" informed his every move. This is an approach to architecture, suggestive of the *ambientismo* of Gustavo Giovannoni, in which a mutually reinforcing relationship is developed between a building and its context—a relationship in which Di Fausto suggests "even the most humble houses . . . now speak, and their words respond in harmony to the new edifices erected by me."[9]

The distinctive qualities of Di Fausto's argument can be found in his assertion that a contemporary architecture could be grounded in its physical context and related to a set of historical building traditions without losing its sense of modernity. While the relationship to the indigenous architecture was one of direct incorporation, he argued that in so doing the artist is ultimately interested in what he called the "continuity between yesterday and tomorrow."[10] Seen in this way, his architecture was a mediation between innovation and imitation, between modernity and tradition—an approach that he regarded as outside of the current tendencies in architectural discourse. Freely employing historical forms like the arch, Di Fausto argued that his projects were based on "the fundamental character of clarity and structural organicity, of sobriety and simplicity of form, of perfect adhesion to function."[11]

This was a theoretical approach to colonial architecture that called for the direct incorporation and synthesis of local references into a contemporary architectural expression, a formulation that was related to the indigenous politics of the Balbo era and, accordingly, was amenable to and determined by the tourist demands for the preservation of indigenous culture. The theoretical position of Di Fausto, which proposed a more literal relationship to the native architecture, was, however, no less problematic with respect to its Arab identity than that offered by the architects of Italian Rationalism, who evinced an abstract and typological connection to these local forms. In the work of Di Fausto, the Arab identity of the Libyan vernacular became merely one of a series of possible regional manifestations of a larger geographical concept. Through a direct incorporation of the traditional architecture of North Africa, this identity was reenacted in his projects, through an eclectic architectural vocabulary, for the purposes of its harmonizing with the spirit of the place.

The writings of Di Fausto indicate that a complex understanding of the Libyan architecture as theorized in the writings of Carlo Enrico Rava was lost or abandoned in the late 1930s. Under the weight of Italian imperial politics, a more sophisticated interest in indigenous Libyan architecture was displaced to the margins. Notably, after 1935 the interest in indigenous forms in the design of a contemporary architecture was the object of some criticism. In an essay entitled "Orientamenti della moderna architettura italiana in Libia," Ottavio Cabiati singles out the work of Rationalist architect Giovanni Pellegrini, noting that "the continuing attempt to derive lessons from what the Arabs, Berbers and Saharans have made and are making is almost folkloristic" (fig. 6.1).[12] In pursuing a more general Mediterranean character, the most significant public buildings in Libya were left to be constructed in a Fascist-inspired colonial style. The theoretical trajectory that had been initiated by Rava had dissipated in favor of a narrower reading of the indigenous architecture. This approach, however, was no less modern, as the preservationist view of indigenous forms in Di Fausto's writings was supported by an equally modern set of premises—that of the emerging discourse on the study of native culture.

This kind of "scientific" interpretation of Libyan architecture was advanced in contemporary scholarly discourse in essays like Fabrizio Maria Apollonj's "L'architettura araba della Libia," which was published in *Rassegna di Architettura* in December 1937. In discussing the monumental architecture of Libya, Apollonj argues that it "appears induced by a thousand influences" that allowed it to "reach very picturesque effects and also sometimes of notable beauty."[13] However, the multiplicity of its sources was ultimately viewed as a sign of weakness rather than a sign of strength and, as such, Libyan monumental architecture was deemed to be of a lesser importance than the Western tradition. In examining the vernacular architecture, Apollonj finds some positive qualities, observing that "this minor architecture, precisely for its purity of art springing from within the land and the people, gives us with inexpressible vividness the sense of exoticism and picturesqueness that our avid Western sensibility asks of Tripolitania."[14] At the same time, he specifically rejects the idea that such buildings should inspire a contemporary colonial architecture, stating that "it may be absurd to attempt to resolve the problem of modern colonial architecture in Libya by means of a plain and simplistic utilization of local motifs."[15] The connection between these views and the indigenous politics of the Italian colonial authorities is particularly apparent in a passage where Apollonj draws an analogy between the indigenous architecture in Libya, which he describes as having "a primitivism, frank and free of any real artistic consistency," and the Libyan people, whom he characterizes as "a poor and static population" (fig. 6.2).[16]

The reading of architecture as the direct expression of a people and its culture was closely tied to contemporary research into the culture of the Libyan populations by anthropologists and ethnographers like Emilio Scarin. His book, *L'insediamento umano nella Libia occidentale* (1940), was the culmination of a program of research on the housing and patterns of living in western Libya that began as early as the first Congress of Colonial Studies in 1931.[17] One of the important subjects of research to Scarin and others was the so-called Troglodyte houses of the Gharyan and Jabal regions, which were seen to be an authentic repository of the primitive customs and practices of the local populations. Notably, it was for this same reason that these houses were one of the more desirable tourist sites. However, this apparently neutral and scientific reading of the Libyan people through their cultural artifacts must be understood as having significant political connotations specific to Fascist Italy in the late 1930s. This connection is clearly apparent in an essay by anthropologist Lidio Cipriani entitled "Razzismo e possessi coloniali," which argues that "the racist doctrine permits us to say the truth without hypocrisy: Europeans dominate in Africa because they have the duty and the right to do so."[18]

Seen in the context of racist arguments offered by authors like Lidio Cipriani, the theories and works of Florestano Di Fausto represent a decisive shift in the discourse on a modern colonial architecture. By pursuing a direct

A sinistra: 1) Pozzo arabo - In centro e a destra: 2-3) Marabutti nei dintorni di Tripoli

L'architettura indigena costituisce la nota più caratteristica del paesaggio tripolitano, quella che lo differenzia da molte altre regioni, pur simili per struttura geologica e per flora. Essa rappresenta il fatto umano ed etnico, ambientato e tuttavia essenzialmente diverso, che dà risalto e pieno valore alle bellezze dell'oasi

L'ARCHITETTURA ARABA DELLA LIBIA

Fra i fattori che contribuiscono a conferire una sua caratteristica fisionomia alla Tripolitania uno dei più importanti è certamente l'architettura indigena. Il paesaggio libico è naturalmente essenziale a tal fine; la splendida feracità delle oasi, gli aspetti orridi o idillici del Gebel, la desolazione della Hammada, della Ramla e del Serir, costituiscono delle visioni indimenticabili. Tuttavia, nelle sue manifestazioni di vita e in particolare nella regione costiera, la natura della Libia non differisce essenzialmente da quella italica, che anzi è spesso richiamata alla memoria da molti aspetti della Gefàra e del Gébel e sembra quasi continuarsi in essi al di là del Mediterraneo. D'altra parte lo squallore dei deserti è un elemento in sè negativo e non può perciò costituire da solo il volto della nostra colonia. Di questo sono anche un fattore decisivo gli indigeni stessi nelle loro varietà etniche: Arabi, Berberi, Tuaregh, Fezzanesi; la loro stessa apparenza, i loro modi di vita, le loro tradizioni storiche e religiose ci danno la sensazione vivida e immediata della diversità di questa terra dalla Madre Patria e ce ne fanno comprendere lo spirito e l'essenza meglio di qualunque visione di paesaggi, per quanto prolungata e attenta.

Tuttavia, al di sopra del paesaggio e delle popolazioni, sono le manifestazioni architettoniche che assumono addirittura il valore di simboli e che anche nel ricordo rimangono a rappresentare in modo indelebile la Tripolitania differenziandola da altre regioni africane e asiatiche. Ed è logico e naturale che sia così, per varie ragioni. In primo luogo l'architettura, che dovunque è fra tutte le arti quella che meglio esprime l'anima di un popolo e la sua vita storica e quotidiana, nei paesi di immigrazione araba, per la mancanza di ogni forma di pittura e di scultura che non sia decorativa, acquista un significato ancor più fondamentale. Inoltre è caratteristica particolare dell'architettura araba qui in Tripolitania, come si vedrà meglio più avanti, di essere intimamente intonata con l'ambiente climatico e paesistico, così da costituire una espressione e quasi una continuazione di esse. Infine gli edifici arabi sono complessivamente così lontani da noi quanto a spirito e a forme che non possono non impressionarci profondamente per il loro stesso valore esotico.

Così sarebbe addirittura impossibile scindere, nel pensiero, dalle costruzioni arabe che vi sorgono, il ricordo di quelle splendide oasi, della costa, che hanno fatto esclamare giustamente a Fazio degli Uberti: « La fama è chiara per queste contrade. Chè la terra vi è tanto buona e pingue. Che per un cento ne fruttan le biade ». Il rigoglio dei palmizi altissimi e diritti e degli ulivi vetusti, dei melograni verdi e vermigli e dei fichi d'India, delle floride culture di cereali, che fanno di questi orti, conclusi dalle « tàbie » di terra battuta, dei giardini dalle mille sfumature di verde, forma la naturale cornice della caratteristica casa araba dalle alte mura nude, dagli eleganti portali, e raccolta spesso con due o tre lati sul verde specchio d'acqua del serbatoio, posto a paro della veranda a mo' di piscina, e sormontato dall'inconfondibile sovrastruttura bianca del pozzo (Ill. 1).

È la casa che rivela la finalità familiare e intima del giardino e ne fa risaltare la freschezza; è il biancheggiare delle case disseminate nell'oasi che ci fa vedere quanto intensamente questa sia abitata e coltivata, richiamando alla nostra mente le città-giardino propugnate e attuate dall'urbanistica moderna. Similmente si può dire che sia impossibile ripensare alla ricchezza di motivi pittoreschi e folkloristici dell'oasi, senza riferirsi inconsciamente a qualcuno dei marabutti candidi e solitari che vi sorgono, ombreggiati dalle palme snelle, sormontati dai tipici voltoni e dalle cupole, spalleggiati a volte dai forti speroni, ingentiliti dai cortili sereni per l'armonia degli archi e delle colonne. Così la visione dell'indigeno, dignitosamente drappeggiato nel suo barracano, che camminando sulla soffice via sabbiosa dell'oasi vicino al suo asino carico di merci transita dinanzi alle case e ai marabutti (Ill. 3) o che indolente-

455

Fig. 6.2. Title page of essay, "L'Architettura araba della Libia," published by Fabrizio Maria Apollonj in Rassegna di Architettura (December 1937).

recourse to the indigenous architecture of Libya under the guise of creating an architectural regionalism, Di Fausto was not merely following the current tendency in Italian and French colonial architecture to carefully assimilate local references. The lack of any apparent process of abstraction of the original source in the projects would seem to give them the status of anthropological studies or works of historic preservation—where the Libyan people and their culture are removed from the temporal flow of the modern West. Indeed, no less so than the *mediterraneità* of Rava, the "Mediterranean vision" of Di Fausto constitutes a modernist and imperialist project. The buildings of this architect are modernist through their allegiance with contemporary scientific practices, while their imperialist allusions derive from their association with an indigenous politics that was increasingly coded according to racial difference. The search for a regionalist expression in Libya in the work of architects like Florestano Di Fausto found its own particular manifestation of an ambivalent modernism—an ambivalence that through its direct imitation of indigenous forms was linked to the modernity of historic preservation and the racially motivated politics of Fascist imperialism.

A MEDITERRANEAN VISION

The public architecture constructed in Libya during the governorship of Italo Balbo was directly influenced by his quite decisive intervention in the realm of architecture and planning. Of particular importance to the changing building politics was the formation of a commission charged with the responsibility to preside over all matters relating to building in the colony. The architectural approach that was favored by this commission was one that proffered a modern and Fascist aesthetic that was carefully integrated with Libya's Mediterranean (and thus Italian) context. The "Visione mediterranea" of Di Fausto, which called for the establishment of a reciprocal relationship between his buildings and their site, was the most important theoretical expression of this new political program—a connection that is attributable to the fact that he was the only prominent architect appointed to a commission dominated by members of various technical and administrative offices of the colonial government.[19]

In the major public projects of Di Fausto in Tripoli, the idea of a Mediterranean architecture was explored through a general urban character that was adjusted to fit with the indigenous forms and environmental demands of the context. The most significant of these built works was the eventual construction of his submission to the Piazza della Cattedrale competition of 1930. The original entry of Di Fausto, which was discarded by the jury, proposed a monumental portico in the building opposite the existing cathedral so as to induce a spatial movement that linked the piazza with the waterfront (fig. 6.3).[20] In a manner that is responsive to

Fig. 6.3. Proposal for the competition for Piazza della Cattedrale in Tripoli (1930), by Florestano Di Fausto.

Fig. 6.4. The Boulevard du IVᵃ Zouaves in Casablanca (1917-22), by Henri Prost.

the competition brief, the project created a setting that was both urban metropolitan and colonial through a symmetrical ordering of public space with a series of regularized and highly articulated building volumes. This urban colonialism has much in common with the development of Casablanca under Lyautey, whose grand boulevards were intended to give a more monumental scale to the redesign of this French colonial city (fig. 6.4).[21]

In its eventual realization as the offices of the National Insurance Institute, the project of Di Fausto creates a monumentality through the uniform and repetitive nature of its facades at the same time as deriving some of its scale and elements from local references—an approach that sets this project apart from the proposals of both the Pentagono Group and Rationalist architect Libera (fig. 6.5). The two elements that seem to refer to indigenous North African forms, the central portico and its flanking towers, serve to reinforce this monumentality by assuming the urban scale of the gesture of connecting this site to the seafront. Like a number of Di Fausto's public buildings realized in Tripoli, the project for the National Insurance Institute combines an urban-scaled neoclassicism and North African colonialism, thus expressing a general Mediterranean quality derived from vernacular constructions of the region. In so doing, this urban project by Di Fausto would seem to have been consciously referring to an already established architectural language—metropolitan colonial—that had itself become a regional style worthy of appropriation, with its own identity, its own historical development. As the preferred image for a public architecture in Libya, it was rightly recognized by the Italians and the Libyans as the architecture of colonialism.

Fig. 6.5. The
National Insurance
Institute in Tripoli
(1938), by Flores-
tano Di Fausto.

The tourist architecture constructed in Libya during this period
was closely related to this more general discourse for a colonial
architecture proper to Italy's Imperial and Mediterranean status.
This was, at least in part, due to the influence of the Libyan
Tourism and Hotel Association (ETAL), under whose scrutiny
the aesthetic appearance of the tourist system was given a more
decisive direction. Immediately following its formation, the group
assumed control of all the municipal and governmental hotels that
had been constructed up until that time.[22] In incorporating the
most recently constructed tourist facilities, it was able to offer a
coherent system through which the foreign traveler could experience the indigenous culture of Libya. Through a careful attention
to design in relation to the native architectural styles, the system
of hotels in Libya provided a continuous experience of "the native"
that was intended to act as an analogue to the actual experience of
the colonial landscape.

The creation of an organized tourist experience of indigenous culture, however, was not limited to Libya. A very similar
tourist system had already been realized in North Africa by the
Compagnie Générale Transatlantique. This steamship company
directed a coordinated system of tourist services in the French
colonies beginning around the end of World War I.[23] Although the
designs varied, a number of the hotels adopted the indigenous
architecture of the region in a very direct way. One of the best
examples of this tendency is the Hôtel de la Mamounia (1923)
in Marrakech, designed by the architects Henri Prost and A.
Marchisio. This project was located on the edge of the Mamounia,
a sumptuous sixteenth-century garden with olive and orange
groves that was located within the walls of the medina to the

immediate west of the famous twelfth-century Al Koutoubia mosque. The hotel was a veritable palace, providing luxury accommodation to the most wealthy travelers with a dining hall, a bar, and a large terrace with a swimming pool facing the garden.[24] The garden facade of the building shows its careful intonation with its immediate context, in addition to revealing the direct formal references to the palace architecture of Marrakech in elements like the twin-columned portico (figs. 6.6, 6.7). Notably, the same palaces were being documented in Jean Gallotti and Albert Laprade's *Le Jardin et la Maison Arabes au Maroc*, which was published in 1926.[25] The connection to these historic buildings is particularly apparent in the interior entrance hall, which provides a sophisticated re-enactment of the decorative wood interiors of the sixteenth-century palaces of Marrakech.

Fig. 6.6. The Hôtel de la Mamounia in Marrakech, Morocco (1923), by Henri Prost and A. Marchisio.

Fig. 6.7. Interior entry hall of the Hôtel de la Mamounia in Marrakech.

In responding to the characteristic aspects of the native culture of Libya, the hotel system of the ETAL and its related tourist attractions were divided into two distinct tourist experiences. The first was associated with the *strada litoranea* that linked up the Roman archeological sites like Leptis Magna and Cyrene with the major and minor population centers throughout the coastal region. In reporting on the recent accomplishments of the Balbo administration in favor of tourism in the journal *Rivista della Colonie*, this coastal network was described as constituting "a new splendid tourist itinerary of almost 2,000 kilometers from one border to the other of the colony"—an itinerary that was "adapted to the new demands created by the opening of this great artery."[26] The hotels and service centers were designed to provide a continuous system of amenities that would facilitate private automobile excursions—an independence that was until this time only possible in the metropole. The second tourist experience that was a feature of the ETAL system followed an itinerary that went south from Tripoli to the city of Ghadames. This route was presented in the tourist literature as "carrying the tourist through the desert zones on the edge of the Sahara, showing them all of the fascination of the African world."[27] Using the two largest cities of Tripoli and Benghazi as their base, the ETAL was able to offer excursions that visited all of the archeological sites along the Mediterranean and the Jabal plain and pre-Saharan region. The brochure that presents these itineraries for the 1936-37 tourist season shows the careful balance between conveying the Roman attractions of the coastal region and the mysteries of the Libyan interior (figs. 6.8, 6.9).

The Mediterranean segment of the tourist system in Libya included the two largest coastal cities, Tripoli and Benghazi, both of which enjoyed the most substantial and elaborate tourist amenities. Tripoli was well furnished with a variety of hotels, from the newly constructed luxury Uaddan (1935) and tourist-oriented Mehari (1935) to the Grand Hotel and more modest Hotel

Fig. 6.8. (Below) Cover of the brochure Escursioni nella Libia (Tripoli: Stabilmento Poligrafico P. Maggi, 1936), published by the Libyan Tourism and Hotel Association.

Fig. 6.9. (Right) Travel itineraries from the brochure Escursioni nella Libia (1936).

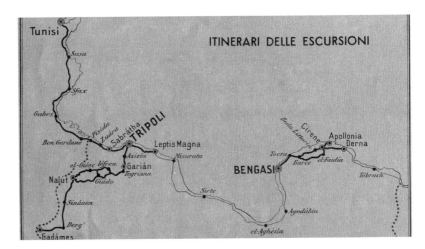

Fig. 6.10. Exterior view of the Hotel of the Gazelle in Zlitan (1935), designed by Umberto Di Segni.

Tripolitania. Benghazi, which was a slightly less desirable tourist destination, had the recently completed Hotel Berenice (1936). The other major attractions supervised by the ETAL in these two cities were the Uaddan Theater, Arab Café, Arena (Sharah al-Shatt), and beach facilities in Tripoli, and the Berenice Cinema and Theater, Italia Cinema, and beach facilities in Benghazi.[28] Most of the other key centers along the coast had hotels, from Zuwarah on the west to Tobruk on the east, which provided a continuous system of accommodation.[29] In the case of the major archeological sites in Libya, the ETAL system included the already constructed hotels at Leptis Magna and Cyrene, which accommodated the demands of travelers to these ancient sites.

The architectural language of the coastal system of attractions was largely related to the indigenous rural constructions of the Libyan countryside—a reference that was clearly aimed at reinforcing the Mediterranean character of the coastal region. One such example is municipal architect Umberto Di Segni's Hotel of the Gazelle in Zlitan, a project that was originally constructed in 1929 and substantially renovated in 1935. It was the smallest tourist facility in western Libya, offering a modest second-class accommodation with ten rooms and four baths.[30] The exterior of the building is described in the tourist literature as "creating new and original lines, at the same time inspired by the most nimble forms of Eastern art" (fig. 6.10).[31] The connection between this hotel and the indigenous constructions is evident in the combination of simple massing and applied wooden lattice work on the exterior terraces. These references reveal a relatively direct use of local forms—an approach that is clearly responsive to the contemporary tourist demands for an authentic experience. In contrast with such indigenous references, the interior of the hotel presents a more conventional and comfortable environment that is much closer to metropolitan precedents.[32]

A second example in the design of hotels along the Mediterranean coast is the Hotel Tobruk (1937), which was located at the entrance to the city with a picturesque view of the port. As the last stopping point before the Egyptian border, this hotel offered first-class accommodation with twenty rooms, most with private baths, a restaurant, tennis courts, and a garage for automobile travelers. In its publicity material, the Hotel Tobruk was described as a "simple, sober, but comfortable hotel," having the most modern furnishings and being fitted with an air-conditioning system to deal with the summer climate of Libya.[33] The exterior of the building provides an even more direct adaptation of the local architecture, the massing scheme and details of the exterior walls suggesting the monolithic quality of the battered earth construction found in Libya. In particular, the arches on the ground floor and the second-floor screened patio allude to a Mediterranean character that seems derived from the massive wall construction of the local architecture (fig. 6.11).

A very different tourist experience was to be found in the two hotels constructed in the city of Tripoli, where the local architecture had a stronger and more monumental tradition. These buildings were the Uaddan Hotel and Casino and the Hotel Mehari, both of which were designed by Florestano Di Fausto with the collaboration of Stefano Gatti-Casazza. In the case of the Uaddan, it was described as "appearing luminous and fantastic on the green strip of the Lungomare Badoglio." The Mehari was similarly identified as relating to its Mediterranean context through "resolving the problem of building in accord with the sun, with the sea and with the multiform play of light and color."[34] Both of these buildings explore a vocabulary of forms and massing that refers quite directly to the architecture of the coastal region of Libya, thereby demonstrating an eclecticism that is grounded in a regionally and culturally specific Mediterranean language.

The Uaddan Hotel and Casino was the most elaborate tourist-oriented project by Di Fausto in Tripoli. Constructed in 1935, its scale and sophistication were clearly recognized in contemporary tourist literature, which referred to this project as a "jewel of modern African architecture."[35] As the only luxury-class hotel in this colony, the Uaddan provided extensive support facilities that included a five-hundred-seat theater and a gaming casino while only accommodating fifty guest rooms. The exclusive nature of the hotel is evident in the fact that it was open only during the winter months, which were the high tourist season.[36] Located along the eastern seafront of Tripoli, this project can, at one level, be understood as a direct expression of the contextualism suggested in the "Mediterranean Vision" of Di Fausto—an approach that implies both a close reading of context and a synthesis of its indigenous forms. As a complex assembly of different building elements, this project was a response to both its seafront location and the diverse architectural heritage of the city of Tripoli. Through the formation of a large terrace on which these elements were grounded, this project created a monumental balcony that linked the hotel to the seafront, while also acting as a transition from the seafront into the city. This quality can be seen in one of the publicity photographs taken from the rear of the hotel, which provides a compel-

Fig. 6.11. Exterior view of the Hotel Tobruk (1937).

Fig. 6.12. View toward the Mediterranean of the Uaddan Hotel and Casino in Tripoli (1935), designed by Florestano Di Fausto and Stefano Gatti-Casazza.

ling image of its engagement with its Mediterranean setting (fig. 6.12). The relationship between the Uaddan and the old city of Tripoli is more by way of analogy than by any literal connection. The composite nature of its forms and stylistic references can be seen as comparable to those of the old city, which was marked by a combination of Roman, Spanish, Arab, and Ottoman interventions.

However, the Uaddan Hotel and Casino was more than a contextual gesture related to the seafront of Tripoli or a synthesis of the complex history of the local architecture. As a rich and luxurious interior world that was intended to satisfy the desires of the most discriminating traveler, it was also an expression of the exoticism often associated with colonial literature.[37] This specifically literary quality was not lost on writers of tourist commentary, one of whom described this project as a "fantastical construction of a fabulous Eastern taste" that "in admiring it . . . one is moved by the fantasy to attempt to discover the key, as in a labyrinth."[38] The exoticism of this project is particularly evident in the popular representations, such as a vividly colored post-card put out by the ETAL in 1937. This tourist image depicts the Uaddan in a somewhat fictive oasis setting that is considerably more spacious than its waterfront location actually provided (fig. 6.13). Through the various promotional materials, the image of the Uaddan was constructed as a place of luxurious accommodation that offered the same opportunity to experience a different culture that was provided by colonial literature. Where the Hotel at the Excavations of Leptis Magna was clearly situated within the more specifically architectural discourse of the early 1930s, this project participates in a tourist discourse that was aimed at the experience of the exotic in which the invitation to travel was provided by the hotel itself.

The complex assembly of exterior forms and interior spaces of the Uaddan was simultaneously a contextual response to the site and the city of Tripoli and a reflection of tourist demands to experience the unfamiliar. These qualities are to a great extent

Fig. 6.13. Postcard view of the Uaddan Hotel and Casino in Tripoli. (See also Plate 15.)

a product of the program of this project. As luxury accommodation for the most discriminating colonial traveler this building combined the hotel proper with a restaurant, a bar, a theater, party rooms, tennis courts, Roman baths, and a gaming casino. Notably, several of these activities, like the theater, casino, and baths, were operated independently from the hotel by the Theater and Performance Service.[39] The composite nature of this complex tourist program was architecturally reinforced through the tactic of housing each of these different activities in a separate volume or space. The gesture of articulating the program volumetrically is, in turn, held together in two specific ways. The first of these is through a uniform treatment of stucco and stone that refers to the local context on the exterior volumes—something that gives the project a Mediterranean image that is in keeping with the character of the old city of Tripoli. These elements are equally contextualized through the large podium that acts as a base for the hotel wing, theater, restaurant, and casino at the back of the site. This podium is, in turn, carved out to create a courtyard that links the baths at the far eastern end of the site with the remainder of the hotel complex. These qualities were noted in the promotional material, which stated that "the whole structure has the virtue of being perfectly contextualized, that is, of almost blending with the attractive surrounding landscape."[40]

The exterior appearance of the project is that of an eclectic assembly of independent buildings that, while clearly linked to their immediate site, create their own self-contained context (fig. 6.14). The analogy between this approach and the indigenous architecture is especially strong with regard to its monumental buildings, and in particular, its mosques and other religious structures. One contemporary commentator on Arab architecture argued that the monumental architecture of Tripolitania was not only subject to a number of heterogeneous influences, but that each building was designed with elements and motifs that were "collected from every place and every time."[41] In the case of the Uaddan, it can be argued that it makes a direct analogy with projects like the sixteenth-century Mosque of Sidi Darghut, which like most of the religious architecture of Tripoli was a composite of independent elements that bore the marks of successive additions and restorations.[42] Moreover, the carefully staged massing of the Uaddan seems to be directly derivative of the exterior profile of these Islamic precedents, which tend to be composed of a combination of minarets, domes, and simple cubic masses (fig. 6.15).

The variable character of the exterior of the Uaddan, which seems to have an analogous relationship to these religious complexes, is more radically expressed on the interior. Designed in collaboration with Stefano Gatti-Casazza, each major component of the program was given an independent expression within the overall composition of spaces. The resulting interior space provides a diverse array of references and materials that explores the eclectic potential of what is suggested on the exterior of the hotel. This approach to the design of the interior spaces is evident in the contrast between the theater, which appears to follow a metropolitan precedent, and the bright and more purely Mediterranean interior of the casino, which was advertised as being similar to the casino at San Remo.[43] The composite nature of the interior is even more apparent in the atrium of the Roman bath complex, where the architects attempted to reconcile two different

Fig. 6.14. View from seafront of the Uaddan Hotel and Casino in Tripoli.

architectural languages with a combination of Roman mosaic floor patterns and a spatial frame that provided an abstract reinterpretation of Ottoman precedents (fig. 6.16).[44]

Although entirely consistent with Di Fausto's polemical writings on the nature of a Mediterranean architecture, which implied a direct process of assimilation of references to a particular context, the Uaddan Hotel and Casino pursued that approach to its breaking point. By creating an analogy to the heterogeneity of the monumental architecture of Tripoli and connecting that eclecticism with the diversity of the tourist program, the project explored the limits of his theoretical premises. It created an elaborate and extravagant interior that was shaped by a combination of diverse activities and unique settings, each of which pursued its own independent qualities. This hotel created a hybrid space where the tourist was able to comfortably explore a variety of sensations, but without ever leaving the hotel. This phenomenon is one that best simulates the space of colonial literature, where, in a romantic search for the experience of the exotic, the reader engages with a constantly changing series of encounters with unfamiliar situations and cultures. In the case of the Uaddan, however, just like in the monumental architecture of Tripoli, these lands and these cultures were largely outside of the purview of the colony. In providing luxury accommodation for a wealthy tourist audience, and creating appropriate settings to these various activities, this hotel had itself become the space of tourism—a self-contained interior world that allowed the traveler to escape the colonies for more distant times and locations. This liminal space—a space both deeply connected to and removed from the colonial context—is the perfect expression of the ambivalence of the colonial relationship in Libya.

Fig. 6.15. Postcard view of the Mosque of Sidi Darghut in Tripoli (1580).

In contrast with this approach to a Mediterranean architecture, the Hotel Mehari, also completed in 1935, represents a more restrained and faithful exercise in the exploration of the indigenous architecture of Tripoli.[45] To some extent, this difference is attributable to the more modest program of this hotel, which was aimed at a more economically minded mass tourist audience. This status is reflected in the location of this building along the east waterfront in Tripoli beyond the Uaddan Hotel. While the hotel did not appear monumental in size, it was by far the largest hotel in Libya, housing over 250 visitors.[46] In response to a program for a tourist hotel that could provide modern accommodation at a reasonable price, the Mehari was a synthesis of local references that were part

Fig. 6.16. Interior view of the Roman baths at the Uaddan Hotel and Casino in Tripoli.

of the tradition of the minor architecture. At the same time, this project, as one commentator noted, responded to the demands to provide "everything that a large modern hotel offers of comfort, of hygiene and of rationality."[47] In addition to providing private or shared baths for every guest room, the hotel offered a long list of amenities, including writing and entertainment rooms, a bar, telephone rooms, a laundry room, and a barber shop (fig. 6.17).

The relationship between the Hotel Mehari and the indigenous architecture of this region is grounded in a common approach to planning (fig. 6.18). The hotel was located on a triangular piece of land on the Passeggiata Maresciallo Badoglio, which was a continuation of the Lungomare Conte Volpi that had for many years defined the seafront of Tripoli. Di Fausto developed the project as

Fig. 6.17. Exterior view of the Hotel Mehari in Tripoli (1935), by Florestano Di Fausto.

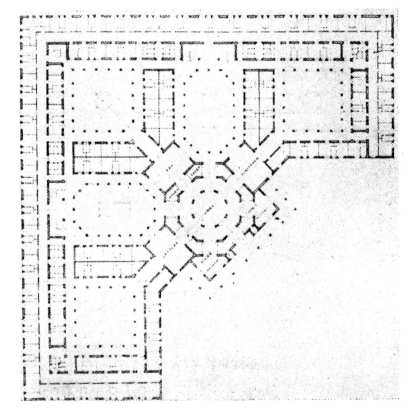

Fig. 6.18. Floor plan of the Hotel Mehari in Tripoli.

a two-story L-shaped block of rooms that was enlivened by five separate courtyard spaces. This horizontal block was intersected at its midpoint by a large octagonal atrium space that formed the main entrance and contained many of the support facilities for the hotel.[48] An aerial view of the hotel taken immediately after its completion indicates that there would seem to be a very direct relationship between this project and the pattern of continuous low-scale housing blocks that were located directly behind the site of the new hotel. Indeed, the indigenous housing of Tripoli was very similar to the Mehari in its mute exterior volumes, utilization of interior courtyards, and extreme modesty of means (fig. 6.19).

By appropriating the indigenous domestic architecture of Tripolitania in the Hotel Mehari, Di Fausto had found a historical precedent that was proper to the unpretentious program of this project. This hotel was thus a reenactment of the local culture

Fig. 6.19. Aerial postcard view of the Hotel Mehari in Tripoli.

Fig. 6.20. View of the courtyard of the Hotel Mehari in Tripoli.

of this region that was staged for the benefit of a mass tourist audience. A closer examination of the plan of the hotel bears out this observation, as these courtyards were not merely used for visual relief. While the perimeter rooms were served by a continuous corridor system, all of the rooms facing the courtyard were accessible from this space. In this sense, a stay in this hotel would be a way of experiencing the characteristic courtyard space of the indigenous domestic architecture. However, rather than the vernacular houses of this region, a more accurate reference for this project in the local architecture is the *funduq*, a form of temporary accommodation and workspace typical to North Africa that had served the merchant populations of Tripoli for many centuries.[49] These buildings were widely regarded as being among the most important works of minor architecture in the old city of Tripoli. This status provoked historian Francesco Corò to call for their preservation in the aftermath of the restoration of the Arch of Marcus Aurelius, a project that threatened many of these structures. In discussing the value of these buildings, Corò referred to these two-story courtyard buildings as "curious hotels, that recall the caravansary, from which they certainly derive" and which accordingly "merit the major consideration of the tourist who visits the old streets of the Libyan capital."[50]

As a careful and studied use of the courtyard typology, the Hotel Mehari was a direct and conscious appropriation of the minor architecture of this region (fig. 6.20). However, in employing such local precedents this project did not sacrifice any of the efficiency and comfort that was expected of this kind of hotel. In addition to ample general facilities, the individual rooms were described as possessing "all of the technical means for the comfort of the guests" while being "furnished with simple yet elegant lines."[51] It is also clear in the various discussions of this hotel that, despite its debt to Muslim vernacular architecture, the aesthetic of the exterior of the building was understood as modern. In one press release that was published at the time of the 1937 visit of Mussolini to Libya, the hotel was purported to have "a sober Novecento style that is simple, restful and solid." The author proceeds to remark that the hotel was "adherent to an architecture made of agile and clear volumes, of light and of luminous courtyards."[52] These qualities are particularly evident in the advertising images of this hotel, which emphasize the strong play of light and shadow on its white planar surfaces.

The Hotel Mehari provided a fusion of the indigenous architecture of Tripoli with a modern aesthetic that responded to the demand for a metropolitan standard of comfort typical to colonial tourism. However, when considering the means of reinterpretation of those vernacular constructions, it is important to recognize that Di Fausto almost literally recreated both the form and function of the courtyard space of the *funduq*. This approach to the appropriation of indigenous forms is fundamentally different from that employed by Larco and Rava in the Hotel at the Excavations in al-Khums, where the courtyard was an abstract point of reference that was transformed to accommodate the program of this building.[53] The courtyard of the Hotel Mehari is more closely related to Di Fausto's restoration project at the Suq al-Mushir—a new facility in the artisanal quarter that directly employed traditional forms. However, in the case of the Mehari, which was designed for a mass tourist audience, the gesture of incorporation involves a form of displacement. That displacement, however, was quite different from that employed in the Uaddan Hotel and Casino, which was based on the space of colonial literature. By creating a living environment that was closely related to that of the indigenous populations, the Hotel Mehari was a kind of living museum of anthropology. It provided a vicarious way for the traveler to experience the native culture of Tripoli in a modern and hygienic environment.

FROM TRIPOLI TO GHADAMES

A second group of hotels was designed by Di Fausto that followed a tourist itinerary that led southwest from Tripoli to the edge of the Sahara. These projects were the Hotel Rumia in Yifran of 1934, the Hotel Nalut of 1935, and the Hotel 'Ain el-Fras in Ghadames of 1935. In contrast with the Mediterranean language explored in the design of the Uaddan and the Mehari, these projects respond to the extreme cultural differences of the architecture of Jabal and pre-Saharan regions of Libya. As part of a coordinated route of travel and accommodation that was organized and run by the Libyan Tourism and Hotel Association, these projects represent an unprecedented effort to create a continuous tourist experience in the colony. In examining this itinerary, the role of architecture in the creation of this seamless tourist panorama is the central and most important question.

The route from Tripoli to Ghadames had been understood, at least from the time of the automobile *raid* of Volpi, as one of the most desirable and characteristic tourist experiences in the Tripolitanian region.[54] To a great extent this interest was linked to the fact that Ghadames had been a crucial stopping point along the caravan routes that linked the Sudan to Tripoli and the Mediterranean. This fascination was then fueled by a combination of literary speculation and reportage that reached a mass audience, and scientific exploration and research that informed and influenced these various representations. In the first case, these more popular publications cultivated an image of places like Ghadames that is reminiscent of the exoticism that has come to be associated with the more romantic strains of colonial literature. One such example is the book *La Porta magica del Sahara*, published by Angelo Piccioli in 1931—a book that was widely disseminated in Italy and that was eventually translated into German and English. In this publication, Piccioli offers the following poetic description of the experience of the oasis of Ghadames: "Everywhere around us, and also within us, a marvelous silence—a silence as transparent as the water."[55]

The image of Ghadames, and of the interior of Libya, was constructed in literary discourse as that of a mysterious and timeless repository of the most primitive origins of Libyan culture. These popular representations were parallel to and supported by a considerable body of research in the field of anthropology, which by concentrating on the historical traditions of this region and its people, ultimately created a scientific justification for the Italian colonization[56] The most significant scientific study of the indigenous architecture of Libya was produced by Emilio Scarin, a professor from the University of Florence who published *L'Insediamento umano nella Libia occidentale* in 1940. What is interesting to note is that the objects of greatest scientific interest to researchers like Scarin, like the Berber castle in Nalut and the oasis of Ghadames, were also important

elements of the tourist itinerary. In the case of this latter settlement, Scarin gives considerable attention to the characteristic
grouping of housing, for which, in an effort to produce a minimal
exterior surface in a severe climate, "one is placed over another
in a way to form a single unity."[57] He then elaborates on the social
patterns of the houses in Ghadames in relation to this typical
arrangement, noting how the privacy of women is maintained
through a very different hierarchy than that offered by the courtyard house of the coastal regions (fig. 6.21).

These literary representations and scientific activities occurred
parallel to the tourist development of the region. It was, however,
not until the control of the Fezzan region in 1932 that such travel
was viable. The military conquest of the colonial landscape coincided with a program of improvement of the road network of
this region under the governorships of De Bono and Badoglio—a
program that was referred to as "a durable work of domination,
as it is the true taking into possession of the colony."[58] These road
improvements were quickly followed by the initiation of bimonthly
transportation service between Tripoli and Ghadames in January
of 1929. One example of such an itinerary was the scheduled bus
service to the southern regions of Libya—a trip whose attraction was the desire to experience an unfamiliar landscape. In the
presentation of this system in *L'Italia Coloniale*, it was referred to
as a "great attraction of exploration and hunting."[59] This itinerary
was greatly enhanced with the construction of the first hotel in
Ghadames in November 1931, at which time travel in this region
was available to a wider audience.[60]

The subsequent governorship of Italo Balbo placed a major
emphasis on the development of the tourist infrastructure in
Libya. Under the direction of the Building Commission of the

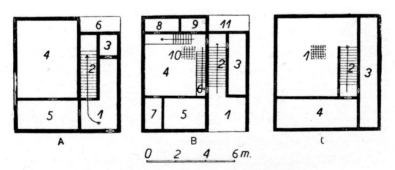

Fig. 6.21. Plan of a house in Ghadames, from Emilio Scarin, L'Insediamento umano nella Libia occidentale (Verona: Officina Grafiche A. Mondadori, 1940).

Fig. 21. - Pianta di una abitazione gadamesina.
A. Pianterreno. Dall'ingresso (1) si accede ai magazzini (5, 4) all'invaso del
locale di decenza (3) e per le scale (2) si sale al I piano (B) in un piccolo
pianerottolo da cui si accede al gabinetto (3) al grande locale di soggiorno
(4) vero centro e vita della casa. Da esso si accede a ripostigli vari (5, 9, 8)
anche per mezzo di una piccola scaletta (presso i numeri 8, 9) e all'alcova
(7) attraverso un arco. Per la scaletta (6) si passa al II piano (C) in un
piccolo pianerottolo da cui si accede a due locali ove si svolge normalmente
la vita delle donne (3, e 4) e per mezzo della scala (2) si passa alla terrazza
(1) in cui v'è il lucernario per il I piano (v. n. 10 di B). Per piccole sca-
lette mobili si sale infine a piccole terrazze sopra il 4 e 3.

Municipality of Tripoli in 1934, the construction of the hotels in Yifran and Nalut and the substantial renovation of the hotel in Ghadames were undertaken. With the creation of the Libyan Tourism and Hotel Association, this route took on the status of a coordinated tourist system. By late 1935, not only had these hotels been completed, but the newly formed Transportation Service had initiated weekly excursions to Ghadames using Saharan motor coaches. This service was prominently featured in all of their publicity material, which noted that the journey involved two travel days in each direction, staying overnight in Nalut and two nights in Ghadames (fig. 6.22).[61] The route thus combined a modern transportation system with a tourist infrastructure that was intended to harmonize with the local environment. The connection between these new hotels and the new system of transportation was noted in an essay in the TCI journal *Le Vie d'Italia* in August of 1936. Combining an intense interest in the technical aspects of the road network with a fascination for the indigenous culture, this article recounts that the hotels along this route were "scrupulously harmonized with the suggestive characteristics of the local constructions," thereby creating an experience that, it argues, "satisfies the demands of the most refined tourist."[62]

The pre-Saharan hotels of Di Fausto in Yifran, Nalut, and

Fig. 6.22. Map of the itinerary from Tripoli to Ghadames, from Itinerario Tripoli-Gadames (1938).

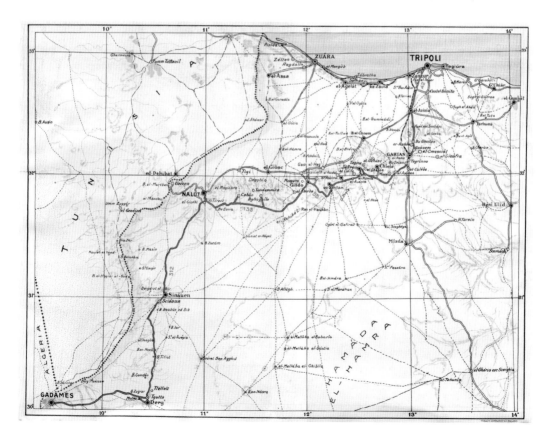

Fig. 6.23. Cover of the guidebook Itinerario Tripoli-Gadames (1938), published by the Libyan Tourism and Hotel Association. (See also Plate 16.)

Ghadames were an integral part of a continuous tourist experience that was organized and run by the ETAL. The importance of this travel route to the identity of this group was evidenced in a postcard series that provides a summary of the most important tourist attractions. Of particular interest is the fact that the hotels in Nalut, Yifran, and Ghadames were included in this series, thereby blurring the distinction between the actual tourist sites and their hotel system. The trip from Tripoli to Ghadames was the subject of a more detailed examination in the 1938 guidebook *Itinerario Tripoli-Gadames*, whose cover conveys an evocative image of its final destination (fig. 6.23).[63] Judging by this representation, the itinerary to Ghadames was a curious hybrid of a modern tourist excursion, a scientific expedition, and a patriotic affirmation of colonial rule. The experience was characterized as providing an efficient and comfortable means of travel supported by hotels which, in addition to being carefully contextualized to their site and the local architecture, provided "the most comfortable hospitality."[64] It is also clear from this book that the journey could provide insights into the traditional architecture, such as the Troglodyte houses of the Gharyan and Jabal regions, and into the history, customs, and practices of its Arab and Berber populations—thus imparting views that were taken from contemporary scientific research (fig. 6.24).[65] Finally, this book did not fail to point out the various improvements brought by Italian colonization, both through the development of agricultural areas, like the tobacco fields near Taghrinnah, and the creation of new urban settlements in the historic centers of the various towns along the route.[66]

The pre-Saharan hotels of Di Fausto were widely recognized for their own assimilation of indigenous sources. In this case, however, the basis of the design was not the monumental architecture of Libya but rather the anonymous rural constructions. In the guidebook *La Libia turistica*, the author noted that in designing the hotels in Yifran, Nalut, and Ghadames, "the small houses that the local necessities allow were studied in their interior and exterior architecture and in their every service with loving care by artists and technicians."[67] The resulting designs were described as being "perfectly harmonized with the environment," an assertion that fuses the tourist interests of the ETAL with the design approach of Di Fausto.

The first of these hotels, the Hotel Rumia in Yifran, was named for a legendary natural spring that existed in the adjacent valley. The hotel was located on the ruins of an existing fortress from the period of Ottoman rule, acting as a simple horizontal block set in relation to the remains of this existing structure (fig. 6.25). In general terms, the hotel seems to have little in common with the

Fig. 6.24. Entrance to a troglodyte house in Gharyan, from Itinerario Tripoli-Gadames (1938).

forms of the adjacent settlements, which were a series of super-imposed circular forms that ascended the sloping terrain. The Rumia is equally distinct from the Berber castle, which was called "a magniloquent mountain of gray limestone in ruin."[68] Rather, its form was generated out of a careful reading of the surrounding natural landscape. Its battered walls and blank stucco surfaces establish a dialectical relationship to the remaining bastion and the horizontality of the plateau on which it was located. As noted in *Itinerario Tripoli-Gadames*, this hotel was designed in rela-tion to the rugged landscape of which it provided a spectacular view, a landscape whose naturally eroded geological stratifica-tion was described as "a piece of Africa that comes apart in crude cuttings" (fig. 6.26).[69] Its horizontal profile can thus be understood as a response to similar qualities in the site and the surrounding landscape and as a physical manifestation of the view for which it became a self-conscious framing device.

Although the Hotel Rumia in Yifran does not directly reflect the local forms of the Berber settlements, it is a product of the same process that produced these kinds of indigenous constructions.[70] In this regard, Di Fausto was extremely attentive to the harsh climate of this region, to which he responded with a largely solid exterior wall, and the discreet use of loggias and arched recesses to protect the various entrances. Equally well considered in rela-tion to climatic exigencies were the various window openings, which employed a combination of shutters and screening devices, both of which are based on those found in the local constructions. Like the Hotel Mehari in Tripoli, there is a certain simplicity and

Fig. 6.25. Exterior view of the Hotel Rumia in Yifran (1934), by Flores-tano Di Fausto and Stefano Gatti Casazza.

Fig. 6.26. Valley of Rumia near Yifran, from Itinerario Tripoli-Gadames (1938).

modesty that links this hotel project to the minor architecture. This quality is particularly evident in the tower and entrance pavilion, which employs a tapered rectangular form found in minarets in the southern parts of Libya.[71] The interior of the project, which was executed in conjunction with the architect Gatti-Casazza, employs rich materials and patterns to create a stark contrast with the stucco exterior volume. This extreme contrast re-creates the sense of intimacy and repose often found in interior spaces in the Libyan domestic architecture (fig. 6.27). Finally, and perhaps most important for its status as a modern tourist facility, the Hotel Rumia provided all of the conveniences that might be expected of a first-class hotel. Although it was an extremely modest size, with only fifteen guest rooms, the hotel contained a restaurant and bar and provided private baths with each room.

In the design of the Hotel Nalut, which was the virtual twin of the project in Yifran, Di Fausto employed a similar site strategy, where a low horizontal building was located on the edge of a large plain, with the restaurant and guest rooms overlooking an immense valley. However, in this case the project faced this surrounding landscape and the adjacent Berber town. In so doing, a relationship was created that by proximity and view alone established a more direct connection between the new construction and the adjacent settlement. This connection is given poetic expression in *Itinerario Tripoli-Gadames*, which asserts that the hotel enjoys "a stupendous panorama not only towards the primitive Berber town . . . but to that prodigious precipitate of cliffs . . . that slope to the plain in a flooding outburst."[72] The link between the hotel and the adjacent settlement is enhanced by an unmistakable similarity between the gently sloping walls of the indigenous constructions and those of the Hotel Nalut. The visual connection between the hotel and the town is particularly well conveyed in the publicity material—the strong horizontal profile of the hotel and its simple rectangular massing appearing superimposed with that of the abandoned Berber castle. This relationship is one of opposition, the white smooth surfaces of the hotel acting as a dramatic counterpoint to the ruinous state of the adjacent settlement.

This dialectical relationship between the Hotel Nalut and the Berber town is conveyed in two postcards that were part of the series that ETAL issued to document this travel itinerary. The first postcard shows the town of Nalut while the second is of the hotel facade that faced this very landscape (figs. 6.28, 6.29). These images suggest a strong connection between the buttressed base of the rear facade of the hotel and the tapered forms of the indigenous constructions of the Berber settlement. They also communicate the unqualified modernity of the building. This effect is the result of the strong horizontal line of the roof, which was designed to provide shade for a series of recessed spaces in front

Fig. 6.27. Interior of the Hotel Rumia in Yifran.

of the guest rooms. The detailed development of the facade, which included the careful design of its openings, made it quite clear that this tourist facility was conceived according to the view of what was described as an "abysmal landscape, that seems to have existed and been uninhabited for millennia."[73] Although, just like the Rumia in Yifran, this project was unquestionably a response to the demands of the tourist audience—providing the most modern comforts in the harsh climate of pre-Saharan Africa—this was not its most important role within the tourist experience. Through the various relationships that it established with the Berber settlement and surrounding landscape, from the conscious framing of views, to direct references to its forms, the Hotel Nalut became a kind of instrument through which the town could be represented to the traveler.

A final relationship between the Hotel Nalut and the adjacent town can be found in its representation in the publication *Itinerario Tripoli-Gadames*, where the discussion of its facilities is accompanied by a historical and ethnographic description of its people. This publication is an indication of the intersection of the tourist discourse in the colonies with contemporary activities in various fields of scientific research—studies in which this region and the Berber people were important subjects.[74] It is also quite apparent that, in this presentation, an analogy is being made between the "heroic resistance" of these people against the Ottoman invaders and the rugged forms of their ancient castle, which was referred to as "a sort of petrified myth."[75] Through reenacting these indigenous forms, this tourist project was participating in a contemporary ethnographic discourse—the stark and primitive qualities of this project suggesting the stern resistance of the Berber people and the perceived timeless quality of their culture.

Fig. 6.28. Postcard panorama of Nalut, ca. 1935.

The pre-Saharan hotels in Yifran and Nalut share a site specificity and a common reference to the native architecture of the region that link them quite directly to the arguments of Di Fausto about a Mediterranean regionalism. However, a critical aspect of these two designs that distinguishes them from the projects he constructed in the coastal region of Libya is that they are almost exactly identical. The repetition even extends beyond their forms to the relationships that each of them established with their respective contexts. Their use of local forms was thus general, not specific. The central tower was derived from religious architecture in this region, but did not refer to the town in which it was built. While the modernity of these hotels can certainly be found in the amenities they provided to the tourist audience, it can also be argued that the most modern aspect of these two projects was their repetition. Through a process of displacement, the authenticity and originality of pre-Saharan architecture is at once celebrated and severely challenged. As a consequence the metropolitan traveler exists in a liminal space—a space that is both connected to and alienated from the experience of the indigenous culture.

The final hotel along this organized travel itinerary was the Hotel 'Ain el-Fras in Ghadames built in 1935. In a manner similar to the Rumia, this tourist facility was named after the celebrated natural spring which provided water to this oasis town on the edge of the Sahara. The project by Di Fausto and Gatti-Casazza was a renovation of the original hotel of 1931; however, in so doing, it was able to provide first-class accommodation with a restaurant and bar and fifteen rooms, each with a private bath.[76] As with the previous pre-Saharan hotels, this project is a mediation between its physical and environmental context and references to the local architecture on the one hand

Fig. 6.29. Postcard view of the Hotel Nalut (1935), by Florestano Di Fausto and Stefano Gatti-Casazza.

and the modern demands of tourist accommodation in this region on the other. This relationship was described in *Itinerario Tripoli Gadames* as one where "the technical perfection of the west merges effortlessly with a picture of pure oriental poetry."[77]

The Hotel 'Ain el-Fras responds to the formal language of the city of Ghadames, which is a complex labyrinth of narrow passages, covered courtyards, and terraces shaped by dense walled structures, by creating a massive exterior wall behind which is a series of courtyard spaces (fig. 6.30). The modernity of this project, while less apparent in its exterior appearance than the other hotel projects of Di Fausto, is in the technical aspects of what looks like an indigenous construction.[78] Forming one edge of a large piazza in front of one of the main gates of the old city that is characterized by its luxuriant landscape, this project establishes a metonymic relationship to this oasis setting. The relationship between the building and its context is particularly well expressed in the so-called portico of the palms, where columns shaped like the trunks of palm trees mingle with those of its own verdant landscape (6.31).[79]

This literal incorporation of an element of landscape into architecture is an indication of the fact that with the Hotel 'Ain el-Fras, the means of appropriation of local references was much more direct than that of the hotels in Yifran and Nalut. In these other pre-Saharan hotels, their forms were an abstract synthesis of a more general, regional expression. A more detailed examination of the Ghadames hotel would seem to confirm this observation. When looking at the arcaded wings that flank the central body of this building, there is an unmistakable relationship between this element and the detailed articulation of openings in the Piazza of the Large Mulberry. This very intimate urban space in the old town of Ghadames was described in *Itinerario Tripoli-Gadames* as an "intersection of gloomy caves, vaults, and large niches that pierce the four white walls of the piazza with their shade" (figs. 6.32, 6.33).[80] The mimetic relationship between the building and the town of Ghadames can also be seen in the interior spaces of the hotel, whose timber ceilings, rich wall coverings, and minimal use of furnishings was intended to suggest the characteristic experience of the indigenous houses. These buildings, which were largely inaccessible to tourists, were described as being like "jewel boxes," as they contained all of the family treasures (fig. 6.34).[81]

While at one level, Di Fausto's direct appropriation of the forms of the town of Ghadames in the Hotel 'Ain el-Fras can be understood as a more consistent manifestation of his "Mediterranean Vision"—which calls for a careful and measured process of design in relation to the Mediterranean context and its various building traditions—this project must also be understood and analyzed

Fig. 6.30. View of the Hotel 'Ain el-Fras in Ghadames (1935), by Florestano Di Fausto and Stefano Gatti-Casazza.

Fig. 6.31. Portico of the palms at the Hotel 'Ain el-Fras in Ghadames.

in relation to its function within the tourist panorama. Through the direct incorporation of the indigenous forms of Ghadames in this tourist facility, Di Fausto created a seamless relationship between the building and its pre-Saharan context. Such a faithful representation of native forms is something that, for the tourist, would have served to blur the relationship between the hotel and its historical setting. Moreover, due to the siting of the hotel just outside one of the main gates of the town, it functioned as a means of introduction to the experience of the architecture and culture of Ghadames. As was stated in the publication *Itinerario Tripoli-Gadames*, the hotel was "an anticipation, for the traveler who does not know the city and the oasis, of its delights, of its enchantment of colors, of its profound effects on the spirit."[82]

The use of local forms in this project was not merely a way of better contextualizing this work of tourist architecture in

Fig. 6.32. Post-card view of the courtyard of the Hotel 'Ain el-Fras in Ghadames.

Fig. 6.33. Piazza of the Large Mulberry in Ghadames, from Itinerario Tripoli-Gadames (1938).

relation to its oasis setting. The hotel was an integral part of a self-conscious staging of the image and the patterns of living of Ghadames that a tourist could comfortably experience. The attempt to simulate the indigenous culture through architecture was enhanced by the fact that the entire hotel staff were dressed in local costume (fig. 6.35).[83] In so closely replicating the culture of this town, however, the Hotel 'Ain el-Fras became its more perfect replacement. Indeed, to experience the indigenous architecture and culture of the oasis of Ghadames, it may have no longer been necessary to see the actual town.

The hotel in Ghadames by Di Fausto represents a crisis in the status of architecture, and in its relationship to its context. While the intention was to create a regional expression within a contemporary architecture, the implications of the project are quite different. The 'Ain el-Fras so closely imitates the identity of the traditional forms of the town of Ghadames that it calls into question the line between restoration and innovation and challenges the identity of these historical forms. However, rather than consider this an anti-modern approach, when looking at this project it is quite clear that it is the opposite. The Hotel 'Ain el-Fras is the logical outcome of the modern tourist demand for historical authenticity. It is related to, and a product of, contemporary scientific research into the form and the culture of the Berber people—a so-called primitive culture which held a particular fascination for a tourist audience.[84] It also reflects the ambivalence of colonial politics in Libya under Italo Balbo—where all indigenous cultural expressions were under the strictest supervision and control. In so carefully reenacting the forms of Ghadames, this project was both tourist facility and ethnographic museum,

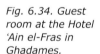

Fig. 6.34. Guest room at the Hotel 'Ain el-Fras in Ghadames.

Fig. 6.35. Tourists in the courtyard of the Hotel 'Ain el-Fras in Ghadames.

where the Libyans and their culture could be experienced outside of the passage of time. As a consequence, the politically motivated racial discourses that were already infused into modern scientific and political practices—discourses that viewed Libyan culture as primitive and backward in relation to the West—were here beginning to be mapped onto the architecture of tourism.

Garian - Le grotte
Abitazione degli
Arari

CONCLUSION

*With the development of Libya, the problem of tourism has in
fact become real and alive. Much has taken place in the twenty
years of the Fascist regime, yet without spoiling any of the local
color, the indigenous customs and practices that open a new
world to the visitor in search of impressions and sensations,
desirous of experiencing the wonders of the Arab world. You
have all of this in Libya, you have that which feeds the fantasy
of poets and that which illuminates the colors of a painter.—
Eros Vicari, "L'Ente Turistico ed Alberghiero della Libia
(E.T.A.L.)," 1942.*[1]

Fig. C.1. Photo-
graphs of tourists
visiting cave dwell-
ings in the Gharyan,
ca. 1930.

Looking carefully, and in retrospect, at the tourist experience
in Libya during the period of Italian colonization, it seems quite
simple to detect a set of preoccupations that continue to inform
the design of tourist environments today. These issues include,
but are not limited to, valuing the authentic, preserving the
physical environment, and even inventing these same experiences
and environments to feed the demands of the modern tourist,
whose thirst for new sensations seems never to be satiated. This
line of thinking would suggest that the tourist system in Libya
is the precursor to consciously preserved tourist sites generated
by the mass tourist movement of recent decades, such as Salem,
Massachusetts, or Santa Fe, New Mexico.[2] It might also seem

quite appropriate to look at such tourist environments as veritable architectural museums, a phenomenon that has been linked to nineteenth century World's Fairs and the far more curious (and contrived) occurrence of the heritage village.[3] Was the tourist experience in Libya merely a foreshadowing of Colonial Williamsburg—where American colonial culture is staged for the benefit of a mass tourist audience?

To some extent the answer to this question is yes. It is at least provisionally productive to think about how such carefully contrived tourist environments as were put in place in Libya are indebted to nineteenth- and early-twentieth-century precedents of fairs and exhibitions while also being a point of reference for the far more extensive reshaping of the environment under the aegis of mass tourism. And yet there are some important and quite significant differences that give the Libyan example its own qualities. The creation of a tourist system in Libya was entirely dependent upon the political initiatives of a regime whose modernization program was responsible for the introduction of a network of roads and public services that transformed the region. Moreover, the modernization program was supported by a military presence whose impact was a formative part of the tourist experience. Finally, and perhaps most important, due to the colonial situation itself, a rather ambivalent relationship was established between the protagonists of the tourist system and the heritage that was being re-presented to the tourist audience.

Even in the most carefully orchestrated tourist environment in Italian colonial Libya, the authentic experience of native culture was always framed by the means and mechanisms of the metropole. The Western traveler was attempting to escape their cultural standards for the purpose of confronting an "other" culture—understood as primitive, savage, backward—while never quite leaving behind those very standards. This can be said for the expectations of organization and comfort that went along with colonial tourism. To create a viable tourist system in the colonies it was necessary to offer a level of amenity that was equal to that found in metropolitan Italy. It is also quite clear that the framing of the Libyan people and their culture as primitive and backward in relation to the West puts the viewer in a privileged position that denies the object of their attention a temporal coevality—an argument, and indeed a relationship, that is essentially a modern (racist) one. In this way the liminal experience of the Western traveler in Libya is perfectly matched in the ambivalent colonial politics that was applied to the native body.

The condition of liminality that was part of the tourist experience is infused into many of the personal records that exist of the early travels in Libya—including postcards, photographs, and souvenirs. One such example is a collection of photographs and postcards of an individual traveler, who visited Libya in the late 1920s.[4] The photographs are all printed in a small format and mounted on a backing sheet that contains the cursive notes of the traveler. The two images show a group of tourists along with an indigenous soldier visiting the cave dwellings in the Gharyan region. Like the typical tourist photograph, the modern experience of travel is documented through the mechanism of the camera—which seems to always locate the tourist within the frame (fig. C.1). The second set of images, which are also photographs, are printed as postcards—images that presumably could eventually be sent back to friends and family in Italy. The image in this case is of a series of boys who carry water and other items for a fee. The title, typed over the photograph, classifies the boys: "Tripoli: Ragazzi pora-tori." Interestingly, the traveler is largely absent in these postcard views, the focus being upon the seemingly objective presentation of the indigenous culture (fig. C.2). These two modes of representation—one a subjective account of the experience of the place and the other an objective documentation of the indigenous body— reflect the conflicted relationship of the tourist in Libya. Despite the visceral qualities of such first-person accounts of travel, the colonial tourist seems always connected to, yet distanced from, the very experience of difference they were seeking.

The architecture of the tourist system in Libya was, at least in part, a product of the same political and cultural forces that deter-mined the tourist experience. Just as tourism in Libya offered a direct encounter with an unfamiliar situation and culture, so did the tourist facilities—but by no means in a uniform manner. The Hotel at the Excavations of Leptis Magna by Larco and Rava was a product of a theoretical position that viewed the indig-enous architecture of Libya as a product of Latin, Mediterranean, and African influences (fig. C.3). The means of appropriation of these references into a contemporary architecture followed a path of simplification and abstraction. It proposed the embrace of a formal aesthetic of Mediterranean origin and the adoption of typological references that were deemed to reflect Roman

Fig. C.2. Photo-graphic postcard of carrying boys in Tripoli, ca. 1930.

Fig. C.3. Postcard of the Hotel at the Excavations of Leptis Magna in al-Khums, ca. 1935.

models. The project is a perfect demonstration of this theoretical approach, alluding to the massing of indigenous constructions while transforming their characteristic forms through its rational organization and the application of a quintessentially modern aesthetic. Even the most common tourist representations of this hotel do not fail to reveal the fusion of its local references with a contemporary architectural language.

The "Mediterranean Vision" of Di Fausto proposes an architecture that is more closely related to the technical and scientific practices of historic preservation. According to this view, a complete understanding of the existing context is the necessary precondition to the proposition of any modern project—an understanding that would also include a careful attendance to the regional building traditions and the use of indigenous materials. In contrast with the *mediterraneità* of Rava, the means of appropriation of local forms proposed by Di Fausto have no mediating processes, leading in some cases to a set of building forms that reenacted the local characteristics. These views found their most clear expression in his tourist-oriented works, which included projects constructed both along the Mediterranean coast and in the most remote regions of the interior. The function of projects like his Hotel 'Ain el-Fras in Ghadames within the tourist panorama is one of quite literally demonstrating the native forms of the town for the Western traveler (fig. C.4).

At one level, the line of difference between the approaches of Rava and Di Fausto reveals the ambivalence of modernity in the Italian colonial context. This ambivalence is the product of the shift from a modernist appropriation in the early 1930s, where the indigenous culture is fused with a modern aesthetic sensibility, to a historicist one in the latter part of the decade, where the indigenous is reenacted as a racially encoded project of historic preservation. What the difference between the views of these two architects tells us is that there was no single and dominant mode with which modernity and indigenous culture interacted. This negotiation was part of a shifting cultural ground that transformed along with the politics of Italian colonialism—which were by no means uniform through this period. In this sense, we can look at "ambivalent modernism" as a hegemonic construction, in the terms of Gramsci, that was neither uniform nor unchanging. In this case, it is a displacement between two distinct views of modernity that evolved out of the conflicted and constantly shifting political and cultural terrain of Italian colonial Libya.

What is also apparent in this book is that *each* of these manifestations of the interaction between modern and indigenous produces its own kind of ambivalent modernism. In the case of the tourist project of Rava, he offers a fusion of local forms into a quintessentially modern language—an approach that would seem to aspire to the Gramscian ideal of a "national-popular" expression. This effort, however, is not without its contradictions, as was pointed out by Edoardo Persico in the 1930s. He argued that the most crucial aspect of the initial manifestos of Italian rationalism was "an intuition for the necessity of new forces that insert themselves in a European state of affairs, not only as an aesthetic idea, but also as a cultural, economic, social and political force."[5] The writings of Rava of 1931 were, for Persico, representative of a more general lack of faith which Italian Rationalism expressed toward European tendencies during the period before and after the second Rationalist exhibition. Persico concludes this critique by stating that "the relationship between architecture and politics . . . had overturned the nature of the debate."[6] This certainly can be said of the Hotel at the Excavations in al-Khums, which reflects the imperialist project of claiming the Libyan cultural legacy as mere transmitters of Latin (that is, Italian) civilization. It is, perhaps, this conflict that represents the ambivalence of Rava's work. In its fusion of seemingly opposite forces—modernity and the indigenous—this work not only erases cultural difference (and in so doing constitutes an imperialist project), it has the capacity to destroy the aesthetic coherence of the very modernity that it set out to create.

The tourist projects of Di Fausto offer their own form of ambivalent modernism—one that relates to the changing political discourse in the latter part of the 1930s. It was at this time that anthropologists and ethnographers were involved in the systematic study of Libyan culture, an effort that was quite clearly linked with an emerging racial discourse in the realm of Fascist colonial politics. In this context, such a direct appropriation of indigenous forms has quite specific political and architectural connotations. The reenactment of the local architecture would effectively destroy any sense of authenticity or originality. In its place, what is offered is an experience of indigenous culture that corresponds with a contemporary scientific view of Libyan culture—effectively stripped of all the dangers that such encounters might bring. In the case of the work of Di Fausto, it is instructive to revisit the writings of Antonio Gramsci on modern Italian literature during the Fascist period. He speaks of the idea of "folkloristic provincialism," which he describes as a subversive technique of satisfying the desire for authentic regional manifestations through their imposition *from above*. The appropriation of indigenous forms in the pre-Saharan hotels of Di Fausto and the construction of the larger tourist panorama in Libya under the aegis of Italian colonialism was a "project" of historic preservation that afforded the Libyans and their culture a liminal status—both connected to and removed from modern metropolitan society. However, in performing what Homi Bhabha describes as an act of colonial mimicry, this ambivalent modernism threatens to undermine the temporal hierarchy of modernity itself.[7]

The apparent difference between these two modernities—a difference largely based on the changing rhetoric of Italian colonial politics—must itself also be interrogated. The emergence of a racially encoded reading of the architecture and culture of Libya was not limited to the work of Di Fausto, as it can also be traced in the continuing intellectual production of Rava. One such essay, entitled "Architettura di razza italiana," appeared in the journal *L'Architettura Italiana* in January of 1939—less than two months after the passage of the Italian racial laws.[8] In this essay, Rava traces a continuous line of thinking in his programmatic writings that relates to the question of Italian racial identity and asserts a purity in Italian architecture that he links to the contemporary

Fig. C.4 . Postcard of the Hotel 'Ain el-Fras in Ghadames, ca. 1935.

GADAMES - Nella calma riposante dell'oasi, sorge l'Albergo di ''Ain El Frass,,

campaign for the defense of the Italian race. One of his primary motivations in linking Italian Rationalism with racist politics was to legitimize this movement in the face of the scrutiny of the Fascist authorities, who were increasingly critical of the European outlook of Italian architecture. Rava was also quite clearly highlighting his own unique contribution to Rationalist discourse—defending himself against accusations of internationalism by distinguishing his writings from the more intransigent views. In so doing, he consistently underscored what he called "the perfect orthodoxy of our new architecture, *born of Italian thought and race.*"[9] "Architettura di razza italiana" exposes a fault line in Rava's theoretical practice in the late 1930s and reveals certain problems that exist in any attempt to create a national or regional identity for modern architecture in the colonies through a recourse to local sources. The indigenous architecture of Libya was not only constructed by Italian architects as a repository of traditional culture, it was also the material basis from which an identity could be produced, whose designation as "Italian" disguised an oppressive politics of exclusion and racial purification.

What remains to be asked about these two forms of ambivalent modernism is how this work can impact current historiography on modern architecture. At one level, all architecture reflects the ambivalent status of the modern condition that Marshall Berman describes as simultaneously liberating and modernizing and a source of alienation and loss. In this case, however, this work cannot be understood as a mere dialectical exchange between modernity and tradition— the theoretical model that dominates much of the current historiography of the modern movement. In part because of the colonial context, the specific political and racial connotations of modernity are quite different. Instead of a dialectical space of interaction between opposed forces, this work offers a liminal space in which modern and indigenous, West and non-West, are linked in a complex relationship of repetition and displacement. In the case of the work of Larco and Rava, that displacement is an aesthetic one. With the projects of Di Fausto, the displacement is temporal.

The ambivalent modernism of Rava has a considerable significance to the historiography of the modern movement in Italy. Despite the embrace of the work of Giuseppe Terragni and Italian Rationalism in histories of modern architecture and the considerable scholarship in English and Italian on architecture during the Fascist period, Rava and his work are relatively unknown. His writings in *Domus*, which theorize a Mediterranean identity for modern Italian architecture, pose an alternative solution to the struggle to create a contemporary architecture that addressed the political demands of Fascist Italy to that offered by his Rationalist colleagues. Moreover, given the colonial and tourist dimensions of the Hotel at the Excavations of Leptis Magna, the discussion of his work has the potential to expand the modernist canon. Not only does this project raise serious questions about any attempt to create a regional expression out of a recourse to indigenous sources, it also compels us to ask whether the Western origin of modern architecture has been problematized by its contact with the colonial "other."

In contrast with the work of Rava, the potential impact of Di Fausto's ambivalent modernism on the history of modern architecture would seem initially somewhat difficult to articulate. How can one historicize projects that seem to have no obvious references to modern aesthetic practices? A more accurate point of reference for these projects would be the theory of modern historic preservation—a subject that has a rich and substantial history in Italy. One of the key protagonists in this discourse is the architect Camillo Boito, who authored some of the most seminal writings on this topic. One such essay, entitled "Conservare or restaurare?" outlines a clear distinction between the act of conservation, where a historic building is virtually complete and can be maintained, and one of preservation, where the completion of the building becomes a contemporary work.[10] The writings of Boito had a profound effect on Gustavo Giovannoni, who in his own quite influential writings argues that contemporary architecture should be related to its physical context, establishing a relationship of mutual dependence.[11] However, in the process of reinterpretation of the legacy of Boito, Giovannoni introduces the idea of *ambientismo* or contextualism—a concept that results in the removal of any clear distinction between new and old in favor of asserting the value of the "architectural environment."[12]

With regard to the history of modern architecture, while a considerable body of theory has informed the modern practice of historic preservation, including the writings of Eugène-Emmanuel Viollet-le-Duc, Alois Riegl, and Camillo Sitte, little attention has been paid to the projects that resulted from these theories.[13] Moreover, if recognized at all as works of architecture, these projects have rarely if ever been considered contemporary works. The few examples that have found some place on the margins of the history of modern architecture—most of which were realized in post–World War II Italy, like the Museum of the Sforzesco Castle in Milan by BBPR architects (1956) or the Castelvecchio Museum in Verona by Carlo Scarpa (1958–64)—have been understood as the product of a particular historical moment (the time of postwar reconstruction) or the ideas of an idiosyncratic architect. When we look at the town of Carcassonne, France, is it understood as a nineteenth-century restoration project that was directed by Viollet-le-Duc rather than as an authentic thirteenth-century walled town? How will future generations understand the numerous environments that have been invented by the field of historic preservation? As a product of this preservation discourse, the tourist projects of Di Fausto in Libya are part of the history of modern architecture—but according to a very different concept of modern. It is not an aesthetic modernism but rather a modernism of scientific research and preservation practices—a modernism that is the metonymic reenactment of a primitive (and timeless) "other."

As a final reflection on the ambivalent status of the tourist experience in Libya, I offer an anecdote on the state of the tourist system under the condition of war—a situation that was much less sanguine than the status it attained during the 1930s. The entry of Italy into World War II was quickly followed by the British campaign in Africa and the subsequent death of governor Italo Balbo, who was shot down by his own forces in the skies over Tobruk in eastern Libya in June of 1940.[14] It was at this same time that the hotels of the ETAL in eastern Libya were either closed or given over to the Italian military authorities. The advance of the British army beyond Benghazi in late 1940—a campaign that was waged against the forces of General Rodolfo Graziani—resulted in the sacking of tourist facilities like the Hotel Berenice.[15] The subsequent entry of the German army into the North African campaign resulted in another set of transformations of the tourist system in Libya. One of the most disturbing of these was the conversion of the Arab Café at the Suq al-Mushir into a German consulate and meeting place for the National Socialist Party.[16] The mutation of the tourist system in Libya under the conditions of war represents a somewhat ironic return to origins. Like the automobile *raid* in which Governor Giuseppe Volpi traveled with General Rodolfo Graziani from Tripoli to Ghadames in May of 1925—an expedition that took the form of a military exercise rather than a tourist excursion—the tourist system in Libya during the early part of the 1940s was once again fused with the military control of the territory.

NOTES

INTRODUCTION

1. Telegram from Volpi to the Minister of the Colonies, May 31, 1925. ASMAE–MAI 3–154. Fasc. Raid automobilistico. The Italian term "raid" means both an automobile race and a military raid. I left the term untranslated to retain this dual significance.

2. Ibid.

3. In addition to his other military activities on behalf of Volpi's administration between January 1922 and December 1924, Graziani led a successful mission to capture Ghadames from February 7–15, 1924. Angelo Del Boca, *Gli Italiani in Libia. Dal fascismo a Gheddafi* (Bari-Rome: Gius. Laterza & Figli, 1991), 36–37.

4. This first *raid* was held from February 26 to March 14, 1925, with arrival in Ghadames on the evening of March 4 and departure in the morning of March 8. See Babini, "Relazione del raid," 16 March 1925. ASMAE–MAI 3–154. Fascicolo–Raid automobilistico.

5. Ibid. The civilian passengers were newspaper correspondent Raffaele Calzini and a professional photographer.

6. "Da Bengasi a Tripoli in Automobile. Come 38 macchine nel deserto annunciano che la Libia è unificata," *Giornale d'Oriente* (28 June 1931).

7. Del Boca, *Gli italiani in Libia. Dal fascismo a Gheddafi*, 207, 213.

8. "Da Bengasi a Tripoli in Automobile."

9. In the book *La rinascità della Tripolitania*, which commemorated the four years of the governorship of Giuseppe Volpi (1921–25), the tourist industry was discussed under the general category of the problem of the industrial development of Tripolitania. Tourism is also discussed under the "politics of transportation," where it is seen as a "new source of prosperity and movement for the Colony." Angelo Piccioli, ed., *La rinascità della Tripolitania. Memorie e studi sui quattro anni di governo del Conte Giuseppe Volpi di Misurata* (Milan: Casa Editrice A. Mondadori, 1926), 260, 511–12.

10. For a detailed discussion of colonial literature see Giovanna Tomasello, *La letteratura coloniale italiana dalle avanguardie al fascismo* (Palermo: Sellerio Editore, 1984). A similar presentation is made on scientific research in Libya during the governorship of Italo Balbo in Del Boca, *Gli italiani in Libia. Dal fascismo a Gheddafi*, 271–78.

11. Pollock, *Avant-Garde Gambits 1888-1893: Gender and the Color of Art History* (New York: Thames and Hudson, 1992), 62. In this essay, she states that "the structures and practices of tourism constitute a unifying consciousness by which the fragmented and complex forms of modern society can be reassembled, but in a displaced form, as spectacle."

12. Giuseppe Bruni, "Il nuovo assetto politico-amministrativo della Libia," in *Viaggio del Duce in Libia per l'inaugurazione della litoranea: Orientamenti e note ad uso dei giornalisti* (Rome: Stabilimento Tipografico *Il Lavoro Fascista*, 1937), 1–14. See also Del Boca, *Gli italiani in Libia. Dal fascismo a Gheddafi*, 279–80.

13. Claudio Segrè argues that Balbo was well aware of the French attempts to assimilate their local populations in their North African colonies, and of the relative lack of success of these efforts in Algeria and Tunisia. Segrè, *Italo Balbo: A Fascist Life* (Berkeley: University of California Press, 1987), 324.

14. Fabian, *Time and the Other: How Anthropology Makes Its Object* (New York:

Columbia University Press, 1983), 31.

15. For a discussion of the display of people in World's Fairs, see Burton Benedict, *The Anthropology of World's Fairs* (London and Berkeley: Scholar Press, 1983), 43–45.

16. Berman, *All That Is Solid Melts into Air: The Experience of Modernity* (New York: Simon & Schuster, 1982), 15.

17. Said, *Orientalism* (New York: Vintage Books, 1978), 12.

18. Bhabha, "Of Mimicry and Man: The Ambivalence of Colonial Discourse," in *The Location of Culture* (London and New York: Routledge, 1994), 86.

19. Ibid., 86.

20. Bhabha, "Signs Taken for Wonders: Questions of Ambivalence and Authority under a Tree outside Delhi, May 1817," in *The Location of Culture*, 120.

21. Lowe, *Critical Terrains: French and British Orientalisms* (Ithaca: Cornell University Press, 1991), 11.

22. See Roland Sarti, "Fascist Modernization in Italy: Traditional or Revolutionary?" *American Historical Review* LXXV, 4 (April 1970): 1029–45. Other arguments include: Philip V. Cannistraro, "Mussolini's Cultural Revolution: Fascist or Nationalist?" *Journal of Contemporary History* 7, 3–4 (July-October 1972): 115–39.

23. Herf, *Reactionary Modernism: Technology, Culture, and Politics in Weimar and the Third Reich* (Cambridge: Cambridge University Press, 1984), 1. In the introduction of this book, Herf states: "Before and after the Nazi seizure of power, an important current within conservative and subsequently Nazi ideology was a reconciliation between the antimodernist, romantic, and irrationalist ideas present in German nationalism and the most obvious manifestation of means-end rationality, that is, modern technology."

24. Ghirardo, "Italian Architects and Fascist Politics: An Evaluation of the Rationalist's Role in Regime Building," *Journal of the Society of Architectural Historians* 39, 2 (May 1980): 109–27. This essay is principally aimed at Italian scholars whose attempts to rescue Italian Rationalism from political concerns have clouded their judgment on these works. It is also an explicit critique of theorists like Peter Eisenman, whose writings from that time on Terragni represent pure formal analysis aimed at producing a contemporary architecture. See Eisenman, "Dall'oggetto alla relazionalità: la Casa del Fascio di Terragni," *Casabella* 344 (January 1970): 38–41; and "From Object to Relationship II: Giuseppe Terragni–Casa Giuliani-Frigerio," *Perspecta* 13-14 (1971): 36–61. This essay was quickly followed by a second, more detailed argument. See Ghirardo, "Politics of a Masterpiece: The Vicenda of the Decoration of the Facade of the Casa del Fascio, Como, 1936–1939," *The Art Bulletin 62* (September 1980): 466-78. See also Ghirardo, *Building New Communities: New Deal America and Fascist Italy* (Princeton: Princeton University Press, 1989).

25. MacCannell, *The Tourist: A New Theory of the Leisure Class*, 3d ed. (Berkeley: University of California Press, 1999), 4.

26. Ibid., 99.

27. The idea of Libya as part of Italy's Mediterranean empire was extremely pervasive in Mussolini's speeches. See Mussolini, "Dal malinconico tramonto liberale all'aurora fascista della nuova Italia, Discorso alla Sciesa di Milano, 4 ottobre 1922," in *Opera Omnia di Benito Mussolini. Volume XVIII. Dalla conferenza di Cannes alla Marcia su Roma (14 gennaio 1922–30 ottobre 1922)*, ed. Edoardo and Dulio Susmel (Firenze: La Fenice, 1956), 433–40.

28. Edensor, *Tourists at the Taj: Performance and Meaning at a Symbolic Site* (London and New York: Routledge, 1998), 25.

29. Edensor and Kothari, "Sweetening Colonialism: A Mauritian Themed Resort," *Architecture and Tourism: Perception, Performance and Place*, eds. D. Medina Lasansky and Brian McLaren (Oxford, UK: Berg Press, 2004), 204.

30. Gramsci, "Appunti per una introduzione e un avviamento allo studio della filosofia e della storia della culture. 1. Alcuni punti preliminari di riferimento," *Quaderno* 11, §12, 1932–33, in *Quaderni del Carcere. Volume secondo. Quaderni 6 (VIII)–11 (XVIII)* (Turin:

Giulio Einaudi Editore, 1975), 1375.

31. Gramsci, "Concept of National-Popular," *Quaderno* 21, §5, 1934–35, in *Quaderni del Carcere. Volume terzo*, 2314. In this discussion, Gramsci argues that "folklore must not be considered an eccentricity, an oddity or a picturesque element, but as something which is very serious and is to be taken seriously. Only in this way will the teaching of folklore be more efficient and really bring about the birth of a new culture among the broad popular masses, so that the separation between modern culture and popular culture or folklore will disappear. An activity of this kind, thoroughly carried out, would correspond on the intellectual plane to what the Reformation was in Protestant countries."

32. William E. Simeone, "Fascists and Folklorists in Italy," *Journal of American Folklore* XCI, 359 (January–March 1978): 543–57.

33. Gramsci, "Passato e presente," *Quaderno* 14, §7, 1932–35, in *Quaderni del Carcere. Volume terzo*, 1660–61.

34. Edensor, *Tourists at the Taj*, 13.

35. Tafuri, "Introduction: The Historical Project," in *The Sphere and the Labyrinth: Avant-Gardes and Architecture from Piranesi to the 1970s*, translated by Pellegrino d'Acierno and Robert Connolly (Cambridge: The MIT Press, 1987), 14.

1. THE INCORPORATION OF LIBYA INTO METROPOLITAN ITALY

1. Balbo, "La Litoranea libica," *Convegno di scienze morali e storiche, 4–11 ottobre 1938, XVI. Tema: l'Africa. Vol. II* (Rome: Reale Accademia d'Italia, 1939), 1194.

2. Segrè, *Italo Balbo: A Fascist Life* (Berkeley, CA: University of California Press), 230–65.

3. Balbo, "La Litoranea libica," 1206.

4. John Wright, *Libya* (London: Ernest Benn Limited, 1969), 127.

5. Ibid., 122–23.

6. For a general discussion of the issue of Italian colonization during the late nineteenth and early twentieth century, see Claudio Segrè, *Fourth Shore: The Italian Colonization of Libya* (Chicago: The University of Chicago Press, 1974), 3–19. The author notes that with regard to the Libyan conquest, a good deal of impetus was created by Nationalist political commentators like Corradini and poets like Carducci and D'Annunzio.

7. Mussolini, "Dal malinconico tramonto liberale all'aurora fascista della nuova Italia," in *Opera Omnia di Benito Mussolini. Vol. XVIII. Dalla conferenza di Cannes alla Marcia su Roma (14 gennaio 1922–30 ottobre 1922)*, 434.

8. Mussolini asserted that "by completing this difficult and patient work, of cyclopean lines, we will truly inaugurate a great period in Italian history." Ibid., 439.

9. "La visita del Duce in Tripolitania nel 1926 e lo 'Scossone' coloniale," in *Viaggio del Duce in Libia per l'inaugurazione della litoranea. Anno XV. Orientamenti e note ad uso dei giornalisti* (Rome: Stabilimento Tipografico Il Lavoro Fascista, 1937), 1–11.

10. Roberto Cantalupo, "Mussolini e l'Africa," *Gerarchia* VI, 4 (April 1926): 209–16.

11. Mussolini, "Speech to Primo Convegno Agricolo Nazionale Coloniale, April 15, 1926," in *Scritti e discorsi di Benito Mussolini. Vol. V. Dal 1925 al 1926* (Milan: Ulrico Hoepli Editore, 1934), 321.

12. Mussolini, "Ai camerati di Tripoli" (March 17, 1937), in *Opera omnia di Benito Mussolini. Vol. XXVIII. Dalla proclamazione dell'Impero al viaggio in Germania (10 maggio 1936–30 settembre 1937)* (Florence: La Fenice, 1959), 145.

13. Ibid., 144.

14. For a general discussion of the public works projects undertaken by the Fascist Regime, see Donatella Calabi, "The Idea of the City and Technical Knowledge in Modern Italy: Public Works," in *Modern Italy: Images and History of a National Identity. Vol. 2. From Expansion to the Second World War* (Milan: Electa Editrice, 1983), 263–70.

15. Ali Abdullatif Ahmida, *The Making of Modern Libya: State Formation, Colonization*

and Resistance, 1830–1932 (Albany: State University of New York Press, 1994), 31, 61.

16. Marida Talamona, "Libya: an Architectural Workshop," *Rassegna* 51 (September 1992): 62–69.

17. Luiggi, "Le opere pubbliche a Tripoli," *Nuova Antologia* 47, 965 (March 1, 1912): 115–30.

18. Ibid., 123.

19. Ibid., 127.

20. Ahmida, *The Making of Modern Libya,* 103–40 passim.

21. A detailed account of the Libyan war and the initial years of colonial rule is provided in Wright, "A Historic Destiny" and "The Years of Accord," in *Libya,* 118–38, 139–46.

22. "Tripolitania. Rapporto Gr.Uff. Niccoli e Governatore Volpi sulla situazione politica della Tripolitania," November 23, 1924. ACS-PCM 1924, 17–4–3093.

23. Wright, *Libya,* 164.

24. The reconquest of coastal areas of Tripolitania was done through a series of military campaigns between January 1922 and November 1924. See Sergio Romano, *Giuseppe Volpi. Industria e finanza tra Giolitti e Mussolini* (Milan: Bompiani, 1979), 102–12. For a more detailed account, see Del Boca, *Gli italiani in Libia. Dal fascismo a Gheddafi,* 5–76.

25. Volpi was the first and only governor of Tripolitania who was not a military officer. Following his appointment in Tripolitania, he became the finance minister under Mussolini from 1925 to 1928. Edoardo Savino, *La Nazione Operante. Albo d'oro del fascismo* (Novara: Istituto geografico De Agostini, 1937), 98–99.

26. Segrè, *Fourth Shore,* 47-56. The changes in land policy under Volpi allowed for a substantial growth (over ten times) in the amount of land available for agricultural colonization.

27. Romano, *Giuseppe Volpi. Industria e finanza tra Giolitti e Mussolini,* 115–16.

28. Ernesto Queirolo, "La politica delle comunicazioni," in *La rinascità della Tripolitania,* 259–83.

29. Ibid., 259.

30. Ernesto Palumbo Cardella, "Le opere pubbliche," in *La rinascità della Tripolitania,* 353–80.

31. See *La rinascità della Tripolitania.* The book was subtitled "Memories and studies on the four years of governing of Count Giuseppe Volpi of Misurata," and was published by the prestigious Mondadori of Milan.

32. Ibid., xvii.

33. Del Boca, *Gli italiani in Libia. Dal fascismo a Gheddafi,* 93–103.

34. For information on the propaganda efforts of the Ministry of the Colonies, see Angelo Piccioli, "La Ricognizione scientifica e la propaganda," in *La nuova Italia d'oltremare* (Milan: A. Mondadori Editore, 1933), 1717–57. For general information on the Colonial Day, see "Giornata coloniale sotto l'alto patronato di S.A.R. Luigi di Savoia, President d'onore a S.E. Mussolini." ACS — PCM 1926, 17.1.934.

35. De Bono, "Le mie idee sulla colonizzazione," *L'Oltremare* II, 8 (August 1928): 293–95.

36. Segrè, *Fourth Shore,* 57–81.

37. The following statement was made in the program that was sent to prospective participants: "The Exhibition will have a strictly national character because only products of Italian labor will be exhibited—whether from any part of the world where people of our nation live and work." *Prima Esposizione Fiera Campionaria di Tripoli. Programma* (Spoleto: Arti Grafiche Panetto & Petrelli, 1927), 6.

38. Tajani, "La giornata inaugurale. Impressione sulla mostra," *Corriere della Sera* (16 February 1927): 1. This assertion ignores the much earlier Franco-Moroccan Exhibition, held in Casablanca in September of 1915.

39. The reality of this event was rather less sanguine. After only two years, Mussolini

was ready to make it a triennial event. See Mario Bevilacqua, "A proposito di Fiere campionarie." *Il Giornale Economico* 8 (August 1929). In this essay, Bevilacqua notes that in 1928, 700,000 lire was invested in new buildings while the total sales were only 100,000 lire.

40. Angelo Piccioli, "L'opera di S.E. Emilio De Bono in Tripolitania," in *Vigor di vita in Tripolitania (Anno 1928–VI)* (Tripoli: Ufficio Studi e propaganda del Governo della Tripolitania), 17–22.

41. L.V. Bertarelli, *Guida d'Italia del TCI, Possedimenti e colonie* (Milan: Touring Club Italiano, 1929), 330–31, 335–36, 340.

42. Ibid., 325.

43. Piccioli, "Le comunicazioni," in *Vigor di vita in Tripolitania (1928, VI)*, 75–85. See also A. Fantoli, "Le strade della Tripolitania," *Le Vie d'Italia* XL, 4 (April 1934): 274–87.

44. His position as general secretary in Tripolitania was under Emilio De Bono, remaining to work under Pietro Badoglio, who promoted him to vice governor in October 1930. He left this post in July 1931 to become governor of Somalia. Savino, *La Nazione Operante. Albo d'oro del fascismo*, 90.

45. For a concise account of the military operations under Badoglio, see Wright, *Libya*, 160–68. The final conquest of these colonies began in the Fezzan of Tripolitania in 1929–30 and concluded in Al-Jaghbub and Al-Kufra in Cyrenaica in 1930–31.

46. Maurizio De Rege, "Il nuovo piano regolatore di Tripoli," *Urbanistica* III, 3 (May–June 1934): 121–28.

47. Rabinow, "Colonialism, Modernity: The French in Morocco," in *Forms of Dominance: On the Architecture and Urbanism of the Colonial Experience* (Brookfield: Ashgate Publishing Company, 1992), 167–82.

48. In Tripoli six centers were identified, each of which was to have its own area of services. De Rege, "Il nuovo piano regolatore di Tripoli," 127.

49. Ibid., 123–27. The plan called for a zone of more intensive building (up to four stories), with the remaining area up to two stories. Within this general framework, particular zones were highlighted as industrial, indigenous, and agricultural.

50. Segrè, *Fourth Shore*, 69–81.

51. Virgilio Testa, "Il Padiglione di Roma alla Fiera di Tripoli," *Capitolium* V, 5 (March 1929): 225–28.

52. During De Bono's governorship the total support for infrastructure averaged around 13.5 million lire per year. The first year under Pietro Badoglio, 27 million lire were spent. Piccioli, *La nuova Italia d'oltremare*, 910–16.

53. "Tripolitania e Cirenaica — Notiziario d'Informazioni economico-agrario, politico, militare ecc., di dette Colonie." ACS — PCM 1931-33, 17.1.6267.

54. Piccioli, *La nuova Italia d'oltremare*, 914. See also Pellegrineschi, "Le nuove strade della Libia," *Rivista delle Colonie Italiane* VII, 11 (November 1933): 888.

55. Fantoli, "Le strade di Tripolitania," 279.

56. These hotels were constructed in Ajdabiya (1932), Cyrene (1932), Ghadames (1931), al-Khums (1931), Yifran (1930), Misurata (1930), Sirt (1933), and Zuwarah (1930). "Tripolitania e Cirenaica—Notiziario d'Informazioni economico-agrario, politico, militare ecc., di dette Colonie." ACS — PCM 1931–33, 17.1.6267.

57. Piccioli, *La nuova Italia d'oltremare*.

58. Mussolini, Preface, *La nuova Italia d'oltremare*, xii.

59. Piccioli, Conclusione, *La nuova Italia d'oltremare*, 1762.

60. Giuseppe Bruni, "Il nuovo assetto politico-amministrativo della Libia," in *Viaggio del Duce in Libia per l'inaugurazione della litoranea. Anno XV. Orientamenti e note ad uso dei giornalisti* (Rome: Stabilimento Tipografico Il Lavoro Fascista, 1937), 1–14.

61. For a more detailed examination of this process in the form of drafts of this legislation and the various negotiations between Balbo and Alessandro Lessona and Emilio De Bono at the Ministry of the Colonies, see ASMAE — MAI, Dir.Gen. AA.Cartella 54 and 56.

62. The main administrative bodies of colonial government continued to be the General

Council and the Government Council. This legislation substantially transformed the role and constitution of this first group, which became an investigative body whose members were chosen by the administration to represent all of the various economic interests in the colony. The advisory function of the Government Council did not change, while its membership was limited to individuals from within the administration. Bruni, "Il nuovo assetto politico-amministrativo della Libia," 10.

63. Ibid., 5.

64. In a letter dated December 7, 1934, Balbo describes the idea of decentralization as follows: "the position of the General Provincial Councils in the administrative regulation of Libya effectively represents . . . the central colonial government in all of its interests and the complexities of its powers and attributions." Letter from Governor of Tripolitania to the Ministry of Colonies. Tripoli, 7 December 1934. ASMAE — MAI, Dir.Gen. AA.Cartella 54, Fascicolo 30.

65. Bruni, "Il nuovo assetto politico-amministrativo della Libia," 8.

66. The law is Regio Decreto Legge 29 April 1935, n. 2006. Mario Scaparro, "Origini e sviluppi dell'ordinamento corporativo libico," *Rassegna Economica dell'Africa Italiana* XXV, 3 (March 1937): 362–67.

67. This legislation was Regio Decreto Legge 9 January 1939, n. 70, which incorporated the four provinces of Libya into metropolitan Italy. For a detailed discussion of the debate concerning this law, see ASMAE — MAI, Dir.Gen.AA.PP. Cartella 54–56.

68. *Italia meridionale e insulare—Libia. Guida Breve, Volume III* (Milano: Consociazione Turistica Italiana, 1940), 385–434.

69. There had already been a significant increase during the governorship of Badoglio (28.5 million lire/year) from that of De Bono (13.5 million lire/year). With regard to the first two years of Balbo's governorship, the average expenditure was around 54 million lire/year (all of these figures are for Tripolitania alone). See MAI. Dir.Gen. AA.EE. e FF. Riassunto delle spese per opere pubbliche o di pubblica utilità. 1913/14–1936/37. ASMAE — MAI 3-56, Fascicolo–OO.Servizi.

70. *Suddivisione politico-amministrativo del territorio della Libia* (Tripoli: Plinio Maggi, 1935).

71. Between 1934 and 1940, housing and barracks related to this new administrative structure were constructed in Tripoli, Misurata, Bani Walid, Bin Ghashir, Gharyan, Jadu, al-Khums, Yifran, Nalut, Surman, Tarhunah, Az Zawiya and Zlitan. See Le Opere Pubbliche in Libia. ASMAE — MAI 3–56, Fascicolo OO.PP.-Servizi.

72. A. Giovannangeli, "Cenni sull'attività municipale di Tripoli," in *Viaggio del Duce in Libia per l'inaugurazione della litoranea. Anno XV. Orientamenti e note ad uso dei giornalisti* (Rome: Stabilimento Tipografico Il Lavoro Fascista, 1937), 1–13.

73. A.V. Pellegrineschi, "Le nuove strade della Libia," *Gerarchia* XV, 10 (October 1935): 866–71.

74. G. Bucciante, "Lo sviluppo edilizio della Libia," in *Viaggio del Duce in Libia per l'inaugurazione della litoranea. Anno XV. Orientamenti e note ad uso dei giornalisti* (Rome: Stabilimento Tipografico Il Lavoro Fascista, 1937), 4–5.

75. Ibid., 4.

76. This plan was adopted by the Municipality of Tripoli in a meeting on May 7, 1934. See Municipio di Tripoli—Ufficio Tecnico, "Relazione sul piano regolatore e d'ampliamento della città di Tripoli," 1934, 1–30. ACS — MAI 114.

77. Bucciante, "Lo sviluppo edilizio della Libia," 5.

78. While the entire length of this highway was listed at 1,822 kilometers, by their own admission this project involved only 813 kilometers of new construction. *La strada litoranea della Libia* (Verona: Officine Grafiche A. Mondadori, 1937), 33.

79. Ibid., 127–34.

80. Ibid., 16–17.

81. This project was, by all accounts, both on time and on budget. This work was

accomplished through a well-organized process that divided the road into segments and called for competitive bids. Segrè, *Italo Balbo: A Fascist Life*, 296–98.

82. Balbo, "La strada litoranea," 11–12.

83. The two bronze statues were executed by the sculptor Ulderico Conti. The travertine bas-reliefs, located over the archway with one facing each direction, were by the artists Quirino Ruggeri (foundation of the road) and Ercole Drei (foundation of the Italian Empire). *La strada litoranea della Libia*, 134–48.

84. "Viaggio del Duce in Libia per l'inaugurazione della Litoranea — Programma Sommario." Tripoli, 18 February 1937. ACS — MCP, Busta 105 Sottofascicolo 4.

85. Segrè, *Italo Balbo: A Fascist Life,* 309.

86. The ECL was a para-state organization that was specifically created to resettle unemployed farm workers in this colony, while the INFPS was a social welfare organization that was involved in land reclamation projects in Italy. Segrè, *Fourth Shore*, 82–111.

87. This plan was formalized with Regio Decreto Legge, n. 701 of May 17, 1938. Del Boca, *Gli italiani in Libia. Dal fascismo a Gheddafi*, 260.

88. Segrè, *Italo Balbo: A Fascist Life*, 311–12.

89. Four such villages were constructed in Cyrenaica for the 1938 mass colonization project: Baracca, Battisti, D'Annunzio, and Oberdan. Wright, *Libya*, 172–73. Six were constructed in Tripolitania in 1938: Bianchi, Giordani, Oliveti, Breviglieri, Crispi, and Gioda. Segrè, *Fourth Shore*, 117.

90. The entire process of departure was organized with military precision. Not only was each family identified and given clear directions at every step in this process, but the various celebrations relating to their departure were meticulously planned. See "Trasferimento in Libia di famiglie coloniche." ACS — PCM 1937–39, 17.4.6001.

91. Martin Moore, *Fourth Shore: Italy's Mass Colonization of Libya* (London, 1940); and Herbert Bailey, "The Colonization of Libya," *Fortnightly Review* 145 (February 1939): 197–204. The manipulative aspects of this event were not lost on Bailey, who stated that "from the time that we left Genoa until the colonists entered their new homes, we lived in an unreal world of propaganda."

92. Balbo, "Coloni in Libia," *Nuova Antologia* (November 1, 1938): 3–13.

93. Bhabha, "Of Mimicry and Man: The Ambivalence of Colonial Discourse," in *The Location of Culture*, 86.

94. Ibid., 86.

2. COLONIAL TOURISM AND THE EXPERIENCE OF MODERNITY

1. Brunelli, "Ospitalità e turismo in Libia," *Viaggio del Duce per l'inaugurazione della litoranea. Anno XV. Orientamenti e note ad uso dei giornalisti* (Rome: Stabilimento Tipografico Il Lavoro Fascista, 1937), 1.

2. This press release was one of several published just prior to Mussolini's visit under the same title, *Viaggio del Duce in Libia per l'inaugurazione della litoranea. Anno XV. Orientamenti e note ad uso dei giornalisti*. All of these documents are bound into two volumes in the library of the ISIAO in Rome.

3. Brunelli, "Ospitalità e turismo in Libia," 1.

4. Ibid., 7.

5. The chapters of this book are as follows: I. La città nuova; II. La Baladìa (Il Municipio); III. Un decennio di opere pubbliche in Tripolitania; IV. Le scuole nella Tripolitania; V. Le ricerche archeologiche; VI. L'Istituto Agrario; VII. Le ferrovie della Tripolitania; VIII. Il bilancio civile, 1921–22; IX. Qualche dato economico sulla Tripolitania; X. La «Dante Alighieri»; and XI. La chiesa cattolica a Tripoli. *Guida di Tripoli e dintorni* (Milano: Fratelli Treves Editori, 1925).

6. Ibid., 2.

7. Of the twenty-eight photographs in this guidebook, only two—a panorama of Tripoli

and a view of the castle—show the local architecture. Nine of the photographs show Roman statuary and ruins.

8. The relationship between these two volumes and the intent of their presentation cannot be underestimated. Particularly notable is the focus on financial and economic data in *Guida di Tripoli e dintorni,* in no small part due to the economic focus of Volpi's governorship.

9. *Guida di Tripoli e dintorni,* 10.

10. Gennaro Pistolese, "Turismo d'Oltremare," *Rivista delle Colonie Italiane* III, 6–7 (June–July 1929): 552–53. In remarking on the recent Mediterranean cruises, he argues that "such visitors to our colonies . . . will return to Italy as proponents of the beauty and value of those lands."

11. Ibid., 555.

12. Giuseppe Borghetti, "Turismo coloniale," *L'Italia Coloniale* VIII, 9 (September 1931): 141–42. The author remarks on the deficiency of the Italian popular tourist propaganda effort in relation to Britain, France, and even Germany, stating: "The publications of this type [by these nations] count in the dozens every year."

13. One article in particular, published in 1933, while recognizing that "all of the conditions exist in Tripolitania for making a higher tourist yield," looked at the tourist infrastructure of the *Compagnie Générale Transatlantique* in the French colonies. See XXX, "Turismo coloniale. Possibilità di sviluppo e necessità di un comando unico," *L'Italia Coloniale* X, 10 (October 1933): 182.

14. The larger context of this statement is as follows: "To obtain a substantial development of tourism in relation to our colonies, we must above all provide for the necessity of organization: that is, to graft the Libyan itineraries into the network of Mediterranean tourist crossings." Giuseppe Borghetti, "Turismo coloniale," 141.

15. XXX, "Turismo coloniale," 182.

16. Ibid., 182.

17. Bertarelli, *Guida d'Italia del TCI. Possedimenti e Colonie.* In addition to Tripolitania and Cyrenaica, this volume presents the colonies of the Italian Aegean Islands, Eritrea, and Somalia. There was an earlier guidebook published on Tripolitania and Cyrenaica by the TCI in 1923. Touring Club Italiano, *Guida della Libia* (Milan: The Club, 1923).

18. Ibid., 250–69. The main topics of this section bear striking resemblance to the earlier publication on the governorship of Volpi. They include: Public works; Building renovations; Politics of communication; Telephone and telegraph service; Railways; Air and maritime travel; Politics of agricultural colonization; Water reclamation; Provisions for livestock. The final section, called the Moral conquest, is a literal reference to this earlier volume, comprising subtopics of Justice, Schools, Sanitary works, Archeological research, Propaganda, the Tripoli Trade Fair, Tourist development, and the Work of tomorrow.

19. Ibid., 268.

20. Giuseppe Vedovato, *Colonizzazione e turismo in Libia* (Salerno: Prem. Stamperia Raffaello Beraglia, 1934). Vedovato was a student of colonial studies at the Cesare Alfieri Institute of Social and Political Science in Florence who took part in an instructional trip to Libya that led to this research project and its eventual publication.

21. Ibid., 8.

22. Ibid., 11–12.

23. The TCI published its other colonies in the following volumes: *Guida dell'Africa Orientale Italiana,* 1938 (comprising Italy's empire in East Africa: Eritrea, Somalia, and Ethiopia) and *Albania,* 1940. A volume on the Italian Aegean Islands was projected for publication in 1937, but was never published.

24. Bertarelli, *Guida d'Italia del Touring Club Italiano. Libia* (Milan: Touring Club Italiano, 1937), 5–6.

25. The term "valorizzazione" is not easily translated into English. It means bringing out the value of something, exploitation, or utilization.

26. Professor Emanuele De Cillis, "Valorizzazione della Libia," in *Guida d'Italia del*

Touring Club Italiano. Libia, ed. Bertarelli, 127.

27. Marida Talamona, "Libya: An Architectural Workshop," *Rassegna* 51 (September 1992): 69.

28. Queirolo, "La politica delle comunicazioni," *La rinascità della Tripolitania*, 260.

29. Enrico Niccoli, "Il problema industriale in Tripolitania," *La rinascità della Tripolitania*, 511–12.

30. See "Il Governatore invia lettera dell'Istituto Coloniale Italiano (sez. Tripoli) sul trattamento che sarebbe usato a Siracusa ai viaggiatori ed alle merci da e per la Libia." ACS — PCM 1921, 13–3–1707.

31. "Il Convegno archeologico di Tripoli," *Rivista della Tripolitania* I, VI (May–June 1925): 417–23.

32. *Guida di Tripoli e dintorni*, vii–xii.

33. Piccioli, "La valorizzazione turistica," in *La nuova Italia d'oltremare*, 1562.

34. For the original statute of the Italian Colonial Institute and information on its activities until 1932, see ASMAE — MAI, Vol. 3 – 46, Fascicolo 13.

35. ASMAE — MAI, Vol. 3 – 39, Fascicolo – Istituto Coloniale Fascista.

36. Bertarelli, *Guida d'Italia del Touring Club Italiano. Possedimenti e colonie*, 277. In addition to the Grand Hotel, which had 120 beds, there were the Grand National Hotel, with 80; the Excelsior, with 40; the Italia, with 50; and the Savoia. Other hotels of a medium-quality range were the Miramare pensione, with 20 beds; the Moderno, with 50; and the Patria, with 60. The most modest were the Commercio, with 30; the Mignon, with 50; and the Marco Aurelio, with 45.

37. Bertarelli, *Guida d'Italia del Touring Club Italiano. Possedimenti e colonie*, 313, 364.

38. "Alle porte del Sahara in autobus," *L'Italia Coloniale* VI, 3 (March 1929): 46.

39. Piccioli, "La valorizzazione turistica," *La nuova Italia d'oltremare*, 1564.

40. Ibid., 1564. Both government employees and agricultural workers were forbidden to use the facility.

41. Ibid., 1564.

42. "La linea aerea Roma—Tripoli," *L'Oltremare* II, 11 (November 1928): 431.

43. Letter from "Italia" company to the Ministry of the Colonies, 8 March 1933. ASMAE – MAI, Vol. 2 – 150/29 fasc. 134.

44. The TCI also held a "National Excursion" in Cirenaica in October of 1933, in this case commemorating the pacification of this region. Giuseppe Vota, ed., *I sessant'anni del Touring Club Italiano* (Milan: Touring Club Italiano, 1954), 259–60.

45. ASMAE – MAI, Vol. 3 – 39, Fascicolo—Istituto Coloniale Fascista. This group which was founded in 1906 was called the Italian Colonial Institute (ICI) until 1928.

46. See Società Nazionale "Dante Alighieri," *Guida programma del viaggio a Civitavecchia - Cagliari - Tunisi - Tripoli - Malta - Siracusa – Napoli* (Milan: Edizioni Turisanda, 1927). The *Avanguardisti* held cruises in June 1928, July 1930 (Trapani, 150 members), April 1933 (Forli, 150 members) and September 1933 (Trieste, 130 members). "Tripolitania e Cirenaica – Notiziario d'Informazioni." ACS—PCM 1931–33—17.1.6267.

47. The annual arrivals in Tripolitania are as follows: 1927: 5,478 Italians, 1,054 foreigners, totaling 6,532; 1930: 7,641 Italians, 1,504 foreigners, totaling 9,145; 1933: 8,541 Italians, 3,038 foreigners, totaling 11,579. "Movimenti negli alberghi di Tripoli." ASMAE – MAI, Vol. 3 – 44, fasc. 10.

48. "Ministero dell'Interno—Pro-memoria—Facilitazioni per lo sbarco nei porti del Regno di crocieristi stranieri," 1932-33. ASMAE – MAI, Vol. 2 – 129, Fascicolo 135.

49. Piccioli, "L'azione dell'Ente Turistico Tripolitano," in *La nuova Italia d'oltremare*, 1565–66. For a comprehensive examination of tourism in Italy, see Taina Syrjämaa, *Visitez l'Italie: Italian State Tourist Propaganda Abroad 1919–1943* (Ph.D. dissertation, Department of General History, University of Turku, 1977), in *Turun Yliopiston Julkaisuja. Annales Universitatis Turkuensis*, Ser. B, Tom 217 (1977). For a description of ENIT, see Luigi Rava, "Che cosa e l'ENIT," *Rassegna Italiana del Mediterraneo* V, 59 (December 1925): 397–400.

50. See "Cronache coloniali. L'organizzazione dell'Ente turistico tripolitano," *Rivista delle Colonie Italiane* V, 1 (January 1931): 53. See also "Il turismo coloniale. Un Ente centrale per coordinare le varie attività," *L'Italia Coloniale* X, 9 (September 1933): 170.

51. A government statute was passed in June 1933, which gave a 50 percent reduction on the cost of rail and maritime travel to Tripoli between October one year and May of the next. Piccioli, "L'azione dell'Ente Turistico Tripolitano," *La nuova Italia d'oltremare*, 1565.

52. "Il Congresso delle Agenzie di viaggio," *Rivista delle Colonie Italiane* V, 12 (December 1931): 963–64.

53. R. Matignon, *La Compagnie Générale Transatlantique depuis la guerre*, Ph.D. thesis, University of Bordeau, 1937 (Bordeaux: Imprimiere-Librairie Delmas, 1937).

54. Compagnie Générale Transatlantique, *North African Motor Tours of the Compagnie Générale Transatlantique* (London: Hill, Siffken & Co., 1928).

55. Carlo Bonardi, "L'avvenire turistico della Libia," *Le Vie d'Italia* XLIII, 6 (June 1937): 434.

56. M. A. Loschi, "L'autostrada del deserto libico," *Le Vie d'Italia* XLII, 8 (August 1936): 529–37.

57. Bucciante, "Lo sviluppo edilizio della Libia," 5.

58. Ibid., 5. The new hotels constructed during the Balbo era were eight in total: the Berenice in Benghazi (1935); the Cussabat (1936); the Derna (1937); the Rumia in Yifran (1934); the Nalut (1934–35); the Tobruk (1937); and the Uaddan (1934–35) and the Mehari (1934–35) in Tripoli. The renovation projects were the 'Ain-el Fras in Ghadames (1934–35), the Sirt (1934–37), and the Gazelle in Zlitan (1935).

59. Bertarelli, *Guida d'Italia del Touring Club Italiano. Libia*, 144.

60. Ibid., 147–49. See also Corso Fougier, "Attrezzatura aeronautica della Libia dal punto di vista del traffico e del turismo aereo," in *Viaggio del Duce per l'inaugurazione della litoranea. Anno XV. Orientamenti e note ad uso dei giornalisti* (Rome: Stabilimento Tipografico *Il Lavoro Fascista*, 1937), 1–11.

61. Francesco Geraci, "Cronache di politica coloniale," *Gerarchia* XIV, 4 (April 1934): 353.

62. "Oltre 30,000 turisti in Libia nei primi mesi del 1934," *Rivista delle Colonie Italiane* VIII, 9 (September 1934): 772–73.

63. The number of OND cruises that visited Libya in 1934 was taken from "Tripolitania e Cirenaica – Notiziario d'informazioni." ACS – PCM 1934–36, 17.1.498. The number of ICF cruises in 1934 is listed in "Letter from Ministro delle Colonie to Governo della Libia." MAI – Archivio Segreto – 200, Fascicolo – Libia, turismo.

64. The company "Lloyd Triestino" operated an eight day cruise to visit Tripoli and the Tripoli Trade Fair in March 1934. ASMAE – MAI 150/28, Fascicolo 130, "Italia Cosulich" offered a fourteen-day Mediterranean cruise from August 1–14, 1934. See *Estate sul Mare. Crociere 1934–XII* (Milan: S.A. Stab. Alfieri & Lacroix, 1934).

65. Piccioli, "La Fiera di Tripoli," *Gli Annali dell'Africa Italiana* I, 2 (August 1938): 541–66.

66. The Grand Prix race was greatly enhanced during the Balbo era with both an improvement of its facilities and expansion of its scope. An annual lottery associated with the race provided funding for these improvements. Segrè, *Italo Balbo: A Fascist Life*, 304–5. For information on these other activities, see "Tripolitania e Cirenaica – Notiziario d'informazioni." ACS – PCM 1934–36, 17.1.498, and "Letter from Ministro delle Colonie to Governo della Libia." MAI – Archivio Segreto – 200, Fascicolo – Libia, turismo.

67. These conferences included a tropical and subtropical agricultural conference linked with the Tripoli Trade Fair in March of 1939.

68. Touring Club Italiano, *Manuale del turismo* (Milan: TCI, 1934), 30. This group was instituted with Regio Decreto Legge N. 1485, dated November 2, 1933.

69. Memorandum of meeting between the Minister of the Colonies and the Libyan Tourism Commission, March 1934. MAI – Archivio Segreto – n. 200/24, Fascicolo – Libia I – Commissariato per il turismo in Libia.

70. "Il Consiglio del Commissariato del turismo," *Rivista delle Colonie Italiane* VIII, 7 (July 1934): 594–95.

71. "Report of Ente turistico ed alberghiero della Libia," 1938. ASMAE – MAI 4–29, Fascicolo 210.

72. ETAL, "Realizzazioni fasciste. Gli sviluppi del Turismo Libico." ASMAE – MAI 5–5, Fascicolo 18.

73. "Report of Ente turistico ed alberghiero della Libia," 1938, 1.

74. Mussolini, "Discorso per lo stato corporativo," November 14, 1933. *Opera Omnia di Benito Mussolini, Vol. XXVI. Dal patto a quattro all'inaugurazione della provincia di Littoria (8 giugno 1933–18 dicembre 1934)*, edited by Edoardo and Dulio Susmel (Florence: La Fenice, 1958), 85–96.

75. "L'insediamento del Consiglio di Amministrazione dell'Ente turistico ed alberghiero," *L'Avvenire di Tripoli* (13 October 1935): 3.

76. The Libyan Tourism and Hotel Association was instituted with Regio Decreto Legge 31 May 1935, n. 1410. This legislation came into law with its publication in the *Gazzetta Ufficiale del Regno* n. 181, dated 5 August 1935.

77. "Istituzione dell'Ente turistico ed alberghiero della Libia," R. Decreto 31 May 1935, XIII, n. 1410. ASMAE – MAI 4-29, Fascicolo 210.

78. "Schema di R.D. relativo alla costituzione dell'Ente turistico ed alberghiero della Libia." ASMAE – CSC 19 (1935) N. 29 (20/5/1935).

79. "Approvazione dello statuto dell'Ente turistico ed alberghiero della Libia," Decreto Ministeriale 24 June 1935 — XIII. ASMAE – MAI 4-29, Fascicolo 210.

80. Ibid.

81. A report produced by the Tourism Commission in Italy in September of 1933 recommends the policing of the boundaries between these areas of activity. See Report from Commissioner of Tourism to the chair of the Council of Ministers, September 7, 1935. ACS – PCM 1934–36, 3.2.1–950. Sottofascicolo 1.

82. See "Approvazione dello statuto dell'Ente turistico ed alberghiero della Libia." See also "L'insediamento del Consiglio di Amministrazione dell'Ente turistico ed alberghiero," 3.

83. ETAL, "Realizzazioni fasciste. Gli sviluppi del turismo libico."

84. "Relazione tecnica del Direttore Generale al bilancio dell'esercizio 1936–37," 16–17. ASMAE – MAI 4–29, Fascicolo 210.

85. Letter from the ETAL dated February 26, 1936 ACS–ETAL [4], Fascicolo. Pubblicità. See also Eros Vicari, "L'Ente turistico ed alberghiero della Libia (E.T.A.L.)" Gli Annali dell 'Africa Italiana, V.4 (December 1942): 968.

86. ETAL,"Realizzazioni fasciste. Gli sviluppi del turismo libico" 3.

87. Riccardo Francaglia, "Il turismo libico e la grande opera dell'E.T.A.L.," 7. ASMAE – MAI 5–17, Fascicolo 219.

88. "Relazione tecnica del Direttore Generale al bilancio dell'esercizio 1936–37," 24–31.

89. Dante Frigerio, *Organizzazione e nuovi mezzi di potenziamento del turismo in Italia* (Bellinzona: Istituto Editoriale Ticinese, 1940), 33–34.

90. "Relazione tecnica del Direttore Generale al bilancio dell'esercizio 1936–37," 12.

91. Ibid., 18–20.

92. Vicari, "L'Ente turistico ed alberghiero della Libia" 962–67.

93. "Concessione in uso all'Ente turistico ed alberghiero della Libia di tutti gli alberghi governativi e municipali," Decreto governatoriale 15 novembre 1935 — XIV, n. 16454. ASMAE – MAI 4–29, Fascicolo 210.

94. Francalangia, "Il turismo libico e la grande opera dell'ETAL," 9.

95. "Relazione tecnica del Direttore Generale al bilancio dell'esercizio 1936–37," 21–22.

96. Vicari, "L'Ente turistico ed alberghiero della Libia," 967–68, 970–71.

97. "Organizzazione ETAL." ACS-ETAL [3] 36. Prospetti vari.

98. The number of tourists visiting Libya rose from around 28,000 in 1933 to almost 44,000 in 1938. Vicari, "L'Ente turistico ed alberghiero della Libia," 958. For information

on the financial state of this company and occupancy rate, see "Relazione tecnica del Direttore Generale al bilancio dell'esercizio 1936–37," 39.

99. All of the hotels in Libya were published in *Annuario Alberghi d'Italia* (originally called *Gli Alberghi in Italia*), a guidebook to hotels in Italy put out by ENIT on a yearly basis. Ente Nazionale Industrie Turistiche, *Annuario Alberghi in d'Italia, 1939* (Milan: Turati Lombardi E.C., 1939).

100. Ibid., 26.

101. Ente Autonomo Fiera Campionaria di Tripoli, *X Manifestazione Internazionale Intercoloniale in Africa. 9 marzo 9 maggio MCMXXXVI–XIV. Catalogo* (Milan and Rome: S. A. Arti Grafiche Bertarelli, 1936), 150–51.

102. ETAL, "Combinazioni di soggiorno," in Ente Autonomo Fiera Campionaria di Tripoli, *XI Manifestazione Internazionale Intercoloniale. Prima mostra dell'Impero Fascista* (Rome: Arti Grafiche Fratelli Palombi, 1937), 89.

103. ETAL, "Attrezzatura alberghiera," in Ente Autonomo Fiera Campionaria di Tripoli, *XI Manifestazione Internazionale Intercoloniale*, 90–91.

104. "Relazione tecnica del Direttore Generale al bilancio dell'esercizio 1936–37," 24.

105. ETAL, *La Libia* (Milan: F. Milan, 1936), 1.

106. Ibid., 3.

107. Ibid., 14.

108. Giovanni De Agostini, *La Libia Turistica* (Milano: Prof. G. De Agostini, 1938), 14–17.

109. Ibid., 19–28, 79–80, 100–109.

110. Ibid., 19.

111. "Nel nome del Duce," *Libia* I, 1 (March 1937): 2.

112. Gaspere Ambrosini, "Ragioni e carattere della grande riforma civile in Libia," *Libia* III, 1 (January 1939): 5–11.

113. Balbo, "La Litoranea. Opera Romana," *Libia* I, 1, (March 1937): 3–9.

114. Aner, "Edificare in tempo Fascista." *Libia* I, 1 (March 1937): 33.

115. Ibid., 35.

116. "Relazione tecnica del Direttore Generale al bilancio dell'esercizio 1936–37," 19, 29–31. See also "Report of Ente turistico ed alberghiero della Libia," 1938, 3–4.

117. "Relazione tecnica del Direttore Generale al bilancio dell'esercizio 1936–37," 23.

118. Vicari, "L'Ente turistico ed alberghiero della Libia," 971.

119. Ibid., 964.

120. ETAL, *Itinerario Tripoli-Gadames* (Milan: Tipo-Litografia Turati Lombardi, 1939), 60.

121. Ibid.

122. ETAL, "Realizzazioni fasciste. Gli sviluppi del turismo libico," 2.

123. ETAL, *La Libia*, 13.

3. THE INDIGENOUS POLITICS OF ITALIAN COLONIALISM

1. Balbo, "La politica sociale fascista verso gli arabi della Libia," *Convegno di scienze morali e storiche. 4–11 ottobre 1938, XVI. Tema: L'Africa*, vol. 1, 733–34.

2. Ibid., 733.

3. Ibid., 733.

4. Ibid., 735.

5. The so-called scramble for Africa began with a conference organized by Leopold of Belgium in 1876, which set up an "International organization for the Exploration and Civilization of Africa." Following the explorations of Stanley in Africa and those of a French explorer de Brazza, there was a great impetus to formalize already established treaties and make new agreements. This resulted in the conference in Berlin, held in November of 1884. For more detail, see J. M. Roberts, "The Beginning of Imperial Rivalry, 1880–90," in *Europe 1880–1945*, 2d ed. (New York: Longman Inc., 1989), 105–18.

6. Malvezzi, *La politica indigena nelle colonie* (Padua: Casa Editrice Dott. A. Milani, 1933), 236.

7. For a detailed discussion of the French under Lyautey, see Gwendolyn Wright, *The Politics of Design in French Colonial Urbanism* (Chicago: University of Chicago Press, 1991), 85–160.

8. Mario Ratto, "I grandi problemi della Libia. La conquista morale degli indigeni," *Rivista Coloniale* VII, II, 2 (July 31, 1913): 34.

9. Ibid., 34.

10. Cantalupo, "Mussolini e l'Africa," 209.

11. "La visita del Duce in Tripolitania nel 1926 e lo 'Scossone' coloniale," 1.

12. Ibid., 8.

13. "Speech by Mussolini to the Muslims of Tripoli," March 18, 1937, in *Il Duce in Libia*, (Milan: S. A. Stab. arti grafiche Alfieri & Lacroix, 1937), 47.

14. "La politica islamica dell'Italia," in *Viaggio del Duce in Libia per l'inaugurazione della litoranea. Anno XV. Orientamenti e note ad uso dei giornalisti* (Rome: Stabilimento Tipografico *Il Lavoro Fascista*, 1937), 4.

15. For a detailed outline of this visit, including this ceremony, see *Il Duce in Libia*.

16. This provision, which was called the "Regio decreto-legge 17 novembre 1938, XVII, n. 1728, recante provvedimenti per la difesa della razza italiana," was presented to the chair of the Council of Ministers for passage into law on November 25, 1938.

17. Zavattari, "Italia e Islam di fronte al problema razzista," *Difesa della Razza* I, 2 (20 August 1938): 14–15.

18. Luiggi, "Le opere pubbliche a Tripoli," 123. See Mia Fuller, "Preservation and Self-Absorption: Italian Colonization and the Walled City of Tripoli, Libya," *Journal of North African Studies* 5, 4 (Winter 2000): 121–54.

19. Ibid., 123.

20. Ibid., 124.

21. Piccioli, "Le ricerche archeologiche," *La nuova Italia d'oltremare*, 1170.

22. Roberto Paribeni, "La ricerca archeologica," *La rinascità della Tripolitania*, 337–49.

23. Ibid., 343–45.

24. Renato Bartoccini, "Gli edifici di interesse storico, artistico ed archeologico di Tripoli e dintorni," *La rinascità della Tripolitania*, 350–52.

25. Pietro Romanelli, "Restauri alle mura barbaresche di Tripoli," *Bolletino d'Arte* II, 12 (June 1923): 570–76.

26. Bartoccini, "Restauri nel Castello di Tripoli," *Bolletino d'Arte* IV, 6 (December 1924): 279–84. Romanelli was Superintendent of monuments and excavations in Tripolitania until 1923.

27. Francesco M. Rossi, "Le Piccole industrie indigene," *La rinascità della Tripolitania*, 517.

28. Ibid., 518.

29. Piccioli, "La conquista morale: La scuola," *La rinascità della Tripolitania*, 285–319.

30. Ibid., 296.

31. Ibid., 296. Notably, in addition to two levels of instruction for boys, this system provided for a five-year course of education for girls and an advanced education in Islamic law.

32. For a brief discussion of the scholarly and research activities of Aurigemma, see A. Gabucci, "Aurigemma, Salvatore," in *Dizionario biografico degli Italiani, volume XXXIV, Primo supplemento* (Rome: Istituto della Enciclopedia Italiana, 1988), 205–7.

33. Aurigemma, "La moschea di Ahmad al-Qarâmânlî in Tripoli," *Dedalo* VII, 8 (January 1927): 504–5.

34. Bartoccini, *Le Terme di Lepcis (Leptis Magna)* (Bergamo: Istituto Italiano d'Arte Grafiche, 1929). This book was the fourth in the series "Africa Italiana – Collezione di monografie a cura del Ministero delle Colonie."

35. Piccioli, "Le richerche archeologiche," *La nuova Italia d'oltremare*, 1167–1239.

36. Mussolini, "For the Grandeur of Rome" (December 31, 1925), in Luciano Morpurgo, *The Rome of Mussolini* (Rome: Luciano Morpurgo, 1933), vii–x. In discussing the importance of Roman and early Christian monuments, Mussolini states that "the millennial monuments of our history should stand out gigantically in monumental solitude."

37. Rava, "Dobbiamo rispettare il carattere dell'edilizia tripolina." *L'Oltremare* 3, 11 (November 1929): 458–59.

38. De Rege, "Il nuovo piano regolatore di Tripoli," 123.

39. Giuseppe Miano, "Florestano di Fausto," in *Dizionario biografico degli italiani. Volume 40* (Rome: Istituto della Enciclopedia italiana, 1991), 1–5.

40. The list of these projects is as follows: Belgrade (1924–26), Cairo (1928–30), Algiers (1931), Ankara and Tunis (1931–32). He also did work in Copenhagen, Stockholm, the Hague, Istanbul, Oslo, Salonica, Nice, Lisbon, Brussels, Buenos Aires, Rio de Janeiro, and London. Ibid., 1–2.

41. Piccioli, "Le opere pubbliche in Tripolitania," *La nuova Italia d'oltremare*, 880–86.

42. F. M. Rossi, "La Fiera e le piccole industrie tripolitane," *L'Italia Coloniale* IV, 4 (April 1927): 67–70.

43. "La mostra delle Tripolitania," *L'Italia Coloniale* V, 11 (November 1928): 226–27.

44. See "Progetto per la trasformazione dell'Ufficio di Arte Applicata in Azienda Autonoma," ASMAE – Archivio Segreto. Cartella 209. Tripolitania IV. Ufficio di Arte Applicate.

45. Guglielmo Quadrotta, "Appunti sull'artigianato libico," in *Viaggio del Duce in Libia per l'inaugurazione della litoranea. Anno XV. Orientamenti e note ad uso dei giornalisti* (Rome: Stabilimento Tipografico *Il Lavoro Fascista*, 1937), 16.

46. Piccioli, "La scuola e le istituzioni educative," *La nuova Italia d'oltremare*, 1108, 1118.

47. Ibid., 1112.

48. Piccioli, "Conclusione," *La nuova Italia d'oltremare*, 1762.

49. The files that pertain to what was called the "Campagna islamica antitaliana" can be found in the ASMAE, Affari Politici–Libia.

50. A telegram from the Italian Consulate in Damascus to the Ministry of Foreign Affairs dated February 9, 1935, states: "In conformity with the instructions sent by Your Excellency, this Office has not forgotten to give to the provisions of clemency recently prepared by S. E. Balbo, governor of Tripolitania, the greatest diffusion, both by way of the press, and with any other opportune means at its disposition." ASMAE – AP – Libia 13 (1935), Fascicolo 2, Sottofascicolo 1.

51. A meeting between Balbo and forty prominent leaders among the local populations was held in the governor's palace on September 13, 1935. As reported in *Agence d'Egypte et d'Orient*, this meeting was to "study important problems in favor of the Arab population." The decree of Balbo that allowed for the return of this property, from October 10, 1936, was published in *La Voix Indigène* (Constantine) on December 17. This policy was continued into 1937, in part due to Mussolini's visit to Libya in March of 1937. ASMAE – AP – Libia 17 (1937), Fascicolo 2.

52. Two such publications can be found in ASMAE – Affari Politici 17 (1937).

53. Malvezzi, *La politica indigena nelle Colonie*, 343–47, 375.

54. Balbo, "La politica sociale fascista verso gli arabi della Libia," 746.

55. Ibid., 738–39.

56. Ibid., 739.

57. Ibid., 734.

58. Ibid., 734–35.

59. Renzo Sertoli Salis, "Problemi indigeni sul piano dell'Impero," *Atti del Terzo Congresso di Studi Coloniali. Firenze–Roma, 12–17 April 1937, vol. II* (Florence: G. C. Sandoni, 1937), 112. See also Alexander DeGrand, "Mussolini's Follies: Fascism in Its Imperial and Racist Phase," *Contemporary European History* 13, 2 (May 2004): 127–47.

60. The *waqfs* are donations given by individuals to the larger Muslim community

for religious institutions and activities. While this organization had already been legally recognized by the Italians in 1917, it was under the Balbo administration that this group was reorganized and given more support. See "Institutions musulmanes," in *L'Italie pour les populations islamiques* (Rome: Società Editrice "Novissima," 1940), 29–32.

61. "L'oeuvre de l'Italie dans le domaine religieux," in *L'Italie pour les populations islamiques*, 16–28.

62. Luigi Turba, "La Moschea dei Caramanli a Tripoli," *Le Vie d'Italia* XL, 8 (August 1934): 583–91. The author notes that the restoration of the building included the domes, walls, and floors, involving repairs and restoration of stucco, marble, metal, wood, and ceramic tile. The material for the ceramic tile work was executed by the Ceramic School of Faenza according to models derived from the site.

63. MacDonald, "Excavation, Restoration and Italian Architecture in the 1930s," in *In Search of Modern Architecture: A Tribute to Henry-Russell Hitchcock*, edited by Helen Searing (New York: The Architectural Foundation, 1982), 298–320.

64. Municipio di Tripoli, "Relazione sul piano regolatore," 5. ACS – MAI 114.

65. The proposed amendment was discussed in "Verbal excerpt from meeting of the Building Commission," August 8, 1935; and "Report of the Municipality of Tripoli," October 12, 1935. ACS – MAI 114.

66. Giacomo Caputo, "Il consolidamento dell'arco di Marco Aurelio in Tripoli," *Africa Italiana* VII, 1–2 (April 1940): 46–66.

67. The projects that were partially demolished were the *Fonduk dei Maltesi* (restored in 1738), the *Fonduk Gheddara* (restored 1850) and the *Fonduk er-Raccah* (restored 1773). Francesco Corò. "Alla scoperta dei vecchi 'Fondugh' tripolini," *Le Vie d'Italia* XLV, 2 (February 1939): 201–10. For information on Di Fausto's proposal, see Micacchi, "L'Arco di Marco Aurelio in Tripoli e la sistemazione della zona adiacente," *Rivista delle Colonie Italiane* VIII, 10 (October 1934): 824–39.

68. Spiro Kostof, *The Third Rome, 1870-1950: Traffic and Glory* (Berkeley, CA: University Art Museum, 1973), 68–69.

69. "L'oeuvre italienne dans le domaine scolaire," in *L'Italie pour les populations islamiques*, 44–48.

70. For the legislative deliberations and presentation related to this school, see ASMAE – Consiglio Superiore Coloniale 19 (1935), N. 30. April 15, 1935, "Istituzione in Tripoli di una Medresa."

71. For a more detailed outline of the curriculum of this school and the general perception of Muslim women by the Italians, see "L'Evoluzione delle condizioni della donna musulmana in Libia," 1–8. ASMAE – MAI 5, Pacco 14, Fascicolo 182.

72. Quadrotta, "Appunti sull'Artigianato Libico," *Viaggio del Duce in Libia per l'inaugurazione della litoranea*, 13-14. For a copy of this legislation, see "Costituzione dell'Istituto Fascista dell'Artigianato della Libia," 25 November 1938. ASMAE – Consiglio Superiore Coloniale, Pacco 27 (1938), n. 135.

73. Quadrotta, "Sviluppo e realizzazioni dell'artigianato in Libia," *Rassegna Economica dell'Africa Italiana* XXV, 7 (July 1937): 952–67.

74. Quadrotta, "Appunti sull'Artigianato Libico," 6–8, 16–24.

75. Balbo, "La politica sociale fascista verso gli Arabi della Libia," 741–42.

76. Federico Cresti, "Edilizia ed urbanistica nella colonizzazione agraria della Libia (1922–1940)," Storia Urbana XI, 40 (July-September 1987): 220–25.

77. Segrè, *Fourth Shore: The Italian Colonization of Libya*, 144–57.

78. Branzoli-Zappi, "La 'Gioventù araba del Littorio' nuova ardita realizzazione coloniale del Fascismo," *Il Lavoro Fascista* (11 August 1935): 1. The law that pertains to the constitution of this group was Decreto Governatoriale, 29 giugno 1935, Serie A, n. 282. See *Bollettino Ufficiale del Governo della Libia*, 16 September 1935, n. 26.

79. Letter from Balbo to Mussolini, dated June 3, 1935. ASMAE – MAI – AP 92, Fascicolo 302.

80. Letter from Italo Balbo to Benito Mussolini, 11 December 1935, ASMAE – AP Cartella 91, Fascicolo 291. The main outlines of this proposal are that it would only be for two years, and would be eliminated after the annexation of Libya's four provinces by Italy.

81. This argument was made by Professor Alfonso Nallino, a member of the Italian Academy and expert on Islamic law, in a report on behalf of the Ministry of the Colonies dated January 1, 1936. ASMAE – AP Cartella 91, Fascicolo 291.

82. This new citizenship was a modified version of the previous provision from 1934, which provided for: 1. Guarantee of individual liberty; 2. The inviolability of the home; 3. Inviolability of property; 4. Right to compete for civic jobs in the colonies; 5. Right to hold a profession in Libya. In addition to these, the law of 1939 added: 1. The right to bear arms in the military; 2. The right to belong to the Muslim Fascist Association; 3. The right to have a military career; 4. The right to take the job of a mayor of a Libyan community; 5. The right to exercise directive functions in a syndical organization. See Gaspare Ambrosini, "La condizione giuridica dei libici dall'occupazione all'avvento del Fascismo," *Rivista delle Colonie* XIII, 1, 2 (January, February 1939): 188.

4. TOURISM AND THE FRAMING OF INDIGENOUS CULTURE

1. L.V. Bertarelli, "Turismo e Comunicazioni," in *Guida d'Italia del Touring Club Italiano. Libia* (Milan: Touring Club Italiano, 1937), 135.

2. Calzini, *Da Leptis Magna a Gadames* (Milan: Fratelli Treves Editori, 1926).

3. Ibid., vi.

4. Ibid., 172.

5. Ibid., 202.

6. Niccoli, "Il problema industriale in Tripolitania," *La rinascità della Tripolitania*, 512.

7. Ibid., 512.

8. ENIT and FFSS, *Tripoli* (Rome: Novissima, 1929), 1. In addition to noting the ancient and modern qualities of Tripoli and mentioning its favorable climate, the introductory page of this guidebook suggests visiting the agricultural concessions—undoubtedly a gesture of recognition of the accomplishments of Fascist colonization.

9. Ibid. The structure of the text of the guidebook is as follows: Introduction; Tripoli in History; Arrival in Tripoli; The City; Notable Sights; The Trade Fair; Trips and excursions—Tripoli–Leptis Magna, Tripoli–Sabratha, Tripoli–Gharyan; and Useful information.

10. Bertarelli, *Guida d'Italia del TCI. Possedimenti e Colonie*, 169–271. This overview is nearly one hundred pages and presents the following information: 1. Naming of the colony; 2. Physical characteristics; 3. Climate; 4. Geology and Morphology; 5. Fauna; 6. Flora; 7. History; 8. Geographical knowledge and exploration; 9. Artistic history; 10. History of excavations; 11. Demographic information; 12. Languages; 13. Islamic religion in Tripolitania; 14. Customs and manners of Muslims and Jews; 15. Economic information; 16. Political and administrative regulations; 17. Sanitary conditions; 18. The Rebirth of Tripolitania; 19. Tourism.

11. Ibid., 340.

12. Commissariato per il turismo in Libia, *Libia itinerari* (Milan: S. A. Arti Grafiche Bertarelli, 1935).

13. Ibid., 12.

14. Angelo Del Boca, "L'Italia e la spartizione dell'Africa. In nome della scienza," in *L'Africa nella coscienza degli Italiani* (Bari-Rome: Giuseppe Laterza & Figli, 1992), 7–22.

15. Società italiana di esplorazioni geografiche e commerciali, Milan, *Pionieri italiani in Libia. Relazioni dei delegati, 1880–1896* (Milano: F. Vallardi, 1912).

16. Martin Clark, *Modern Italy, 1871–1982* (New York: Longman Inc., 1984), 204–5.

17. Tomasello, *La letteratura coloniale italiana dalle avanguardie al fascismo* (Palermo: Sellerio Editore, 1984), 25–38.

18. D'Annunzio, *Più che l'amore* (Milan: Fratelli Treves, Editori, 1906).

19. Caroline Tisdall and Angelo Bozzolla, "Futurism and Fascism: Marinetti and Mussolini," in *Futurism* (New York and Toronto: Oxford University Press), 200–209.

20. Marinetti, *Mafarka le futuriste. Roman africain* (Paris: E. Sansot & C.ie, 1909).

21. Tomasello, *La letteratura coloniale italiana*, 39–50.

22. The values of the protagonist are revealed very early in the novel, where he states that the realities of life are "God, family, Country and man." As the "son of the first three," man is above all dedicated to "his Country and collectivity." Dei Gaslini, *Piccolo amore Beduino* (Milan: L'Eroica, 1926), 34.

23. Tomasello, *La letteratura coloniale italiana*, 70.

24. Dei Gaslini, *Piccolo amore Beduino*, 82.

25. See Ente autonomo fiera campionaria di Tripoli, *I. Mostra internazionale d'arte coloniale. Catalogo* (Rome: Fratelli Palombi, 1931), 321–23.

26. As the narrator himself states: "This love is based on clay, on clouds, on impossible reality. A white official cannot love a black woman." Dei Gaslini, *Piccolo amore Beduino*, 166.

27. Nica always refers to the protagonist as "il mio signore" or "signore cristiano." Tomasello attributes the end of the relationship between Nica and the author to the "incompatibility of his civilizing destiny with that of the woman conquered by love and by civilization." Tomasello, *La letteratura coloniale italiana*, 71.

28. Dei Gaslini, *Natisc fiore dell'oasi. Romanzo coloniale* (Bologna: L. Cappelli Editore, 1928). The monthly journal *Esotica* was relatively short-lived, beginning in October of 1926 and ceasing publication some time early in 1928.

29. Bieppi, "Estetica maschile e gusto latino," *Esotica* I, 1 (October 1926): 54.

30. Dei Gaslini, "Le Ombre dell'harem," *Esotica* I, 2 (November 1926): 64.

31. Bertarelli, *Guida d'Italia del Touring Club Italiano. Possedimenti e colonie*, 270.

32. Ibid., 340–41.

33. Cristina Delvecchio, "Icone d'Africa: Note sulla pittura coloniale italiana," in *Architettura italiana d'oltremare 1870–1940*, ed. Giuliano Gresleri, Pier Giorgio Massaretti, and Stefano Zagnoni (Venice: Marsilio Editori, 1993), 68–81. See also *Il Mito e l'immagine: Capri, Ischia e Procida nella pittura dal '600 ai primi del '900* (Turin: Nuova ERI Edizioni Rai, 1988).

34. Del Boca, *Gli italiani in Libia. Dal fascismo a Gheddafi*, 271.

35. Surdich, "Le spedizioni scientifiche italiane in Africa Orientale e in Libia durante il periodo fascista," in *Le guerre coloniali del fascismo*, ed. Angelo Del Boca (Bari: Editori Laterza, 1991), 449–51, 460–61. The government-sponsored research included Colonel Enrico de Agostini in Cyrenaica (1922–23), Nello Puccioni in Cyrenaica (1928–29), and a large expedition to Jufra sponsored by the vice governor of Libya, Rodolfo Graziani (1933). Other expeditions were in Ghadames (1933), Fezzan (1935), and Jadu (1937).

36. Marco Mozzati, "Gli intellettuali e la propaganda coloniale del regime," in *Le guerre coloniali del fascismo*, 99–111.

37. Beguinot, "Libia. Etnografia antica," *Enciclopedia italiana di scienze, lettere ed arti. Vol. XXI* (Milan: Istituto Giovanni Treccani, 1934), 59–62.

38. The conferences all took place with the patronage of King Vittorio Emanuele III and the Fascist government. In addition to representation from local officials, the honorary committee included the Ministry of the Colonies and the Ministry of Education. The research presented was organized according to broad categories of study, including history, archeology, geography, ethnography, philology, sociology, law, economy, agriculture, hygiene, and medicine.

39. Valensin, "Primo congresso di studi coloniali," *L'Oltremare* V, 2 (February 1931): 75.

40. These publications are as follows: *Atti del Primo Congresso di studi coloniali. Firenze, 8–12 April 1931* (Florence:Sicc. B Seeber, 1931), *Atti del Secondo Congresso di studi coloniali. Napoli, 1–5 October 1934* (Florence: Tip. Giuntina di L.S. Olschki, 1934) ; and *Atti del Terzo Congresso di studi coloniali. Firenze-Roma, 12–17 April 1937*.

41. De Agostini, "Etnografia delle popolazione libiche." *Atti del Primo Congresso di studi coloniali, Vol. IV*, 7–23.

42. Di Marzo, "L'atteggiamento psicologico degli indigeni nord-Africani di fronte alla colonizzazione." *Atti del Primo Congresso di studi coloniali, Vol. IV*, 218–26.

43. Scarin, "Tipi indigeni di insediamento umano e loro distribuzione nella Tripolitania settentrionale." *Atti del Primo Congresso di studi coloniali, Vol. IV*, 24–44.

44. See "Antropologia," *Enciclopedia italiana*. Vol. III, 580–97; "Etnologia," *Enciclopedia italiana*. Vol. XIV, 495–504; Folklore, *Enciclopedia italiana*. Vol. XV, 606–9.

45. Cipriani, "Una missione scientifica italiana nel Fezzan," *Le Vie d'Italia* XXXIX, 9 (September 1933): 679–91. This expedition went south from Tripoli via Gharyan and Mizdah to the oases of Brak and Sabha, then heading west to Ghat, circling back east to Murzuq and then back to Tripoli via Suknah and Misurata. The TCI excursion visited some of these oases, missing only Ghat in the far southwestern region near the Algerian border.

46. Carlo Bonardi, "Col touring nel Fezzan," *Le Vie d'Italia* XLV, 7 (July 1935): 485–96.

47. Graziosi, "Preistoria," in *Guida d'Italia del Touring Club Italiano. Libia*, 63–65. The material for this section was taken from the archeological mission to the Fezzan region headed by Graziosi and sponsored by the *Reale Società Geografica Italiana* in 1933.

48. "Etnografia e demografia," in *Guida d'Italia del Touring Club Italiano. Libia*, 84–88.

49. Ahmida, *The Making of Modern Libya*, 114.

50. This provision, which was called the "Regio decreto-legge 17 novembre 1938–XVII, n. 1728, recante provvedimenti per la difesa della razza italiana," was presented at the Presidency of the Council of Ministers for passage into law on November 25, 1938.

51. Raffaele Corso, *Africa Italiana. Genti e costumi* (Naples: Casa Editrice Raffaele Pironti, 1940), 16–17.

52. Cipriani, "Razzismo Coloniale," *Difesa della Razza* I, 2 (20 August 1938): 18–20.

53. Dei Gaslini, *Paradiso nell'inferno. Uso e costumi abissini* (Milan: Zacchi ambrosiana, 1937); *L'Italia su mar rosso* (Milan: La prora S.A.S.T.E., 1938); and *Le richezze dei Galla-Sidama* (Milan: Popolo d'Italia, 1940).

54. Marinetti, "L'Africa generatrice e ispiratrice di poesia e arti," in Reale Accademia d'Italia, *Convegno di scienze morale e storiche. 4–11 ottobre 1938–XVI. Tema: Africa. Volume 1* (Rome: Reale Accademia d'Italia, 1939), 198–201.

55. Renato Bartoccini, "Il Museo di Tripoli," *La rinascità della Tripolitania*, 565–72.

56. *Guida di Tripoli e dintorni*, ix.

57. M.M. "L'Esposizione di Tripoli," *L'Italia Coloniale* III, 12 (December 1926): 232.

58. "Chronache coloniali. L'organizzazione dell'Ente turistico tripolitano," *Rivista delle Colonie Italiane* V, 1 (January 1931): 53.

59. Piccioli, "L'azione dell'Ente Turistico Tripolitano," in *La nuova Italia d'oltremare*, 1565.

60. Istituto Coloniale Fascista, *Prima Crociera Nazionale in Cirenaica – 23 maggio – 7 giugno – X* (Rome: Istituto Coloniale Fascista, 1933), 3. ASMAE – MAI.3–39, Fascicolo Istituto Coloniale Fascista.

61. Untitled memorandum of meeting between the Ministry of the Colonies and the Libyan tourism commissioner, March 1934. ASMAE – MAI – Archivio Segreto 200, Fascicolo Libia I – Commissariato Turismo in Libia.

62. Telegram from the government in Tripoli to the minister of the colonies, dated March 19, 1934. ASMAE – MAI–Archivio Segreto 200, Fascicolo – Libia, turismo.

63. Commissariato per il Turismo in Libia, *Libia Itinerari*, 101.

64. On the telegram from the government in Tripoli to the Ministry of the Colonies, this ceremony was underlined and marked with an emphatic no. Telegram from government in Tripoli to the Ministry of the Colonies, dated March 19, 1934.

65. "Decreto che vieta in Libia ceremonie biasimevoli di alcune confraternite religiose musulmane," (Decreto Governatoriale, June 16, 1935), 2. ASMAE – MAI 2. Posizione 150/39, Fascicolo 174.

66. The Berber castle in Nalut, which was constructed to protect the provisions of the Berbers at the time of the Arab incursions into this region, was in a semi-ruined state. Its restoration was completed in March of 1935, just two months after the completion of

the Hotel Nalut. "Governo della Libia, Gabinetto del Governatore Generale – Notiziario Informazioni" (Tripoli, 31 March 1935), 8. ACS – PCM 1934–1936, 17.1.498.

67. Ibid., 7.

68. "Istituzione dell'Ente turistico ed alberghiero della Libia," R. Decreto 31 maggio 1935, XIII, n. 1410.

69. The relative statute is: D.G. 15 November 1935, n. 16454, "Concessione in uso all'Ente turistico ed alberghiero della Libia di tutti gli alberghi governativi e municipali," ASMAE – MAI 4, Pacco 29, Fascicolo 210. ETAL – Materiale illustrativo ed informazioni.

70. The ETAL system of hotels were as follows: in Tripoli, the Uaddan, the Grand, the Mehari, and the Tripolitania; the Gebel in Gharyan; the Rumia in Yifran; the Nalut; the 'Ain el-Fras in Ghadames; the Hotel at the Excavations of Leptis Magna in al-Khums; the Gazelle in Zlitan; the Misurata; the Sirt; the Zuwarah; the Ajdabiya; the Berenice in Ben ghazi; the Grand Hotel at the Excavations in Cyrene; the Derna and the Tobruk. Vicari, "L'Ente turistico ed alberghiero della Libia," 955–75.

71. "Report of Ente turistico ed alberghiero della Libia," (1938), 1.

72. Ente autonomo fiera campionaria di Tripoli, *XI Manifestazione internazionale-intercoloniale. Prima mostra coloniale dell'Impero fascista*, 85.

73. Patricia A. Morton, *Hybrid Modernities: Architecture and Representation at the 1931 Colonial Exposition, Paris* (Cambridge, MA: MIT Press, 2000), 220–21, 251–69. Morton rightly observes that such pavilions as the French West African one were an amalgam of African styles—pointing out its connection to both Timbuktu in the Sudan and Djenné in the upper Niger region.

74. One early example of the use of the diorama is the "paesaggio Somalo" at the colonial exhibition in Genoa in 1914. ASMAE – MAI 3–40–8, Foto-esposizioni, musei.

75. Ente Autonomo Fiera Campionaria di Tripoli, *XII Manifestazione Internazionale-Intercoloniale. 20 febbraio–5 aprile 1938–XVI. Seconda Mostra dell'Impero* (Rome: Società anonima tipografica Luzzatti, 1938), 140.

76. ETAL, *Combinazioni di soggiorno in Libia* (Tripoli, ETAL, 1937).

77. Ibid., 1.

78. De Agostini, *La Libia turistica*, 14.

79. A number of essays on indigenous culture deal with its past, including: Michele Scaminaci, "Conclusione sullo studio del grande musulmano emulo di Marco Polo. Importante storica d'Ibd Batutah," *Libia* IV, 9 (September 1940): 31–33; Mario Caramitti, "Una magnifica casa del '700 a Tripoli," *Libia* I, 4 (July 1937): 24–26; Enrico Insabato, "La vita di Maometto secondo la tradizione," *Libia* I, 6 (January 1938): 5–7.

80. This author states: "the Regime has already called Italian woman to an extremely lofty understanding of their duties as wife and mother, has developed all of her best gifts, having taken care that also in the external life her delicate femininity would be integrally preserved." Valori, "Femminismo arabo," *Libia* I, 6 (September 1937): 23–28.

81. The author states: "It is important to note to the Arabs that the number of children, to which they justifiably aspire, are not dependent on the number of wives but are instead a consequence of the good hygienic and sanitary conditions of the family," Ibid., 26.

82. ETAL, *Itinerario Tripoli-Gadames*, 6.

83. Ibid., 13.

84. From 1937 the ETAL began producing postcard itineraries that described the major population centers and travel routes in this colony. Packaged in a group of twelve, these postcards were photographs taken within a strict documentary style of representation. See "Relazione tecnica del Direttore Generale al bilancio dell'esercizio 1936–37," 26.

85. The larger context of this statement is as follows: "The meeting places and recreation facilities, which constitute one of the most appreciated attractions for the foreigner and are patronized with great pleasure by the most wealthy native elements, should not be forgotten." "Report of the ETAL," (1938), 4.

86. Bucciante, "Lo sviluppo edilizio della Libia," in *Viaggio del Duce in Libia per l'inaugurazione della litoranea*, 4.

87. Ibid., 10–11.

88. Quadrotta, "Sviluppo e realizzazioni dell'artigianato in Libia," 955. The entrance hall further illustrates this connection, containing a Byzantine fragment found at the archeological site at Sabratha.

89. Vicari, "L'Ente Turistico ed Alberghiero della Libia," 971.

90. "Relazione tecnica del Direttore Generale al bilancio dell'esercizio, 1936–37," 23.

91. Ibid., 17. The Tobacco Shop and Office in Rome is reported under the Tourism Service section of this document, where it is noted that "the sales of artisanal objects are continually increasing, and the profits of this operation are fair, enough to cover the costs." This gives some indication that as a business its role was more for propaganda than profit.

5. TOWARD A MODERN COLONIAL ARCHITECTURE

1. Rava, "Di un'architettura coloniale moderna – Parte seconda," *Domus* 42 (June 1931): 36.

2. "Di un'architettura coloniale moderna" was published in two parts in May and June of 1931. These were the fifth and sixth of the eight essays to be published under the title "Panorama del Razionalismo." The first four essays (published January–April 1931)—"Svolta pericolosa. Situazione dell'Italia di fronte al razionalismo europeo," "Spirito latino," and "La necessità di selezione" (part 1 and 2)—contained all the essential aspects of his theory for a modern Italian architecture. In the final two essays, Rava provides further detail in "Giovani architetti nordamericani" (July 1931) and reacts to the criticism of his arguments in "Conclusione" (November 1931).

3. The original members of the *Gruppo Sette* were Ubaldo Castagnoli, Luigi Figini, Guido Frette, Sebastiano Larco, Gino Pollini, Carlo Enrico Rava, and Giuseppe Terragni. The manifestos of this group were published in this journal as follows: "Architettura," *Rassegna Italiana* XVIII, 103 (December 1926): 849–54; "Architettura II: Gli Stranieri," *Rassegna Italiana* XIX, 105 (February 1927): 129–37; "Architettura III: Impreparazione, Incomprensione, Pregiudizi," *Rassegna Italiana* XIX, 106 (March 1927): 247–52; and "Architettura IV: Una nuova epoca arcaica," *Rassegna Italiana* XIX, 108 (May 1927): 467–72.

4. Gruppo Sette, "Architettura," 852.

5. Rava, "Di un'architettura coloniale moderna – Parte prima," *Domus* 41 (May 1931): 89.

6. Rava, "Di un'architettura coloniale moderna – Parte seconda," 32.

7. Rava, "Di un'architettura coloniale moderna – Parte prima," 41.

8. Rava's first visit to Tripolitania was from December 24, 1927 to February 9, 1928; his second and third visits were April 18 to May 3 and November 1–17, 1928; the fourth visit was from January 24 to April 10, 1929; and his fifth visit was from November 14, 1929 to March 18, 1930. Information collected from: Carlo Enrico Rava, Album di viaggio, 1928–30 and 1931–32. Rava family, private collection.

9. "Concorso per il Padiglione delle Colonie alla Fiera Campionaria di Milano. Relazione della Commissione giudicatrice," *Rivista Coloniale* XXII, 3 (May–June 1927): 179. The following are the jury's comments: "It is the project that has more character than all of the others. An animated plan, variable and practical. The facades are inspired by elements of Arab minor architecture, elements more technical than decorative, due to ethnic reasons, and then developed with a completely modern clarity and refinement, although there are some less satisfying details to raise."

10. Piacentini, "Due lavori di C.E. Rava e S. Larco," *Architettura e Arti Decorative* VII, 11 (July 1928): 528.

11. Rava, "Svolta pericolosa. Situazione dell'Italia di fronte al razionalismo europeo," *Domus* 37 (January 1931): 39.

12. Ibid., 39.

13. Ibid., 44.

14. For a general discussion of this debate, see Silvia Danesi, "Aporie dell'architettura italiana in periodo fascista – mediterraneità e purismo," in *Il razionalismo e l'architettura in Italia durante il fascismo* (Milan: Electa Editrice, 1976), 21–26.

15. Rava, "Conclusione," *Domus* 47 (November 1931): 40.

16. Silvia Danesi, "Aporie dell'architettura Italiana in periodo fascista—mediterraneità e purismo," 21. Danesi has commented on the concept of *mediterraneità*, arguing that this term was permeated with ambiguities that resulted from its use by artists and architects attempting to get work within the official structures of the Fascist bureaucracy.

17. Persico, "Punto e da capo per l'architettura," *Domus* 83 (November 1934): 3.

18. These essays include the following: Pietro Romanelli, "Restauri alle mura barbaresche di Tripoli," *Bolletino d'Arte* II, 12 (June 1923): 570–76; Renato Bartoccini, "Restauri nel Castello di Tripoli," *Bolletino d'Arte* IV, 6 (December 1924): 279–84; and Salvatore Aurigemma, "La moschea di Ahmad al-Qarâmânlî in Tripoli," *Dedalo* VII, 8 (January 1927): 504--5.

19. Aurigemma, *Tripoli e le sue opere d'arte* (Milan, Rome: Luigi Alfieri & Co. Editori, 1927).

20. Ibid., 33.

21. For a detailed discussion of this issue, see Henry Millon, "The Role of the History of Architecture in Fascist Italy," *Journal of the Society of Architectural Historians* 24 (March 1965): 53–59.

22. For a biography of Ricard's early career, see C.E. Curiner, "Ricard, Prosper-Marie-Eugène," in *Dictionnaire national des contemporains, contenant les notices de toutes les personnalités vivantes, françaises ou demeurant en France, qui se sont fait connaître*. 6 tom (Paris : Office Général d'Édition, 1901–18).

23. Alfred Bel and Prosper Ricard, *Le travail de la laine a Tlemcen* (Alger : Typ. A. Jourdan, 1913); and Prosper Ricard, *Corpus de Tapis Marocains* (Paris: Geunther, 1923), eight vols.

24. Ricard, "Il rinnovamento artistico del Marocco," *Dedalo* IX, 12 (May 1929): 742–70. The activities of the indigenous arts service included study, instruction, and an exhibition program that was largely the basis for the renewal of artisanal industries in Tripolitania.

25. Ricard, *Le Maroc* (Paris, Hachette, 1919); *Les merveilles de l'autre France; Algerie, Tunisie, Maroc; le pays—les monuments—les habitants* (Paris: Hachette, 1924); and *Algérie, Tunisie, Tripolitaine [et] Malte* (Paris: Hachette, 1930). Ricard also published an earlier guidebook to the town of Fez: *Guide de Fes: renseignements pratiques, apercu historique, organization municipal, principaux monuments, excursions urbaines et suburbaines* (Fez: Impr.Municipale, 1916).

26. Ricard, *Pour comprendre l'art musulman dans l'Afrique du Nord et en Espagne* (Paris: Hachette, 1924), 8.

27. Ricard, "Les arts tripolitains, pte I," *Rivista della Tripolitania* II, IV, & V (January–February, March–April 1926): 203–35, 275–92; Ricard, *Les arts tripolitains* (Rome: Tipografia del Senato del Dott. G. Bardi, 1926).

28. In discussing the architectural traditions of Tripolitania, Ricard notes that "we are, as in Tunisia, at the point of contact between East and West, where Turkish and Maghreb civilizations have penetrated while leaving them profoundly influenced by Italy." Ricard, "Les arts tripolitains, pte I," 205.

29. Ricard, "Les arts tripolitains, pte I," 286–87.

30. For a detailed analysis of the activities of the *Associazione artistica fra i cultori di architettura*, see Richard Etlin, *Modernism in Italian Architecture, 1890–1940* (Cambridge: MIT Press, 1991), 129–61. For an investigation of the planning implications of this group's activities, see Etlin, *Modernism in Italian Architecture, 1890–1940*, 101–28.

31. In the first year of this journal, these historical presentations included: Corrado Ricci, "La porta di San Pietro di Perugia," *Architettura e Arti Decorative* I, 1 (September–October 1921): 17–31; and Papini, "Il chiostro delle majoliche in Santa Chiara di Napoli,"

Architettura e Arti Decorative I, 4 (March–April 1922): 325–38. In addition to these essays, this journal contained a monthly *"Cronaca dei monumenti,"* gave titles of recent publications, and reported on the activities of the *Associazione artistica*.

32. Although many more volumes were planned, only three of these publications were produced between 1926 and 1940. The first two of these were on the city of Rome, while the third was on the province of Lazio. See Associazione artistica fra i cultori di architettura in Roma, *Architettura minore in Italia* (Turin: C. Crudo & Co., 1926–40). Vol. I. Roma; Vol. II. Roma; Vol. III. Lazio e suburbio di Roma.

33. See Giovannoni, "Vecchie città ed edilizia nuova," *Nuova Antologia* XLVIII, 995 (June 1, 1913): 449–72; and "Il diradamento edilizio dei vecchi centri – il Quartiere della Rinascenza in Roma," *Nuova Antologia* XLVIII, 997 (July 1, 1913): 53–76. Giovannoni argues that in order to respond to the need for hygiene within historic centers while preserving the local artistic aspect, the *diradamento* is the preferred solution.

34. See Piacentini, "Il momento architettonico all'estero," *Architettura e Arti Decorative* I, 1 (September–October 1921): 32–76. In this article, Piacentini provides a general survey of foreign architecture, characterizing these tendencies as all deriving from the same impulse for simplification, the suppression of false structure, and the reduction of decoration.

35. Piacentini, "Il momento architettonico all'estero," 72. In concluding this article, Piacentini states: "We have seen what the differences are between the various national schools and what are the new laws common to all. We must persuade ourselves of this and find in our past, and even more in our homes, the fundamental and permanent principles of our race. With only these two elements we must find our way."

36. Piacentini, "Influssi d'arte Italiana nel Nord-America," *Architettura e Arti Decorative* I, 6 (July–August 1922): 536–55.

37. In an article reporting on this exhibition, Antonio Mariani argues that rustic architecture "is something more than a picturesque moment in the landscape, it is an architecture in its own right." "L'Architettura rustica alla Cinquantenale romana," *Architettura e Arti Decorative* I, 4 (March–April 1922): 379–85.

38. Bartoccini, "La moschea di Murad Agha in Tagiura (Tripolitania)," *Architettura e Arti Decorative* III, 8 (April 1924): 345. Bartoccini notes that despite the fact that the founder of the building, Murad Agha, was the first governor after the reconquest of Tripoli by the Ottomans in 1551, the building conformed to Maghreb typologies, rather than Ottoman ones.

39. Romanelli, "Vecchie case arabe di Tripoli," *Architettura e Arti Decorative* III, 5 (January 1924): 193–211.

40. Ibid., 195. In discussing the Roman origins of the Arab house, Romanelli argues that "fundamentally this is the general and recognized type of the house in all of the countries of the East." At the same time, he asserts that this type developed, amplified, and modified itself "to better correspond to the necessities and particular habits of the people who the house served." Ibid., 195–96.

41. Ibid., 211. In discussing the craftsmanship of these houses, Romanelli notes: "Another influence was exercised on the Tripolitanian masters, and not in small measure, and it was that of the coeval art in Europe, and more particularly that of Italy." He then later explains that "many of these unknown masters, or at least their most valid and able collaborators, were without a doubt Italian, slaves taken by the barbaric ships, taken to Tripoli, and there obliged to work for the Pasha or their ministers."

42. Sergio Romano describes the architecture of the Volpi period as a "literary pastiche, attempting to give a historic depth and civic legitimacy to the Italian presence." He proceeds to call these projects "Moorish and Roman, Byzantine and Neoclassical, Pisan and Venetian"—a clear reference to the Venetian origins of Volpi, which can be detected in the particular mode of appropriation of Eastern architecture. Romano, *Giuseppe Volpi*, 117.

43. Béguin, *Arabisances. Décor architectural et tracé urbain en Afrique du Nord, 1830–1950* (Paris: Dunod, 1983), 1.

44. For information on Brasini, see Mario Pisani, *Architetture di Armando Brasini* (Roma: Officina Edizioni, 1996). He was trained as an artist and craftsman in the Institute of Fine Arts in Rome and the Industrial Arts Museum before apprenticing as an architect.

45. Gian Paolo Consoli, "The Protagonists," *Rassegna* 51 (September 1992): 54.

46. Pisani, *Architetture di Armando Brasini*, 47. Pisani connects the project of Brasini with "the first tombs of martyrs that subsequently are transformed into churches, like Santa Costanza in Rome . . . but also to the Mausoleum of Theodoric in Ravenna read as a moment of joining between East and West, in tune with what was proposed by the Roman architect on the occasion of the film *Teodoro* (1919)."

47. Bertarelli, *Guida d'Italia del Touring Club Italiano, Possedimenti e colonie*, 438, 440.

48. Vicari, "L'Ente Turistico ed Alberghiero della Libia," 965. The hotel was also advertised to have hot and cold running water, an elevator and car park. For Tripoli, this would be considered a luxury hotel. Bertarelli, *Guida d'Italia del Touring Club Italiano. Possedimenti e Colonie*, 277.

49. Ibid., 962–63, 966. See also, ENIT and FFSS, *Tripoli*, 25–26.

50. Gian Paolo Consoli characterizes Limongelli's work as follows: "He evolved his language in search for an architecture both Classical and Mediterranean, reinterpreting Romanity in light of the version given to it by local architecture: horizontality of line, simplicity and clarity of volumes, the elimination of decoration, neatness and whiteness of the surfaces are the constants of Limongelli's mature works." Consoli, "The Protagonists," 57.

51. Quoted in Piccioli, "La Fiera di Tripoli," *Gli Annali dell'Africa Italiana* I, 2 (August 1938): 511.

52. In this essay, Rava argues that "the simple house of local architecture . . . born in the same locus, offers an exemplary and characteristic example of how one can construct in North Africa." Rava, "Dobbiamo rispettare il carattere dell'edilizia tripolina," *L'Oltremare* 3, 11 (November 1929): 462.

53. Ibid.

54. Ibid., 463–64.

55. "Notiziario," *Rivista delle Colonie Italiane* III, 11 (November 1929): 1214–15.

56. "Nuovi Concorsi. Concorsi di edilizia in Tripoli," *Architettura e Arti Decorative* IX, 12 (August 1930), n.p. This statement was an explicit part of the instructions for the competition and was made in reference to the task of creating an Italian colonial architecture.

57. "Il concorso per la sistemazione di piazza della Cattedrale in Tripoli," *Architettura e Arti Decorative* X, 9 (May 1931): 447. The Pentagono group were Natale Morandi, Mario Lombardi, Giambattista Cosmacini, Alberto del Corno, Oddone Cavallini, and Dante Alziati.

58. Ibid., 444.

59. Consoli, "The Protagonists," 55–58.

60. The premature death of Limongelli is noted in Piccioli, *La nuova Italia d'oltremare*, 880.

61. Piccioli, *La nuova Italia d'oltremare*, 928. This discussion of the activities of the municipality in Cyrenaica provides the most detailed description of the facilities of the Grand Hotel at the Excavations.

62. Bertarelli, *La guida d'Italia del Touring Club Italiano. Libia*, 398.

63. Consoli, "The Protagonists," 57. As an architect of the so-called Roman school, Consoli argues that his use of Libyan vernacular references is through a classical filter. He describes the later colonial projects by Limongelli, including the Grand Hotel at the Excavations in Cyrene, as part of a search for an architecture that was "both Classical and Mediterranean."

64. Rava, "Di un'architettura coloniale – Parte prima," 43.

65. Ibid., 41–42.

66. Rava visited Ghadames for the first time from February 3-15, 1929, his second visit beginning on March 17, 1931. Notably, this second trip was at the same time that he was publishing his "Panorama of Rationalism."

67. Ibid., 89. Rava notes that "the mysterious and very distant Ghadames . . . as it was the

greatest caravan junction through which the Mediterranean communicated with the basin of the Niger, has also been, in some small way, the place of transition and of exchange between the architectural forms of *latinità* and those of Saharan-Sudanese Africa."

68. Ibid., 42.

69. Ibid., 89. Rava argues that the Ottomans "introduced the use of wooden loggias and roof terraces, elements of a character essentially colonial, much in tune with the landscape of Mediterranean Africa and befitting the necessities of its climate—thus renewing and varying the possibilities of the Arab patio inherited from the porticoed courtyard of the ancient Roman house."

70. Ibid., 89. Rava enumerates this first source as follows: "The Roman influence (the true, that is, the one of the practical and organizing spirit of Rome, not that of archeology, of style, of the ruins, is also imperial), is still very vital in the scheme of the Arab-Turkish house, whose very rational plan is the exact reproduction of that of the ancient classical house."

71. Ibid., 89. The second source is described as "the impulse of a vigorous primitivism that, superimposing itself on the Roman scheme, it derives from its relations with the populations of the South (Sahara, Niger, Sudan), which leave their trace in that predilection for simple forms."

72. Ibid., 89. These final qualities were described as follows: "The general mediterranean characteristic that, as much through the Roman scheme of the house, as through the composition of simple and linear geometric masses which has been spoken of, composing blank rhythms of cubes and parallelepipeds, opposing the cool shade of the patio, to the sun and to the blue of the large superposed and alternating verandahs or roof terraces."

73. Rava, "Di un'architettura coloniale moderna – Parte seconda," 34.

74. Ibid., 35.

75. It is quite evident from the two photographic albums of his travels in Tripolitania that Rava utilized a process of selection not unlike that employed in *Vers une architecture* (Paris: les Editions G. Cres, 1923). Rava's photographs of the mosque of Qasr al-Hajj show an interest in white walls and pure solids similar to that espoused by Le Corbusier in this famous publication.

76. Mussolini, "Speech at Municipio di Tripoli," April 11, 1926. *Scritti e discorsi di Benito Mussolini. Vol. V. Scritti e discorsi dal 1925 al 1926* (Milan: Ulrico Hoepli Editore, 1934), 318–19. The following is the larger context of this statement: "It is not without significance that I draw my wish to this shore of the sea that was Roman and returns to Rome and it is particularly significant that I spread out all of the Italian people around me, a united people of soldiers, of colonists, of pioneers."

77. Rava, "Di un'architettura coloniale moderna—Parte seconda," 36.

78. N.D.R., "Un progetto per il Concorso della Piazza della Cattedrale di Tripoli," *Architettura e Arti Decorative* IX, 12 (August 1930): 571–76.

79. Ibid., 575.

80. Letter from Rava to Papini, dated March 30, 1930. Archivo Roberto Papini – 453. Concorso Piazza Cattedrale e Piano Regolatore di Tripoli.

81. Gruppo Sette, "Architettura," *Rassegna Italiana* XVIII, 103 (December 1926): 851–52.

82. N.D.R., "Architetture libiche degli Arch. Carlo Enrico Rava e Sebastiano Larco," 682. The larger context of this quotation is as follows: "It is interesting to look at the realized project (looking at the plans of the previously cited article) that is certainly one of the most clear affirmations of Italian avant-garde architecture. In it, in fact, we can see pursued some of the so-called rationalist aesthetic postulations and, additionally, among the most sane and acceptable, particularly in constructions of this type. Above all the fundamental ones of pure architectonic constructivity and functionality, that is of the total and exclusive response of the external expression to the internal organism, that which was thought of and felt in its two-fold and contemporary technical-artistic and aesthetic representation."

83. Ibid., 682.

84. Ibid., 682. This article is clearly arguing that this project avoids the fashion-able tendencies of the International style in architecture. Some of the manners that it attaches to this movement are "the adding of massing elements extraneous to the compo-sition of useful volumes, or the systematic use of voids that are more long than high, or corner windows."

85. Ibid., 682. A more complete context to these quotations is as follows: "The authors have instead conserved in the voids the sense of proportion typical to the houses of Libya: small windows, just a little higher than a square; doors of a long size, of a measure scarcely sufficient. It is curious and symptomatic to observe how from the objective and well-intended application of modern ideas an architecture completely contextualized to a Mediterranean country has resulted."

86. "L'Albergo agli Scavi di Leptis Magna," *Domus* 44 (August 1931): 21–23. This project was published in *Domus* in August of 1931, during the midst of the "Panorama del razionalismo" that Rava published in this same magazine that year and just two months after his second article on colonial architecture appeared.

87. Rava, "Di un'architettura coloniale moderna—Parte seconda," 36.

88. The publication of this project in *Domus* explains that it was intended for groups of fifty to sixty tourists who would be there just for the day and a smaller number of guests who would stay overnight. This programmatic demand helps to clarify the development of the sequence of rooms on the ground floor and the proportionally small number of guest rooms located on the upper floor (fourteen). "L'Albergo agli Scavi di Leptis Magna," 21.

89. Rava, "Di un'architettura coloniale moderna—Parte seconda," 32.

90. "L'Albergo agli Scavi di Leptis Magna," 21, 23. In its publication in *Domus*, the environmental concerns of this project were well noted. Recognizing that Larco and Rava took advantage of its seafront location with a series of verandahs, terraces, and loggias, this article remarks that this series of elements have "in their spirit some char-acteristics of a steamship." This comment shows the delicate balance between climatic concerns that grounds the project in its context and the modernist or rationalist refer-ences of the project.

91. Bucciante, "Lo sviluppo edilizio della Libia," 5.

92. Fulvio Suvich, memorandum to Benito Mussolini, 18 November 1931. ASMAE – Archivio Segreto – 200. Fasc. Libia – turismo. Written upon Suvich's return from the XII Conference of Travel Agencies (held in Tripoli February 10–14, 1931), this report outlines the urgent problems with tourism in this region, which were: (1) The creation of a tourist season for Tripolitania; (2) the organization of tourist propaganda; (3) the institution of attractions of local culture; and (4) the connection by land to Tunisia. The question of modern architecture and local color is part of a general discussion of the need to preserve these qualities in this colony.

6. IN SEARCH OF A REGIONALIST EXPRESSION

1. Di Fausto, "Visione mediterranea della mia architettura," *Libia* I, 9 (December 1937): 16.

2. Clark, *Modern Italy, 1871–1982*, 266, 281–82.

3. Giuliano Gresleri, "La 'nuova Roma dello Scioa' e l'improbabile architettura dell'Impero," *Architettura italiana d'oltremare 1870–1940*, 164–77. Gresleri notes that the Ministry of the Colonies created the Central Council for Architecture and Urbanism in November of 1936.

4. "I voti conclusivi del Congresso," *Urbanistica* VI, 3 (May–June 1937): 146–48.

5. De Grand, "Mussolini's Follies," 127–47.

6. Pellegrini, "Manifesto dell'architettura coloniale," *Rassegna di Architettura* VIII, 10 (October 1936): 349–67. The two-page essay was followed by a series of fifty-one photo-graphs, twenty-nine of which were taken by Pellegrini. Each image was accompanied by a

title and brief commentary related to its particular applicability to the task of creating a contemporary colonial architecture.

7. Di Fausto, "Visione mediterranea della mia architettura," 16.

8. Ibid., 18. Di Fausto further notes: "Here was the culmination of three great civilizations; Greek, Roman and Christian. Coming from Nordic, Asiatic or African distances, the populations that were attracted there, immediately had the influence of a mitigation of customs and in an artistic industry that has had its own marks of beauty and enjoys the greatest radiant clarity."

9. Ibid., 17.

10. Ibid., 17.

11. Ibid., 17–18.

12. Cabiati, "Orientamenti della moderna architettura italiana in Libia," *Rassegna di Architettura* VIII, 10 (October 1936): 344.

13. Apollonj, "L'Architettura araba della Libia," *Rassegna di Architettura* IX, 12 (December 1937): 459.

14. Ibid., 459.

15. Ibid., 459.

16. Ibid., 461. The larger context of these statements is as follows: "While the contemporary [Italian] building art is the final point of arrival of a long aesthetic evolution . . . in the forms of Arab architecture we find ourselves in the presence of a primitivism, frank and free of any artistic consistency, which cannot but be that proper to the spontaneity of the constructive spirit that inspired it and to the effective immediacy of means with which it is explained. On the one hand we have the extreme refinement of a civilization that has reached a position, if not final, certainly extremely advanced and often utopian; on the other the intuitive spontaneity of a poor and static population."

17. Scarin, *L'Insediamento umano nella Libia occidentale* (Verona: A. Mondadori, 1940).

18. Cipriani, "Razzismo e possessi coloniali," *Difesa della Razza* I, 2 (5 September 1938): 17.

19. Bucciante, "Lo sviluppo edilizio della Libia," 4–6. The commission was created by a gubernatorial decree on February 21 and was composed of members from the colonial administration, the municipality, the technical office, the superintendency to the monuments and excavations, and two consultants: the architect Florestano Di Fausto and his partner Stefano Gatti-Casazza.

20. Giuliano Gresleri, "L'architettura dell'Italia d'oltremare: Realtà, finzione, immaginario," in *Architettura italiana d'oltremare 1870–1940*, 33.

21. Wright, *The Politics of Design in French Colonial Urbanism*, 101–2. The project for the Boulevard du IVª Zouaves by Marcel Prost from 1914 was part of a new regulatory plan for Casablanca from this same year. As Wright notes, this monumental boulevard was a key part of the Prost plan, which was intended to link the port to the commercial center of the city, the Place de France.

22. The relative statute is: D.G. 15 November 1935, n. 16454. "Concessione in uso all'Ente turistico ed alberghiero della Libia di tutti gli alberghi governativi e municipali." ASMAE – MAI 4 – Pacco 29, Fascicolo 210. ETAL – Materiale illustrativo ed informazioni.

23. R. Matignon, *La Compagnie Générale Transatlantique depuis la guerre*, Ph.D. thesis, University of Bordeau, 1937 (Bordeaux: Imprimiere-Librairie Delmas, 1937).

24. Prosper Ricard, *Les Guides Bleus. Le Maroc* (Paris: Librairie Hachette, 1930), 123, 127. A more recent guidebook notes that this building was the stopping point for the most famous figures, including Winston Churchill; *1994 North African Handbook*, ed. Anne and Keith McLachlan (Chicago: Passport Books, 1994), 268.

25. Gallotti and Laprade, *Le Jardin et la Maison Arabes au Maroc* (Paris: Éditions Albert Levy, 1926). This book provides detailed documentation of buildings like the Pavilion of Rodoane.

26. "Nuovi alberghi in funzione nella Libia orientale," *Rivista delle Colonie* XII, 2 (February 1938): 235.

27. ETAL, *Combinazioni di soggiorno in Libia*, 1.

28. Report of the ETAL, 1938, Tables 4 and 6.

29. The ETAL hotels along the Mediterranean coast were in the following cities (from west to east): Zuwarah, Tripoli, al-Khums (Leptis Magna), Zlitan, Misurata, Sirt, Ajdabiya, Benghazi, Cyrene, Derna, and Tobruk.

30. "Relazione tecnica del direttore generale al bilancio dell'esercizio, 1936–37," 7.

31. Vicari, "L'Ente turistico ed alberghiero della Libia," 966.

32. Ibid., 966. The restaurant is described as "divided in various environments, it is modernly decorated, with characteristic rope chairs and a grandiose diffuse light."

33. Vicari, "L'Ente turistico ed alberghiero della Libia," 967. For a more detailed account of the facilities of this hotel, see "Nuovi alberghi in funzione nella Libia orientale," 235.

34. Claudio Brunelli, "Ospitalità e turismo in Libia," 2, 4.

35. Brunelli, "L'organizzazione turistica della Libia," 328.

36. Vicari, "L'Ente turistico ed alberghiero della Libia," 963, 965, 971. The price of staying at the Uaddan was almost three times that of the Mehari, the first being 55–70 lire/day for single room with bath, the second hotel being 18–25 lire/day.

37. Tomasello, *La letteratura coloniale italiana*, 70. In discussing the novels of Mario dei Gaslini, Tomasello notes that *Piccolo amore beduino* "presents itself as the typical expression of D'Annunzian literature. . . . If on the one hand, in fact, the author undergoes a fascination and charm of a foreign land, on the other he seeks a confrontation with a different culture."

38. Vicari, "L'Ente turistico ed alberghiero della Libia," 965.

39. Brunelli, "Ospitalità e turismo in Libia," 4. The theater of this project was operated by the Theater and Performance Service, which organized events involving Italian theatrical companies and orchestras throughout the tourist season. The casino, though also catering to hotel guests, was also treated as a separate attraction and was, in fact, a replacement of an earlier municipal casino that was also located along the eastern waterfront.

40. Bucciante, "Lo sviluppo edilizio della Libia," 7.

41. Apollonj, "L'Architettura araba della Libia," 459. In this essay, the author states: "This Tripolitanian monumental architecture, although naturally presenting a general structure that inserts itself in the great trunk of Arab art, appears induced by a thousand influences, prevalently of Roman and Western origin: nevertheless not missing heterogeneous influxes like, for example, Persian or Turkish. It reaches very picturesque effects and also sometimes of notable beauty, as in the principal mosques of Tripoli and in the mosque of al-Khums."

42. The mosque of Sidi Darghut, named after a sixteenth-century governor, is one of the largest in Tripoli. It is formed by a T-shaped sanctuary, which is connected to a series of surrounding tomb-chambers and a bath that was built on the remains of Darghut's original palace. The mosque is flanked by several irregular courtyard spaces, one of which contains the minaret and several graves, and then an encircling wall that links it to the larger context. This building is a composite of separate buildings and different historical periods, such as Roman and early and late Ottoman. Muhammed Warfelli, "The old city of Tripoli," in *Art and Archeology Research Papers* (Tripoli: Dept. of Antiquities, 1976), 8–9.

43. Bucciante, "Lo sviluppo edilizio della Libia," 7. Bucciante comments on the interior finishing: "The interior is luxuriously yet soberly finished with marble and stucco, and countless plays of light cause the structures to stand out. The small theater, with a seating capacity of about 500 spectators, is one of the most exquisite buildings of its type."

44. Although several sources including Vicari refer to the hotel having both Roman and Turkish baths, their advertisement in *Libia* magazine show them as *Terme romane*.

45. "Governo della Libia – Notiziario d'informazioni" (31 May 1935). ACS - PCM 1934–36, 17.1.498. Both of these hotels were, in fact, inaugurated on April 29, 1935, by the principe di Piemonte, who was in Tripoli with his wife for an official visit that included seeing the Tripoli Trade Fair.

46. Vicari, "L'Ente turistico ed alberghiero della Libia," 962–64. Vicari notes that "the Albergo del Mehari, that takes its name from the characteristic racing camel, is the tourist hotel, with large capacity, and every convenience, but respecting the economy of space the most."

47. Ibid., 964.

48. Ibid., 964. Vicari notes: "With a triangular plan, sober in style, more gracious than elegant, crowned in the front with a small cupola that corresponds to the atrium, ample and luminous, with five small cool and fascinating courtyards, low in construction, all in white, it presents itself brightly to the sea."

49. *Islamic art and architecture in Libya* (London: The Architectural Association, 1976), 28. This catalogue notes that the *funduqs* were important to the commerce of the city, often directly associated with suqs (or markets). These buildings functioned as hotels for merchants, in addition to providing storage and workshop space.

50. Corò, "Alla scoperta dei vecchi Fondugh tripolini," 201–10.

51. Bucciante, "Lo sviluppo edilizio della Libia," 7.

52. Brunelli, "Ospitalità e turismo in Libia," 2.

53. The courtyard in the Hotel at the Excavations at Leptis Magna did not appear to be a courtyard, given that it was covered with a glass roof, nor did it function as one. On the ground floor it acted as one of a series of interconnected public rooms, and on the upper level it was a light well for the corridor linking the guest rooms.

54. Bertarelli, *Guida d'Italia del Touring Club Italiano. Libia*, 221. Before the definitive conquest of Ghadames by General Graziani in February of 1924, this town was only sporadically under the control of the Italians after the initial invasion of 1911.

55. Piccioli, *La Porta magica del Sahara* (Tripoli: Libreria Edit. Minerva, 1931). The other editions of the book are: Piccioli, *The Magic Gate of the Sahara*, translated by Angus Davidson (London: Methuen, 1935); Piccioli, *Die magische Pforte der Sahara*, translated by Helly Steglich-Hohenemser (Hamburg: Verlag Broschek & Co, 1941). Vicari notes the great success of the book in Germany. Vicari, "L'Ente turistico ed alberghiero della Libia," 965.

56. Del Boca, *Gli italiani in Libia. Dal fascismo a Gheddafi*, 271–78. Del Boca notes that much of this research was either conducted under the support of the Ministry of the Colonies or by one of several colonial organizations whose interest it was to support Fascist government policy.

57. Scarin, *L'Insediamento umano nella Libia occidentale* (Verona: Off. Grafiche A. Mondadori, 1940): 120. In this section, Scarin notes that the upper portions of the house were dedicated to women, including the exterior terraces above the street level, which he describes as a kind of market exclusively for women.

58. Piccioli, *La nuova Italia d'oltremare*, 912.

59. "Alle porte del Sahara in autobus," 46.

60. Bertarelli, *Guida d'Italia del Touring Club Italiano. Possedimenti e Colonie*, 321, 336. A twice-monthly transportation service from Tripoli to Ghadames using buses began in 1929, with four days' travel in each direction and three days in Ghadames. In addition to the hotel in Ghadames, the modest Hotel Nefusa was opened in Nalut in October 1928.

61. ETAL, *La Libia*, 16–17. The cost for this trip was a rather steep 575 lire for transportation and 250 lire for food and accommodation per person.

62. Loschi, "L'autostrada del deserto libico," 529.

63. ETAL, *Itinerario Tripoli-Gadames*. This seventy-two page book was translated in separate editions in English, French, and German.

64. ETAL, *Itinerario Tripoli-Gadames*, 29.

65. ETAL, *Itinerario Tripoli-Gadames*, 14. For a detailed scientific discussion of these same houses, see Scarin, *L'Insediamento umano nella Libia occidentale*, 144–59. While dismissing the fact that these are primitive dwellings, Scarin still manages to essentialize their defensive purpose: "the principal aim of the troglodyte house . . . consists in creating

an efficient defense against the jump in temperature and the violent winds on the one hand, and probably from sudden attacks of raiding nomads on the other."

66. ETAL, *Itinerario Tripoli-Gadames*, 7.

67. De Agostini, *La Libia turistica*, 69.

68. ETAL, *Itinerario Tripoli-Gadames*, 27. Here is a vivid description of this settlement: "their houses run high in superimposed circles of round walls overflowing; excretions, one could say, of the entrails of the same mountain." Ibid., 26.

69. Ibid., 28. The larger context of the statement is: "Today this [panorama is] enjoyed from the terrace of the hotel and it is the most precious gift that Yifran offers to the visitor: an enchantment of land and sky, unvaried in magic colors from the dawn to sunset; a piece of Africa that comes apart in crude cuttings, in an effusive light of sidereal triumph, where the mountains, the trees, the houses, even the stones and the grass, are enunciated in incredibly definite contours, as they might be under the focus of a lens."

70. Apollonj, "L'architettura araba della Libia," 459. The author notes that "another reason for the fascination provoked by the minor architecture is its intimate response to the Tripolitanian landscape. Rather, this response is thus complete and profound, constituting one of the most important characteristics of this architecture. What I am calling the telluricity of the Arab construction, manifests in the first case with the same material employed, which is generally battered earth."

71. Gaspare Messana, *Architettura Musulmana della Libia* (Castelfranco Veneto: Edizione del Grifone, 1972), 64. Messana points out that one of the characteristic minaret forms, found in the mosque at Suknah, is a tapered square, which he claims is found in the southern regions of the country. Suknah is an oasis, roughly parallel to Ghadames, located directly south of Misurata and Sirt.

72. ETAL, *Itinerario Tripoli-Gadames*, 41.

73. Ibid., 3. Brunelli comments on the building and adjacent landscape: "The windows of the hotel face the view of an abysmal landscape, that seems to have existed and been uninhabited for millennia. The crude enchantment of Nalut is destined to remain in the memory of who reaches this remote village in the interior, like a Dantesque apparition: mysterious and ghost-like, without the murmur of a fountain, without the repose of green."

74. In addition to Emilio Scarin's *L'insediamento umano nella Libia occidentale*, the Berber people are referred to in numerous anthropological studies, such as Raffaele Corso's *Africa Italiana, Genti e costumi* (1940).

75. ETAL, *Itinerario Tripoli-Gadames*, 36. An extensive discussion is provided of the Berber castle in Nalut, one of the most important and significant tourist sites in this region. Later used as a fortified granary, it was said to have functioned as military defense before the conquest of this region. The following is the myth recounted in this publication: "In the Castle the people of Nalut sustained a memorable siege at the time of the second conquest of the Ottomans: the Berbers resisted the harsh assault for months and months, without provisions, without water, almost without weapons. When their enemies got the best of their heroic resistance, in the narrow streets within the castle they found only piles of cadavers, the majority of which were in an advanced state of decay: true hawks of the Jabal, the Berbers preferred death over dishonor." Ibid., 39.

76. Bucciante, "Lo sviluppo edilizio della Libia," 7. While the authorship of this project is represented in several sources as being an engineer with the municipality named Agujari, Bucciante confirms that this project was executed by Di Fausto in conjunction with Gatti-Casazza.

77. ETAL, *Itinerario Tripoli-Gadames*, 56.

78. Vicari, "L'Ente turistico ed alberghiero della Libia," 966. The author notes that to protect the building from its harsh environment, its walls were given air spaces equipped with special heat-refracting material.

79. ETAL, *Itinerario Tripoli-Gadames*, 56. The relationship is described as: "The

building is literally covered by long boughs of palms; from every side their trunks encircle the building, they grow luxuriantly in the internal court and stretch out a thousand arms in front of the glass of the windows. You will be in the magic of green. . . . Do you want to experience the vegetal transparency in which the sweet reflections pour into the main halls, in the rooms, in the corridors? You lead into the garden of the hotel. The palms plunging into the soft ground, are already three years old; if you stay in the date season, you could gather some, at the intersection of the branch and the trunk, the beautiful golden clusters that melt with sweetness: tawny mark among all of this green: the natives call them *deglat en nur*: fingers of light. Every type of fruit bearing tree is within: orange, pomegranate, lemon, carob, pistachio."

80. Ibid., 66.

81. Ibid., 72. One of the few houses accessible to tourists was located near the 'Ain el-Fras and was described as follows: "On the outside it does not differ a lot from the others. Crossing the threshold, a steep stair, with delightful decorations sculpted or etched in the walls, leads to the main floor and flows into the central room, that one can say is representative. No furniture. On the floor are mats and carpets. The richness is on the mantels of the walls where innumerable silver, pewter, and brass vases are collected. This is the jewel box: this is the safe of the family."

82. Ibid., 56.

83. Vicari, "L'Ente turistico ed alberghiero della Libia," 966.

84. Interest in the Berbers was sparked for a number of reasons: they were the most ancient Libyan peoples, having preexisted the Arab invasion of this region, and—as the Italians were quick to point out—they were reluctant converts to Islam, having first been converted to Christianity. The perceived primitivism of their culture was also of considerable interest, both to a tourist audience and for anthropological and ethnographic researchers like Emilio Scarin.

CONCLUSION

1. Vicari, "L'Ente Turistico ed Alberghiero della Libia," *Gli Annali dell'Africa Italiana* V, 4 (December 1942): 956.

2. Lucy Lippard provides an excellent discussion of Santa Fe in her book *On the Beaten Track: Tourism, Art, and Place* (New York: The New Press, 1999).

3. Edward N. Kaufman, "The Architectural Museum, from World's Fair to Restoration Village," *Assemblage* 9 (1989): 21–39.

4. These fifteen pairs of small mounted images and thirty postcards are an incomplete collection of a larger group of images that were purchased at the Porta Portese Market in Rome. The dating of the images is based upon the modes of transportation shown.

5. Persico, "Punto e da capo per l'architettura," 4–5.

6. Ibid., 3.

7. Bhabha, "Of Mimicry and Man: The Ambivalence of Colonial Discourse," in *The Location of Culture*, 86.

8. Rava, "Architettura di razza italiana," *L'Architettura Italiana* (January 1939): 41–42.

9. Ibid., 39. The intention of this article is quite clear from the beginning when Rava states: "It seems to me fundamentally right that today, after the racist principle, as natural corollary of the great autarchic battle in which every aspect of the nation has been engaged, has raised the issue of the italianità of the new architecture." Ibid., 37.

10. Boito, "Conservare o restaurare?" *Nuova Antologia* LXXXVII (1886), in *Testimonianze e polemiche figurative in Italia. L'Ottocento, dal Bello ideal al Pre-raffaellismo*, ed. Paola Barocchi (Messina, Florence: Casa Editrice G. D'Anna, 1972), 383–92. See also Amedeo Bellini, "Camillo Boito," in *Dictionary of Art* (New York: Grove's Dictionaries, 1996), 246–48.

11. Giovannoni, "Vecchie città ed edilizia nuova," 449–72; and "Il diradamento edilizio dei vecchi centri – il Quartiere della Rinascenza in Roma," 53–76.

12. Giovannoni, *Questioni di architettura nella storia e nella vita. Edilizia – estetica architettonica – restauri – ambiente dei monumenti* (Rome: Biblioteca d'Arte Editrice, 1929), 28–29.

13. See Eugène-Emanuel Viollet-le-Duc, "Restoration," in *The Foundations of Architecture: Selections from the Dictionnaire Raisonné*, trans. Kenneth D. Whitehead; Introduction by Barry Bergdoll (New York: George Braziller, Inc., 1990), 195–227; Alois Riegl, "The Modern Cult of Monuments: Its Character and Its Origin," in *Oppositions* 25 (Fall 1982), 2–19; Camillo Sitte, *City Planning According to Artistic Principles* (1889), in George Collins and Christiane Crasemann Collins, *Camillo Sitte: The Birth of Modern City Planning* (New York: Rizzoli, 1986), 243–78.

14. Del Boca, *Gli italiani in Libia. Dal fascismo a Gheddafi*, 297.

15. Vicari, "L'Ente turistico ed alberghiero della Libia," 972–75.

16. Ibid., 973.

BIBLIOGRAPHY

PERIODICALS SURVEYED FOR 1911-43

Africa Italiana (Bergamo, 1938-43)

Architettura e Arti Decorative (Milan, Rome, 1921-43)

Gli Annali dell'Africa Italiana (Rome, 1938-43)

Casabella (Milan, 1928–)

Difesa della Razza (Rome, 1938-43)

Domus (Milan 1928–)

Esotica (Milan, 1926-27)

L'Italia Coloniale (Milan, 1924-43)

Libia (Tripoli, 1937-42)

L'Oltremare (Rome, 1927-34)

Rassegna di Architettura (Milan, 1929-39)

Rassegna Economica delle Colonie (Rome, 1928-43)

Rassegna Italiana (Rome, 1928-43)

Rivista della Tripolitania (Tripoli, Rome, 1924-27)

Rivista delle Colonie Italiane (Rome, 1927-43)

Le Vie d'Italia (Milan, 1917-67)

SELECTED GENERAL REFERENCES ON MODERNITY, FASCISM, AND COLONIALISM

AlSayyad, Nezzar, ed. *Forms of Dominance: On the Architecture and Urbanism of the Colonial Experience.* Brookfield: Ashgate Publishing Company, 1992.

——.*Consuming Tradition, Manufacturing Heritage: Global Norms and Urban Forms in the Age of Tourism.* New York and London: Routledge, 2001.

Béguin, François. *Arabisances. Décor architectural et tracé urbain en Afrique du Nord, 1830–1950.* Paris: Dunod, 1983.

Bel, Alfred and Prosper Ricard. *Le travail de la laine a Tlemcen.* Algiers: Typ. A. Jourdan, 1913.

Benedict, Burton. *The Anthropology of World's Fairs.* London and Berkeley: Scholar Press, 1983.

Ben-Ghiat, Ruth. *The Formation of a Fascist Culture: The Realist Movement in Italy, 1930–1943.* Ph.D. dissertation, Brandeis University, 1990.

——. "Fascism, Writing and Memory: The Realist Aesthetic in Italy, 1930–1950." *Journal of Modern History* 67: 3 (September 1995): 627–65.

——. "Italian Fascism and the Aesthetics of the 'Third Way.'" *Journal of Contemporary History* 31, 2 (April 1996): 293–316.

——. "Envisioning Modernity: Desire and Discipline in the Italian Fascist Film." *Critical Inquiry* 23, 1 (Autumn 1996): 109–44.

Ben-Ghiat, Ruth, and Mia Fuller, eds. *Italian Colonialism.* New York: Palgrave MacMillan, 2004.

Berman, Marshall. *All That Is Solid Melts into Air. The Experience of Modernity.* New York: Simon and Schuster, 1982.

Bhabha, Homi. *The Location of Culture*. London and New York: Routledge, 1994.

Bozdogan, Sibel. *Modernism and Nation Building. Turkish Architectural Culture in the Early Republic*. Seattle and London: University of Washington Press, 2001.

Cannistraro, Philip V. "Mussolini's Cultural Revolution: Fascist or Nationalist?" *Journal of Contemporary History* 7, 3–4 (July–October 1972): 115–39.

Çelik, Zeynep. *Urban Forms and Colonial Confrontations: Algiers under French Rule*. Berkeley: University of California Press, 1997.

Clark, Martin, *Italy 1871–1982*. New York: Longman Inc., 1984.

Cohen, Jean-Louis and Monique Eleb. *Casablanca. Mythes et figures d'une aventure urbaine*. Paris: Editions Hazan, 1998.

Crinson, Mark. *Empire Building: Orientalism and Victorian Architecture*. London and New York: Routledge, 1996.

De Grand, Alexander. "Mussolini's Follies: Fascism in Its Imperial and Racist Phase, 1935–1940." *Contemporary European History*, 13, 2 (May 2004): 127–47.

Edensor, Tim. *Tourists at the Taj: Performance and Meaning at a Symbolic Site*. New York and London: Routledge, 1998.

Fabian, Johannes. *Time and the Other: How Anthropology Makes its Object*. New York: Columbia University Press, 1983.

Falasca-Zamponi, Simonetta. *Fascist Spectacle: The Aesthetics of Power in Mussolini's Italy*. Berkeley: The University of California Press, 1997.

Gallotti, Jean, and Albert Laprade. *Le Jardin et la Maison Arabes au Maroc*. Paris: Éditions Albert Levy, 1926.

Ghirardo, Diane. "Italian Architects and Fascist Politics: An Evaluation of the Rationalist's Role in Regime Building." *Journal of the Society of Architectural Historians* XXXIX, 2 (May 1980): 109–27.

——. "Politics of a Masterpiece: The Vicenda of the Decoration of the Facade of the Casa del Fascio, Como, 1936–1939." *The Art Bulletin* 62 (September 1980): 466–78.

——. *Building New Communities: New Deal America and Fascist Italy*. Princeton: Princeton University Press, 1989.

——. "Architects, Exhibitions, and the Politics of Culture in Fascist Italy." *Journal of Architectural Education* 45, 2 (February 1992): 67–75.

——. "*Città Fascista*: Surveillance and Spectacle." *Journal of Contemporary History* 31, 2 (April 1996): 347–72.

Gramsci, Antonio. "Appunti per una introduzione e un avviamento allo studio della filosofia e della storia della culture. 1. Alcuni punti preliminari di riferimento," *Quaderno* 11, §12, 1932-33. In *Quaderni del Carcere. Volume secondo. Quaderni 6 (VIII) – 11 (XVIII)*, 1375. Turin: Giulio Einaudi Editore, 1975.

——. "Appunti e note sparse per un gruppo di saggi sulla storia degli intellettuali," *Quaderno* 12, §1, 1932. In *Quaderni del Carcere. Volume terzo*, 1513. Turin: Giulio Einaudi Editore, 1975.

——. "Concept of national-popular." *Quaderno* 21, §5, 1934–35. In *Quaderni del Carcere. Volume terzo*, 2113–20. Turin: Giulio Einaudi Editore, 1975.

——. "Osservazioni sul Folklore," *Quaderno* 27, §1, 1935. In *Quaderni del Carcere. Volume terzo*, 2311–12. Turin: Giulio Einaudi Editore, 1975.

Guy, Raphaël. *L'Architecture moderne de style arabe*. Paris: Librairie de la construction moderne, s.d.

Herf, Jeffrey. *Reactionary Modernism: Technology, Culture, and Politics in Weimar and the Third Reich*. Cambridge: Cambridge University Press, 1984.

Hewitt, Andrew. *Fascist Modernism: Aesthetics, Politics, and the Avant-Garde*. Stanford, CA: Stanford University Press, 1993.

Kostof, Spiro. *The Third Rome, 1870–1950: Traffic and Glory*. Berkeley: University Art Museum, 1973.

Lasansky, D. Medina. *The Renaissance Perfected: Architecture, Spectacle and Tourism in*

Fascist Italy. University Park: Pennsylvania State University Press, 2004.

Lowe, Lisa. *Critical Terrains: French and British Orientalisms*. Ithaca: Cornell University Press, 1991.

MacCannell, Dean. *The Tourist: A New Theory of the Leisure Class*. 3d. ed. Berkeley: University of California Press, 1999.

MacDonald, William, "Excavation, Restoration and Italian Architecture of the 1930s," in *In Search of Modern Architecture: A Tribute to Henry-Russell Hitchcock*, edited by Helen Searing. New York: The Architectural History Foundation, 1982.

Millon, Henry, "The Role of the History of Architecture in Fascist Italy," *Journal of the Society of Architectural Historians* 24 (March 1965): 53–59.

Morton, Patricia. *Hybrid Modernities: Architecture and Representation at the 1931 Colonial Exposition, Paris*. Cambridge: The MIT Press, 2000.

Pollock, Griselda. *Avant-Garde Gambits 1888–1893: Gender and the Color of Art History*. New York: Thames and Hudson, 1992.

Rabinow, Paul. *French Modern: Norms and Forms of the Social Environment*. Cambridge: MIT Press, 1989.

Ricard, Prosper. *Guide de Fes: renseignements pratiques, aperçu historique, organization municipal, principaux monuments, excursions urbaines et suburbaines*. Fes: Impr. Municipale, 1916.

——. *Le Maroc*. Paris, Hachette, 1919.

——. *Corpus de Tapis Marocains*. Paris: Geunther, 1923.

——. *Les merveilles de l'autre France; Algerie, Tunisie, Maroc; le pays-les monuments-les habitants*. Paris: Hachette, 1924.

——. *Pour comprendre l'art musulman dans l'Afrique du Nord et en Espagne*. Paris: Hachette, 1924.

——. "Il rinnovamento artistico del Marocco." *Dedalo* IX, 12 (May 1929): 742–70.

——. *Algérie, Tunisie, Tripolitaine [et] Malte*. Paris: Hachette, 1930.

——. *Les Guides Bleus: Le Maroc*. Paris: Librairie Hachette, 1930.

Said, Edward W. *Orientalism*. New York: Vintage Books, 1978.

——. *Culture and Imperialism*. New York: Knopf; distributed by Random House, 1993.

Sarti, Roland. "Fascist Modernization in Italy: Traditional or Revolutionary?" *American Historical Review* LXXV, 4 (April 1970): 1029–45.

Savino, Edoardo. *La Nazione Operante. Albo d'oro del fascismo*. Novara: Istituto geografico De Agostini, 1937.

Simeone, William E. "Fascists and Folklorists in Italy." *Journal of American Folklore* XCI, 359 (January–March 1978): 543–57.

Wright, Gwendolyn. *The Politics of Design in French Colonial Urbanism*. Chicago: The University of Chicago Press, 1991.

SELECTED REFERENCES ON TOURISM AND FASCIST COLONIAL POLITICS IN LIBYA

Ahmida, Ali Abdullatif. *The Making of Modern Libya: State Formation, Colonization, and Resistance, 1830–1932*. Albany: State University of New York Press, 1994.

"Alle porte del Sahara in autobus." *L'Italia Coloniale* VI, 3 (March 1929): 46.

Ambrosini, Gaspare. "Ragioni e carattere della grande riforma civile in Libia." *Libia* III, 1 (January 1939): 5–11.

Atti del Primo Congresso di Studi Coloniali. Firenze, 8–12 April 1931. Florence: Sicc B. Seeber, 1931.

Atti del Secondo Congresso di studi coloniali. Napoli, 1–5 October 1934. Florence: Tip. Giuntina di L.S. Olschki, 1934.

Atti del Terzo Congresso di studi coloniali. Firenze-Roma, 12-17 April 1937. Florence: G.C. Sandoni, 1937.

Bailey, Herbert. "The Colonization of Libya." *Fortnightly Review* 145 (February 1939):

197–204.

Balbo, Italo. "La litoranea libica." *Nuova Antologia* LXXII, 1559 (March 1, 1937): 5–13.

———. "Coloni in Libia." *Nuova Antologia* (November 1, 1938): 3-13.

———. "La Litoranea libica." *Convegno di scienze morali e storiche. 4–11 ottobre 1938–XVI. Tema: l'Africa. Volume II*, 1194–1207. Rome: Reale Accademia d'Italia, 1939.

———. "La politica sociale fascista verso gli arabi della Libia." In Reale Accademia d'Italia, Fondazione Alessandro Volta. *Convegno di scienze morali e storiche. 4–11 ottobre 1938, XVI. Tema: l'Africa. Volume I*, 733–49. Rome: Reale Accademia d'Italia, 1939.

Beguinot, Francesco. "Libia. Etnografia antica." In *Enciclopedia italiana. Vol. XXI*, 59–62. Rome: Istituto della enciclopedia italiana fondata da Giovanni Treccani, 1934.

"Da Bengasi a Tripoli in Automobile. Come 38 macchine nel deserto annunciano che la Libia è unificata." *Giornale d'Oriente* 28 June 1931.

Bertarelli, L.V. *Guida d'Italia del Touring Club Italiano. Possedimenti e colonie*. Milan: Touring Club Italiano, 1929.

———. *Guida d'Italia del Touring Club Italiano. Libia*. Milan: Touring Club Italiano, 1937.

Bonardi, Carlo. "Col touring nel Fezzan." *Le Vie d'Italia* XLV, 7 (July 1935): 485–96.

———. "L'avvenire turistico della Libia." *Le Vie d'Italia* XLIII, 6 (June 1937): 434–37.

Borghetti, Giuseppe. "Turismo Coloniale." *L'Italia Coloniale* VIII, 9 (September 1931): 141–42.

Brunelli, Claudio. "L'organizzazione turistica della Libia." *Rassegna Economica delle Colonie* 25, 3 (March 1937): 327–30.

———. "Ospitalità e turismo in Libia." In *Viaggio del Duce per l'inaugurazione della litoranea. Anno XV. Orientamenti e note ad uso dei giornalisti*, 1–7. Rome: Stabilimento Tipografico *Il Lavoro Fascista*, 1937.

Bruni, Giuseppe. "Il nuovo assetto politico-amministrativo della Libia." In *Viaggio del Duce in Libia per l'inaugurazione della litoranea. Anno XV. Orientamenti e note ad uso dei giornalisti*, 1–14. Rome: Stabilimento Tipografico *Il Lavoro Fascista*, 1937.

Cantalupo, Roberto. "Mussolini e l'Africa." *Gerarchia* VI, 4 (April 1926): 209–16.

"Chronache coloniali. L'organizzazione dell'Ente turistico tripolitano." *Rivista delle Colonie Italiane* V, 1 (January 1931): 53.

Cipriani, Lidio. "Una missione scientifica italiana nel Fezzan." *Le Vie d'Italia* XXXIX, 9 (September 1933): 679–91.

———. "Razzismo Coloniale." *Difesa della Razza* I, 2 (20 August 1938): 18–20.

Commissariato per il turismo in Libia. *Libia itinerari*. Milan: S.A. Arti Grafiche Bertarelli, 1935.

Compagnie Générale Transatlantique. *North African Motor Tours of the Compagnie Générale Transatlantique*. London: Hill, Siffken & Co., 1928.

"Il Congresso delle Agenzie di viaggio." *Rivista delle Colonie Italiane* V, 12 (December 1931): 963–64.

"Il Consiglio del Commissariato del turismo." *Rivista delle Colonie Italiane* VIII, 7 (July 1934): 594–95.

Corso, Raffaele. *Africa Italiana. Genti e costumi*. Naples: Casa Editrice Raffaele Pironti, 1940.

Costa, G.B. "Gadames, metropoli sahariana." *Ospitalità Italiana* III, 1 (January 1928): 50–53.

De Agostini, Giovanni. *La Libia Turistica*. Milan: Prof. G. De Agostini, 1938.

D'Annunzio, Gabriele. *Più che l'amore*. Milan: Fratelli Treves, Editori, 1906.

De Bono, Emilio. "Le mie idee sulla colonizzazione." *L'Oltremare* II, 8 (August 1928): 293–95.

Del Boca, Angelo. *Gli italiani in Libia. Dal fascismo a Gheddafi*. Rome-Bari: Giuseppe Laterza & Figli, 1991.

———"L'Italia e la spartizione dell'Africa. In nome della scienza." In *L'Africa nella coscienza degli Italiani*. 7–22. Rome-Bari: Giuseppe Laterza & Figli, 1992.

Il Duce in Libia. Milan: S.A. Stab. arti grafiche Alfieri & Lacroix, 1937.

Ente Nazionale per le Industrie Turistiche and Ferrovie dello Stato. *Tripoli*, Rome: Novissima, 1929.

Ente Nazionale per le Industrie Turistiche. *Annuario Alberghi in d'Italia, 1939*. Milan: Turati Lombardi E.C., 1939.

Ente Turistico ed Alberghiero della Libia. *La Libia*. Milan: F. Milani, 1936.

——. *Combinazioni di soggiorno in Libia*. Rome: ETAL, 1937.

——. *Itinerario Tripoli-Gadames*. Milan: Tipo-Litografia Turati Lombardi, 1938.

——. *Tripoli e dintorni*. Milan: Tipo-Litografia Turati Lombardi, 1939.

Federazione Nazionale Fascista Alberghi e Turismo. *Politica Turistica*. Rome: Stabilimento Tipografico Ditta C. Colombo, 1928.

Federzoni, Luigi. "La nuova vita dell'Istituto Coloniale Fascista dell'Africa Italiana." *Rivista delle Colonie* XIII, 1 (January 1939): 3–12.

Fougier, Corso. "Attrezzatura aeronautica della Libia dal punto di vista del traffico e del turismo aereo." In *Viaggio del Duce per l'inaugurazione della litoranea. Anno XV. Orientamenti e note ad uso dei giornalisti*, 1–11. Rome: Stabilimento Tipografico *Il Lavoro Fascista*, 1937.

Frigerio, Dante. *Organizzazione e nuovi mezzi di potenziamento del turismo in Italia*. Bellinzona: Istituto Editoriale Ticinese, 1940.

Gaslini, Mario Dei. *Piccolo amore Beduino*. Milan: L'Eroica, 1926.

——. *Natisc fiore dell'oasi. Romanzo coloniale*. Bologna: L. Cappelli Editore, 1928.

——. *Paradiso nell'inferno. Uso e costumi abissini*. Milan: Zacchi ambrosiana, 1937.

Gaslini Mario Dei and L.F. De Magistris. *L'Oltremare in terra d'Africa. Visioni e sintesi*. Bergamo: Istituto Italiano d'Arti Grafiche, 1930–31.

Ghisleri, Arcangelo. *La Libia nella storia e nei viaggiatori. Dai tempi omerici all'occupazione italiana*. Turin: G. B. Paravia & Co., 1928.

Giovannangeli, A. "Cenni sull'attività municipale di Tripoli." In *Viaggio del Duce in Libia per l'inaugurazione della litoranea. Anno XV. Orientamenti e note ad uso dei giornalisti* 1–13. Rome: Stabilimento Tipografico *Il Lavoro Fascista*, 1937.

Gray, Ezio Maria. "L'opera del CIT in Tripolitania." *Ospitalità Italiana* III, 1 (January 1928): 55–56.

Guida, Osvaldo. "Questa letteratura coloniale." *L'Oltremare* III, 8 (August 1929): 358–60.

Guida di Tripoli e dintorni. Milano: Fratelli Treves Editori, 1925.

"L'insediamento del Consiglio di Amministrazione dell'Ente turistico ed alberghiero." *L'Avvenire di Tripoli* (13 October 1935): 3.

Insabato, Enrico. "Islam." *Libia* I, 5 (August 1937): 9–11.

Interlandi, Dante. "La Tripolitania e il suo sviluppo turistico." *Ospitalità Italiana* III, 1 (January 1928): 86–87.

L'Italie pour les populations islamiques de l'afrique italienne. Rome: Società Editrice "Novissima," 1940.

"La linea aerea Roma – Tripoli." *L'Oltremare* II, 11 (November 1928): 431.

Loschi, M.A. "L'autostrada del deserto libico." *Le Vie d'Italia* XLII, 8 (August 1936): 529–37.

Malvezzi, Aldobrandino. *La politica indigena nelle Colonie*. Padua: Casa Editrice Dott. A. Milani, 1933.

Marchetti, Ugo. "Saper viaggiare in Libia." *Libia* I, 1 (March 1937): 38–40.

Marinetti, Filippo Tommaso. *Mafarka le futuriste. Roman africain*. Paris: E. Sansot & C.ie, 1909.

——. "L'Africa generatrice e ispiratrice di poesia e arti." In Reale Accademia d'Italia, *Convegno di scienze morale e storiche. 4-11 ottobre 1938-XVI. Tema: Africa. Volume 1*, 198–201. Rome: Reale Accademia d'Italia, 1939.

Matignon, R. *La Compagnie Générale Transatlantique depuis la guerre*. Ph.D. dissertation, University of Bordeau, 1937. Bordeaux: Imprimiere–Librairie Delmas, 1937.

Mitrano Sani, Gino. *Malati di Sud*. Naples: Edizioni Trinchera, 1928.

——. *La reclusa di Giarabub*, with preface by F.T. Marinetti. Milan: Alpes, 1931.

——. *Femina somala*. Naples: Edizioni Dekten e Rocholi, 1933.

Moore, Martin. *Fourth Shore: Italy's Mass Colonization of Libya*. London, 1940.

Mozzati, Marco. "Gli intellettuali e la propaganda coloniale del regime." In *Le guerre coloniali del fascismo*, 99–111. Bari: Editori Laterza, 1991.

Mussolini, Benito. "Speech to the Italian Fascists of Tripoli" and "Speech at Municipio of Tripoli," April 11, 1926. In *Scritti e discorsi di Benito Mussolini. Volume V. Scritti e discorsi dal 1925 al 1926*, 318–19. Milan: Ulrico Hoepli Editore, 1934.

——. "Ai camerati di Tripoli," 17 March 1937. *Opera omnia di Benito Mussolini. Vol. XXVIII. Dalla proclamazione dell'Impero al viaggio in Germania (10 maggio 1936–30 settembre 1937)*, edited by Edoardo and Dulio Susmel, 143–45. Florence: La Fenice, 1959.

——. "Alla prima riunione delle Corporazione dell'Ospitalità." 25 January 1936. In *Opera Omnia di Benito Mussolini. Vol. XXVII. Dall'inaugurazione della provincia di Littoria alla proclamazione dell'Impero (19 dicembre 1934–9 maggio 1936)*, edited by Edoardo and Dulio Susmel, 214–15. Florence: La Fenice, 1959.

——. "Le direttive agli esponenti del turismo," 14 December 1936. In *Opera omnia di Benito Mussolini. Vol. XXVIII. Dalla proclamazione dell'Impero al viaggio in Germania (10 maggio 1936–30 settembre 1937)*, edited by Edoardo and Dulio Susmel, 92–93. Florence: La Fenice, 1959.

"Nuovi alberghi in funzione nella Libia orientale." *Rivista delle Colonie* XII, 2 (February 1938): 235.

"Oltre 30,000 turisti in Libia nei primi mesi del 1934." *Rivista delle Colonie Italiane* VIII, 9 (September 1934): 772–73.

Paloscia, Franco. *Storia del turismo nell'economia italiana*. Città di Castello: Editore Petruzzi, 1994.

Pellegrineschi, A.V. "Le nuove strade della Libia." *Gerarchia* XV, 10 (October 1935): 866–71.

Piccioli, Angelo. *La Porta magica del Sahara*. Tripoli: Libreria Edit. Minerva, 1931.

——. *La nuova Italia d'oltremare*. Milan: A. Mondadori Editore, 1933.

"La politica islamica dell'Italia." In *Viaggio del Duce in Libia per l'inaugurazione della litoranea. Anno XV. Orientamenti e note ad uso dei giornalisti*, 1–6. Rome: Stabilimento Tipografico *Il Lavoro Fascista*, 1937.

Pistolese, Gennaro. "Turismo d'Oltremare." *Rivista delle Colonie Italiane* III, 6–7 (June–July 1929): 552–53.

Pozzi, Mario. "Arte e propaganda nella letteratura coloniale." *L'Oltremare* III, 5 (May 1929): 210–12.

Quadrotta, Guglielmo. "Appunti sull'artigianato libico." In *Viaggio del Duce in Libia per l'inaugurazione della litoranea. Anno XV. Orientamenti e note ad uso dei giornalisti*, 1–31. Rome: Stabilimento Tipografico *Il Lavoro Fascista*, 1937.

——. "Sviluppo e realizzazioni dell'artigianato in Libia." *Rassegna Economica dell'Africa Italiana* XXV, 7 (July 1937): 952–67.

Rava, Carlo Enrico. *Viaggio a Tunin*. Bologna: Luigi Cappelli Editore, 1932.

Rava, Luigi. "Che cosa e l'ENIT." *Rassegna Italiana del Mediterraneo* V, 59 (December 1925): 397–400.

Ricard, Prosper. *Les arts tripolitains*. Rome: Tipografia del Senato del Dott. G. Bardi, 1926.

La rinascità della Tripolitania. Memorie e studi sui quattro anni di governo del Conte Giuseppe Volpi di Misurata. Milan: Casa Editrice A. Mondadori, 1926.

Romano, Sergio. *Giuseppe Volpi. Industria e finanza tra Giolitti e Mussolini*. Milan: Bompiani, 1979.

Rosselli, Giovanna. "Turismo e colonie. Il Touring Club Italiano." In *Architettura italiana d'oltremare*, edited by Giuliano Gresleri, Pier Giorgio Massaretti and Stefano Zagnoni, 100–107. Venice: Marsilio Editori, 1993.

Scaparro, Mario. "Origini e sviluppi dell'ordinamento corporativo libico." *Rassegna Economica dell'Africa Italiana* XXV, 3 (March 1937): 362–67.

Scarin, Emilio. *L'Insediamento umano nella Libia occidentale*. Verona: A. Mondadori, 1940.

Segrè, Claudio. *Fourth Shore: The Italian Colonization of Libya*. Chicago: The University of Chicago Press, 1974.

———. *Italo Balbo: A Fascist Life*. Berkeley: University of California Press, 1987.

Società italiana di esplorazioni geografiche e commerciali, Milan. *Pionieri italiani in Libia. Relazioni dei delegati, 1880-1896*. Milan: F. Vallardi, 1912.

"La stagione teatrale di Tripoli." *Libia* I, 9 (December 1937): 42.

La strada litoranea della Libia. Verona: Officine Grafiche A. Mondadori, 1937.

Surdich, Francesco. "Le spedizioni scientifiche italiane in Africa Orientale e in Libia durante il periodo fascista." In *Le guerre coloniali del fascismo*, edited by Angelo Del Boca, 449–61. Bari: Editori Laterza, 1991.

Suvich, Fulvio. *Relazione a S.E. il Capo del Governo sui problemi del turismo*. Rome: Soc. Tip. Castaldi, December 1930.

Syrjämaa, Taina. *Visitez l'Italie: Italian State Tourist Propaganda Abroad 1919–1943*, Ph.D. dissertation, Department of General History, University of Turku, 1977. In *Turun Yliopiston Julkaisuja. Annales Universitatis Turkuensis*. Ser. B, Tom 217 (1977).

Tomasello, Giovanna. *La letteratura coloniale italiana dalle avanguardie al fascismo*. Palermo: Sellerio Editore, 1984.

Touring Club Italiano. *Guida della Libia*. Milan: the Club, 1923.

———. *Manuale del Turismo*. Milan: TCI, 1934.

"Il turismo coloniale. Un Ente centrale per coordinare le varie attività." *L'Italia Coloniale* X, 9 (September 1933): 170.

U.T.E. *Rodi: Guida del Turista*. Milan-Rome: Casa Editrice d'Arte Bestetti & Tumminelli, 1928.

Valensin, Guido. "Primo congresso di studi coloniali." *L'Oltremare* V, 2 (February 1931): 75.

Valori, Francesco. "Femminismo arabo." *Libia* I, 6 (September 1937): 23–28.

Vedovato, Giuseppe. *Colonizzazione e turismo in Libia*. Salerno: Prem. Stamperia Raffaello Beraglia, 1934.

Vicari, Eros. "L'Ente turistico ed alberghiero della Libia (E.T.A.L.)." *Gli Annali dell'Africa Italiana* V, 4 (December 1942): 955–75.

Vigor di vita in Tripolitania (Anno 1928–VI). Tripoli: Ufficio studi e propaganda del Governo della Tripolitania, 1928.

"La visita del Duce in Tripolitania nel 1926 e lo Scossone coloniale." In *Viaggio del Duce in Libia per l'inaugurazione della litoranea. Anno XV. Orientamenti e note ad uso dei giornalisti*, 1–11. Rome: Stabilimento Tipografico *Il Lavoro Fascista*, 1937.

"Vita e attrazione a Tripoli. Movimento turistico del mese." *Libia* I, 2 (May 1937): 55–56.

Vota, Giuseppe, ed. *I sessant'anni del Touring Club Italiano, 1894–1954*. Milan: Touring Club Italiano, 1954.

Wright, John. *Libya*. London: Ernest Benn Limited, 1969.

XXX. "Turismo coloniale. Possibilità di sviluppo e necessità di un comando unico." *L'Italia Coloniale* X, 10 (October 1933): 182.-

Zavattari, Edoardo. "Italia e Islam di fronte al problema razzista." *Difesa della Razza* I, 2 (20 August 1938): 14–15.

SELECTED REFERENCES ON MODERN ARCHITECTURE IN ITALY AND LIBYA

"L'Albergo agli Scavi di Leptis Magna." *Domus* 44 (August 1931): 21–23.

"Alcune opere recenti dell'architetto Giovanni Pellegrini a Tripoli." *Rassegna di Architettura* X, 10 (October 1938): 415–26.

Aner. "Edificare in tempo Fascista." *Libia* I, 1 (March 1937): 33.

Apollonj, Fabrizio Maria. "L'Architettura araba della Libia." *Rassegna di Architettura* IX, 12 (December 1937): 455–62.

"L'architettura razionale italiana, 1931." *Casabella* 40 (April 1931): 67–82.

Associazione artistica fra i cultori di architettura in Roma. *Architettura minore in Italia.* Turin: C. Crudo & Co., 1926–40.

Aurigemma, Salvatore. *Tripoli e le sue opere d'arte.* Milan, Rome: Luigi Alfieri & Co. Editori, 1927.

——. "La moschea di Ahmad al-Qarâmânlî in Tripoli." *Dedalo* VII, 8 (January 1927): 504–5.

Bartoccini, Renato. "La moschea di Murad Agha in Tagiura (Tripolitania)." *Architettura e Arti Decorative* III, 8 (April 1924): 345.

——. "Restauri nel Castello di Tripoli." *Bolletino d'Arte* IV, 6 (December 1924): 279–84.

——. *Le Terme di Lepcis (Leptis Magna).* Bergamo: Istituto Italiano d'Arte Grafiche, 1929.

Bongiovanni, Giannetto. "Le moschee di Tripoli." *Ospitalità Italiana* III, 1 (January 1928): 28–29.

Bosio, Gherardo. "Future città dell'Impero." *Architettura* XVII, 7 (July 1937): 419–31.

Brunetti, Fabrizio. *Architetti e fascismo.* Florence: Alinea Editrice, 1993.

Bucciante, G. "Lo sviluppo edilizio della Libia." In *Viaggio del Duce in Libia per l'inaugurazione della litoranea. Anno XV. Orientamenti e note ad uso dei giornalisti,* 1–17. Rome: Stabilimento Tipografico *Il Lavoro Fascista,* 1937.

Cabiati, Ottavio. "Orientamenti della moderna architettura italiana in Libia." *Rassegna di Architettura* VIII, 10 (October 1936): 343–44.

Caputo, Giacomo. "Il consolidamento dell'arco di Marco Aurelio in Tripoli." *Africa Italiana* VII, 1–2 (April 1940): 46–66.

Ceretti, Claudio. "Teneo te, Africa: L'immaginario, l'esplorazione, la rappresentazione." In *Architettura italiana d'oltremare,* edited by Giuliano Gresleri, Pier Giorgio Massaretti and Stefano Zagnoni, 51–67. Venice: Marsilio Editori, 1993.

Ceretti, G. P. "Per un efficiente organizzazione di Stato della industria turistica Italiana." *La Gazzetta* (Verbano) (8 Marzo 1930): 1–2.

Cipriani, Lidio. *Abitazioni indigene dell' Africa orientale italiana.* Naples: Edizioni della Mostra d'oltremare, 1940.

Ciucci, Giorgio. *Gli architetti e il fascismo. Architettura e città 1922–44.* Turin: Piccola Biblioteca Einaudi, 1989.

Consoli, Gian Paolo. "The Protagonists," *Rassegna* 51 (September 1992): 52–61.

Corò, Francesco. "Alla scoperta dei vecchi Fondugh tripolini." *Le Vie d'Italia* XLV, 2 (February 1939): 201–10.

Cresti, Federico. "Edilizia ed urbanistica nella colonizzazione agraria della Libia (1922–1940)." *Storia Urbana* XI, 40 (July-September 1987): 189–231.

Danesi, Silvia. "Aporie dell'architettura italiana in periodo fascista - mediterraneità e purismo." In *Il razionalismo e l'architettura in Italia durante il fascismo,* edited by Silvia Danesi and Luciano Patetta, 21–26. Milan: Electa Editrice, 1976.

De Rege, Maurizio. "Il nuovo piano regolatore di Tripoli." *Urbanistica* III, 3 (May–June 1934): 121–28.

Di Fausto, Florestano. "Visione mediterranea della mia architettura." *Libia* I, 9 (December 1937): 16.

Doordan, Dennis Paul. *Architecture and Politics in Fascist Italy: Il Movimento Italiano per l'Architettura Razionale, 1928–1932.* Ph.D. dissertation, Columbia University, 1983.

——. *Building Modern Italy: Italian Architecture 1914-1936.* New York: Princeton Architectural Press, 1988.

"Elenco degli architetti aderenti al Movimento Italiano per l'Architettura Razionale." *Casabella* 40 (April 1931): 68.

Etlin, Richard. *Modernism in Italian Architecture, 1890–1940.* Cambridge: The MIT

Press, 1991.

Fariello, Francesco. "Edifici a Tripoli: architetto Giovanni Pellegrini." *Architettura* XIV, 3 (March 1935): 150.

Figini, Luigi, and Carlo Enrico Rava. "Polemica mediterranea." *Domus* (January 1932): 66.

Fuller, Mia. "Building Power: Italian Architecture and Urbanism in Libya and Ethiopia." In *Forms of Dominance: On the Architecture and Urbanism of the Colonial Enterprise*, edited by Nezzar alSayyad, 211–39. Brookfield: Ashgate Publishing Company, 1992.

——. *Colonizing Constructions: Italian Architecture, Urban Planning, and the Creation of Modern Society in the Colonies, 1869–1943*. Ph.D. dissertation, University of California, Berkeley, 1994.

——. "Wherever You Go, There You Are: Fascist Plans for the Colonial City of Addis Ababa and the Colonizing Suburb of EUR'42." *Journal of Contemporary History* 31, 2 (April 1996): 397–418.

——. "Preservation and Self-Absorption: Italian Colonisation and the Walled City of Tripoli, Libya." *Journal of North African Studies* 5, 4 (Winter 2000): 121–54.

Giovannoni, Gustavo. "Vecchie città ed edilizia nuova." *Nuova Antologia* XLVIII, 995 (June 1, 1913): 449–72.

——. "Il diradamento edilizio dei vecchi centri - il Quartiere della Rinascenza in Roma." *Nuova Antologia* XLVIII, 997 (July 1, 1913): 53–76.

——. "Case del quattrocento in Roma." *Architettura e Arti Decorative* V, 6 (February 1926): 241–57.

Gresleri, Giuliano. "L'architettura dell'Italia d'oltremare: Realtà, finzione, immaginario." In *Architettura italiana d'oltremare 1870–1940*, edited by Giuliano Gresleri, Pier Giorgio Massaretti and Stefano Zagnoni, 22–47. Venice: Marsilio Editori, 1993.

——. "La 'nuova Roma dello Scioa' e l'improbabile architettura dell'Impero." *Architettura italiana d'oltremare 1870–1940*, edited by Giuliano Gresleri, Pier Giorgio Massaretti and Stefano Zagnoni, 164–77. Venice: Marsilio Editori, 1993.

——. "Classico e vernacolo nell'architettura dell'Italia d'oltremare." In *Classicismo Classicismi. Architettura Europa/America 1920–1940*, edited by Giorgio Ciucci, 68–87. Milan, Venice: Electa, C.I.S.A. Andrea Palladio, 1995.

Gruppo Sette. "Architettura." *Rassegna Italiana* XVIII, 103 (December 1926): 849–54.

——. "Architettura II: Gli Stranieri." *Rassegna Italiana* XIX, 105 (February 1927): 129–37.

——. "Architettura III: Impreparazione, Incomprensione, Pregiudizi." *Rassegna Italiana* XIX, 106 (March 1927): 247–52.

——. "Architettura IV: Una nuova epoca arcaica." *Rassegna Italiana* XIX, 108 (May 1927): 467–72.

"Il concorso per la sistemazione di piazza della Cattedrale in Tripoli." *Architettura e Arti Decorative* X, 9 (May 1931): 447.

Islamic Art and Architecture in Libya. London: The Architectural Association, 1976.

"I voti conclusivi del Congresso." *Urbanistica* VI, 3 (May–June 1937): 146–48.

Luiggi, Luigi. "Le opere pubbliche a Tripoli." *Nuova Antologia* 47, 965 (March 1, 1912): 115–30.

Ma, Pa. "Due lavori dell'arch. Rava a Mogadiscio." *Architettura* XIV, 1 (January 1934): 26–30.

Marconi, Plinio. "L'architettura nella colonizzazione della Libia. Opere dell'Arch. Giovanni Pellegrini." *Architettura* XVIII, 12 (December 1939): 715.

Mariani, Antonio. "L'Architettura rustica alla Cinquantenale romana." *Architettura e Arti Decorative* I, 4 (March–April 1922): 379–85.

Messana, Gaspare. *Architettura Musulmana della Libia*. Castelfranco Veneto: Edizione del Grifone, 1972.

Miano, Giuseppe. "Florestano Di Fausto." In *Dizionario biografico degli italiani. Volume 40*, 1–5. Rome: Istituto della Enciclopedia italiana, 1991.

Micacchi, Rodolfo. "L'Arco di Marco Aurelio in Tripoli e la sistemazione della zona adiacente." *Rivista delle Colonie Italiane* VIII, 10 (October 1934): 824–39.

N.D.R. "Un progetto per il Concorso della Piazza della Cattedrale di Tripoli." *Architettura e Arti Decorative* IX, 12 (August 1930): 571–76.

——. "Architetture libiche degli architetti Carlo Enrico Rava e Sebastiano Larco." *Architettura e Arti Decorative* X, 13 (September 1931): 682–87.

Pellegrini, Giovanni. "Manifesto dell'architettura coloniale." *Rassegna di Architettura* VIII, 10 (October 1936): 349–50.

"Per la moderna architettura coloniale italiana." *Domus* VII, 6 (June 1934): 11–12.

Persico, Edoardo. "Punto e da capo per l'architettura." *Domus* 83 (November 1934): 1–9.

Piacentini, Marcello. "Il momento architettonico all'estero." *Architettura e Arti Decorative* I, 1 (September–October 1921): 32–76.

——. "Influssi d'arte Italiana nel Nord-America." *Architettura e Arti Decorative* I, 6 (July–August 1922): 536–555.

——. "Due lavori di C.E. Rava e S. Larco." *Architettura e Arti Decorative* VII, 11 (July 1928): 528.

——. "Prima internazionale architettonica." *Architettura e Arti Decorative* VI, 12 (August 1928): 544–62.

Piccinato, Luigi. "Edilizia coloniale." In *Enciclopedia italiana di scienze, lettere ed arti. Volume 10*, 826–27. Milan: Istituto Giovanni Treccani, 1931.

——. "La casa in colonia. Il problema che si prospetta ai nostri architetti." *Domus* 101 and 102 (May and June 1936): 22–25, 12–17.

——. "Un problema per l'Italia d'oggi, costruire in colonia." *Domus* 105 (September 1936): 7–10.

Pisani, Mario. *Architetture di Armando Brasini*. Rome: Officina Edizioni, 1996.

"Proclama del Raggrumpamento Architetti Moderni Italiani." *La Tribuna* (May 5, 1931).

"A proposito della mostra di architettura razionalista." *Architettura e Arti Decorative* X, 9 (May 1931): n.p.

Rava, Carlo Enrico. "Di un'architettura coloniale moderna - Parte prima." *Domus* 41 (May 1931): 39–43, 89.

——. "Di un'architettura coloniale moderna – Parte seconda." *Domus* 42 (June 1931): 32–36.

——. "I. Svolta pericolosa: situazione dell'Italia di fronte al razionalismo europeo." *Domus* 37 (January 1931): 39–44.

——. "II. Spirito latino." *Domus* 38 (February 1931): 24–9.

——. "III. Necessità di selezione, parte prima e seconda." *Domus* 39 and 40 (March and April 1931): 36–40, 84; 39–43, 88.

——. "V. Giovani architetti nordamericani." *Domus* 43 (July 1931): 33–6, 88.

——. "VI. Conclusione." *Domus* 47 (November 1931): 34–40.

——. "Politica edilizia coloniale." In *Problemi di architettura coloniale. In occasione del Congresso Nazionale degli Architetti Italiani – Napoli, ottobre 1936-XIV*, 24–30. Naples: Assoc. Cultori di Architettura del S.I.F.A della Lombardia, 1936.

——. "Problemi di architettura coloniale." *Rassegna Italiana* XIX, 216 (May 1936): 398–402.

——. "Architettura coloniale. Una lettera di C.E. Rava." *Rassegna Italiana* XIX, 219–20 (August–September 1936): 680–82.

——. "Costruire in Colonia I, II and III." *Domus* 104, 106, 109 (August, October 1936, January 1937): 8–9, 28–30, 23–27.

——. "Alcuni punti di urbanistica coloniale." In *Atti del primo congresso nazionale di urbanistica, Volume 1. Urbanistica coloniale*, 90-93. Rome: Istituto Nazionale di Urbanistica, 1937.

——. "Architettura coloniale." *Gli Annali dell'Africa Italiana* I, 3–4 (December 1938): 1293–1300.

——. "Architettura di razza italiana." *L'Architettura Italiana* (January 1939): 41–42.

——. "Attrezzatura coloniale." *Domus* 138 (June 1939): n.p.

——. "Abitare e vivere in colonia." *Domus* 145 (January 1940): 21–23.

Rava, Maurizio. "Dobbiamo rispettare il carattere dell'edilizia tripolina." *L'Oltremare* 3, 11 (November 1929): 45?–464.

Rigotti, Giorgio. *L'edilizia nell'Africa orientale italiana. La zona di Addis Abeba.* Turin: Editrice libreria italiana, 1939.

Romanelli, Pietro. "Restauri alle mura barbaresche di Tripoli." *Bolletino d'Arte* II, 12 (June 1923): 570–76.

——. "Vecchie case arabe di Tripoli." *Architettura e Arti Decorative* III, 5 (January 1924): 193–211.

Sartoris, Alberto. *Gli elementi dell'architettura funzionale. Sintesi panoramica dell'architettura moderna. Terza edizione.* Milan: Ulrico Hoepli Editore, 1941.

Talamona, Marida. "Libya: an Architectural Workshop." *Rassegna* 51 (September 1992): 62–69.

——. "Primi passi verso l'Europa (1927–1933)." *Luigi Figini Gino Pollini. Opera completa,* 61–73. Milan: Electa, 1996.

Turba, Luigi. "La Moschea dei Caramanli a Tripoli." *Le Vie d'Italia* XL, 8 (August 1934): 583–91.

Von Henneberg, Krystyna. "Piazza Castello and the Making of a Fascist Colonial Capital." In *Streets: Critical Perspectives on Public Space,* ed. Zeynep Çelik, Diane Favro, and Richard Ingersoll, 135–50. Berkeley: University of California Press, 1994.

——. *The Construction of Fascist Libya: Modern Colonial Architecture and Urban Planning in Italian North Africa (1922–1943).* Ph.D. dissertation, University of California, Berkeley, 1996.

——. "Imperial Uncertainties: Architectural Syncretism and Improvisation in Fascist Colonial Libya." *Journal of Contemporary History* 31, 2 (April 1996): 373–95.

Warfelli, Muhammed. "The Old City of Tripoli." In *Art and Archeology Research Papers.* Tripoli: Department of Antiquities, 1976.

FIGURE CREDITS

Color Plates

1. L.V. Bertarelli, *Guida d'Italia del Touring Club Italiano. Possedimenti e colonie* (Milan: Touring Club Italiano, 1929)
2. The Mitchell Wolfson Jr. Collection – Fondazione Regionale Cristoforo Colombo, Genoa
3. Giovanni De Agostini, *La Libia turistica* (Milan: Prof. G. De Agostini, 1938)
4. The Mitchell Wolfson Jr. Collection – Fondazione Regionale Cristoforo Colombo, Genoa
5. *Uaddan Hotel Casino Teatro* (Tripoli: P. Maggi, 1937)
6. *Itinerario Tripoli-Gadames* (Milan: Tipo-Litografia Turati Lombardi, 1938)
7. *Libia* 2, 3 (March 1938)
8. Ministry of Foreign Affairs Archive, Rome – Political Affairs, Libya
9. Mario dei Gaslini, *Piccolo amore Beduino* (Milano: L'Eroica, 1926)
10. *Esotica* 1, 1 (October 1926)
11. National Association of Tourist Industries and Italian State Railway, *Tripoli* (Rome: Novissima, 1929)
12. *Difesa della Razza* 1, 2 (20 August 1938)
13. Author's collection
14. *Combinazioni di soggiorno in Libia* (Tripoli: ETAL, 1937)
15. Author's collection
16. *Itinerario Tripoli-Gadames* (Milan: Tipo-Litografia Turati Lombardi, 1938)

Black and White

I.1. Central State Archive, Rome – Photographic archive of Rodolfo Graziani
I.2. Ministry of Foreign Affairs Archive, Rome – Documents of the Ministry of Italian Africa
I.3. Author's collection
I.4. Author's collection

1.1. *La rinascità della Tripolitania. Memorie e studi sui quattro anni di governo del Conte Giuseppe Volpi di Misurata* (Milan: Casa Editrice A. Mondadori, 1926)
1.2. *Nuova Antologia* 242 (March 1, 1912): 120-21
1.3. *La rinascità della Tripolitania. Memorie e studi sui quattro anni di governo del Conte Giuseppe Volpi di Misurata* (Milan: Casa Editrice A. Mondadori, 1926)
1.4. *La rinascità della Tripolitania. Memorie e studi sui quattro anni di governo del Conte Giuseppe Volpi di Misurata* (Milan: Casa Editrice A. Mondadori, 1926)
1.5. *Capitolium* 10 (January 1927): 570
1.6. Ministry of Foreign Affairs Archive, Rome – Documents of the Ministry of Italian Africa
1.7. Alpago Novello and Cabiati, *Relazione sul Piano Regolatore e d'ampliamento della Città di Tripoli* (Milan: Tipografia G. Colombi & Co, 1933), in Roberto Papini Archive, Architecture and Engineering Library, University of Florence
1.8. Léandre Vaillat, *Le Visage Français du Maroc* (Paris: Horizons de France, 1931)
1.9. *Architettura e Arti Decorative* 8, 11 (July 1929): 517

1.10. Ministry of Foreign Affairs Archive, Rome – Documents of the Ministry of Italian Africa

1.11. *La Strada litoranea della Libia* (Verona: Officine Grafiche A. Mondadori, 1937)

1.12. Author's collection

1.13. The Mitchell Wolfson Jr. Collection – Fondazione Regionale Cristoforo Colombo, Genoa

1.14. The Mitchell Wolfson Jr. Collection – Fondazione Regionale Cristoforo Colombo, Genoa

2.1. *La rinascità della Tripolitania. Memorie e studi sui quattro anni di governo del Conte Giuseppe Volpi di Misurata* (Milan: Casa Editrice A. Mondadori, 1926)

2.2. *Italiani, Visitate la Tripolitania!* (Tripoli: Scuola d'Arti e Mestieri, 1926)

2.3. Author's collection

2.4. *La rinascità della Tripolitania. Memorie e studi sui quattro anni di governo del Conte Giuseppe Volpi di Misurata* (Milano: Casa Editrice A. Mondadori, 1926)

2.5. L. V. Bertarelli, *Guida d'Italia del Touring Club Italiano. Possedimenti e colonie* (Milan: Touring Club Italiano, 1929)

2.6. Angelo Piccioli, ed., *La nuova Italia d'oltremare. L'opera del Fascismo nelle colonie italiane* (Milan: A. Mondadori Editore, 1932)

2.7. *The North African Motor Tours of the Compagnie Générale Transatlantique* (London: Hill, Siffken & Co., 1928)

2.8. *Tripoli: Piccola guida pratica e pianta della città* (Tripoli, Unione Coloniale Italiana Pubblicità & Informazioni, 1938)

2.9. The Mitchell Wolfson Jr. Collection – Fondazione Regionale Cristoforo Colombo, Genoa

2.10. The Mitchell Wolfson Jr. Collection – Fondazione Regionale Cristoforo Colombo, Genoa

2.11. *Gli Annali dell'Africa Italiana* 5, 4 (December 1942)

2.12. Ministry of Foreign Affairs Archive, Rome – Documents of the Ministry of Italian Africa

2.13. *Gli Annali dell'Africa Italiana* 5, 4 (December 1942)

2.14. Ministry of Foreign Affairs Archive, Rome – Documents of the Ministry of Italian Africa

2.15. Ente autonomo Fiera campionaria di Tripoli, *XI Manifestazione internazionale intercoloniale. Prima mostra dell'Impero Fascista* (Rome: Arti Grafiche Fratelli Palombi, 1937)

2.16. State Publications Archive, Rome

2.17. Giovanni De Agostini, *La Libia turistica* (Milan: Prof. G. De Agostini, 1938)

2.18. The Mitchell Wolfson Jr. Collection—Fondazione Regionale Cristoforo Colombo, Genoa

2.19. Author's collection

2.20. *Gli Annali dell'Africa Italiana* 5, 4 (December 1942)

2.21. *Uaddan Hotel Casino Teatro* (Tripoli: P. Maggi, 1937), Author's collection

2.22. The Mitchell Wolfson Jr. Collection—Fondazione Regionale Cristoforo Colombo, Genoa

2.23. *Gli Annali dell'Africa Italiana* 5, 4 (December 1942)

2.24. *Itinerario Tripoli-Gadames* (Milan: Tipo-Litografia Turati Lombardi, 1938)

2.25. *Libia* 2, 3 (March 1938)

2.26. Ministry of Foreign Affairs Archive, Rome – Documents of the Ministry of Italian Africa

3.1. Author's collection

3.2. *La rinascità della Tripolitania. Memorie e studi sui quattro anni di governo del Conte Giuseppe Volpi di Misurata* (Milan: Casa Editrice A. Mondadori, 1926)

3.3. *La rinascità della Tripolitania. Memorie e studi sui quattro anni di governo del Conte Giuseppe Volpi di Misurata* (Milan: Casa Editrice A. Mondadori, 1926)

3.4. Author's collection

3.5. *Dedalo* 7, 8 (January 1927): 501

3.6. Author's collection

3.7. Ministry of Foreign Affairs Archive, Rome – Documents of the Ministry of Italian Africa

3.8. Ministry of Foreign Affairs Archive, Rome – Documents of the Ministry of Italian Africa

3.9. Central State Archive – Photographic archive of Rodolfo Graziani

3.10. Ministry of Foreign Affairs Archive, Rome – Political Affairs, Libya

3.11. *L'Italie pour les populations islamiques de l'afrique italienne* (Rome: Società Editrice

"Novissima," 1940)

3.12. Ministry of Foreign Affairs Archive, Rome – Documents of the Ministry of Italian Africa

3.13. *L'Italie pour les populations islamiques de l'afrique italienne* (Rome: Società Editrice "Novissima," 1940)

3.14. The Mitchell Wolfson Jr. Collection – Fondazione Regionale Cristoforo Colombo, Genoa

3.15. *L'Italie pour les populations islamiques de l'afrique italienne* (Rome: Società Editrice "Novissima," 1940)

4.1. Raffaele Calzini, *Da Leptis Magna a Gadames* (Milan: Fratelli Treves Editori, 1926)

4.2. Libyan Tourism Commission, *Libia itinerari* (Milan: S.A. Arti Grafiche Bertarelli, 1935)

4.3. Libyan Tourism Commission, *Libia itinerari* (Milan: S.A. Arti Grafiche Bertarelli, 1935)

4.4. Mario dei Gaslini, *Piccolo amore Beduino* (Milan: L'Eroica, 1926)

4.5. Mario dei Gaslini, *Piccolo amore Beduino* (Milan: L'Eroica, 1926)

4.6. *Esotica* 1, 1 (October 1926)

4.7. National Association of Tourist Industries and Italian State Railway, *Tripoli* (Rome: Novissima, 1929)

4.8. Author's collection

4.9. *Le Vie d'Italia* 39, 9 (September 1933): 679

4.10. *Difesa della Razza* 1, 2 (20 August 1938)

4.11. Author's collection

4.12. *La rinascità della Tripolitania. Memorie e studi sui quattro anni di governo del Conte Giuseppe Volpi di Misurata* (Milan: Casa Editrice A. Mondadori, 1926)

4.13. *La rinascità della Tripolitania. Memorie e studi sui quattro anni di governo del Conte Giuseppe Volpi di Misurata* (Milan: Casa Editrice A. Mondadori, 1926)

4.14. Author's collection

4.15. Ministry of Foreign Affairs Archive, Rome – Documents of the Ministry of Italian Africa

4.16. Author's collection

4.17. The Mitchell Wolfson Jr. Collection – Fondazione Regionale Cristoforo Colombo, Genoa

4.18. Touring Club Italiano – Alinari Archives Management

4.19. The Mitchell Wolfson Jr. Collection – Fondazione Regionale Cristoforo Colombo, Genoa

4.20. *Combinazioni di soggiorno in Libia* (Tripoli: ETAL, 1937)

4.21. *Combinazioni di soggiorno in Libia* (Tripoli: ETAL, 1937)

4.22. *Itinerario Tripoli-Gadames* (Milan: Tipo-Litografia Turati Lombardi, 1938)

4.23. *Itinerario Tripoli-Gadames* (Milan: Tipo-Litografia Turati Lombardi, 1938)

4.24. Author's collection

4.25. Ministry of Foreign Affairs Archive, Rome – Documents of the Ministry of Italian Africa

4.26. The Mitchell Wolfson Jr. Collection – Fondazione Regionale Cristoforo Colombo, Genoa

4.27. Author's collection

4.28. *Gli Annali dell'Africa Italiana* 5, 4 (December 1942)

5.1. *Architettura e Arti Decorative* 7, 11 (July 1928): 526

5.2. Rava family collection, Milan

5.3. *La rinascità della Tripolitania. Memorie e studi sui quattro anni di governo del Conte Giuseppe Volpi di Misurata* (Milan: Casa Editrice A. Mondadori, 1926)

5.4. *Dedalo* 9, 12 (May 1929): 743

5.5. *Nuova Antologia* 48, 997 (1 July 1913): 73

5.6. *Architettura e Arti Decorative* 1, 4 (March-April 1922): 383

5.7. *Architettura e Arti Decorative* 3, 5 (January 1924): 194

5.8. *La rinascità della Tripolitania. Memorie e studi sui quattro anni di governo del Conte Giuseppe Volpi di Misurata* (Milan: Casa Editrice A. Mondadori, 1926)

5.9. *La rinascità della Tripolitania. Memorie e studi sui quattro anni di governo del Conte Giuseppe Volpi di Misurata* (Milan: Casa Editrice A. Mondadori, 1926)

5.10. Author's collection

5.11. Author's collection

5.12. The Mitchell Wolfson Jr. Collection – Fondazione Regionale Cristoforo Colombo, Genoa

5.13. The Mitchell Wolfson Jr. Collection – Fondazione Regionale Cristoforo Colombo, Genoa

5.14. Author's collection

5.15. *Architettura e Arti Decorative* 7, 12 (August 1928), 570

5.16. Ministry of Foreign Affairs Archive, Rome – Documents of the Ministry of Italian Africa

5.17. *Rassegna di Architettura* 5, 9 (September 1933), 391

5.18. *Architettura e Arti Decorative* 10, 9 (May 1931): 436

5.19. *Architettura e Arti Decorative* 10, 9 (May 1931): 441

5.20. The Mitchell Wolfson Jr. Collection – Fondazione Regionale Cristoforo Colombo, Genoa

5.21. *Rassegna di Architettura* 5, 9 (September 1933): 396

5.22. *Gli Annali dell'Africa Italiana* 5, 4 (December 1942)

5.23. Rava family collection, Milan

5.24. Rava family collection, Milan

5.25. Rava family collection, Milan

5.26. *Architettura e Arti Decorative* 9, 12 (August 1930): 574

5.27. Roberto Papini Archive, Architecture and Engineering Library, University of Florence

5.28. *Architettura e Arti Decorative* 10, 13 (September 1931): 684

5.29. *Architettura e Arti Decorative* 6, 12 (August 1928), 561

5.30. Ministry of Foreign Affairs Archive, Rome – Documents of the Ministry of Italian Africa

5.31. Ministry of Foreign Affairs Archive, Rome – Documents of the Ministry of Italian Africa

6.1. *Rassegna di Architettura* 8, 10 (October 1936): 355

6.2. *Rassegna di Architettura* 9, 12 (December 1937): 455

6.3. Angelo Piccioli, ed., *La nuova Italia d'oltremare. L'opera del Fascismo nelle colonie italiane* (Milan: A. Mondadori Editore, 1932)

6.4. Léandre Vaillat, *Le Visage Français du Maroc* (Paris: Horizons de France, 1931)

6.5. *Emporium* 88, 528 (December 1938): 310

6.6. Henri Descamps, *L'Architecture moderne au Maroc, II – Constructions particulières* (Paris: Librairie de la Construction Moderne, 1931), Plate 15B

6.7. Descamps, *L'Architecture moderne au Maroc, II – Constructions particulières* (Paris: Librairie de la Construction Moderne, 1931), Plate 14B

6.8. Author's collection

6.9. Author's collection

6.10. *Gli Annali dell'Africa Italiana* 5, 4 (December 1942)

6.11. *Gli Annali dell'Africa Italiana* 5, 4 (December 1942)

6.12. The Mitchell Wolfson Jr. Collection – Fondazione Regionale Cristoforo Colombo, Genoa

6.13. Author's collection

6.14. The Mitchell Wolfson Jr. Collection – Fondazione Regionale Cristoforo Colombo, Genoa

6.15. Author's collection

6.16. The Mitchell Wolfson Jr. Collection – Fondazione Regionale Cristoforo Colombo, Genoa

6.17. The Mitchell Wolfson Jr. Collection – Fondazione Regionale Cristoforo Colombo, Genoa

6.18. *Libia* 1, 1 (March 1937): 35

6.19. Roberto Papini Archive, Architecture and Engineering Library, University of Florence

6.20. The Mitchell Wolfson Jr. Collection – Fondazione Regionale Cristoforo Colombo, Genoa

6.21. Emilio Scarin, *L'Insediamento umano nella Libia occidentale* (Verona: Officina Grafiche A. Mondadori, 1940)

6.22. *Itinerario Tripoli-Gadames* (Milan: Tipo-Litografia Turati Lombardi, 1938)

6.23. *Itinerario Tripoli-Gadames* (Milan: Tipo-Litografia Turati Lombardi, 1938)

6.24. *Itinerario Tripoli-Gadames* (Milan: Tipo-Litografia Turati Lombardi, 1938)

6.25. The Mitchell Wolfson Jr. Collection – Fondazione Regionale Cristoforo Colombo, Genoa

6.26. *Itinerario Tripoli-Gadames* (Milan: Tipo-Litografia Turati Lombardi, 1938)

6.27. The Mitchell Wolfson Jr. Collection – Fondazione Regionale Cristoforo Colombo, Genoa

6.28. Author's collection

6.29. Author's collection

6.30. The Mitchell Wolfson Jr. Collection – Fondazione Regionale Cristoforo Colombo, Genoa

6.31. The Mitchell Wolfson Jr. Collection – Fondazione Regionale Cristoforo Colombo, Genoa

6.32. Author's collection

6.33. *Itinerario Tripoli-Gadames* (Milan: Tipo-Litografia Turati Lombardi, 1938)

6.34. *Gli Annali dell'Africa Italiana* 5, 4 (December 1942)

6.35. The Mitchell Wolfson Jr. Collection—Fondazione Regionale Cristoforo Colombo, Genoa

C.1. Author's collection

C.2. Author's collection

C.3. Author's collection

C.4. Author's collection

INDEX

Page numbers in bold refer to illustrations.

agricultural development, 19, 23, 26, 31, 39, 48–49. See also *ventimila*

Alba (al-Fager), Libya, 101. *See also* Balbo, Italo: and indigenous politics

Alessandro Volta Foundation Conference, 17, 79, 94–97

Alpago Novello, Alberto, Ottavio Cabiati, and Guido Ferrazza:
—plan of Benghazi, 29
—plan of Tripoli, **29**, 29–31, 35, 89–90, 98, 166, 233n49

ambivalent modernism, 8–11

Apollonia, Libya, 89

Apollonj, Fabrizio Maria, 186, **187**

Arab Café, Suq al-Mushir, 140–41, **141–42**; as German consulate, 227

archeological convention, Tripoli, 50

archeological excavations: Apollonia, 89; Cyrene, 89, 167, 193; Leptis Magna, 83–84, **84**, 89, 106, 178; Sabratha, 84, 89

archeological museums, 89, 124, **124**

architecture and tourism. S*ee* tourist architecture

Architettura e arti decorative (journal), 155–56; and Gustavo Giovannoni, 153; and Marcello Piacentini, 153–54

Arch of Marcus Aurelius, Tripoli, 98, **99**, 149

Arena of Sharah al-Shatt, Tripoli, 64, **72**; activities at, 72–73

Associazione artistica fra i cultori di architettura, 153

Aurigemma, Salvatore, 88–89, 149

Automobile Club of Benghazi, 5

automobile *raid*, 3–5, 74, 134; Tripoli-Benghazi-Tripoli, **3**, 5; Tripoli-Ghadames-Tripoli, 3–5, **4**, 106, 227

Avanguardisti (fascist youth groups), 53

Babini, Major Valentino, 4–5, **105**, 106

Badoglio, Marshall Pietro: and agricultural colonization, 31; and automobile *raid*, 5; education system of, 92–93; military campaigns of, 29, 233n45; modernization program of, 31–32; preservation initiatives of, 91–92; and public works projects, 31–32; and tourist system, 32, 50–54, 233n56. *See also* Libya; modernization; preservation; tourism, Libya

Balbo, Italo: administrative changes of, 32–33; and agricultural colonization, 39, 48–49; and building commission, 35, 188; colonial politics of, 6–7; and corporativism, 60; death of, 226; and indigenous politics, 17–18, 79–80, 94–103, **95**, 127–30, 136, 139, 141, 143, 184, 242n51; modernization program of, 12–13, 18, 32–35; and *strada litoranea*, 35–36, 38, 234n78; tourist system of, 54–58, **56**, 238n58; and transatlantic flight, 17–18; and *ventimila*, 38–39. *See also* indigenous politics; Libya; modernization; preservation; *strada litoranea*; tourism, Libya; *ventimila*

Banco di Roma, 18

Bartoccini, Renato, 85, 107, 155

BBPR architects, 226

Beguinot, Francesco, 118, 119

Benghazi, Libya, 5, 29, 33–34; tourist infrastructure of, 57, 64, 158, 192–93

Berbers, 118, 121, 152, 216, 258

Berman, Marshall, 8, 225

Bhabha, Homi, 8–9

Boito, Camillo, 226

Brasini, Armando, 24, **25**, 85
—Monument to the Fallen and to Victory, Tripoli, 158

Brunelli, Claudio, 43–44

Bruni, Giuseppe, 60

Cabiati, Ottavio, 185. *See also* Alpago

Novello, Alberto, Ottavio Cabiati, and Guido Ferrazza

Calzini, Raffaele, **105**, 106

Carcassone, France, 226

Casablanca, Morocco: master plan of, **30,** 30–31, 90; and urban colonialism under Lyautey, 189, **189**

Castle, Tripoli, 85, **85**. *See also* Brasini, Armando; Bartoccini, Renato

Center of Colonial Studies, 118

Central Council for Architecture and Urbanism, 184

Cesare Alfieri Institute of Social and Political Science, 118

Chamber of Commerce, Tripoli, 50, 126

Cipriani, Lidio, 121–22, 186

Cipriani, Lidio, and Antonio Mordini: and scientific mission to Fezzan, **120,** 120–21

colonial architecture, 189; early works of, 156–58; and influence of Italo Balbo, 184–85; Mediterranean, 170–75; modernist discourse on, 162–66. *See also* Di Fausto, Florestano; Limongelli, Alessandro; Pellegrini, Giovanni; Rava, Carlo Enrico

colonial discourse, 8–9

colonial literature, 110–14; influence on architecture of, 195–98; influence on tourism of, 117; origins of, 110; realism of, 109

colonial politics. *See* Italy: and colonial politics

colonial studies conferences, 118–19

Combinazioni di soggiorno in Libia (brochure), 134–35, **135**

Compagnie Générale Transatlantique, 54, **55**; and Hôtel de la Mamounia, Marrakech, 190–91, **191**

Congress of the International Federation of Travel Agencies, Tripoli, 54

Corso, Raffaele, 118, 121

Crispi, Francesco, 80

Cyrene, Libya, 89, 167, 193

D'Annunzio, Gabriele, 18, 110–12

Dante Alighieri Society, 53

De Bono, Emilio: and agricultural colonization, 26; education system of, 92–93; as Minister of the Colonies, 32, 53, 127; modernization program of, 26–28; preservation initiatives of, 88–89, 91, 92–93; and public works projects, 27–28,

233n52; and tourist system, 50–52. *See also* Libya; Ministry of the Colonies; modernization

Dei Agostini, Colonel Enrico, 119, 136, 245n35

demographic colonization, 18, 20, 21, 32

Derrida, Jacques, 8

Desio, Ardito, 118

Di Fausto, Florestano, 14; and agricultural villages, 39; as "folkloristic provincialism" of Gramsci, 223–24; education and early career of, 91, 242n40; influence on historiography of modern movement, 225–26; and "Visione mediterranea della mia architettura," 183–85, 187–88. *See also* Libyan Tourism and Hotel Association (ETAL)

—Arab Café, Suq al-Mushir, 140–41, **141–42**

—*Arae Philenorum*, 36–37, 235n83

—Arch of Marcus Aurelius, Tripoli, 98, **99.** *See also* Arch of Marcus Aurelius, Tripoli

—Artisanal Quarter, Suq al-Mushir, Tripoli, **90**, 91, 138–39, **140**

—Governor's Palace, Rhodes, **90**, 91

—National Insurance Institute, Tripoli, 189, **190**

—Piazza della Cattedrale, **188**, 188–89

Di Fausto, Florestano, and Stefano Gatti-Casazza:

—Hotel 'Ain el-Fras, Ghadames, 57, 212–17, **214–17**, 222–24, **224**. *See also* Libyan Tourism and Hotel Association (ETAL): Hotel Service

—Hotel Mehari, Tripoli, 57, 199–204, **201–2**

—Hotel Nalut, 57, 210–12, **213**

—Hotel Rumia, Yifran, 57, 208–10, **209, 211,** 212

—Uaddan Hotel and Casino, Tripoli, 57, 73, 194–98, **195–96, 198, 200**

Difesa della Razza (journal), 82, 121, **122**

Di Marzo, Costanzo, 119

Di Segni, Umberto, **38**, 39, 166; and Hotel of the Gazelle, Zlitan, 193–94

East African colonies, 184

Edensor, Tim, 10–11, 14

Eisenman, Peter, 230n24

Enciclopedia italiana: presentation of indigenous culture in Libya, 118

Eritrea, 32, 80
Esotica (journal), 114, **114**, 116–17
Ethiopia, 20, 47, 184

Fabian, Johannes, 8
Fahrenkamp, Emil, 148
Fanon, Frantz, 8
Fascism, preservation policy of, 89
Fascist Arab Youth Club (GAL), 101
Fascist Colonial Institute (ICF), 53, 57
Fascist Institute of Libyan Artisans, 100
Fascist institutions, 20
Fascist modernism, 9–10
Fascist Youth Club, 101
Federzoni, Luigi, 23
Fezzan, the, 22, 31, 47, 118, 120–21. *See also* scientific missions
Fileni brothers, 36, 38
folklore: and Fascist regime, 11–12; and Antonio Gramsci, 11, 231n31
France: colonial tourism of, 45; and colonial urbanism, **30**, 30–31, 189, 254n21; and North African colonies, 45. *See also* Lyautey, Maréchal Hubert
funduqs, Tripoli, 256n49; and Arch of Marcus Aurelius, 98, 203, 243n67; and Hotel Mehari, 203

Gallotti, Jean, and Albert Laprade (*Le Jardin et la Maison Arabes au Maroc*), 191
Gaslini, Mario Dei: influence of, 114; and *Esotica*, 114, **114**, 116–17; later publications of, 122–23; and *Piccolo amore Beduino*, **111**, 112–14
Gatti-Casazza, Stefano. *See* Di Fausto, Florestano, and Stefano Gatti-Casazza
Ghadames, Libya, 3–4, 34–35, 52, 171, 204; indigenous houses of, 214, 258n81; and Piazza of the Large Mulberry, 213, **215**; and preservation, 129
Ghirardo, Diane, 10
Giolitti, Giovanni, 18
Giovannoni, Gustavo: *ambientismo* of, 185; and *Architettura e arti decorative*, 153
—reorganization of Renaissance quarter in Rome (1913), 153, **154**
Government Office of Indigenous Applied Arts: and exhibitions, 86, **87**, 91, **92**; mission of, 85–86; and preservation, 85–86; name changed to School of Arts

and Crafts, 91; and tourism, 125. *See also* indigenous artisanal industries; Muslim School of Indigenous Arts and Crafts; School of Arts and Crafts
Gramsci, Antonio, 9; and folklore, 11, 231n31; and "folkloristic provincialism," 12, 224; and "national-popular," 11–12, 223; and *Prison Notebooks*, 11–12
Grand Hotel, Tripoli, 24, 50, **51**, 56, 160–61, **161**
Grand Hotel at the Excavations, Cyrene, 52, 57, 166–70, **168–69**. *See also* Limongelli, Alessandro
Grand Prix automobile race, Tripoli, 58
Graziani, General Rodolfo: and automobile *raid*, 3–5, and military campaigns, 229n3; and reconquest of Tripolitania, 22–23
Graziosi, Paolo, 121
Great Britain: colonial tourism of, 45
Gropius, Walter, 148
Gruppo Sette, 145–46, 165, 248n3
Guida di Tripoli e dintorni (brochure), 44, 124–25

Hasuna Qaramanli Orphanage and Shelter, 101
Herf, Jeffrey, 9
Hotel 'Ain el-Fras, Ghadames, 57, 129, 212–17, **214–17, 224**
Hotel at the Excavations of Leptis Magna, 52, 57, 175–79, **176–80**. *See also* Rava, Carlo Enrico, and Sebastiano Larco
Hotel Gebel, Gharyan, 161, **162**
Hotel Italia, Benghazi, 158–60, **159**
Hotel Mehari, Tripoli, 57, 199–204, **201–2**; restaurant, 73, **74**
Hotel Nalut, 57, 210–12, **213**
Hotel Nefusa, Nalut, 52, 161, **162**
Hotel of the Gazelle, Zlitan, 57, **193**, 193–94; dining room, 75–76, **77**
Hotel Rumia, Yifran, 57, 208–10, **209, 211**, 212
hotels, construction, 32, 50, 52, 56–57, 233n56, 238n58. *See also* Libyan Tourism and Hotel Association (ETAL): Hotel Service
Hotel Tobruk, 194, **195**

indigenous agriculture, 100–101, **101**
indigenous architecture: pre-Saharan

region, 257n71

indigenous artisanal industries, 85–87, 91–92. *See also* Government Office of Indigenous Applied Arts; School of Arts and Crafts

indigenous ceremonies, 126–27, **128,** 140–41

indigenous culture, 109; French influence on, 150–52; and scholarly discourse, 149–56

indigenous politics, 7, 13; and Muslim world, 81; and Italo Balbo, 94–97; in Britain and France, 80–81; and modernization program, 80; and racist discourse, 97. See also Balbo, Italo; preservation; Volpi, Giuseppe

Istituto Nazionale Luce, 62

Italian citizenship, 101–2, 244n82

Italian Colonial Institute (ICI): and excursions, 50; and Pavilion of Colonies, Milan Trade Fair, 147. *See also* Rava, Carlo Enrico, and Sebastiano Larco

Italian colonies, 20, 32, 47, 80, 184

Italian Fascist Party, 19

Italian Geographic Society, Florence, 18; and scientific missions, 118, 120

Italian Rationalism, 10, 148

Italian Touring Club (TCI), 50, 53, 54, 120; guidebook to Italian colonies, 46–47, 106, 107, 117, 236n17; guidebook to Libya, 48–49, 121

Italian Tourism Company (CIT), 62

Italy: and colonial politics, 18–19, 80–81, 184, 231n6; and Muslim world, 80; and military campaigns in Libya, 22; modernization program of, 20; racial discourse of, 82–83; and scramble for Africa, 18, 80, 240n5. *See also* Balbo, Italo; Badoglio, Marshall Pietro; De Bono, Emilio; Libya; Mussolini, Benito; Volpi, Giuseppe

Itinerario Tripoli-Gadames (guidebook), 136–37, **207;** and Berber culture, 138, **138;** and experience of travel, 74–75, **75,** 207–8; and Fascist colonization, 137, **137,** 208

Kothari, Uma, 11

Lacan, Jacques, 8

Larco, Sebastiano. *See* Rava, Carlo Enrico, and Sebastiano Larco

Lares (journal), 11

Le Corbusier, 148

Leptis Magna, Libya, 83–84, **84,** 89, 106, 178; and coastal itinerary, 193; museum at, 89, 124; and tourist access, 50, 51, 57

Lessona, Alessandro, 5, 39

Libera, Adalberto, 165, **167**

Libia, La (brochure), 66–67, **67**

Libia Itinerari (brochure), 108, 127

Libia (journal), 68–71, 136

Libia turistica, La (guidebook), 68, 136

Libya: building commission of, 35, 188, 254n19; and corporativism, 33, 60; education system of, 86, 92–93, 98–100; and incorporation into Italy, 7, 18, 33, 96–97; as Italy's "fourth shore," 13, 18, 20, 35; military operations of, 3–5, 22–23, 25, 29; modernization programs of, 12–13, 18, 23–28, 31–35; and Ottoman administration, 81; public works of, 23, 27–28, 31–35; resistance of, 22, 81; and Roman archeological sites, 89; as Roman colony, 18; and unification as a colony, 7, 32–33. *See also* Badoglio, Marshall Pietro; Balbo, Italo; De Bono, Emilio; Volpi, Giuseppe

Libyan Colonization Organization (ECL), 39, 235n86. *See also* agricultural development; Balbo, Italo

Libyan Tourism and Hotel Association (ETAL), 13, 43, 60–65, 108; administrative structure of, 61; aesthetic control of, 190; and experience of modernity, 72–77; founding legislation of, 60–61; and indigenous politics, 130–31; and Mediterranean language, 193–94; tourist facilities of, 192–93, 204, 206–8, 255n29; and tourist itineraries, 192, **192;** and tourist system, 71–72. *See also* tourism

—Hotel Service, 61, 63, 65; Grand Hotel, Tripoli, 24, 50, **51,** 56, 160–61, **161;** Grand Hotel at the Excavations, Cyrene, 52, 57, 166–70, **168–69;** Hotel 'Ain el-Fras, Ghadames, 57, 129, 212–17, **214–17;** Hotel at the Excavations of Leptis Magna, al-Khums, 52, 57, 175–79, **176–80;** Hotel Gebel, Gharyan, 161, **162;** Hotel Mehari, Tripoli, 57, 199–204, **201–2;** Hotel Nalut, 57, 210–12, **213;** Hotel of the Gazelle, Zlitan, 57, **193,** 193–94; Hotel Rumia, Yifran, 208–10, **209,**

211, 212; Hotel Tobruk, 194, **195**; and
indigenous sources, 130, 193, 208; and
modernity, 75–76; and *strada litoranea,*
71; and system of hotels, 247n70; Uaddan
Hotel and Casino, Tripoli, 57, 194–98,
195–96, 198, 200
—Publicity and Propaganda Service, 61–62,
65–71; and *Combinazioni di soggiorno
in Libia,* 134–35, **135**; and *Itinerario
Tripoli-Gadames,* 136–37; and *Libia,*
68–71, 136; and *La Libia turistica,* 68,
136; and postcard itineraries, 138, **139**;
and indigenous culture, 131–38; tourist
publications of, 133–38; and Tripoli
Trade Fair, 132–33
—Theater and Performance Service, 61,
63–64, 72–73, 138–41; and Arab Café,
Suq al-Mushir, 140–41, **141–42**; and
Arab music school, Suq al-Mushir, 141;
and Artisanal Quarter, Suq al-Mushir,
139–40, **140**; and Uaddan Hotel and
Casino, **73**, 197, **200**
—Tourism Service, 61; and travel agency,
Tripoli, 62, **62**, 71; and tobacco shop in
Rome, 142, **143**
—Transportation Service, 61, 63, **63**, 74–75;
excursions to Libyan interior, 206
Libyan Tourism Commission, 58, 127
Lido Giuliana, Benghazi, 64, **64**
Limongelli, Alessandro: and architectural
discourse, 164
—competition for Piazza della Cattedrale,
165
—design for Piazza Italia, 28, **28**
—Grand Hotel at the Excavations, Cyrene,
166–70, **168–69**. *See also* Libyan Tourism
and Hotel Association (ETAL): Hotel
Service
—pavilion for the governorate of Rome,
30, 31
—residential project in Tripoli, **163**, 164
—triumphal arch for King of Italy's visit to
Tripoli, 162, **163**
London, England, 21
Lowe, Lisa, 9
Luiggi, Luigi: master plan of Tripoli, **21**,
21–22, 83
Lyautey, Maréchal Hubert, 7, 81

MacCannell, Dean: "staged authenticity,"
10

MacDonald, William H.: archeology and
Fascist architecture, 97–98
madrasa, Tripoli, 99
Marinetti, Filippo Tommaso, 111–12, 123
Mausoleum of Augustus, Rome, 98
Mausoleum of Theodoric, Ravenna, 158.
See also Brasini, Armando
mediterraneità, 148–49, 170–72, 249n16
Melchiori, Alessandro, 58, 127
Mendelsohn, Erich, 148
Mercato di suk tripolino, Turin Interna-
tional Exhibition, 91, **92**
Mies van der Rohe, Ludwig, 148
Ministry of Foreign Affairs, 94
Ministry of Popular Culture, 82
Ministry of the Colonies, 118, 127
Miramare Theater, Tripoli, 50
modernization: and government programs,
12–13, 18, 23–28, 31–35; and tourism,
5–6, 13, 43–44, 49–58. *See also* Badoglio,
Marshall Pietro; Balbo, Italo; De Bono,
Emilio; Volpi, Giuseppe
Morocco: and French colonial politics, 7, 81
Mosque of Ahmad Pasha Qaramanli,
Tripoli, **88**, 88–89, 149; model for Suq al-
Mushir, 139; restoration of, 97, 243n62
Mosque of Murad Agha, Tajura, 155
Mosque of Sharah Bu-Harida, Tripoli, **96**,
97
Mosque of Sidi Darghut, Tripoli, 197, **199**,
255n42
Mosque of Sidi Hamuda, **157**, 158
Mukhtar, 'Umar al-, 29
Municipal Casino, Tripoli, 53
Municipal Palace, Benghazi, 160, **160**
Museum, Tripoli, 124
Muslim School of Indigenous Arts and
Crafts, Tripoli, 99–100, 139–40. *See also*
Government Office of Indigenous Applied
Arts; School of Arts and Crafts
Mussolini, Benito, 17; and preservation, 89,
242n36; and corporativism, 60; Fascist
politics of, 19; Imperial politics of, 20, 32;
and *strada litoranea,* 54, 71; resistance
to unification of Libya, 32; and *ventimila,*
39; and visits to Libya, 19, 20, 35, 38,
81–82

Nalut, 34–35, 52; Berber castle in, 129, 211,
257n75
National Association of Tourist Industries

(ENIT), 50, 53, 61

National Conference of Urbanism, Rome, 184

National Fascist Institute for Social Security (INFPS), 39, 235n86

National identity, in modern Italian architecture, 148

National Museum of Popular Arts and Traditions, Rome, 11

National Socialist Party, 227

Nice, Promenade des Anglaises, 22

Nietzsche, Friedrich, 110

Nori, Felice: Roman pavilion, Tripoli Trade Fair, 26, **27**, 31

North America: and indigenous architecture, 154–55, 172

Nuova Italia d'Oltremare, La (commemorative volume), 32

Oedipus Rex (Sophocles), 63

Office of Public Instruction of Arts and Antiquities, Morocco, 151

Opera Nazionale Dopolavoro (OND), 57

Panteri, Saffo:
—San Cuore del Gesù cathedral, Tripoli, 165

Paribeni, Roberto, 84

Paris, France: boulevards of, 21

Pellegrini, Giovanni, 39, 166, 184

Pentagono Group (Natale Morandi, Mario Lombardi, Giambattista Cosmacini, Alberto del Corno, Oddone Cavallini, and Dante Alziati):
—competition for Piazza della Cattedrale, Tripoli, 165, **166**

Persico, Edoardo, 148, 223

Piacentini, Marcello, 153–55
—Berenice Theater in Benghazi (with Luigi Piccinato), 164, **165**
—Villa in the Parioli Quarter, Rome, 155, **156**

Piazza della Cattedrale competition, Tripoli, 165. *See also* Di Fausto, Florestano; Libera, Adalberto; Pentagono Group; Rava, Carlo Enrico, and Sebastiano Larco

Piccinato, Luigi:
—Berenice Theater in Benghazi (with Marcello Piacentini), 164, **165**

Piccioli, Angelo, 47, 93, 107; and *La Porta magica del Sahara*, 204; as Superinten-

dent of Education in Tripolitania, 86

Piccolo amore Beduino (Gaslini), **111**, 112–14

Pollock, Griselda, 6

Postcards: depiction of characteristic scenes, **116**, 117; and influence of scientific research, 122, **123**

preservation: and government programs, 83–89, 91–93; and tourism, 124–25, 129–30, 136, 141. *See also* Badoglio, Marshall Pietro; Balbo, Italo; De Bono, Emilio; indigenous politics; Volpi, Giuseppe

Prison Notebooks (Gramsci), 11–12

Prost, Henri:
—master plan of Casablanca, **30**, 30–31, 90

Prost, Henri and A. Marchisio:
—Hôtel de la Mamounia, Marrakech, 190–91, **191**

Provincial Council for the Administration of the Waqfs, 97, 129, 242–43n60

Puccioni, Nello: scientific mission in Cyrenaica, 245n35

Qaramanli, Ahmad Pasha al-, 85

Qaramanli house, Tripoli, 155–56, **156**

Qasr al-Hajj, Libya: Berber castle, **170**, 170–71; mosque, 171, **172**, 173

Rabinow, Paul: and "techno-cosmopolitanism," 30–31

Rava, Carlo Enrico: as "national popular" of Gramsci, 223; and "Di un'architettura coloniale moderna," 135–37, **170**, 170–74, **172–73**; early professional career of, 147; and *Gruppo Sette*, 145–46; influence on historiography of modern movement, 225; and "Panorama of Rationalism," 145, 147–48; and political discourse, 173–74; and racial discourse, 224–25; and "Svolta pericolosa: Situazione dell'Italia di fronte al razionalismo Europeo," 147–48; and transformation of ideas, 184; and travel in Libya, **146**, 147, 248n8, 251n66

Rava, Carlo Enrico and Sebastiano Larco:
—competition for Piazza della Cattedrale, **174**, 174–75
—Hotel at the Excavations of Leptis Magna, al-Khums, 175–79, **176–80**, 203, 221–22, **222**, 253n88, 256n53. *See also* Libyan Tourism and Hotel Association (ETAL): Hotel Service
—Pavilion of the Colonies, Milan Trade

Fair, **145**, 147

Rava, Maurizio, 28, 147, 233n44; and report to Mayor of Tripoli, 89, 164

Ricard, Prosper, 150–52, **151**, 249n25

Riegl, Alois, 226

Rinascità della Tripolitania, La (Niccoli), 25–26; and tourist literature, 44, 47, 48; and presentation of tourism, 49, 229n9; and indigenous culture, 106–7

Romanelli, Pietro: and restoration of Leptis Magna, 84; and restoration of walls of Tripoli, 85; and "Vecchie case arabe di Tripoli," 155–56

romanità: definition of, 158; in work of Armando Brasini, 158; in work of Alessandro Limongelli, 162, 164, 168–70

Sabratha, Libya: museum in, 89, 124; and performance of *Oedipus Rex*, 63; and restoration program of Volpi, 84; tourist access in, 50, 51–52

Saharan motor coaches, 52–53, **63**

Said, Edward (*Orientalism*), 8–9

Salem, Massachusetts, 219

Santa Fe, New Mexico, 219

Santi, Bruno: and cover of *Libia*, 70, **70**

Sanusi order, 22, 29; and Balbo administration, 95

Sarti, Roland, 9

Scaparro, Mario, 92

Scarin, Emilio, 119, 186;

—houses of Ghadames, 204–5, **205**

Scarpa, Carlo:

—Castelvecchio Museum, Verona, 226

School of Arts and Crafts, Tripoli, 91–92, **93**. *See also* Government Office of Indigenous Applied Arts; indigenous artisanal industries; Muslim School of Indigenous Arts and Crafts

scientific missions, 118–119, 245n35

scientific research, 117–19; as model for tourist excursion, 119–20; influence on tourism, 119–22

scramble for Africa, 18, 80, 240n5

Sitte, Camillo, 153, 226

Somalia, 32, 80

Soulek, Alfred, 148

steamship companies, 53, 57

strada litoranea, 18, 20, 54; and tourist system of ETAL, 71; description of, 35–36, 234n78; in *Libia*, 70–71; in *La*

Libia turistica, 68

Suq al-Kebir, Tripoli: artisanal workshops in, 125, **126**

Suvich, Fulvio, 54, 180, 253n92

Tafuri, Manfredo, 14

Tessenow, Heinrich, 148

tourism, Libya: and air travel, 53, 57; and colonial literature, 6, 13; and colonial politics 5, 6–7, 44–45, 47–48, 49, 105; and economic development, 47; and military control, 3–5, 226–27; and modernization, 5–6, 12–14, 43–44, 47, 105; and scientific research, 6, 13; and indigenous culture, 4–6, 13; and marine connections, 49–50, 53, 57; and scheduled transportation, 52–53, 57. *See also* Libyan Tourism and Hotel Association (ETAL)

tourist: colonial, 8, **219**, 219–21, **221**

tourist architecture, 7–8; and early eclecticism, 158–62; and Grand Hotel at the Excavations, 166–70; and Hotel at the Excavations of Leptis Magna, 175–80; and indigenous language, 208; influence of ETAL on, 190; and Mediterranean language, 193–94; and modernist discourse, 13–14, 180–81; and regionalist discourse, 14. *See also* Libyan Tourism and Hotel Association (ETAL)

tourist infrastructure, 50–53, 55, 57

tourist itineraries, 57; from Tripoli to Ghadames, 204–8; map, **206**

tourist publications, 45, 47; and ETAL, 61–62, 65–68. See also Libyan Tourism and Hotel Association (ETAL): Publicity and Propaganda Service

tourist system, 32, 45, 49–58. *See also* Badoglio, Marshall Pietro; Balbo, Italo; De Bono, Emilio; Libyan Tourism and Hotel Association (ETAL); Volpi, Giuseppe

Tripoli: and Corso Vittorio Emanuele III, 24, **24**; Italian remaking of, 24–25; master plan of, **29**, 29–31, 35, 166, 233n49; museum in, 50; and Piazza Italia, 24; and tourist infrastructure, 50–51, **51**, 53, 57, 64, 192–93, 237n36

Tripoli (guidebook), 107, **115**, 117

Tripolitania: and preservation commission, 84–85; and reconquest, 3–4, 22–23

Tripolitanian Tourism Association, 53–54,

126–27

Tripoli Trade Fair, 26–27; Colonial Village at, 125; and early problems, 232–33n39; expansion of, 31, 57–58, **59**; and initial tourist interest, 50–51; and ETAL, 65, 132–33, **132–34**; and new location, 53. *See also* Badoglio, Marshall Pietro; Balbo, Italo; De Bono, Emilio; Libyan Tourism and Hotel Association: Publicity and Propaganda Service

Uaddan Hotel and Casino, Tripoli, 57, 194–98, **195–96**, **198**, **200**; theater, 64–65, 73, **73**

Vedovato, Giuseppe (*Colonizzazione e turismo in Libia*), 47, 236n20
ventimila, 38–40, 235n89
Vienna, Austria: and the "Ring," 21
Viollet-le-Duc, Eugène-Emmanuel, 226
Volpi, Giuseppe, 22–23, 44, 157; and archeology, 84; and automobile *raid*, 3–5; biography of, 232n25; education system of, 86; and indigenous arts, 85–86, 125; military operations of, 3–5, 22–23; modernization program of, 23–25; and preservation initiatives, 83–87, 124–25; and scholarly research, 149–50; and tourist system, 49–50. See also Government Office of Indigenous Applied Arts; indigenous politics; Libya; modernization; preservation; *Rinascità della Tripolitania, La*; tourism, Libya
Volta Conference. *See* Alessandro Volta Foundation Conference

Women's School for Instruction and Work, 99

Yifran, Libya, 209, **210**

Zavattari, Edoardo, 82